# American Canopy

*Trees, Forests, and the*
*Making of a Nation*

## ERIC RUTKOW

SCRIBNER

*New York London Toronto Sydney New Delhi*

SCRIBNER

A Division of Simon & Schuster, Inc.
1230 Avenue of the Americas
New York, NY 10020

First Scribner hardcover edition April 2012

SCRIBNER and design are registered trademarks of The Gale Group, Inc.,
used under license by Simon & Schuster, Inc., the publisher of this work.

For information about special discounts for bulk purchases,
please contact Simon & Schuster Special Sales at
1-866-506-1949 or business@simonandschuster.com.

The Simon & Schuster Speakers Bureau can bring authors to
your live event. For more information or to book an event contact the
Simon & Schuster Speakers Bureau at 1-866-248-3049 or
visit our website at www.simonspeakers.com.

*Book by Ellen R. Sasahara*

Manufactured in the United States of America

1   3   5   7   9   10   8   6   4   2

ISBN 978-1-4391-9354-9
ISBN 978-1-4391-9360-0 (ebook)

Endpaper and chapter opener (pp. 1, 11, 40, 71, 99, 129, 168, 201, 228, 268, 308, 345)
art courtesy of the General Research Division, The New York Public Library,
Astor, Lenox and Tilden Foundations. Illustration on p. iii, "The Colonists
Under Liberty Tree" (1861), © Duncan Walker/iStock.

*For my mother and father*

# Contents

# Introduction

## *The Death of Prometheus*

White Pine

O N  T H E  M O R N I N G  of August 6, 1964, thirty-year-old Donald Currey was leading several men up a trail along Wheeler Peak, the highest mountain in Nevada. One of Currey's companions wore a U.S. Forest Service uniform, a second lugged a chainsaw, and a third carried a camera to document the event that would follow. They hiked through the thinning air for several hours, past clusters of piñon pines and Utah junipers. Eventually, the men reached the timberline, a point 10,750 feet high on the mountain, where tall plants yielded to the onslaught of nature's winds and nothing survived beyond scrubby vegetation. There, on the environment's edge, Currey's team would encounter one of the world's more remarkable trees, the bristlecone pine. And there, they would change five thousand years of history.

The bristlecone pine is found only in the mountains of the southwestern United States at altitudes that sustain few other life-forms. The rugged environment sculpts the bristlecones into a dramatic, gnarled form, more horizontal than vertical, the physiognomy of an endless battle against the elements. On the wind-facing side, sand particles sheer away outer bark in a process called die-back. The wood beneath looks almost polished, as though it has been petrified alive. John Muir, the eminent naturalist, wrote that the bristlecone "offers a richer and more varied series of forms to the artist than any conifer I know of." The trees can grow up to thirty feet high and twenty around, but often maintain living needles in only a small section—an indoor Christmas tree's worth of green—which produces the distinctive prickle-tipped purple cones that lend the conifer its name.

In 1958 the bristlecone pine had created a giant measure of excitement within a tiny segment of the scientific community when a *National Geographic* article declared that the species produced the oldest trees on earth. Edmund Schulman, the scientist who wrote the piece, explained that he had used tree-ring dating—literally counting up the annual rings in the trunk—to identify multiple bristlecone specimens in California's Inyo National Forest that were more than four thousand years old. The most impressive find, a tree containing 4,676 rings, was named Methuselah, a nod to the longest-lived figure in the Bible. The *National Geographic* article asserted that the oldest bristlecones were located "at the western limit of their range" where Methuselah grew, suggesting that Schulman's biblically named discovery was quite possibly the world's oldest tree.

Schulman's finding held great promise for a variety of reasons. Tree rings recorded climatic activity with remarkable precision—wetter years generated widely spaced rings, drier periods kept them close, and all trees in a given area corresponded. Consequently, these bristlecones were silent but scrupulous witnesses to several millennia of droughts, floods, shifting rivers, and retreating glaciers. Their rings offered scientists, specifically dendrochronologists (those who study tree rings), a chance to reconstruct the local climate to dates contemporaneous with the building of the Egyptian pyramids.

Currey, a graduate student in geography, was hoping to exploit this relationship between trees and history. He wanted to develop a climatic timeline connected to glacier growth and rock settlements in the Southwest as far back as 2000 BCE. His research centered on geological features in eastern Nevada's Snake Range, a mountain chain capped by the imposing 13,063-foot Wheeler Peak. Bristlecones near the range's timberline held valuable data within the rings of their trunks.

Currey's research site was several hundred miles east of the Methuselah find. Thus, he anticipated finding only specimens much younger than those featured in *National Geographic*. During the summer of 1964, however, he stumbled upon something unexpected. A bristlecone stand in the national forest tract known as the Wheeler Peak Scenic Area appeared to contain trees as old as anything that Schulman had described. An eager Currey began to take samples of the trees using his twenty-eight-inch-long Swedish increment borer, a sophisticated hand tool with an aperture approximately the size of a drinking straw that removed a fragment of the trunk without causing permanent damage. Day after day, he scrambled over the limestone soil and the deposited rock that surrounded the bristlecones, carrying his notebook and Swedish borer alongside, collecting samples that he could later analyze under a microscope.

Currey's 114th specimen was the most spectacular that he encountered. He measured it as having "a dead crown 17 feet high, a living shoot 11 feet high, and a 252-inch circumference 18 inches above the ground." Such a wide base would have required four men with arms outstretched to encircle it. Currey also noted that the tree's bark, which was necessary for its survival, was only "present along a single 19-inch-wide, north-facing strip." The winds and sand had worn away everything else. But the tree was alive and still producing its compact bunches of needles on a three-inch-wide shoot.

Currey attempted to sample this tree, which he labeled WPN-114, but his borer broke. He tried again and damaged his reserve borer. Without equipment, he was suddenly stymied. This ancient specimen stood before him, its rings holding the secrets to several thousand years of climate change, and he had no way to study it, not with his borers, anyway.

Currey appealed to the district Forest Service ranger, explaining that he wanted to cut down WPN-114 and study the cross-section directly. At the time, sawing down trees for dendrochronological research was not uncommon—even Schulman admitted in *National Geographic* to felling three samples, though not Methuselah itself. The Forest Service ranger consulted with his supervisor and determined that the tree "was like many others and was not the type that the public would visit" and that it would better serve science and education. The supervisor concluded, "Cut 'er down."

Shortly thereafter, on that August 6 morning, Currey led the cutting team up Wheeler Peak. When they reached WPN-114, the men took turns sawing away at the tree. Several hours later there was nothing left but an enormous stump.

Currey brought the prepared samples to his microscope and began counting tree rings. Then he made a startling discovery. There were 4,844 rings, nearly two hundred more than in Methuselah. And WPN-114 had been cut down several feet above its true base, losing access to some of the earliest rings. The tree could have easily been five thousand years old. Schulman had been wrong about where the oldest bristlecones lived.

Thirty-year-old Donald Currey had unintentionally felled the most ancient tree ever discovered—an organism already wizened when Columbus reached Hispaniola, middle-aged when Caesar ruled Rome, and starting life when the Sumerians created mankind's first written language.

The next year, Currey quietly published his discovery in the journal *Ecology*. The three-page article, written in the scientific passive voice, acknowledged that WPN-114 was the oldest tree on record but postulated that future research would yield many older specimens.

However, the only thing that the future actually yielded was a growing controversy over why WPN-114 was allowed to be cut down in the first place. The forest ranger who had claimed that the tree held no interest for the public had been wrong. Conservationists knew about the bristlecones and had earlier named WPN-114 "Prometheus" after the Titan who stole fire from Zeus, gave it to man, and then suffered eternally for his action. These conservationists claimed that the Forest Service had acted recklessly in permitting the cutting. Stories that a member of Currey's team had died carrying a slab of Prometheus down Wheeler Peak left some observers suggesting that the tree had taken a life to remedy the injustice. Several dendrochronologists attacked Currey as an ignorant graduate student who didn't know how to handle a borer and had little or no scientific reason to fell this particular sample.

Evidence supported both sides of the controversy, depending on which accounts were used, and new perspectives leaked out over the decades. As late as 1996, the Forest Service ranger who authorized the cutting wrote a memo to correct "the many rumors," and Currey himself gave the occasional interview up until his death in 2004. The only facts that anyone seemed to agree upon were that WPN-114 was the oldest tree ever discovered and that Americans had intentionally killed it.

T HE DEATH OF Prometheus was a tragedy, something to reflect upon with disbelief. Some of us, the more environmentally inclined, may react with anger, even outrage, knowing that scientists discovered such a marvelous tree only to steal it with a hasty and arrogant hand. After all, nothing can bring the elder statesman of the plant kingdom back. Others among us, perhaps more than would admit it in public, may simply shrug. It was one tree hidden on a mountain almost no one visited, whose only distinction was having been there longer than logic would suggest, a literal freak of nature, a sideshow act in wood. There are plenty of other bristlecones.

But to treat the felling of Prometheus in isolation misses much of the story. The controversy was not merely a localized battle between dendrochronologists, conservationists, and the men holding sap-stained chainsaws. It was a tiny chapter in a much larger narrative of trees and America, or trees and Americans, two members of the natural environment who are constantly acting on one another, and over time changing as a result. Trivial details in the Prometheus story represent important shifts in America's relationship with wood, trees, and nature.

Take the location of the tree, for example. Wheeler Peak Scenic Area was part of a national forest, a type of government-controlled land first created in the late nineteenth century. For much of American history, the idea that the government would control some of the forests seemed ridiculous, an affront to the spirit of individualism and private property that helped build the country.

The controversy itself formed part of a long lineage of Americans realizing that they had abused their great renewable resource when it was too late. Sometimes, this awakening involved a single tree, like the Liberty Tree that the Boston patriots could not protect from the axes of the British redcoats. Other times, it was a single species, such as the American chestnut, which was once the mightiest forest tree and now is little more than a legend due to an imported disease. Often, it was an entire forest, like the white pine belts of New England and the Lake States, which fell victim to America's logging industry.

The death of Prometheus offers only the tiniest window into this rich and wide-ranging history of Americans and their trees. The tale of how they shaped each other over time is simply too large, too multilayered, too varied for any single bristlecone on a lonesome timberline in Nevada. This larger story, however, forms the subject of *American Canopy*.

H ow easy it is to forget that much of American history has been defined by trees.

Giovanni da Verrazzano, the first European to leave a detailed account of a journey to North America, marveled in 1524 that "the wooddes [were] so greate and thicke that an armye (were it never so greate) mighte have hydd it selfe therein." He labeled this heavily forested land Acadia, meaning "idyllic place." The trees, in his opinion, were the most useful thing the land had to offer.

But Verrazzano's observation is high praise, for there is simply nothing else in nature quite as helpful to man as a tree. Timber is a universal building material, essential for shelter, furniture, tools, and countless types of transport. The initial English efforts to colonize America depended, in no small part, on a desire to secure timber for construction of the great naval fleet that would soon come to define the British Empire. Once European settlers began to infiltrate America's mighty forests, many would build dwellings that were little more than felled logs, stacked in a pile, sealed with a bit of mud and straw. Even now, most homes are constructed mainly with softwood timbers and sheets of plywood. Trees were also the nation's essential source of fuel for hundreds of years. Wood was used in the forges and furnaces of almost every American manufacturing industry, every steam engine, and every family hearth. Furthermore, the pulp of trees is the source of manufactured paper, an unsung pillar of advanced society. The transition to inexpensive wood-pulp paper, which began in the 1860s, allowed for an explosion in written materials—daily penny papers, dime novels, low-cost stationery—that would forever alter the culture of the country. The creation of every horseshoe, wagon, carriage, gun, bottle, ship, train, and early airplane required trees. Every mine, corral, stockyard, tannery, mill, refinery, dock, barge, telegraph and telephone line, and early oil derrick required trees. James Hall, the famous American geologist, once said, "Well may ours be called a *wooden country*, not merely from the extent of its forests, but because in common use wood has been substituted for a number of the most necessary and common articles—such as stone, iron, and even leather."

But to speak of timber or fuel or pulp is to flatten trees into a single dimension. They also provide sustenance: sap into sugar, seeds into nuts and fruits. Their foliage brings life to desolate landscapes, their roots stability to shaky soils. Finally, on a hot summer day, there are few pleasures that rival hiding in the shade beneath the boughs of a noble oak.

Over the years, technology has obscured the vital role that trees have played in shaping society. Steel and plastic replaced timber. Coal and oil substituted for firewood. Digital screens are crowding out paper copies. Industrial food chains have left almost no one relying directly on the forests for dinner. Sometimes it seems like this was always the way, man's dominion over nature. Americans interact with trees that have been circumscribed, commoditized. Our furniture is a thin veneer of wood placed over synthetic materials. The wooden supports of our homes are tucked away from view with drywall and vinyl siding. Forests are cordoned off in carefully delimited regions, far away from the cities and suburbs. The juice from the fruit of trees has been pasteurized and homogenized.

This separation from nature makes it easy to forget just how important trees are to our lives today. Each year, the average American consumes roughly 250 board feet of timber, 200 square feet of plywood and other structural panel products, and 700 pounds of paper and paperboard. More than 2.5 million Americans hold jobs directly dependent on the country's woodlands. Nearly 20 percent of the nation's freshwater originates in the national forests. And these same national forests provide more than seven billion activity days for vacationers, hunters, fishermen, and hikers. But these are just the most obvious dependencies. Trees also provide raw materials for countless medicines, plastics, technological devices, and artificial food.

Additionally, some believe that our trees will hold the key to the country's future, as they have the past. Our illimitable forests, which extract carbon dioxide from the atmosphere and store much of it as wood and other plant matter, may provide an opportunity to combat global warming. The same is imagined of tree planting. Scientists are also working to develop new processes that might turn trees into sources of renewable energy.

Thus, even as we have found many ways to replace trees, they remain as important as ever.

*A*MERICAN *C*ANOPY explores this remarkable evolution. How trees changed from enemy, to friend, to potential savior. How forests morphed from obstacles to timber reserves to tree farms to sanctuaries of nature. How wood built the country, and apples united it, and trees imbued its great cities with life. How trees became part of the political calculus for westward settlement, as necessary as water and air, valued by settlers, speculators, surveyors, and soldiers. Americans started as people frightened of the woods, transitioned into a nation that consumed these woods for profit—along the way turning the tree into a lifeless, deracinated object—and finally arrived at the present point. Today, few of us understand where timber comes from or what to call any given tree species, but most of us share a sense that to destroy trees is to destroy part of ourselves.

This story is uniquely American. No other country was populated because of its trees quite like the United States. Nowhere else has the culture been so intimately associated with wood. Entire states were peopled specifically for their trees: lumbering in the Northwest; orange growing in Florida and Southern California. Such great American cities as Chicago, Los Angeles, Miami, and Seattle would have looked completely different without the early commercial opportunities that trees provided. The industrial advance of the late nineteenth century—America's great surge forward—may have been exploiting steam trains, telegraphs, and electricity, but it depended on cheap, abundant wood for rail ties, fuel, buildings, and utility poles. The nation's military might also owed its fair debt to trees, unsung heroes of both world wars—for forests were recruited alongside soldiers. And after World War II, when a fast-rising population needed new housing, it was cheap timber that allowed for the sudden emergence of the suburbs, where, it should be noted, a tree could be found in every yard.

It is no surprise that trees would shape America more than other nations. After all, America has some of the most spectacular tree resources on the planet. Forests once covered almost half of the contiguous states, a staggering 950 million acres. The diverse geography across the country gives America ideal soil for almost any type of tree, from the palms of Southern California to the pines of New England. The United States is home to the world's biggest trees (the giant sequoias), the world's tallest trees (the coastal redwoods), and the world's oldest trees (the bristlecone pines). The biggest single organism on earth is also a tree species—and is also American—a stand of quaking aspens in Utah, known as Pando; it reproduces clonally, weighs sixty-six hundred tons, and is tens of thousands if not millions of years old.

*American Canopy* takes these magnificent American trees as its subject, but the story is most often one of personal drama. Americans, after all, are half the equation. The Sons of Liberty used a famous tree as a center for popular protest that helped spark the American Revolution. George Washington and Thomas Jefferson were avid horticulturists who traded tree specimens as they negotiated the Constitution—Jefferson even considered the introduction of the olive tree to South Carolina as one of his greatest achievements. John Chapman, a man most Americans know as Johnny Appleseed, sold his trees to settlers looking to establish residence in the Ohio Valley. Henry David Thoreau helped awaken a nation to the beauty of woodlands. John Muir then used his passion for trees and unbounded nature to champion the creation of national parks. J. Sterling Morton, one of the first settlers in Nebraska, tried to turn the Great Plains into a forest by creating Arbor Day. Later, President Theodore Roosevelt, with his close confidant Gifford Pinchot, struggled to save the great western forests from industrial ruin. And in the following generation, President Franklin Roosevelt—a tree lover if there ever was one—looked to the nation's woody resources as a way to ameliorate the Great Depression. Each man's story tells a small fragment of a much larger tale, a tale that becomes the story of America.

This relationship with trees has been one of the great drivers of national development. It belongs in a conversation with other forces that helped to forge American identity: the endless frontier, immigration, democracy, religion, slavery and its legacy, the struggle for labor rights, the expansion of civil rights, and free market and state capitalism, to name a few. And like all useful cicerones, the trees show us a picture of America at its best and at its worst.

History has lost or buried many of the episodes highlighted in *American Canopy*. To learn about trees is to discover a side of the nation's past that is rarely told. No one has ever treated America's trees in all their dimensions as a subject for historical study. Pieces of the story for certain, but not the story itself. Perhaps it is because trees have been so integral to American history that it becomes easy to overlook them. People notice the unusual, not the ubiquitous. Like so many Americans, historians are guilty of taking trees for granted. But trees are the loudest silent figures in America's complicated history.

M EANWHILE, Prometheus turned out to be one of the loudest trees of all, though only in death. With each year that passed and without the discovery of an older bristlecone, the tree's reputation grew, as did the controversy over its cutting. The felling of Prometheus convinced conservationists to take a more aggressive stand to ensure that such ill-advised chain-sawing was never repeated. Donald Currey even became one of the foremost advocates for greater controls over the region that contained the bristlecones. These efforts helped to create, in 1986, the Great Basin National Park, a heavily protected area that includes Wheeler Peak Scenic Area. And today all bristlecone pines, standing or down, receive federal protection. Thanks to these measures the bristlecones can continue to fight their eternal battle with nature's wind undisturbed and to silently record America and the world as they change. But for Prometheus, all that remains is an unmarked stump and a footnote in history. It is still the oldest tree ever discovered.

# 1

## From Discovery to Revolution

White Oak

## "Wooddes of All Sortes"

I N LATE 1605, Richard Hakluyt, archdeacon of London's Westminster Abbey and the preeminent geographer in Europe, sat in his study preparing for a meeting that he had spent a lifetime awaiting. The newly crowned king of England, James I, had granted Hakluyt and his colleagues an audience to discuss overseas expansion. They were seeking a royal charter that would authorize them to establish permanent settlements in a mysterious land known to some as Norumbega, to others as Acadia, and to others still as Virginia. The territory stretched from thirty-four to forty-five degrees north latitude, the present-day location for most of America's Eastern Seaboard. If King James refused Hakluyt's appeal, the project of English colonization in North America might wither before it could begin. And the central argument that Hakluyt planned to use with the king of England rested on trees.

Hakluyt viewed North American expansion as the key to his country's future. Overseas growth had already been a boon for Spain and Portugal, the two states that had most successfully exploited the New World since Christopher Columbus's famous 1492 voyage. Their western holdings provided mineral wealth and access to raw materials. Spain, in particular, had used these newfound riches to develop the world's strongest navy and administer an ever-growing empire. England, by contrast, had barely participated in the sixteenth-century land grab. In Hakluyt's opinion, westward expansion into the one great Atlantic region that remained unclaimed—the North American continent above Spanish Florida—was necessary to contest Spain's spreading dominion and to boost the English economy.

In the epistle to his first book, a 1582 collection of North American travel literature called *Divers Voyages*, Hakluyt exhorted his countrymen to remedy the situation: "I marvaile not a little . . . that since the first discoverie of America . . . after so great conquests and plantings of the Spaniardes and Portingales there, that wee of Englande could never have the grace to set fast footing in such fertill and temperate places."

In 1584, Hakluyt first set out his thoughts on the whys and hows of North American expansion in a manuscript titled *A Discourse of Western Planting*. The work had been commissioned by Sir Walter Raleigh, a friend of the geographer and one of Europe's most respected explorers. Raleigh had recently received a royal patent from Queen Elizabeth I authorizing him to "discover, search, and find" uninhabited lands, but he wanted additional royal support for a proposed permanent settlement in North America and felt that Hakluyt could make a compelling case.

*Western Planting* advocated Britain's expansion through colonies, often referred to in the sixteenth century as "plantations" or "plantings." The idea was to populate North America with transplanted Englishmen, who would work the land. This approach differed from the early Spanish style of conquest, which focused on precious metal extraction and used native peoples in mining or cash crop production. Hakluyt wanted colonies to be "for the manifolde imploymente of numbers of idle men," a category that had been increasing during the last three decades of the sixteenth century, when England's population grew from 3.25 million to 4.07 million people. North American colonies would turn these unemployed men into producers and traders. They would harvest raw materials and ship them to England in exchange for woolen clothes and other manufactured goods.

*Western Planting*'s colonial ideas corresponded with an economic theory in fashion during Queen Elizabeth's reign. It argued that a country's balance of trade—exports versus imports—determined prosperity. The key was to import raw materials, so-called marketable commodities, and export manufactured goods. North American colonies, Hakluyt argued, could provide a steady stream of marketable commodities to England and in exchange receive goods that the home country manufactured. And colonial importation was vastly preferable to trading between independent states because there would be no duties and no risk of diplomatic problems.

For this idea to work, however, Hakluyt needed to identify marketable commodities in North America. They would need to be raw materials that were plentiful overseas, easy for settlers to obtain, and scarce in England.

Hakluyt's years of studying travel literature had familiarized him with North America's raw materials. The topic appeared frequently in the writings of overseas adventurers, who typically surveyed the land with an eye toward exploitation. John Ribault, one of the first Englishmen to record a voyage to North America, in 1564, wrote "the Contrie . . . is the fairest, frutefullest, and pleasauntest of all the worlde, aboundinge in honye, waxe, venison, wilde fowle, fforrestes, [and] wooddes of all sortes." The potential resource list was long, so much so that Hakluyt suggested, hyperbolically though not insincerely, that the land could yield "all the commodities of Europe, Affrica, and Asia, as far as we were wonte to travel."

One raw material, however, stood out above all the rest in Hakluyt's manuscript: trees. There were certainly others, among them fish and furs, two commodities that different geographers and explorers identified as the most essential resource. And there were the speculative commodities as well, such as gold and silver deposits. But none of these held equal footing with trees for Hakluyt. North America, he wrote, was "infinitely full fraughte with sweet wooddes . . . and divers other kindes of goodly trees." Colonists could immediately be put to work "settynge upp mylles to sawe them" and producing boards "ready to be turned into goodly chests, cupboordes, stooles, tables, desks, etc." Trees would be the ideal marketable commodity for a colonial expedition: unlimited in supply, simple to harvest, and able to serve as the raw material for countless manufactured goods. Hakluyt concluded: "So that were there no other peculier commodities, this onely [wood] I say were ynoughe to defraye all the chardges of all the begynnynge of the enterprise, and that oute of hande." Trees, Hakluyt assured, were the guarantee that the colonial venture would succeed financially.

North America's woody resources, however, fulfilled only the supply half of the economic calculus. For trees to qualify as a marketable commodity, there would also need to be strong demand. And this was the case, because of a problem Hakluyt diplomatically labeled "the present wante of tymber in the Realme." In truth, England was suffering from a severe timber crisis that, at the time of his writing, left the poor literally freezing to death in wintertime for want of firewood.

Originally, the British island had been a woodland. Forests of oak and other hardwoods had filled the southern lands, while conifer stands populated the higher latitudes. Sheepherders over the centuries converted much of this to pastureland, but the domestic wood supply remained great enough to handle timber and firewood demands. Then, beginning in the 1540s, came new manufacturing industries that razed the forests for their fuel. This new wave of deforestation started with the iron industry, an early royal effort to boost manufacturing in accord with the trade-based economic theory—the production of iron required immense amounts of heat and, initially, used charcoal (which is derived from wood) as fuel. In 1543, Parliament first addressed the impending timber shortage with the Act for the Preservation of Woods, which restricted farmers from exploiting woodlands more than two furlongs (440 yards) from their homes. Sherwood Forest was becoming as much a myth as Robin Hood.

The situation worsened during the long reign of Queen Elizabeth I (1558–1603). She promoted numerous other wood-fuel-driven manufacturing industries, including copper smelting, salt making, and glass production. (The coal industry, which was beginning, could not meet the skyrocketing demand for fuel.) One writer from this period commented, "Never so much [oak] hath been spent in a hundred years before as is in 10 years of our time." The price of firewood doubled between 1540 and 1570. This pushed some citizens out of the firewood market, and it became commonplace for the poor to shiver through the winters. The timber shortage had commoditized a product once freely available for the cutting.

But fuel needs did not fully account for England's timber demand. Wood was also necessary in the construction of ships. And Queen Elizabeth, in addition to promoting domestic manufacturing, had championed shipbuilding, part of the Crown's long-term strategy to contest Spanish sea power and strengthen English commercial trade.

Few industries in history have depended on wood quite like shipbuilding (at least before the conversion to iron and steel hulls in the mid-nineteenth century). A large naval warship, known as a ship of the line and constructed almost entirely from wood, weighed over one hundred tons in Hakluyt's day. The bodies of such vessels required about two thousand mature oaks, which meant at least fifty acres of forest had to be stripped. While oak supplied the timber for much of the ship, it was too inflexible and heavy for ship masts, the poles that supported the canvas sails. Instead, these required lighter and more shock-resistant softwoods, such as pines and firs. The largest masts were more than three feet wide at their base and over one hundred feet tall—roughly one yard in height per inch in width. To maintain these wooden cathedrals of the sea, shipwrights relied on a range of forest products, known as naval stores, extracted from pines and firs as well. Most notable were the tar, pitch, and turpentine used to condition and preserve the hull, mast, and other components.

The twin demands of shipbuilding and wood-fuel-hungry manufacturing had turned England into a net wood importer. In particular, the country had to trade for masts and naval stores, since it had no suitably commercial conifer forests. The preferred mast trees, called Riga firs or Scotch pines, came from an Eastern European region around the city of Riga (in present-day Latvia), but several northern countries had giant spruce forests that were also exploited for naval stores. The trade centered on ports in Scandinavia and the Baltic Sea—the latter, which included Riga, was accessible only through narrow straits between Denmark and Sweden. Rulers who controlled the various ports and access to the straits knew that England's sea power depended on forest products and, consequently, kept duties, taxes, and shipping fees high. The Danish, for example, collected tolls for each crossing. If England ever lost access to these ports, it would cripple the entire shipping industry, and with it the Royal Navy.

Hakluyt saw the solution to this potential dilemma in the woods of North America as well. If his travel narratives agreed on anything, they "agreed that the New World was an inexhaustible source of naval supplies," according to historian Howard Mumford Jones. Hakluyt stressed this same point in *Western Planting*: "And England posessinge the purposed place of platinge . . . [will] have plenty of excellent trees for mastes, of goodly timber to builde shippes and to make greate navies, of pitche, tarr, hempe, and all thinges incident for a navie royall, and that for no price and withoute money or request." A foothold in tree-rich North America would shore up the Royal Navy's greatest vulnerability and seemingly do so at little cost.

Viewed more broadly, Hakluyt's *Western Planting* was attempting to translate into economic and political terms a majestic wooded landscape that Europeans could hardly comprehend. Many of the North American tree varieties were unknown on the continent, and even the familiar species possessed inconceivable size and number. Giovanni da Verrazzano, in 1524, wrote of "mightie greate wooddes . . . with divers sorts of trees [as] plesaunte and delectable to beholde as is possible to imagine." The early voyagers simply ran out of adjectives to describe the abundance, grandeur, and range of the virgin forests. Geographers estimate that woodlands covered about 95 percent of presettlement New England and contained three-quarters of a million trees for every ten square miles. The mature specimens in any given stretch generally stood over one hundred feet high and were three feet thick at chest height. They towered above the forest floor, often free of branches for thirty to fifty feet, their leafy crowns floating like green fortresses in the sky. England, by comparison, was a barren wasteland. Sir Thomas Culpepper, a seventeenth-century British economist, lamented that "no man can let his Timber stand, nor his Wood grow to such years growth as is best for the Common-Wealth."

In late 1584, Hakluyt met personally with Elizabeth, the virgin queen, to discuss his book and to make an appeal for colonization on behalf of his patron Raleigh. It was Hakluyt's first royal audience (and the last before his meeting with James I twenty-one years later). During the meeting, the geographer presented the queen a copy of *Western Planting*. They then almost certainly discussed the various colonial arguments: the economic promise of North American forests, the twin political advantages of a New World check on Spain and of a secure naval supply chain, the religious opportunities to spread the reformed Protestant gospel to the infidels, the possibilities of mineral wealth or a direct passage to China and the East Indies spice trade.

Despite Hakluyt's best efforts, however, he failed to secure a charter authorizing permanent settlements. The problem seemed to be that equally compelling reasons against colonization existed. To begin with, such an aggressive undertaking was an incredibly dangerous proposition in the early 1580s. Spain still ruled the seas and showed interest in North America. Committing England to a colonization project risked war with the most powerful nation in Europe. But even without the Spanish menace, the project was precarious. In 1578, Elizabeth had granted a six-year exploratory charter to Sir Humphrey Gilbert, but he never returned from the trip, his crew lost at sea. (Hakluyt had turned down an opportunity to travel with Gilbert, a decision that unquestionably saved his life.)

Perhaps Hakluyt's unwavering enthusiasm struck Queen Elizabeth as zealotry. It was common for colonial propagandists to face charges of exaggeration and mendacity, claims that did not always lack merit. After all, Hakluyt, a man who had never seen North America, was promising the queen resources greater than those of all of Europe. His fantastical-sounding assurances may have outweighed his inchoate reputation for pragmatism and integrity. Still, the geographer must have impressed Elizabeth, for two years later he received a clerical advancement to Bristol Cathedral on her mandate.

Raleigh, meanwhile, pursued his colonial plans without the royal charter he desired. The year after Hakluyt's royal audience, the explorer founded a colony in North America called Roanoke (on an island near present-day North Carolina). The project lasted for two years, but the original settlers all disappeared under mysterious circumstances, this doomed adventure remembered by history as the "Lost Colony."

Hakluyt, in the period between his two royal audiences, continued his colonial advocacy unabated, as scholar, propagandist, and agitator. In 1589 he published the first edition of a massive compendium of North American travel narratives called *Principall Navigations,* which reappeared ten years later in a three-volume expanded format. The revised edition of the book remains the definitive text of precolonial exploration. Many consider it one of the most important documents from the Elizabethan age and have dubbed Hakluyt the "English Homer." Shakespeare is thought to have referenced one of the maps from *Principall Navigations* in his play *Twelfth Night.*

Ever the pragmatist, Hakluyt eventually contributed his unrivaled reputation to a business partnership with seven other men in order to found a permanent settlement in North America. Known as the Virginia Company, they hoped to succeed where Gilbert and Raleigh had failed. And it was with this group that Hakluyt was going to petition King James in 1605.

The circumstances for colonization, meanwhile, had grown more favorable in the two decades since Hakluyt's first royal audience. In 1585, war had erupted between Spain and England with control of the seas the winner's prize. Sir Francis Drake, the famed British explorer, defeated a Spanish fleet in a 1587 preemptive strike, proving that the Spanish were not invulnerable upon the seas and could not defend the extensive territories that they claimed. The following year, a coalition of English naval and merchant ships conquered Spain's great Armada, arguably the most important sea battle in history. In August 1604, King James I signed a peace treaty with Spain, meaning that English-flagged ships could sail through Atlantic waters for the first time without fear of Spanish attack. England suddenly controlled the world's waterways, a position it would maintain into the nineteenth century.

During this sea change, several English voyages to North America had reinforced Hakluyt's claim that timber-trade-based colonization could be profitable and benefit the Crown. In 1602, Bartholomew Gosnold—an eventual member of Hakluyt's Virginia Company—had sailed to North America and returned with a ship weighed down with cuttings of sassafras, a tree that became briefly invaluable amid rumors that its extract cured syphilis. George Weymouth, another English explorer, had traveled to North America two years later and reported that the entire coast was indeed covered with dense woods. He determined, among other things, that the trees produced turpentine in "marvellous plenty" and "so sweet," which "would be a great benefit for making Tarre and Pitch."

Against this backdrop, Hakluyt and his Virginia Company met with King James I. The geographer's arguments, little changed since *Western Planting,* had gained force, especially since the timber crisis had only deepened and the Royal Navy had grown in power. Hakluyt himself had also gained force, no longer the young novitiate, but an asset to his country, the patriotic expert in a field of self-interested explorers and businessmen. Once again he set forth the manifold reasons for colonization that he had earlier given Elizabeth, this time with twenty more years of reputation, knowledge, and favorable political developments to assist him. And this time he succeeded.

On April 10, 1606, James I issued the First Charter of Virginia. It granted the men of the Virginia Company the right "to make habitation, plantation, and to deduce a colony of sundry of our people into that part of America commonly called Virginia." The charter split the Virginia Company into two sections, a London-based group that included Hakluyt (known as the London Company) and a Plymouth-based group (the Plymouth Company). Hakluyt's team received rights to the southern half of the territory. The northern half went to the Plymouth Company. The geographer had finally persuaded the Crown to support North American colonization, and his long-standing dream was on the verge of being realized.

Of course, the charter was nothing more than a document and a promise of governmental assistance. It would have meant little if the Virginia Company had failed like all of the previous unchartered colonization attempts, such as Roanoke.

Almost exactly one year after James issued the charter, on April 26, 1607, the first colonists from the London Company reached Virginia. They formed a small settlement in the Chesapeake region that they called Jamestown, in honor of the king. Captain John Smith, a man contracted to oversee the adventure, proved a gifted leader, able to manage the settlers and negotiate with the native population. Soon, the colonists started to send shipments back to England, especially trees. A 1608 letter stated, "I heare not of any novelties or other commodities she hath brought more then sweet woode."

The early years nonetheless proved difficult. Of the original 214 colonists, only 60 survived a brutal winter in 1609, known as the "Starving Time."

Colonial promotional literature, designed to garner financial support and dampen bad publicity, emphasized the claims Hakluyt had long been making about trees as a commodity. The most famous pamphlet, from the more than twenty the London Company printed, quoted one of the founding company members, who had traveled to the new colony, as swearing under oath "that the country yeeldeth abundance of wood . . . which are the materials, of . . . Clap boards, Pipe-staves, Masts and excellent boardes of forty, fifty and sixtie length." The publication concluded, "[N]either the scattered Forrest of England, nor the diminished Groves of Ireland, will supply the defect of our Navy. When in Virginia there is nothing wanting, but onely mens labours, to furnish both Prince, State and merchant, without charge or difficulty."

Despite these claims, the London Company struggled financially for the next fifteen years, largely because exporting the abundant commodities proved more challenging and expensive than anticipated. Jamestown, however, was the first permanent English settlement in North America and became the foundation of present-day Virginia.

Meanwhile, the Plymouth Company was simultaneously working to colonize the northern territories, which roughly correspond to present-day New England. George Popham, a founding member of the Virginia Company, led an expedition that settled on the shore of present-day Maine on August 13, 1607. Problems such as an unexpectedly cold winter and food shortages plagued the new settlement. The colonists put all their efforts toward constructing a ship—a foreshadowing of New England's future—and produced a thirty-ton vessel named *Virginia*. But Popham died during that first winter, and all forty-five colonists returned to England the next spring. The Plymouth Company was then inactive until a revival in 1620 when, among other activities, it granted settlement rights to a group of religious dissidents known as the Pilgrims, who had earlier negotiated with the London Company but accidentally landed far north of their intended destination and became New England's first permanent English colonists.

As for Hakluyt, he never made it to the New World. The man who devoted his life to studying sea voyages refused to be part of one. The reasons for this remain a mystery. He died in 1616, leaving behind a son and two shares in the London Company worth twenty-one pounds. His grave in Westminster Abbey is unmarked. A commemorative plaque in Bristol Cathedral reads: "The ardent Love of my Country devoured all Difficulties."

Hakluyt had realized his patriotic vision of a colonial England, but in doing so he had also planted the seeds of a new nation. And the trees that he saw bringing so much prosperity to his homeland would soon shape the emigrants to this once-unknown land.

## "Here Is Good Living for Those That Love Good Fires"

ON NOVEMBER 11, 1620, after a two-month journey, the *Mayflower* finally settled in to a harbor near Cape Cod Bay. As carpenters began repairing the ship, sixteen men set out to explore the territory, "necessitie calling them to looke out a place for habitation," according to William Bradford, the future governor of the Pilgrims' colony. The scouting party wandered toward the forests, when they spotted several natives, who fled into the woods like startled deer. The Pilgrims pursued them to ensure that more were not lying in ambush. However, according to Bradford, his companions "soone lost both [the natives] & them selves, falling into shuch thickets as were ready to tear their cloaths & armore in peeces, but were most distressed for wante of drinke." Several days later, while Bradford was lost in the woods with another party, he leaned over to look at a curiously bent sapling, which "gave a sodaine jerk up, and he was immediately caught by the leg" and pulled off the ground by an Indian game trap.

Hakluyt may have been correct about the value of trees as a commodity, but he had not appreciated the challenges of living in the woods. In Bradford's words, the "whole countrie, full of woods & thickets, represented a wild & savage heiw [hue]."

The forests were a frightening place for settlers transported from Europe. Savages lived there, alongside strange beasts, swarming insects, and, quite possibly, the devil himself. But these fears were, in some ways, no more troubling than the trees themselves. The Pilgrims could not begin planting crops nor building homes until they cut them down, one by one, a task near impossible for men who had never handled heavy axes. One potential settlement region the Pilgrims had "a very great liking to plant in" was rejected largely because of the trees. According to Bradford, it was "so incompassed with woods, that we should bee in much danger of the Salvages, and our number being so little, and so much ground to cleare, so as we thought good to quit and cleare [leave] that place."

Eventually, the Pilgrims established their colony near Plymouth Harbor in an outcropping free of woods. The land's natural forest had earlier been cleared by Patuxet Indians, who had been growing corn there until a 1617 plague decimated the population. Hakluyt's travel narratives had described the continent as pristine territory, but in reality the native population had shaped the forests for thousands of years through burnings and tree fellings. Many of the earliest settlement points—Plymouth, Boston, Salem, Medford, Watertown—were actually abandoned Indian fields or natural clearings, ironic for a Yankee culture that would soon be defined by trees.

The forest, while not the Pilgrims' literal home, quickly became their salvation. They had brought stores of food and clothes on the *Mayflower,* but few building materials and no fuel. In the first two years, Bradford and his men hauled great logs and thousands of small trees from the nearby woodlands to construct a fort as well as individual houses. And firewood was their only source of heat in a territory with unexpectedly cold winters—Hakluyt's travel narratives were from summertime voyages, which described the climate accordingly.

Wood gathering "always cost a great deale of labour," according to Bradford. One Pilgrim complained that the colony's location forced him to walk "halfe a quarter of an English myle" to gather wood, not a great distance, but tiresome considering the backbreaking labor and the enormous quantities involved—each family burned through an acre of wood a year. Despite the heavy labor, access to unlimited timber and fuel mitigated the effects of the first brutal winter, which claimed the lives of half the original settlers. A report on the original New England colonies by a minister in Salem, Massachusetts, stated, "Here is good living for those that love good fires," though the Pilgrims who had to carry the logs might have disagreed.

The New England trees were as diverse as they were plentiful. Though most woodlands had several dominant species—such as the oak-chestnut forests of southern New England or the spruce-hardwood forests of Vermont—there was a cornucopia of species variation within any given region. William Wood, the first Englishman to produce a detailed account of New England ecology, in 1634, summed up the situation with a poem:

> *Trees both in hills and plaines, in plenty be,*
> *The long liv'd Oake and mournefull Cypris tree,*
> *Skie towring pines, and Chesnuts coated rough,*
> *The lasting Cedar, with the Walnut tough:*
> *The rozin dropping Firre for masts in use,*
> *The boatmen seeke for Oares light, neate growne Sprewse* [spruce],
> *The brittle Ash, the ever trembling Aspes,*
> *The broad-spread Elme, whose concave harbours waspes . . .*
> *The Diars* [dyer's] *Shumach* [sumac], *with more trees there be,*
> *That are both good to use, and rare to see.*

Collectively, these trees formed the landscape of early New England, one of vibrant springtime blossoms, dense summer foliage, and brilliant autumnal leaves.

Timber was the most conspicuous resource, practically the only resource, the Pilgrims had at first. When they yielded to pressures from their financial backers in 1621 and sent a load of commodities back to England aboard the fifty-five-ton vessel *Fortune,* it contained only "2 hoggsheads of beaver and otter skins" but was "laden with good clapboard as full as she could stowe," according to Bradford.

But this practice of timber export did not last long. The Pilgrims found their wood supply too important, and on March 29, 1626, the colony's leaders restricted overseas sale with the following:

> That for the preventing of such inconveniences as do and may
> befall the plantation by the want of timber, That no man of what
> condition soever sell or transport any manner of workes . . . [that]

may tend to the destruction of timber . . . without the consent approbation and liking of the Governour and councile.

Hakluyt's vision of North American colonies immediately supplying the home country with timber butted up against the reality that survival concerned Bradford's group more than providing commodities. Trees made the task of carving a life out of a new, savage land easier, but only by so much.

By the mid-1630s, following a decade of increased immigration (partly related to the ongoing timber famine in England), the original treeless out-croppings started to become overpopulated. Recent settlers, of necessity, entered the woods to make their property claims. This presented a new series of challenges, aside from the Indian attacks or a visit from Satan. The earliest forest dwellers often did not have the time or resources to construct a proper home. As one colonist explained, for many, forming a shelter meant

> [they would] dig a square pit in the ground, cellar fashion, 6 or 7 feet deep, as long and as broad as they think proper, case the earth inside with wood all around the wall, and line the wood with the bark of trees or something else to prevent the caving in of the earth; floor this cellar with plank and wainscot it overhead for a ceiling, raise a roof of spars clear up and cover the spars with bark or green sods.

Once a shelter was established, at least a year was needed to burn, chop, log, plow, and sow several acres. And that was if the settler was handy with an ax, which practically none were. For the heaviest tasks, like moving logs and building a more permanent shelter, he needed the aid of several neighbors and, ideally, oxen, which had to be imported from Europe.

The more New England colonists lived with trees, however, the more they learned to exploit them for goods beyond timber and fuel. The wood-lands offered the raw material for daily life, replacements for comforts and necessities that had been left behind in England. Early settlers crafted tools and bowls from the hardest woods, like ash, hickory, and hornbeam, which, according to William Wood, required "so much paines in riving [splitting] as is almost incredible." Distinctive woods, like the sweet-smelling, red-hued cedar or the dark, richly textured black walnut, were often selected for fan-cier products, ranging from decorative boxes and carved furniture to cere-monial gunstocks. The trees also provided New Englanders with fruits and nuts, including wild plums, cherries, acorns, chestnuts, and walnuts, which could be "as bigge as a small peare," according to Wood. From the amber sap of maple trees, colonists derived sugar, their main source of sweetness besides honey. And they fermented birch, black walnut, sassafras, and spruce to produce beer. The forest even served as something of a pharmacy: purgatives from nut oils; suppuratives from the bark of alder, birch, oak, and willow; cough medicine from the dark, potato-chip-like bark of black cherry trees; and astringents from white pine or hemlock sap. Additionally, colonists extracted colorful dyes from numerous species, including ash, birch, dogwood, hemlock, hickory, sassafras, and sumac.

These first colonists—Pilgrims, Puritans, and independent settlers—thus started to find refuge among the New England forests, but they were failing to live up to their commercial obligations. Their sponsors, joint-stock companies such as Hakluyt's London Company, were for-profit ventures that expected the colonies to deliver commodities and justify the investment. Pilgrims and Puritans may have arrived in America to discover an uncorrupted life, but that didn't mean their backers shared this enthusiasm. In 1629, the New England Company, a reorganized version of the original Plymouth Company, sent six or seven shipwrights to Salem, Massachusetts, jump-starting a domestic shipbuilding trade. The directors of the Massachusetts Bay Company then sent over their own trained shipwrights, coopers, and woodsmen to begin exploiting the woods for profit. Suddenly, the New England coasts were buzzing with the sounds of hammers, axes, and adzes.

The region seemed to have been designed for the building of ships. White oaks, similar to English oaks, furnished excellent ship timber and planking. Cedars, chestnuts, and black oaks were decay-resistant and provided resilient boards for outdoor and underwater sections of ships. Colonists extracted the ever-important naval stores from pitch pines, a fire-resistant conifer, which populated areas that Indians had burned. But perhaps the greatest asset was the white pine, which grew to prodigious heights in the unspoiled forests of New England and produced larger masts than any of the Riga firs in Europe.

Collectively, these assets bolstered the shipbuilding trade. In turn, this brought about the fishing, shipping, and whaling trades, three staples of New England life. Maritime work would become the second-largest colonial occupation, exceeded only by agriculture and trailed closely by logging.

The natural endowments of New England were so great that colonial shipbuilders gained a competitive advantage over their English counterparts, who had an eighty-year head start and the active support of the Crown. Colonists never needed to import timbers or naval stores. Their shipwrights easily obtained even the naturally curved timbers that were preferred for bows, ribs, stems, and sterns. Ultimately, the abundance of good timber allowed New Englanders to produce ships at least 30 percent cheaper than the English, and it became commonplace to sell New England ships to ship merchants in the mother country. These ships would become New England's most profitable manufactured export in the colonial period.

While the home country showed interest in the colonial ships, it was less enthusiastic about timber itself. Hakluyt had been wrong about wood products' becoming the commodity that would justify colonization for his country. The problem was that American timber was too costly. Part of the issue was that freehold laborers in the colonies earned six times more than their serf counterparts in European timber-producing nations. But a bigger concern was that transatlantic shipping made New England uncompetitive. The Baltic ports charged nine to twelve shillings per shipping ton, while the Boston ports charged forty to fifty shillings for the longer transatlantic journey.

New England's inability to sell one of its most widely available products helped send the colonial economy into serious debt. By 1640, there was a glut of British manufactured goods in the colonies and not enough marketable commodities to sell back in exchange.

The need to develop timber markets and bolster the economy forced the colonists to look beyond England for trading partners, one of the first steps that helped separate New England from the mother country. Boston traders began to establish timber markets in Spain, Portugal, the Canary Islands, the Azores, and Madeira after the 1640 economic downturn. Shipping costs to these locations were relatively neutral between the colonies and the Baltic ports. Madeira, a Portuguese settlement and one of the wine islands, actually translates to "wooden land," but deforestation had made this name ironic. The new Iberian and wine islands trades consisted primarily of oak staves for barrels, but also included building timber, white pine boards, and cedar shingles. Seven Boston vessels sailed to these ports in 1642, and this region became the dominant trading partner by the 1660s.

Timber was not among the "enumerated commodities" in England's Navigation Acts, which restricted trade between the colonies and the rest of Europe. New Englanders, consequently, could continue their wine islands commerce in timber without upsetting the home country. Such was not the case with most of the valuable commodities that the southern colonies produced, such as indigo and tobacco, both regulated under the Navigation Acts.

The next major trade relationship that New England developed was with Barbados, a British colony in the West Indies. The small island was the colonial center for cane sugar, one of the most coveted marketable commodities. The Navigation Acts prohibited Barbados from trading its sugar with other European nations, but allowed unrestricted intracolonial commerce with New England. Sugar production had completely denuded a once-forested ter-

ritory, and Barbadians became wholly dependent on New England. When Bridgetown, the island's capital, burned to the ground in 1668, the city sent a flotilla to New England for timber to rebuild. By the 1670s British West Indian sugar islands depended entirely upon trade with New England, and timber was the most important commodity in terms of tons shipped. A group of Barbadian representatives in 1673 told the British Parliament of "the great necessity the Sugar Plantations had of a trade with [New England] for Boards timbers pipestaves horses & fish, & that they could not mainetaine theire buildings, nor send home theire Sugars, nor make above halfe that quantity without a Supply of those things from New England."

With trading partners on both sides of the Atlantic, Boston ships began participating in various "triangular trades" to address commodity imbalances. In one route, timber and other goods were traded for wine in the wine islands. This was then sold to prosperous sugar planters in exchange for rum, which was then resold in New England. In another variation, New England supplies, mainly timber and low-grade fish for slave food, went to the British West Indies in exchange for rum, which was then used to purchase African slaves or sold to European slave traders. These slaves were then traded back to the British West Indies in exchange for sugar, which was distributed in the colonies or England. In the most historically famous triangle trade, New England ports, which handled almost all international trading from the American colonies, sold southern cash crops like tobacco, indigo, and rice to England; European manufactured goods were then bartered for African slaves, who were shipped back to the West Indies or southern colonies to fuel the various cash crop plantations.

In little more than fifty years, abundant timber resources had transformed New England from a harsh, uninviting land to a wealthy trading outpost. Some of the timber barons were as rich as any man in England, and the Puritans controlled one of the strongest shipping trades outside of the Dutch empire. Hakluyt had been correct about the potential for North America's forests, but he had not foreseen the manner in which it would develop.

Of course, there was one forest commodity, New England masts, about which Hakluyt had been uncannily prescient. Their importance to the Royal Navy was too great for England to ignore, regardless of shipping costs or political consequences.

## The King's Broad Arrow

IN EARLY OCTOBER, 1691, King William III issued a new royal charter governing the Massachusetts Bay Colony. Its final section included a curious provision reserving to the King "all Trees of the Diameter of Twenty

Four Inches and upwards" that were not on lands previously granted to private persons. Anyone who felled such trees would suffer the "penalty of Forfeiting One Hundred Pounds sterling." The Crown had suddenly codified a prediction that Hakluyt had made more than one hundred years earlier: New England pines, according to the charter, were being regulated "for the better provideing and furnishing of Masts for [the] Royall Navy."

During the second half of the seventeenth century Hakluyt's fears about the Baltic mast trade had been realized. It began in the early 1650s when the ascendance of Dutch shipping, combined with that nation's opposition to the English Navigation Acts, led to a series of Anglo-Dutch wars. The Dutch had earlier purchased the rights to the Baltic straits from the Danes for a sum of thirty-five thousand pounds annually and had used this leverage to threaten the supremacy of English shipping. The strait was shut down entirely for a brief period in 1654, and the situation remained tense throughout the late seventeenth century. When England's new rulers, William and Mary, stepped up naval production once more in 1689 in preparation for a struggle with France, the heightened demand, along with the already strained Baltic conditions and growing hostility from Sweden, triggered a new timber crisis, and the Crown finally chose to exert its authority over the great mast resources in the forests three thousand miles away.

The North American mast trade, however, was already well established before the 1691 charter. The initial shipment had occurred in 1609 when Jamestown colonists sent "fower score" masts to the home country. Twenty-five years later, New England sent its first delivery of the enormous pines aboard a ship aptly named *Hercules*. Then, in 1652, during the First Anglo-Dutch War, the British admiralty dispatched a mast transport to New England. This precipitated an annual trade with prices for good masts averaging around one hundred pounds. Samuel Pepys, the seventeenth-century English naval administrator whose daily diaries have made him one of the most famous figures in English history, talked about the New England mast trade on repeated occasions in his journal. On December 3, 1666, he wrote: "There is also the very good news come of four New England ships come home safe to Falmouth with masts for the King; which is a blessing mighty unexpected, and without which, if for nothing else, we must have failed the next year. But God be praised for thus much good fortune, and send us the continuance of his favour in other things!"

Unlike timber or naval stores, colonial masts were not simply an alternative or an insurance policy to the Baltic trade. They were superior to the European equivalents, regardless of shipping costs. To begin with, the North American white pines were generally considered more resilient than the Riga firs and

were one-fourth lighter than the European product. But of infinitely greater importance was the size of the North American trees. Hundreds of years without human intervention had allowed these trees, capable of growing taller than nearly any others on earth, to reach proportions almost incomprehensible to London shipwrights (or, for that matter, modern-day Americans). The tallest white pines soared 250 feet above the forest floor, often a hundred feet straight up without a single branch. They were citadels of twenty-five stories (by comparison, twice the height of the nation's first skyscraper, Chicago's Home Insurance Building, built in 1885). The largest New England pine trees could also be several feet in diameter at their base. While forty inches was the widest mast that English ships of the line required, much broader trees were recorded and rumored to exist. A 1736 article in the *American Weekly Mercury* noted one tree "whose Diameter was seven feet eight Inches, and its Length proportionable." If such an awesome tree ever lived, it would have been twenty-four feet around at the ground.

These grandiose pines grew in a broad swath that stretched from the Connecticut River in the northern half of present-day Connecticut straight into Nova Scotia, a region that included almost all of Massachusetts, New Hampshire, and Maine—in other words, New England. It is nearly impossible to convey in text just what these trees meant for the landscape, though many have tried. To quote Donald Culross Peattie, author of a classic American tree guide, "When the male flowers bloomed in these illimitable pineries, thousands of miles of forest aisle were swept with the golden smoke of this reckless fertility, and great storms of pollen were swept from the primeval shores far out to sea and to the superstitious sailor seemed to be 'raining brimstone' on the deck."

Colonists, for the most part, were less interested in the mast potential of these mighty pine trees than in their value as timber. Boston's powerful shipping business with the West Indies and wine islands ensured a brisk commerce in colonial softwoods. Timber export was the premier, and really only, industry of New Hampshire and later Maine. White pines even served as currency in those territories. Advertisers in New Hampshire papers offered "an Assortment of English and West India Goods, Pork and Molasses, cheap for cash or White Pine Boards." Consequently, whatever bounty the Royal Navy offered to encourage mast production was not incentive enough to preserve the white pines from general cutting. The 1691 charter was seeking to remedy this problem by fiat.

Woodsmen, who were compensated only for their labor whether the product was timber or masts, particularly disliked the mast trade because the felling and transport of whole pine logs was brutal work. First, they had to cut a roadway, free of tree-damaging impediments, from the potential fell site to the nearest watercourse, a distance that increased as these trees became harder to find. Next, the fell site had to be prepared with a springy bed of smaller trees, for the weight of a great pine easily caused the trunk to crack on impact with forest floors. According to a colonial official, the white pines were "of such immense weight it [was] almost beyond the power of man to use any secure management in lowering them." And when trees did fall, they often went in unexpected directions, killing lumbermen or making the massive pines impossible to move. Once on the ground, though, loggers found that "48 out of 50 may happen to be defective, although while standing they appeared to be perfectly sound." Decay in the heart of the wood, common in centuries-old trees, disqualified it for use in shipbuilding. The unsuitable 90-plus percent was simply cut to pieces and sent to the nearest mill. Given what was involved in transport, the only person saddened to find a decayed pine was likely the mast contractor himself.

Felled logs that had not cracked, become immobile, or shown signs of heart rot weighed from fifteen to twenty tons and were as difficult to transport as they had been to cut down. The loggers rigged them up with fifteen-foot-high wooden wheels, connected through heavy chains and axles, in a process known as baulking. Enormous teams of oxen pulled these baulked logs toward the river, an especially precarious journey. A log that rose when cresting a hill could pull the oxen off the ground, at which point the yoke strangled them. Trees rushing downhill on icy roads crushed or injured many animals. The loggers simply cut dead or maimed members of the team from their yokes and replaced them with reserves. Once logs finally reached the river, they floated down, often before crowds who assembled to watch the spectacle, and were eventually loaded onto special transports.

When the 1691 charter first appeared, its white pine reservation clause had little impact on the logging trade or the men involved. The independent-minded colonists simply ignored the restriction on cutting trees with diameters exceeding twenty-four inches, treating it like other mandates that proved nearly unenforceable across an ocean. The only evidence of the clause was a marking on some "protected" trees known as the King's Broad Arrow, three strikes of an ax that looked like a crow's track or an upward facing arrow. Parliament had authorized an official to survey the woods and mark restricted trees, but he also proved ineffectual, unsurprisingly, considering the size of the territory involved. One 1700 survey found more than fifteen thousand logs that violated the twenty-four-inch restriction.

The situation changed, however, upon the arrival of John Bridger on the scene. He had worked as a shipwright in Portsmouth, England, and had visited New England while serving as purser aboard a royal naval vessel. In his opinion, Parliament's failure to enforce the reservation clause was putting the Royal Navy, and with it the Crown, at risk. In 1705, Parliament needed a new surveyor general of His Majesty's Woods, and Bridger got the job—it helped that he was the only applicant. He arrived in North America the following year and began to perform his duties with enthusiasm, seizing timber, prosecuting violators, conducting extensive mast surveys, and blazing the King's Broad Arrow throughout the regions where logging was heaviest.

Colonists, who had lived for generations free from British interference in their timberlands, fought back against Bridger's new regime. They cut down the marked pines and sent them to the mills in secret, where they would be sawed into boards just shy of the punishable twenty-four inches. Prerevolutionary homes in New England contained beautiful pine boards of twenty-two or twenty-three inches, but almost never more, a society-wide wink and nod. Fires also began to mysteriously damage trees that Bridger had emblazoned, rendering them useless as masts but fine for timber. Paper townships appeared, turning public lands private and excepting the pines from Bridger's Broad Arrow. Even when perpetrators were caught, colonial courts dismissed Bridger's prosecutions and lectured him for exceeding the scope of his official mandate. A frustrated Bridger wrote to his superiors in England, "[H]ere everyone's hand is against anything belonging to her Majestie or her Intrest; No such thing as Loyallty ever breed here."

For fifteen years, Bridger petitioned members of Parliament and the British Board of Trade to strengthen the Broad Arrow laws. It became a personal obsession. He sent hundreds of letters asking for more resources, tighter regulations, and the authority to bring prosecutions in vice-admiralty courts, which were considered more loyal to the Crown than colonial courts. "Nothing can Doe it Else Effectually," Bridger pleaded.

Between 1706 and 1729, a series of parliamentary acts shaped a Broad Arrow policy that met Bridger's demands. The surveyor-general's resources and jurisdiction increased. More important, the new legislation brought almost all New England pine trees, not just those above twenty-four inches or on public property, under the control of the Crown. Bridger, however, never benefited from these changes, as he was removed from office under charges of corruption in 1718. His immediate successor as surveyor-general treated the new scheme much as Bridger's predecessor had, with indifference.

Though the new legislation wasn't being enforced, it still bred resentment among colonists. A similar Broad Arrow policy had existed within England a century earlier as part of the policies attempting to combat the timber shortage, but the 1647 civil war that ousted King Charles I had ended royal infringements on personal property. Colonists wanted to own their property on the same terms as their countrymen, but the reformed Broad Arrow policy abrogated their rights. At its strictest interpretation, the policy would have permitted the surveyor-general to arrest a man for building his home out of white pine logs or for clearing his land of trees to plant crops. The lieutenant governor of New Hampshire wrote in 1710 that the Crown "never had right: soil being in the natives, as judges of the Courtt have declared."

In 1734, a new surveyor-general, Colonel David Dunbar, soon found out just how strongly the colonists felt about British claims to their pines. He was not only surveyor, but also the lieutenant governor of New Hampshire, which remained under the authority of Massachusetts through 1741. When he took over from Bridger's replacement, he attempted for the first time to enforce the more expansive Broad Arrow policy and decided to make an example of Exeter Township in New Hampshire.

In March 1734, Dunbar traveled up-country toward Exeter to review the timber situation personally. While there, his team encountered a large supply of white pine logs floating in a mill pond. Dunbar proceeded to interrogate a townsperson about the name and ownership of the nearest mill. When the man refused to cooperate, Dunbar raised his cane and began to beat him vigorously. A second townsman refused to provide the information and received the same treatment. After two canings, Dunbar returned to Portsmouth, New Hampshire, to contemplate his next step.

He procured a decree of seizure for a half million board feet from the vice-admiralty court and hired a brute squad to follow him to Exeter. Several of these men headed there in advance of the surveyor-general to gather information. Upon arrival, they found the town quiet and retired to a lodging house for the evening. Soon, a party of Exeter townsmen, dressed as Indians, descended on the inn and assaulted Dunbar's men with a fury that made the surveyor's canings seem like gentle caresses. These assailants ordered Dunbar's men from the inn, at which point the scouts discovered that their attackers had also burned the seizure boat, forcing them to return to Portsmouth on foot.

The next morning, Dunbar approached the town with his entire enforcement squad. When he encountered his beaten scouts walking toward him, he grew enraged and set upon Exeter, his cane raised in fury, prepared to right the injustice. Two more men suffered lashings from the surveyor. He next destroyed the sawblades of one of Exeter's larger mills with an iron bar. But the Exeter townsmen were not to be intimidated. An armed militia met the surveyor and sent his team fleeing to the sound of gunshots. Dunbar never seized his half million board feet.

His replacement as surveyor-general, Benning Wentworth, had a much different idea about the role of the Broad Arrow policy. Wentworth came from the most prominent timber family in New Hampshire. His brother, Mark Hunking Wentworth, was the primary New England mast contractor and one of the richest men in the colonies. Thanks to these connections, Benning had been appointed governor of New Hampshire in 1741. Two years later he actually paid two thousand pounds for the surveyor title, a remarkable sum considering that the job only provided two hundred pounds salary. The position, in conjunction with his governorship, allowed him to secure his family's monopoly and increase his brother's fortune for the twenty-five years of his reign. Enforcement was superficial or used as a tool to intimidate rivals, though woodsmen still chafed at seizures. The surveyor-general reported that one of his deputies, while "in the Execution of his office, was Seized . . . & thrown into a Mill pond, whereby he was in great danger of being drowned."

In 1767, Benning Wentworth finally lost his titles due to malfeasance and disloyalty to the Crown. His cousin, John Wentworth, took both positions, partly to save face and to preserve the family name. The younger Wentworth, despite the conflict of interest with his family, took his responsibilities seriously. According to Reverend Timothy Dwight, who knew Wentworth, he "was a man of sound understanding, refined taste, enlarged views, and a dignified spirit. His manners, also, were elegant; and his disposition enterprising." New Hampshire citizens respected Wentworth for these qualities as well as for his having been born in the state, which distinguished him from all the other royal governors. He was truly one of their own.

Wentworth marshaled all his resources and personal charisma to enforce a mast policy that he found deeply flawed but necessary. Whereas his uncle had sent deputies to survey the woods, Wentworth went personally, riding on horseback through the forests for days at a time and greeting new settlers and lumberers. One of Wentworth's tours began in South Carolina, which produced naval stores, and stretched all the way back to his home state. When he did encounter violators, he treated them with respect and sympathy, a sharp contrast to Dunbar's cane. In one incident Wentworth patiently explained the mast policy to a group of poor woodsmen who had assumed that they could fell the trees because they owned the land. At the conclusion of the conversation, in Wentworth's words, he "singled out one man who had been the most zealous . . . and required him to . . . help me to seize and mark five hundred logs . . . which he directly performed." This approach to enforcement led to a hundredfold decrease in destruction after one year, at least according to Wentworth. If this were true to any extent, it proved the people's affection for Wentworth, not respect for the mast policy.

As Wentworth's term as surveyor and governor advanced, he was increasingly torn between loyalty to his homeland and loyalty to his home country.

Many colonists shared these concerns in the last decade before the Revolution, when open hostility toward royal authority became commonplace. For every New Hampshire resident who cursed the Crown and its forest policies, another stressed that all colonists were British citizens first. An opinion piece in a New Hampshire paper argued for continued Broad Arrow enforcement, "especially when all that is required of us, is to preserve such trees as nature has provided for the sole use of the Navy, and which the laws of our country enjoin upon us, from falling a sacrifice to the avaricious and unbounded desires of groveling and mean spirited men." The words might as well have been Wentworth's.

Soon, circumstances forced him to choose between his state and his country. In April 1775, eight days before the violence at Lexington and Concord that initiated the Revolutionary War, the Massachusetts Provincial Congress sent word to northern ports instructing them "to make use of all proper and effective measures to prevent" any masts on hand from reaching the enemy. Woodsmen from Portsmouth and from Falmouth and Georgetown in Maine began towing masts from the loading pools and hiding them. The following month, Maine loggers kidnapped the British commander of a mast transport ship. Later on, the British, in retaliation, bombarded the kidnappers' town until there was little left but ashes. The last supply of New England masts—a trade that had sent forty-five hundred white pines to England under the Broad Arrow policy—reached the home country on July 31, 1775.

Wentworth honored his position and stayed loyal to the Crown through the Revolution. Though some in his family sided with the colonists, Wentworth himself left New Hampshire soon after hostilities began, figuring that it was safest to wait out the conflict abroad and return after the English triumphed. But he never saw his beloved New Hampshire again. Halifax, Nova Scotia, became his new home, as was the case with numerous Loyalists. He once more was surveyor-general, only in a different Majesty's Woods, the forests of the region that would become Canada.

Ironically, the policies meant to protect England from a mast shortage would trigger one during the Revolutionary War. The Royal Navy had used New England pines almost exclusively as their mainmasts in ships of the line, and the sudden outbreak of hostilities, and consequent cessation of mast shipments, forced England to turn back to the Baltic ports. While the Eastern European ports quickly filled the demand, the Riga firs they provided almost never exceeded twenty-seven inches. Nearly all of the new mainmasts that English ships of the line used in the eight-year Revolutionary War were inferior composite or "made" masts, and the British were unable to produce a wartime effort's worth of made masts on schedule after several generations of relying on colonial white pines.

Without New England masts, the Royal Navy was weakened, if not crippled. During the war, many ships were stuck in port with broken masts, and masting problems also delayed the outfitting of multiple British fleets throughout the war, leaving the British at a disadvantage. New Englanders, meanwhile, sold their masts to the French, whose navy assisted the colonial army during the conflict. Robert Albion, one of the greatest naval historians, has argued that "the lack of masts deserves more of a place than it has yet received among the various reasons for England's temporary decline in sea power" during the American Revolution. Some think he overreaches, but his basic point is true: New England white pines, in their role as naval masts, were an unsung hero in America's gaining its independence.

Regardless of what role masts played in the naval history of the American Revolution, England's colonial mast policy proved an outright disaster for deeper reasons. The disrespect for private property rights, draconian cutting laws, and generally shoddy enforcement drove a wedge between the colonists and the Crown. England might have saved itself money and aggravation by simply purchasing a gigantic masting nursery from the colonists. In the lumbering regions of New England, white pine masts became a symbol of English repression.

But in the cities and towns of the colonies another type of tree was becoming a symbol of something different—American liberty. Trees, it turned out, would help unify the colonies around the belief that liberty was an ideal to hold above all others.

## The Tree of Liberty

THE BOSTON TOWNSPEOPLE who walked past Deacon Eliot's house on the morning of August 14, 1765, encountered something unexpected. Hanging from the branches of a great elm at the corner of Essex and Newbury Streets was the body of a man. Closer inspection revealed it to be a straw-stuffed dummy wearing the letters "A.O.," the initials of Andrew Oliver, secretary of the province. Next to the effigy, swinging in the breeze, was a boot with a little devil "peeping out and thrusting the [effigy] with an Horrid Fork," according to one account.

Oliver was not only secretary of the province but also the royal official commissioned with distributing papers for a new English tax on the colonies, the Stamp Act. The legislation had not gone into effect yet, but when it did it would require that almost all colonial papers carry a stamp that showed payment of a tax. The range of documents covered was staggering, everything from legal transactions and licenses down to dice and playing cards. Boston already had economic problems that summer, and the threat of new taxes enraged nearly all the colonists. The words written near Oliver's hanging effigy summed up the sentiments: "How Glorious is it to see, a Stamp officer hang on a Tree."

Oliver's dummy remained in the great elm for all to observe throughout the day. At one point, according to an eyewitness, "[t]hree Guineas was offerd to any one that should take it down and no one dard to make the Tryall." People openly mocked Oliver and the act, pantomiming stampings on various goods. As evening approached, a spontaneous crowd gathered under the tree. Witnesses counted one thousand participants, a massive number in a town of fifteen thousand. They cut the effigy from the tree and "with great solemnity" placed it in a coffin. Then a procession, led by about fifty well-dressed tradesmen, paraded the two dummies through the streets of Boston, past the house of the royal governor. They continued toward the newly built stamp office and leveled the brick building with a makeshift battering ram. The mob scene concluded with a bonfire in front of Oliver's house, where the crowd burned the effigy and broke all the windows in his house. By 11:00 p.m. the rioters had dispersed. Oliver made it known the next day that he would not serve as stamp distributor.

Though the riots failed to dissuade Parliament from enforcing the Stamp Act, they succeeded in forging a new folk hero: the large American elm where the entire affair began. The tree, in many respects, had grown up in tandem with colonial Boston. Early Massachusetts Bay colonists had planted it in 1646 on a spot near the city's common. During the intervening six score years, it matured into a mighty elm around one hundred feet tall, its leafy crown towering above the nearby houses. And by the 1760s, it had become one of the greatest trees in the entire city, just as Boston had become one of the greatest cities in all of the colonies.

The elm was formally recognized as a symbol of public protest the month after the anti–Stamp Act riot, on September 11, 1765. That day, the Boston Sons of Liberty, a group of leading patriots that included Samuel Adams and Paul Revere, affixed a copper plate to the mighty tree at Deacon Eliot's house that read "The Tree of Liberty" in gold letters. The cause of liberty suddenly had an icon. Soon everyone knew of Boston's Liberty Tree, even members of Parliament in London, who talked of "the Affair at Liberty Tree." Local carpenters pruned the elm for free as "it was for the public good" and "they were always ready to serve the true-born Sons of Liberty."

The American colonies had a long tradition of using trees as meeting spots. John Eliot, a Puritan missionary who reached Massachusetts Bay in 1631, had spent much of his life preaching to Indians beneath a great white oak, known as Eliot's Oak until its death in the twentieth century. William Penn had signed a peace treaty with the Lenape Indians in 1683 beneath the grace-ful branches of an American elm. Black slaves often met in "hush arbors" in the woods, where their activities were shielded from the eyes of white masters. In colonial New York City, businessmen routinely gathered around a buttonwood tree (better known in the modern day as an American sycamore) to meet and trade stocks—the New York Stock Exchange would formally begin in 1792 with the signing of the Buttonwood Agreement.

And trees had also served as symbols of the colonies themselves. Connecti-cut's Charter Oak, for instance, took its name from a story, considered apoc-ryphal, stating that in 1687 a Connecticut colonist had successfully secreted the state's charter inside an oak tree when King James II attempted to seize it. Early Massachusetts colonists minted a shilling with the image of a pine tree—the coin's designer observed, "What better thing than a tree to portray the wealth of our country?" In the eighteenth century, New Englanders began using a flag with a pine tree emblem, a practice that became commonplace during the Revolutionary War. A pine tree flag would wave at Bunker Hill and also when the Massachusetts navy sailed down the Charles River to attack British-held Boston.

The newly christened Liberty Tree was both symbol and stage. It became an active participant in the decade of activity leading up to rebellion in 1775. The Sons of Liberty claimed the tree as their own and used it as an outdoor meeting spot, an area dubbed Liberty Hall. This became an egalitarian point of organization capable of holding thousands of people and excluding none. The Sons of Liberty also erected a flagpole "a good deal above the Top of the Tree," and they would hoist a flag to signal meetings. The tree enfranchised the mobs and functioned as the locus of popular rebellious actions, the first place Bostonians looked for news and demonstrations against the more opprobri-ous policies of Parliament. Official meetings occurred in nearby Faneuil Hall, but the so-called lower-class mobs held court around the elm in Liberty Hall. One disgruntled American Tory referred to the Liberty Tree as "an Idol for the Mob to Worship."

The de facto custodian of the tree, at least at the outset, was a man drawn from the lower classes, twenty-seven-year-old Ebenezer Mackintosh. His sta-tus as a shoemaker distinguished him from merchants like Adams and Revere, who formed the core of colonial resistance. Mackintosh donned the title "First Captain General of the Liberty Tree," a half-mocking allusion to the royal governor's official moniker. His biggest job qualification was his captaining the South End company, a neighborhood artisans' group that participated in the annual Pope's Day festival, a celebration in November when various artisan factions paraded through the streets. Mackintosh had led the festival before, and he would apply this experience to directing angry mobs that formed around the Liberty Tree.

Such was the situation on November 1, 1765, the next time that the Liberty Tree made international news. The Stamp Act went into effect that day, and in the morning two new effigies, those of the prime minister and a member of Parliament associated with the act, appeared hanging from the boughs of the Liberty Tree. A crowd of "several thousand" formed around the site during the day, and at 3:00 p.m. the dummies were cut down from the tree, with Mackintosh leading the protesters through the streets. Eventually, "in token of their utmost Detestation," members of the crowd "tore [the effigies] in Pieces & flung their Limbs with Indignation into the Air," according to one witness.

More Liberty Tree protests followed during the subsequent months. On December 17, 1765, upward of two thousand people gathered to hear Oliver reaffirm for the third time his commitment not to enforce the Stamp Act: "I do hereby in the most explicit and unreserved Manner declare . . . that I never will . . . take any Measures for enforcing the Stamp-Act in America; which is so grievous to the People." Two months later, in February, the Sons of Liberty erected a stage below the Liberty Tree with a gallows. A representation of the devil lay along the top, handing a copy of the Stamp Act to two new effigies below, one of which was the prime minister. A crowd of between two and three thousand assembled around the tree and followed the Sons of Liberty, along with the gallows, a half mile to a spot where they set the entire structure ablaze.

The Liberty Tree gained mythic status in late May 1766, when news reached Boston that Parliament had finally repealed the Stamp Act. The Sons of Liberty gathered around the tree and, according to a contemporary account, "regailed themselves on the Occasion with firing Guns, drinking loyal Toasts, & other decent expressions of Joy." On nearby Boston Common, an oiled-paper obelisk designed by Paul Revere glowed with 280 interior lamps and entertained the reveling crowds. One side of the obelisk showed an image of the Liberty Tree with an angel above and an eagle nesting in the upper branches. The Sons of Liberty meant to move the obelisk in front of the Liberty Tree "as a standing monument of this glorious era," but the object caught on fire and was consumed. The following night, they hung 108 lanterns on the Tree of Liberty, the number representing the members of the "glorious majority" in Parliament. The Sons of Liberty, it must be noted, remained loyal to the Crown at this point—it was tyranny and oppression they had been contesting with the Stamp Act protests.

Soon the Liberty Tree concept began to spread to the other colonies, establishing outdoor, public forums for the various Sons of Liberty groups that dotted the Eastern Seaboard. The earliest such copycat—the only known imitator preceding the repeal of the Stamp Act—was a buttonwood tree in Newport, Rhode Island. The grantor stated that he was bequeathing a "Tree of Liberty" as "a Monument of the spirited and noble Opposition made to the Stamp-Act" that should be "considered as emblematical of Public Liberty." Colonists later dedicated trees at such wide-ranging locations as Norwich, Connecticut; Braintree, Roxbury, and Salem, Massachusetts; Providence, Rhode Island; and Charlestown (Charleston), South Carolina.

In New York, the Liberty Tree took on a different, though related, form. There, Sons of Liberty had erected a wooden pole in City Hall Park, near the city's British barracks, upon hearing the news of the Stamp Act's repeal. This irritated the English soldiers, who chopped it down repeatedly, only to see it spring up once again. In March 1767, the New York Sons of Liberty reinforced their most recent pole with ironwork around the base. A letter posted in the colonial papers warned that those who dared to cut this pole down were "volunteers of Satan" who "may be almost assured New York will be too hot to hold [them] long." Liberty Poles, typically pine masts or flagstaffs, soon rivaled Liberty Trees as symbols opposing British oppression.

Back in Boston, the original Liberty Tree became a self-perpetuating generator of antityrannical sentiment. The twin dates of the original August anti–Stamp Act protests and the act's repeal (celebrated in March instead of May) were now semiannual holidays. In August 1766, at the first of these new rituals, the Sons of Liberty gathered at Liberty Hall to the sound of ceremonial cannon fire. While there they drank a series of fourteen toasts that presaged the conflicts of the next decade. At first, cheers rang out for King George III, the Prince of Wales, and the British Empire, and revelers raised their glasses that "the Union between Great Britain and the Colonies never be dissolved." But later, the Sons of Liberty asked that "the Colonies ever be watchful to obviate any evil Designs, or clandestine Measures to disturb their Harmony." The closing toast demanded that "the everlasting Remembrance of the 14th of August, serve to revive the dying 'Sparks of Liberty,' whenever America shall be in Danger of Slavery." Soon these sparks set the colonists' anti-British sentiment aflame.

One of the first violent clashes before the Revolution began took place around the Liberty Pole in New York. On the night of January 16, 1770, a group of redcoats managed to fell the ironclad pole that had been erected in 1767. Colonists called for justice the next day at a meeting that three thousand people attended. A street fight broke out two days later between soldiers and colonists, the scene threatening to explode into an uncontrollable battle before British officers arrived and dispersed the soldiers. Both sides, however, suffered serious injuries and at least one New Yorker died of a stab wound. The clash became known as the Battle of Golden Hill and preceded the better-known Boston Massacre by six weeks.

These sorts of bloody encounters hardened many of the Sons of Liberty against the British Parliament. However, their antityrannical passion was tempered by Parliament's abandoning nearly all colonial taxes in 1770 with the repeal of the Townshend duties, a series of revenue-raising measures that it had imposed on the colonies three years earlier. All that remained was a tax on tea, which had been retained as a symbolic assertion of British authority. But in May 1773, Parliament revived the simmering hard-line opposition when it granted the East India Company a functional monopoly over the colonial tea market. The Boston Sons of Liberty, like those of the other colonies, now demanded an outright boycott on tea imports and directed their anger toward the colonial tea importers.

On the morning of November 3, 1773, a flag was again waving atop the Liberty Tree. The Sons of Liberty had called a meeting to insist that the local traders swear to reject and return any East India tea shipments. The traders posted their own opposition flyers, also supposedly signed by the Sons of Liberty, that labeled the day's gathering "the deceitful Bait of those who falsely stile themselves Friends of Liberty." This counternotice insisted that traders were entitled "to Buy and Sell when and where we please." Its authors urged Bostonians to avoid the protest altogether.

The Liberty Tree, however, had become the most respected representation of the Sons of Liberty, and no public postings could undermine its flag-flying call to order. A crowd several hundred strong gathered throughout the morning and decried the traders who would not comply with the boycott. As with the events of August 1765, the mob insisted that these tradesmen appear at the Liberty Tree to declare their fealty to the nonimportation of tea. But this time it was not to be. The traders sent letters explaining that it was "impossible for [them] to comply with the Request of the Town." Repeated attempts to coerce these businessmen failed, and eventually, on December 16, the rebuffed Sons of Liberty, dressed as an Indian party, snuck onto the tea ships sitting in Boston Harbor and dumped their supplies overboard, a sabotage known, of course, as the Boston Tea Party.

Over the next eighteen months the situation devolved rapidly. Parliament, reacting to the Tea Party, adopted the Intolerable Acts in the spring of 1774. The following fall, representatives of the thirteen colonies convened in Philadelphia for the First Continental Congress. Liberty Poles now began to shoot up throughout the colonies like cornstalks in July. They appeared at too many new sites to mention individually. In Plymouth, colonists attempted to erect one pole on their famous rock, but split the mighty stone in the process, a fitting metaphor perhaps of the spirit of revolution cracking open the legacy of colonialism. Hostilities formally began on the morning of April 19, 1775, at the town of Lexington in Massachusetts.

One of the war's earliest casualties was the original Liberty Tree itself, the great elm near Deacon Eliot's house that had first enlivened the Boston mobs a decade before. A party of British soldiers decided in August 1775 that they needed to fell this tree that gave the rebels so much inspiration. According to a newspaper account, "After a long Spell of laughing and grinning, sweating, swearing and foaming, with Malice diabolical, they cut down a Tree, because it bore the Name of Liberty." One of the redcoats, while working to sever a branch, fell to the ground and died instantly.

The following year, in August, Bostonians erected a pole atop the Liberty Tree's stump. The location had not changed, but this new sign of liberty was no longer rooted in English soil. One month before, the nation's founders had signed the Declaration of Independence.


IN 1787 THOMAS JEFFERSON famously said, "The tree of liberty must be refreshed from time to time, with the blood of patriots and tyrants. It is its natural manure." Liberty Trees and Liberty Poles would remain symbols of popular protest in America long after the last British soldier departed. Pennsylvania farmers would raise poles during the Whiskey Rebellion, a 1794 reaction to the federal whiskey tax. Another wave of poles would appear in protest of the 1798 Sedition Act, which made it illegal to libel the government. In the 1832 presidential election, supporters of Andrew Jackson, known as Old Hickory, would erect Hickory poles, while those who favored Henry Clay, from Ashland, Kentucky, would use Ash poles. Other isolated incidents would continue up until the Civil War, when the practice seemed to finally die out, a timely end to a tradition that assisted the nation in taking its first steps.

But while the original Liberty Tree helped to unite the colonies in their opposition to tyranny, that did not mean the thirteen colonies were united otherwise. The diverse groups that banded together to defeat the English came from different cultures, religious beliefs, and geographies. A lumberer in Maine, after all, shared little with a Virginia tobacco grower.

This new land of promise would soon rely on trees to help bridge its many gaps.

# 2

## The Fruits of Union

Crab Apple

### Seeds of American Science and Exploration

IN THE MID-EIGHTEENTH CENTURY Peter Collinson, a London merchant, Quaker, and an avid gardener, found himself at the center of a thriving intercolonial plant trade. Of the many specimens available from the numerous British colonies, the ones most in demand were American trees. Because of America's similar latitude, its trees thrived in Europe more than those from other, less temperate territories. Aristocrats coveted these "exotics" for their ornamental gardens, nobility wanted them for their palaces and forests, and botanists sought New World discoveries for study and classification. Prices were high, and the financial and scientific potential of this trade was phenomenal. Unfortunately, reliable suppliers were difficult, if not impossible, to locate. By the 1720s, the prosperous and savvy Collinson was desperately trying to find a botanist in America who traded in trees and could fill the orders that piled up.

Collinson's supply dilemma arose largely because the American colonies lagged behind Europe in all matters scientific. Most colonists were more preoccupied with taming the forested landscape than with assimilating the ideas of the Enlightenment and the Scientific Revolution, those twin engines of progress in Europe. Eighteenth-century America possessed few centers of learned discourse, no significant libraries, and only a handful of colleges, nothing to rival the centuries-old traditions of England or elsewhere on the Continent. The absence of an aristocracy or royalty exacerbated this deficiency, as their patronage traditionally financed full-time scientists in Europe. Even the rare educated colonist with income and a predisposition toward science still lacked both adequate tools, which were manufactured abroad, and ways to communicate and discuss his findings. In such a poor scientific environment, few men could develop the skills necessary for a trading partner in trees: botanical expertise; funds to support collecting trips; and a commercial nursery.

One potential solution to this problem was to send a European botanist. However, the cost of maintaining an overseas infrastructure made this prohibitively expensive for any significant length of time. The most useful partner, at least from Collinson's perspective, had to be a permanent colonist who somehow overcame the obstacles of American life.

John Bartram, the man who would soon fill this role, was a Quaker born in Pennsylvania in 1699. He was of average height, with an upright posture and a face long yet dignified. He was hardworking and resilient, but possessed a demeanor that was gentle and good-natured. His earliest biography, written by one of his sons, noted that Bartram was also an abolitionist who "zealously testified against slavery."

Growing up in William Penn's newly settled colony, Bartram had limited access to formal schooling, but he was inclined toward self-education and managed to learn basic Latin, a necessity for scientists. According to his son, "[h]e seemed to have been designed for the study and contemplation of nature, and the culture of philosophy." The industrious Bartram initially showed an interest in medicine, but shifted toward botany in his twenties. The reason for this, his son speculated, was that "most of his medicines were derived from the vegetable kingdom." Many colonial physicians indeed doubled as botanists, including famous early Americans like Cadwallader Colden, Benjamin Smith Barton, David Hosack, and Caspar Wistar, for whom the plant genus *Wisteria* is named. But Bartram was unique. He alone devoted himself exclusively to the study of plants.

In September 1728, Bartram purchased a plot of land off the Schuylkill River near Philadelphia and turned it into an eight-acre botanical garden, the first of its kind in America. He began to travel the surrounding countryside at his own expense, searching for new trees, shrubs, and other plants. This was difficult work. Trips lasted for days or weeks, as it was slow going to reach the remotest specimens. Most exploration was done on horseback along river-courses. The densest forests and swamps, however, could only be traversed on foot. Such circumstances meant that Bartram was able to carry few provisions in and precious few specimens out. The forests were also dangerous, home to disease-carrying insects, wild animals, hostile Indians, and treacherous terrain. One early botanist in the colonies actually fell to his death while climbing over rocks during a 1680 excursion. Bartram nearly met a similar fate at least once, writing:

> I was on top of the tree, when the top that I had hold of and the branch I stood on, broke—and I fell to the ground . . . . [M]y pain was grievous; afterwards very sick; then in a wet sweat, in a dark thicket, no house near, and a very cold, sharp wind, and above twenty miles to ride home.

Bartram's curious botanical garden, full of exotic American specimens, quickly attracted the visits and notice of "many virtuous and ingenious persons," as described by his son. These men "encouraged [him] to persist in his labours," but like most Americans, Bartram was disconnected from the vibrant scientific networks of Europe. To remedy this, the Pennsylvania botanist began communicating his discoveries "to the curious in Europe, and elsewhere, for the benefit of science, commerce, and the useful arts."

In 1730, one of Bartram's correspondents brought his work to the attention of Collinson. The Londoner, excited to discover a true botanist living within the colonies, began writing with requests for American specimens. To his delight, Bartram proved a reliable and faithful supplier. The two men gradually developed a partnership that blossomed into a friendship and mentorship. Collinson and his cohort became de facto patrons of the American Quaker, financing his travels and supplying him with European texts. Collinson also integrated Bartram into a dynamic European intellectual circle devoted to natural history. Soon the Pennsylvania botanist was routinely corresponding with men of science and letters across Europe, including Carl Linnaeus, the great Swedish botanist whose work had introduced the modern system of taxonomy.

The Bartram/Collinson relationship, while sustained through amity and a mutual love for learning, was, in many respects, a by-product of the international commercial and scientific tree trade. Rarely did a letter arrive or depart during their voluminous correspondence without addressing Bartram's activities gathering specimens. Sometimes Collinson's missives read like little more than work orders, as with this 1735 example:

> Thee need not collect any more Tulip cones, Swamp Laurel cones, Hickory, Black Walnut, Sassafras, nor Dogwood, Sweet Gum, White Oak acorns, Swamp Spanish Oak, nor Red Cedar berries; but all other sorts of acorns, Firs, Pines, Black Gum, or Black Haw, Judas tree, Persimmon, Cherries, Plums, Services, Hop tree, Benjamin, or Allspice; all the sorts of Ash, Sugar tree, Wild Roses, Black Beech, or Hornbeam; all sorts of flowering and berry-bearing shrubs, Honey Locust, Lime tree, Arrow-wood, a particular Locust, Guelder Rose: not anything can come amiss to thy friends, and in particular to thy true friend, P. Collinson.

The always-polite Londoner sometimes discouraged Bartram from "exert[ing] thyself out of reason to serve us," but such courtesy made the extensive requirements no less real.

European demand for American trees was simply insatiable. Partly this was driven by a growing interest in natural history in general, but the real impetus behind the trade was a landscape gardening fad that swept the landed classes of Europe, especially England, during the eighteenth century. The preferred style favored naturalistic environments that incorporated diverse trees—one of the most popular guides, Batty Langley's 1728 *New Principles of Gardening*, stated, "There is nothing more agreeable in a Garden than good *Shade*, and without it *a Garden is nothing*." Englishmen, often using Collinson as their go-between, fanatically pursued America's most fashionable resource. One collector, Lord Petre, "planted out about ten thousand Americans," according to Collinson. Both the Prince of Wales and the Duke of Richmond likely died due to their passion. About this, Collinson wrote Bartram:

> [They] are suspected both to have lost their lives by it, by being out in their gardens, to see the work forwarded, in very bad weather. The Prince of Wales . . . manifestly lost his life by this means. He contracted a cold, by standing in the wet to see some trees planted . . . which brought on a pleurisy, that he died of, lately.

Parliament eventually passed legislation to punish anyone caught stealing American plants by "transport[ing] the rogues," fittingly, to America. Mark Catesby, a British botanist, when reflecting on the situation years later, noted:

America had, "within less than half a century, furnished England with a greater variety of trees than [had] been procured from all the other parts of the world for more than a thousand years past."

Aided by this booming tree trade, Bartram developed as a botanist and explorer. And the more his knowledge grew, the more he longed for the scientific sophistication of Europe. America, he felt, needed a formal organization, like the Royal Society of London, where colonists could exchange ideas, encourage one another, and finance promising research. In 1739 he suggested this to Collinson in a letter that has since been lost. Collinson wrote back:

> As to the Society that thee hints at, . . . to draw learned strangers to you, to teach sciences, requires salaries and good encouragement; and this will require public, as well as proprietary assistance,—which can't be at present complied with—considering the infancy of your colony.

Such was the sorry state of American science, disorganized and utterly dependent on Europe. Bartram was a true outlier, far ahead of his time.

Although his initial proposal went no farther than Collinson, Bartram persevered. The Pennsylvania Quaker next enlisted the help of Benjamin Franklin, a printer who soon developed a reputation as America's greatest scientist. On March 17, 1742, Franklin's *Pennsylvania Gazette* published "A Copy of the Subscription Paper, for the Encouragement of Mr. John Bartram." It called for an annual contribution to support Bartram, arguing:

> And as the Wildernesses, Mountains and Swamps in America, abound with Variety of Simples [herbal medicines] and Trees, whose Virtues and proper Uses are yet unknown to Physicians and curious Persons both here and in Europe; it should be esteem'd fortunate, and a general Benefit, if a Man could be found sufficiently skilful and hardy, who would undertake, as far as in his Power, a compleat Discovery of such Herbs, Roots, Shrubs and Trees, as are of the Native Growth of America.

This announcement was one of the first colonial efforts to promote coordinated science. And it came as no surprise that this appeal originated with the tree trade and botany—natural history, after all, was the only branch of eighteenth-century science where America had an advantage over Europe thanks to the abundant and largely unexplored forests that served as one giant laboratory.

Franklin's appeal on behalf of Bartram, however, fell flat. The Pennsylvania botanist lamented that the "Americans have not zeal enough to encourage any discoveries . . . at their expense."

But the request for funding had not been entirely in vain. Less than six months later, on May 14, 1743, Franklin issued a formal proposal requesting that "one Society be formed of *virtuosi* or ingenious men, residing in the several colonies, to be called *The American Philosophical Society*." Of the enumerated topics for discussion, the first was "all new-discovered plants, herbs, trees, roots, their virtues, uses, &c." This time, the subscription idea finally took hold, and Franklin's American Philosophical Society (APS) became the first organization of its kind in the colonies, an intellectual space where men of science could learn from one another and discuss their work. Bartram, the first to call for this idea, was one of nine founding members and the official botanist. According to a historian of the society, "nearly the whole load was carried by Franklin, with zealous but rather artless help from Bartram, and almost none from anybody else." By the late 1760s a flourishing APS became the hub of American science, with Franklin at the helm and Bartram by his side.

However, just as the APS was finding its footing the colonies plunged headlong into war with England. The Revolution upended life in America for almost a decade, and science was no exception. Many had to decide between their homeland and their home country. Bartram, who had gained the title of king's botanist in 1765, chose his native flora over his British office, a sharp contrast to John Wentworth, the surveyor-general of His Majesty's Woods, who had fled to Canada.

A wartime embargo with England temporarily crippled Bartram's trade in American trees and plants. At one point, Franklin stepped in to resolve this challenge personally. In May 1777, he wrote to Bartram from Paris, where he was serving as secretary of state for the recently unified colonies:

> The communication between Britain and North America being cut off, the French botanists cannot, in that channel, be supplied as formerly with American seeds, &c. . . . . [Y]ou may, I believe, send the same number of boxes here . . . I will take care of the sale, and returns, for you.

Bartram, by this point, was old and in poor health. And he would not live long enough to see his tree trade fully restored. He died in 1777—Collinson, his dear friend, had passed on nine years earlier. It was a remarkable life for a Quaker farmer with no formal education. He had become a member, in addition to the APS, of the Royal Societies of London and Sweden. His botanical garden still exists on its original site. Though he published no seminal works, during the course of his career he had botanized across almost all of eastern North America, including Florida. In 1763 he had declared to Collinson that he knew "more of the North American plants than any others." But perhaps this was being too modest. The incomparable Carl Linnaeus supposedly described Bartram as "the greatest natural botanist in the world."

His death came just as a new age of American science was dawning. Men like Bartram and Franklin had paved the way for the next generation, ready to channel the energy of independence toward science, discovery, and exploration. Philadelphia, home of the APS, became the nation's scientific, intellectual, and political center, second only to London among the English-speaking cities of the world. In the wake of the Revolution, Americans began making contributions in fields as diverse as astronomy, chemistry, zoology, and physical anthropology. Nonetheless, botany—and the European tree trade—remained central to American science in this period.

Bartram's death had left a void in the scientific community, and no one person could replace him. The man who came closest was his protégé and cousin, Humphry Marshall. Like Bartram, he was a Quaker botanist with interests in almost all aspects of the natural world. His botanical garden, founded in 1773, was older and better-known than all others aside from his elder cousin's. After Bartram's death, he quickly became the nation's leading seedman.

In 1785, Bartram's protégé published a work that cemented both their legacies and put American botany officially on the map, *Arbustrum Americanum: The American Grove*, an alphabetical catalogue of native forest trees and shrubs. Though little remembered today, this was the first work on American botany published by an American and one of the earliest scientific texts published in the new nation. Marshall dedicated the manuscript to the APS, the organization that Bartram helped found, now the locus for all important scientific writing. The book contained a straightforward catalogue of the country's roughly 350 known trees and shrubs, according to their classification under the taxonomic system that Linnaeus had devised. The emphasis on trees reflected the continued influence of the international commercial trade, which was still supporting botanists such as Marshall. At the back of the book appeared an advertisement that read: "Boxes of seeds, and growing plants, of the Forest Trees, Flowering Shrubs, &c. of the American United States; are made up in the best manner and at a reasonable rate by the Author." Marshall's book sold poorly in America but was popular abroad, with French and German translations appearing by 1788.

• • •

SHORTLY AFTER MARSHALL published his seminal work, André Michaux, a celebrated French botanist, appeared on the American scene. The king of France, Louis XVI, had sent him to America with instructions to "study the productions and collect with care for His Majesty the plants, seeds, and fruits of all trees and shrubs." France was interested in America's trees for many reasons, particularly one similar to that of England nearly two centuries earlier—their navy depended on timber and, as most of their slow-growing domestic oaks had been felled, they sought faster-growing American varieties for reforestation. According to a French report from the period, France had only thirty-seven species of forest trees that reached thirty feet, while America possessed ninety species that grew past forty feet. Additionally, of the eighteen predominant French forest trees, only seven were suitable for naval and civil construction, while America boasted fifty-one suitable varieties.

Michaux reached New York in mid-November 1785, carrying letters of introduction. As both a man of science and a representative of America's foremost ally during the Revolutionary War, he was quickly embraced by leading American politicians and scientists, including Franklin, George Washington, and Marshall.

Michaux's approach to botany mirrored that of the American seedmen. A man of indefatigable industry and dedication, he spent months traveling through the forests of the various states and operated two botanical gardens for study and trade. The quantities he began sending back to France were massive. One shipment from March 1786 included 525 red maples, 190 magnolias, 260 hickories, 112 silver bell trees, 100 holly trees, and lesser quantities of innumerable other varieties. During the next ten years, he would ship more than 60,000 trees to his homeland.

Such an elaborate operation was, not surprisingly, expensive to maintain. Unlike that of the American botanists, Michaux's work was primarily noncommercial—his specimens went directly to the royal gardeners in Paris—and depended entirely on French patronage. For the first several years, he received generous support, being funded to live "on a par with all . . . agents for France, public or private, under the protection and immediate safeguard of His Majesty." Soon, however, the French Revolution changed the political scene. Support for Michaux dissipated and by 1792 his personal funds were running dangerously low. Like Bartram fifty years earlier, he wished to find other funding and support within the United States, both for the sake of scientific advancement and to fulfill his original mandate.

At the same time that Michaux was struggling financially, Thomas Jefferson, the secretary of state and a member of the APS, began vigorously lobbying his colleagues to finance an excursion past the western limits of the new nation.

Such a mission had enormous potential for future trade and natural history. Jefferson, best remembered as a statesman, was also a leading natural historian and botanist, with an especial love for trees. He once wrote, "The greatest service which can be rendered any country is, to add an useful plant to its culture." The only book he published, *Notes on the State of Virginia,* thoroughly described the territory's natural history and vigorously counterattacked a pernicious but popular European theory of "cultural degeneracy," which claimed that inherent inferiorities in the climate and soil of North America degraded the quality of all plant and animal life.

Jefferson's idea of western exploration was a familiar one. Explorers since the days of Hakluyt had sought the fabled western passage to Cathay. In 1763, Bartram had even contemplated a western trip in a letter to Collinson, but dismissed it out of hand as impractical: "Before this scheme can be executed, the Indians must be subdued or drove about a thousand miles back. No treaty will make discovery safe." Jefferson himself had first attempted to organize an ill-fated trip in 1786. But none of these endeavors came especially close to being realized.

By 1792, Jefferson, in conjunction with the APS, was actively seeking qualified men to lead his proposed western excursion. His preference was for natural historians, specifically botanists, whose scientific and field expertise made them best equipped to handle such an ambitious journey. In June, Caspar Wistar, on Jefferson's behalf, reached out to Moses Marshall, a botanist who worked closely with his uncle, Humphry. Wistar's letter stated that "Jefferson and several other gentlemen are much interested, and think they can procure a subscription sufficient . . . as a compensation to any one who undertakes the journey . . . to have our continent explored in a western direction." Marshall, however, passed on the opportunity. Meriwether Lewis, a young Virginian with a promising future in exploration, applied for the spot but was rejected.

In December, Michaux of his own initiative contacted the APS and Jefferson, who had thus far been unable to find any worthy explorers. According to the botanist's journal, "I proposed to several members of the Philosophy Society the advantages to the United States in having geographic information west of the Mississippi. I asked for the sum of 3,600 francs" to undertake such a mission. If the APS agreed, it would be the first journey of its kind to push west beyond any known settlements. It would also resolve Michaux's financial difficulties. And the Frenchman was explicit in his priorities: "Bound by all manner of consideration to my country, I owe to her my services, and the primary objective of my researches on natural history is to fulfill my obligations in this regard; the second objective is to be useful to America." In other words, Michaux's foremost concern was seeking out useful trees for his homeland.

Shortly after receiving the French botanist's request, the members and affiliates of the APS—effectively the leaders of the new republic—seized on the proposal. Michaux's reputation matched or exceeded that of any other botanist in the colonies. He appeared to be an ideal candidate to lead the previously unachievable mission. In early 1793, the society produced a document endorsing Michaux's proposal and guaranteeing funds. The signatories included Washington, Jefferson, John Adams, Alexander Hamilton, and seven other members of the Constitutional Convention.

The trip was about to begin when Michaux had the misfortune of crossing paths with a French ambassador named Edmond-Charles Genêt. Better remembered as Citizen Genêt, the ambassador had been sent to America to garner official support for France's war against Spain and Britain, but he immediately proved impossible to control. One of his subversive acts was an unauthorized campaign to free Spanish Florida and Louisiana, and Michaux was solicited for this doomed conspiracy plot. Torn between his love for botany and his love for his country, Michaux chose the latter. His landmark western excursion collapsed once authorities learned of his involvement in the Citizen Genêt Affair.

After Michaux's western expedition was aborted, the idea of transcontinental exploration idled for another decade until Jefferson, now president of the country and the APS, revived his long-standing dream once more. In January 1803, he sent a confidential message to Congress recommending another western exploring party, and the legislature eventually appropriated five thousand dollars for its execution. Jefferson commissioned Meriwether Lewis, now a captain in the army, to lead the mission, with William Clark as his second in command. The language authorizing this new expedition was practically identical to the instructions Jefferson had earlier sent to Michaux—the Lewis and Clark trip was essentially a repackaging of the 1793 proposal. In fact, one of Jefferson's greatest concerns was that while Lewis had "a remarkable store of accurate observation" he was "no regular botanist." Consequently, the president insisted that Lewis spend several months before his departure in Philadelphia with Benjamin Smith Barton, a botanical professor, physician, and member of the APS, who had recently published *Elements of Botany*, the nation's first botanical textbook.

On August 31, 1803, Lewis and Clark set out from Pittsburgh and embarked on an adventure more than two centuries in the making. They spent three years exploring the western limits of the continent, collecting geographical, anthropological, and botanical information. Though the mission is best remembered for its symbolic, almost spiritual, importance in the formation of the idea of a continent-spanning nation, it was also a major scientific triumph.

Lewis and Clark sent back numerous specimens, including the Osage Orange tree, which later became a staple of natural hedges throughout the prairie states.

America, by the early nineteenth century, had shifted from a botanical curiosity for European scientists into an increasingly independent scientific nation, especially in the realm of natural history. Americans began to produce important manuscripts across a wide range of scientific topics, building on the tradition that Marshall started in 1785. The nation was now adjusting to a new political and cultural paradigm in which science and discovery progressed, even in the absence of European assistance.

## The Founding Gardener

I N  T H E  H I S T O R Y  of America, few anecdotes are more familiar than one involving a young George Washington and an ill-fated cherry tree. The original version was first published in a popular biography of the president from the early nineteenth century. In it, six-year-old George received a hatchet and quickly used it to dispatch an English cherry tree. His father confronted him, and George hesitated but soon produced perhaps the most famous admission in the history of America: "I can't tell a lie, Pa; you know I can't tell a lie. I did cut it with my hatchet." The moral of the story, which millions of schoolchildren subsequently internalized, was that the nation's founding father was an honest man, one obliged to admit his wrongs, a model worth emulating. The problem, of course, was that this incident never took place. Washington's biographer invented the story, along with many others, to help boost sales and humanize a man often perceived as cold and distant.

The irony in this famous fabrication was that Washington, like several of the Founding Fathers, spent much of his domestic life planting trees. He would no more have needlessly destroyed a fine English cherry than he would have disbanded the Continental Army at Valley Forge. A proper introduction to the young Washington was not the apocryphal cherry tree tale, but a snippet from the journal he kept at sixteen, his earliest writing: "[W]e went through the most beautiful Groves of Sugar trees and spent the best part of the Day admiring the Trees and the richness of the Land." This was the true disposition of the nation's first president. He was a man enraptured by the aesthetic beauty and utility of trees, always content to pass a day among them, something he did often during his early years as a surveyor in Virginia.

As with many of the Founding Fathers, especially those from the southern states, Washington was a planter, meaning that he owned more than twenty slaves and earned his living from the cash crops he grew. Southern planters, who composed the top 1 or 2 percent of the white population in mid-eighteenth-century Virginia, used slaves to handle the majority of farming's pedestrian tasks, which left them time to pursue creative endeavors. Washington devoted much of his domestic energy to beautifying and cultivating his Virginia estate, Mount Vernon, which he had inherited in 1752. The same landscape gardening fad that had swept England in the mid-eighteenth century was beginning to captivate the Virginian planter class, and Washington was at the movement's forefront. He, along with Jefferson and several other Founding Fathers, displayed a passion for tree planting equal to that of British aristocrats like the Duke of Richmond, the Prince of Wales, and Lord Petre.

In 1783, shortly after the Treaty of Paris had been signed and officially ended the Revolutionary War, Washington, having guided the Continental Army to victory and riding a wave of popular approval, announced that he wished to return to his farm. King George III, disbelieving that any leader would yield power so easily, reportedly said of Washington: "If he does that, he will be the greatest man in the world." George III may have been justified in his claim, but he failed to understand that Washington was a planter by disposition. Warcraft was a public responsibility that he had performed grudgingly. Washington's greatness in walking away from the temptations of power stemmed largely from a desire to retreat into the pleasures of rural life. Shortly after returning to Mount Vernon, he wrote:

> I am become a private citizen on the banks of the Potomac, and under the shadow of my own Vine and my own Fig-tree, free from the bustle of a camp and the busy scenes of public life, I am solacing myself with those tranquil enjoyments. . . . I am not only retired from all public employments, but I am retiring within myself; and shall be able to view the solitary walk, and tread the paths of private life with heartfelt satisfaction.

Now free to pursue his own interests, Washington devoted himself entirely to landscape gardening. In January 1785, he wrote to a friend, "Plantations . . . are now become my amusement and I should be glad to know where I could obtain a supply of such sorts of trees as would diversify the scene." For the next two years, the selection and transplanting of ornamental and shade trees became a quotidian affair, his primary leisure activity. Washington would mount his horse and ride through his properties, spotting potential specimens with the practiced eye of a surveyor and general. His journal read like an inventory of native specimens: "thriving ash trees," "very fine young Poplars—Locusts—Sasafras and Dogwood," "thriving plants of the Magnolio," and "young Crabtrees of all sizes & handsome." By February 1785, according to his journal, he was "[e]mployed all day in marking the ground for the reception of my Shrubs." The following month, he was spending "the greatest part of the day in pruning and shaping the young plantation of Trees & Shrubs." Washington persevered throughout 1785 and 1786, overseeing Mount Vernon's transformation into a sylvan paradise. By 1787, the developed portion of his estate included two groves, two wildernesses, shrubberies, a mount, a deer park, serpentine drives, a bowling green, a botanical garden, and symmetrical flower and vegetable gardens. At this point, however, national affairs reclaimed Washington, first as president of the Constitutional Convention in 1787 and then as president of the United States from 1789 to 1797.

History tends to separate Washington's life at Mount Vernon from his roles as general or president, but in truth they were never far apart. The statesman could be taken out of the farm, but not the farm out of the statesman. For example, in August 1776, as Washington was days away from the Battle of Long Island, the first and largest fight of the war, he wrote to his estate manager with great specificity about the way that new trees were to be distributed in Mount Vernon:

> [T]hese Trees [are] to be Planted without any order or regularity (but pretty thick, as they can at any time be thin'd) and to consist that at the North End, of locusts altogether. & that at the South, of all the clever kind of Trees (especially flowering ones) that can be got, such as Crab apple, Poplar, Dogwood, Sasafras, Lawrel, Willow (especially yellow & Weeping Willow, twigs of which may be got from Philadelphia) and many others which I do not recollect at present—these to be interspersed here and there with ever greens such as Holly, Pine, and Cedar, also Ivy—to these may be added the Wild flowering Shrubs of the larger kind, such as the fringe Tree & several other kinds that might be mentioned.

A decade later, during the summer of 1787 that Washington spent in Philadelphia for the Constitutional Convention, he made two trips to Bartram's famous garden, noting that the site, "tho' stored with many curious plants, shrubs and trees, many of which are exotics, was not laid off with much taste, nor was it large." As president, he traveled to Flushing, Long Island, to see Prince Nurseries, the oldest commercial nursery in the country. Washington wrote that the outfit "did not answer my expectations. The shrubs were trifling, and the flowers not numerous." Perhaps it was difficult to impress a man whose own estate was fast becoming the national sanctuary of tree culture.

Washington had company among the Founding Fathers in mixing political culture with plant culture. Many of them, including Jefferson and James Madison, possessed great estates. Washington was certainly not the only one who snuck off to Bartram's garden during the Constitutional Convention; Jefferson, another avid horticulturist and landscape gardener, visited frequently, as did many others. Questions of statecraft for these men routinely blended with discussions of seeds, grafting, and landscape gardening. Recall, for example, that Benjamin Franklin, while in France on a diplomatic mission, acted to protect the seed trade even though his mandate was to acquire French support for the cause of independence. Subsequently, Jefferson, during his own diplomatic turn in France, spent significant time visiting farms and gardens in search of domesticated plants to introduce to America.

When people sought to curry goodwill or political favor with Washington and Jefferson, they customarily sent a choice tree specimen as a gift. Washington received grafts and seedlings from political cohorts, including fellow participants in the Constitutional Convention, such as Governor George Clinton of New York and Henry "Light-Horse Harry" Lee, the governor of Virginia and father to General Robert E. Lee. This practice of gifting plants was also common for visiting foreign dignitaries. When Michaux arrived in America, he stopped at Mount Vernon with a phenomenal cache of rare specimens that included seventy-five pyramidal cypresses and four Ramnus trees, a type of evergreen. The head gardener of the Jardin Royal in Paris sent Jefferson an annual tree offering for several decades.

In 1797, Washington, after finishing his second term as president, again walked away from public life. Few could believe that once more he ceded power so easily, but Washington desired a return to the pastoral existence that history so frequently denied him. His Virginia estate had finally matured into a sylvan oasis, with mighty tulip poplars lining the entry path and more than sixty native species spread throughout. After arriving at Mount Vernon for this final stay, he wrote: "I am once more seated under my own Vine and fig tree, and hope to spend the remainder of my days . . . in peaceful retirement, making political pursuits yield to the more rational amusement of cultivating the Earth."

It was fitting, perhaps, that for a nation cut from among the trees, dependent on their abundance, its first hero was their champion and benefactor. As Washington once wrote to a friend, "[T]hose trees which my hands have planted . . . by their rapid growth, at once indicate a knowledge of my declining years, and their disposition to spread their mantles over me before I go hence to return no more. For this, their gratitude, I will nurture them while I stay."

## Johnny Appleseed and the Old Northwest

O NE MIDAUTUMN DAY in 1797, twenty-three-year-old John Chapman was hiking west across the Allegheny Plateau in north central Pennsylvania when an early-winter storm overtook him. Lacking all but the most basic provisions, he quickly selected a sheltered site and made his camp. The snow piled up until it was knee deep and impassable, but the young man, who was no stranger to the wilderness, gathered a supply of beech tree switches and moosewood bark and set about constructing snowshoes. These proved sturdy enough to sustain him the rest of his way, and around the first of December he arrived in the town of Warren, Pennsylvania, which had been founded two years earlier. The knapsack he'd been carrying contained a cargo of apple seeds, and the following spring he used them to plant a small nursery about six miles south of the frontier outpost. This, history or tradition suggests, was the first link in a chain of apple nurseries that soon blanketed the Old Northwest.

According to those who claimed to have met Chapman, his physical appearance reflected the simple, almost primitive, way he conducted his life. He stood about five feet nine inches tall, with a wiry frame, long unkempt hair, and a scraggly beard. His dress was often little more than the cast-off articles he received, and in later life nothing more than a coffee sack with arm and neck holes. Most days he went barefoot, even in the coldest weather. His hat was, at one point, an upturned tin vessel and later a homemade swatch of pasteboard with an immense brim to protect his eyes.

Outfitted in such an unusual manner, Chapman seemed to have emerged from nature itself, but in truth his roots traced back to New England. He was born in Leominster, Massachusetts, on September 26, 1774, the second child of a farmer who was one of the original Minutemen. Chapman's father apparently fought at the Battle of Bunker Hill and later served with Washington's Continental Army. In 1776, while Chapman's father was still away fighting, his mother died, and he and his older sister were effectively orphaned, raised in the care of a neighboring family.

Between this point and Chapman's 1797 appearance in Warren, painfully few details survive, leaving only questions about where he attained his interest in the undeveloped frontier or his love for apples.

With regard to the first issue, territorial developments in the new nation offered some insight. On July 13, 1787, when Chapman was twelve years old, the United States incorporated an enormous stretch of land north and west of the Ohio River known as the Northwest Territory. Its more than 260,000 square miles included the modern states of Ohio, Indiana, Illinois, Michigan, and Wisconsin as well as the northeastern section of Minnesota. Most of this was federal land, and government policy in the period favored transferring such property to private hands as quickly as possible. Some lands were given to war veterans and some allotments were purchased by private investors, but for most of the first decade Native American threats inhibited settlement. This changed in 1795, when a peace treaty was signed in the wake of General "Mad" Anthony Wayne's victory over the affiliated tribes of the Western Confederacy at the Battle of Fallen Timbers.

Developers soon began promoting cheap lands—in the regions around Pittsburgh and countless other areas throughout the West—to the growing and often debt-ridden populations of Massachusetts and the Connecticut Valley. Soon enterprising Americans, willing to hack out a new life from the great hardwood forests of the interior, started pushing into the frontier, first along the Susquehanna Valley of western Pennsylvania and eventually into Ohio, Indiana, and Illinois. When Chapman appeared at Warren in 1797, he was arriving with this first wave of settlers.

But why, even if he was following this westward push, did he show up hauling a store of apple seeds?

A PPLES, THE QUINTESSENTIAL American fruit, are thought to have originated primarily in the forested foothills of the Tien Shan Mountains, along the border between northwest China, Kazakhstan, and Kyrgyzstan. Apple seeds are a bit like snowflakes in that no two are exactly alike. Any given apple tree can produce offspring whose fruits differ markedly from those of their parents: seeds from a sweet apple can yield bitter apples, large apples can yield small, and so on through an infinite list of possibilities. This quality has made them among the most adaptable and durable fruits in the entire plant kingdom, but it also meant that no desirable fruits lasted longer than the life span of a specific tree. Eventually prehistoric farmers learned that apples, like many trees, could reproduce through grafting or budding, processes where preexisting plant matter was attached to a new rootstock. This allowed a degree of control over variation.

By the time the first colonists reached North America, the fruit already had a long and rich history throughout the known world. An apple from the Tree of Knowledge had tempted Eve in the mainstream translations of the Old Testament. A golden apple of discord had sparked a contest between Greek gods that led to the Trojan War. A falling apple had helped Isaac Newton recognize the force of gravity.

The cultivated apple—as opposed to native crab apples that some Native Americans may have used—emigrated to North America as seeds that the earliest colonists carried. The man thought to have introduced them to New England was an eccentric Plymouth minister named William Blackstone (or Blaxton), who arrived in 1623. Tradition suggests that he saddle-trained a bull and rode it through the countryside distributing apples and flowers. Peter Stuyvesant, the last administrator of New Netherland (present-day New York City), likely imported the first apple graft—in the mid-seventeenth century his orchard in the Bowery district featured the Summer Bonchretien apple, a Dutch variety.

Apples soon thrived in the colonies thanks, in large part, to their method of propagation. Whereas many European plant species suffered in the New World (and prompted continental natural historians to posit the theory of "cultural degeneracy" that Jefferson rebuffed), European apple trees successfully adapted to their new environs (and also cross-bred with native crab apples). Farmers planted seeds on newly cleared land, hoping for a few palatable specimens, which they could then graft if desired. The first named American variety was, quite possibly, Blaxton's Yellow Sweeting (known today as the Sweet Rhode Island Greening), which the bull-riding minister grew as far back as 1635. Another contender for this crown is the Roxbury Russet, named for the Massachusetts town of its origin and the russet, or brownish, color of its skin.

By the mid-eighteenth century, apple cultivation had progressed to the point where England was importing New World varieties. A letter that Collinson sent Bartram in 1759 noted that "Our friend Benjamin [Franklin had] a fine parcel of . . . apples [brought] over, this year,—in which I shared." The variety that Franklin had carried over was the most popular apple in the colonies, the Newtown Pippin, pips being apple trees grown originally from seed. This fruit must have made a strong impression on Collinson, for he freely expressed his displeasure in Bartram's failure to include any specimens in his latest shipment: "We were sadly disappointed,—being in hopes of seeing some grafts of the true Newtown Pippin; but there was none." Later, Jefferson wrote from France to James Madison, "They have no apple here to compare to our Newtown Pippin."

Palate-pleasing varieties like the Newtown Pippin, however, played only a small part in the fruit's American history. Most planted trees came from seeds, not grafts, and the large majority, well over 99 percent, produced fruit far inferior to a Yellow Sweeting or a Roxbury Russet. These infinite barrels never made it to the dining table. Many became food for the hogs that most American farmers raised. Others were dried until needed for sauces, or converted into vinegar, or cooked down into preserves. But the most popular use was in fermentation. Far and away, the factor that allowed the apple to dominate the landscape and affect the economy was its role in the first great American drink: hard cider.

Colonists prized alcoholic beverages. Strong drafts were often safer than drinking water, which could be unpalatable and polluted, and they palliated a harsh life spent fighting the forests and taming the land. Seventeenth-century New England already had a well-developed cider culture, and, with apples quickly acclimating to the American landscape, the beverage was a natural fit. Many other, less successful alternatives were concocted in the early years of colonization, including beers made from spruce, pumpkin, and persimmon, and so-called health beers produced from just about anything else available. Another rival, rum, was imported from the sugar-producing islands—part of the many triangle trades that New England ships participated in—but nothing competed with cider in scope and availability. It was one of the few aspects of American culture that all the colonies shared.

The drink peaked in popularity during the century that framed the American Revolution. The average New England family was consuming seven barrels annually by 1767, roughly thirty-five gallons per person. One in ten New England farms owned and operated a cider mill. On July 4, 1788, when seventeen thousand Philadelphians assembled to celebrate the establishment of the Constitution, they drank nothing but beer and cider, prompting the newspaper report to comment, "Learn, reader, to prize those invaluable Federal liquors [i.e., cider and beer], and to consider them as the companions of those virtues that can alone render our country free and respectable." John Adams, the nation's second president, reportedly began each morning with a tankard of hard cider. Frenchman St. John de Crèvecoeur, who traveled throughout the new nation and wrote a series of widely read essays and letters, once stated bluntly, "Cider is to be found in every house." The drink even became a common unit for exchange, much as white pine boards were in New Hampshire and Maine.

Thus, the American apple orchard was really a cider orchard, and it was an ever-present feature of farms for all classes of citizens. Jefferson's Monticello orchards contained about 265 cider apple trees, mostly of the Taliaferro and Hewes Crab varieties. Washington's Mount Vernon orchards produced a staggering 120 gallons of cider or mobby (apple or peach brandy) each day throughout the autumn. Crèvecoeur once noted that on his own farm he had prepared "a new apple orchard of five acres consisting of three hundred and fifty-eight trees."

Planting a cider orchard was not only something that every farmer chose to do; in many circumstances, it was something that every farmer had to do, often before they even constructed their dwellings. Possession of an orchard indicated that land was being settled and productively used. When Washington offered portions of his own land for lease, he mandated:

> [W]ithin three years there shall be planted an orchard of 100 apple
> trees . . . and 100 peach trees, the same to be kept always during
> the continuance of said lease well pruned, fenced in and secured
> from horses, cattle and other creatures that might hurt them.

The Ohio Company, one of the land development firms operating in the
Northwest Territory, required settlers seeking one-hundred-acre lots to plant
not less than fifty apple trees and twenty peach trees within three years. The
planting of apple seeds or peach stones often served as a guarantee to warrant
land titles. Apple trees (along with peach trees) were the only trees that settlers
and typical farmers actually planted on their property. Everything else met the
ax, ornamental plantings being the province of wealthy men like Washington
and Jefferson. The first apple crop meant settlement had been achieved, both
culturally and often legally.

The problem for settlers in the interior was how to acquire these all-
important trees, the providers of food, drink, and, most important, title to land.
Carrying seedlings or grafting scions from their homes back East was impractical and a waste of precious space. Besides, few could have afforded to buy
the stock in the first place. Starting a tree from seed was troublesome in its
own right. The maturation process took five years, a dangerously long stretch of
time for men looking to cultivate the land and claim title as fast as possible in a
notoriously corrupt system.

A GAINST THIS BACKDROP appeared John Chapman and his satchel
of apple seeds at Warren, Pennsylvania, in late 1797. He was not the first
to bring apples into the Old Northwest, nor was he the only nurseryman to
set up shop, but what made Chapman unique, aside from his comportment,
was a lifetime spent pursuing the frontier, anticipating the waves of settlers,
always ready with young seedlings and a concern for his fellow man's well-
being. Though apple nurseries were a business, he treated it more like a mission, happy to give his seedlings to needy families, insisting that the only true
way to raise an apple was from seed, and arguing that budding and grafting
were perversions of nature.

By 1804, Chapman, now thirty years old, began shifting his operations
from western Pennsylvania to the north central Ohio frontier, the region
where he would spend much of his life. One year earlier, the federal government had opened U.S. military lands to the general public, paving the way for
a new rush of pioneers. Chapman's nurseries soon spread out along the lanes of

a great triangle of early Ohio trails and watercourses: The nadir was the town of Marietta, which sat at the intersection of the Ohio and Muskingum Rivers and, in 1788, was the first permanent settlement established within the Northwest Territory.

Chapman traveled along these footpaths and byways, stopping to plant nurseries wherever the forest, population density, and legal circumstances permitted. According to the earliest American written description of Chapman, after taking time to sow a sufficient number of seeds, "he would go off some twenty miles or so, select another favorable spot, and again go through the same operation." Every so often he swung east to inspect his older nurseries and collect apple seeds from the cider mills of Pennsylvania, then return, as one story claimed, in two canoes lashed together, with him lying supine in one, a cache of seeds in the other.

The challenges of frontier life seemed to present no difficulties for Chapman. He often slept outside beneath the leaves of the giant hardwoods that blanketed the region. Even when neighbors offered him quarters he preferred to sleep on the floor near the fire. His need for companionship was modest. He never married and, while some rumors surfaced of a fondness for young girls, they appeared to be grounded in Rabelaisian gossip rather than actual fact. His endurance was remarkable, an almost superhuman disposition toward sweat and toil. One of the most famous tales, embellished but grounded in truth, had Chapman running through the forests for dozens of miles one night during the War of 1812 to spread the news of oncoming British and Native American attacks. An 1871 biography from *Harper's New Monthly Magazine* commented, "Refusing all offers of food and denying himself a moment's rest, he traversed the border day and night until he had warned every settler of the approaching peril." The Native Americans, despite their hostility toward settlers, were said to respect Chapman as a holy man, and he walked freely among them. The Ohioan pioneers soon took to calling this strange figure John Appleseed, which later became Johnny Appleseed.

There was, however, another side to Chapman. The bowdlerized versions of his legend styled him an inscrutable lover of nature with a passion for apple seeds. A fuller picture included his devotion to Swedenborgianism, a small Christian sect based on the teachings of Emanuel Swedenborg, a Swedish theologian. Chapman, as an adherent, believed that a spiritual continuity linked his world to the one beyond; they shared a physical geography and natural phenomena, such that everything present in the real world was also found in the afterlife. Perhaps this worldview helps explain his ascetic behavior and his devotion to spreading the seeds of America's great utilitarian fruit.

Chapman's religious beliefs were as well known among settlers as his nurseries. Though he carried few possessions, he always kept religious literature handy for distribution. In one of the earliest eyewitness accounts of Chapman's life, an Ohio settler wrote:

> After talking about his nurseries and relating some of his wild wood scenes, encounters with rattlesnakes, bears and wolves, he changed the conversation and introduced the subject of Swedenborg; at the same time he began to fumble in his bosom and brought forth some three or four old half-worn-out books. As we were fond of reading, we soon grabbed them, which pleased Johnny. I could see his eyes twinkle with delight. He was much rejoiced to see us eager to read them.

The first published account of Chapman, from 1817, came from a Swedenborg society in England. It described him as "a very extraordinary missionary of the New Jerusalem" and claimed that the profits from his nurseries were "intended for the purpose of enabling him to print all the writings of Emanuel Swedenborg, and distribute them through the western settlements of the United States." To the extent that Swedenborgianism took root in Ohio, Chapman deserved the credit.

But few settlers actually warmed to his dogma. Some even thought he was crazy or possessed by the devil, though perhaps this was understandable given his singular lifestyle. Swedenborgianism was simply too intellectually rigorous for a largely illiterate population. Nonetheless, many of these pioneers, living on the rough edges of society with little respite from the ravages of nature and one another, were easily swayed by emotional revivalism and sensationalism, and the Old Northwest hosted one of the greatest flowerings of heterodox Protestantism in the history of the nation. There was an exhausting list, far too long to recount, that included Adventists, Congregationalists, Free-Will Baptists, Jerkers, Millerites, Mennonites, Mormons, Restorationists, Sabbatarians, Unitarians, and Universalists.

Over the course of a generation, these numerous pioneers filled up Chapman's beloved Ohio forests. Along the rivers and footpaths, once-untamed woodlands fell before the settler's ax, and townships sprang up to fill the spaces that had earlier betrayed few signs of Western civilization beyond Chapman's nurseries.

Again, he turned westward. The nation's inhabitable boundaries, which tended to grow in parallel with the retreat of Native Americans, had expanded in 1817 following the Treaty of Maumee Rapids, when confederated tribes relinquished a further four million acres in the Northwest. This new terrain of forests, swampland, and transitional prairie included the spot where, more than twenty years earlier, the Battle of Fallen Timbers had been won. Within this latest frontier Chapman spent the last third of his life, spreading his nurseries along a roughly east-west corridor that stretched from Mansfield, Ohio, located north of the Muskingum River, out toward Defiance, Ohio, and Fort Wayne, Indiana, beyond.

In 1845, after almost fifty years of following the Northwest frontier, Chapman's life came to an end near Fort Wayne. Though he had lived as a pauper, he did not die as one. His land holdings totaled several hundred acres spread across more than twenty properties in the Old Northwest. This was not a great fortune, but it exceeded that of most early settlers. Chapman's true legacy, of course, were the millions of apple seeds he had sown throughout Pennsylvania, Ohio, and Indiana. For this he was enshrined in the pantheon of early American heroes, though most of the context was lost in the twentieth century, when he became, among other things, a Disney character.

Apples, meanwhile, suffered something of a similar blanching. Consumption of hard cider declined dramatically in the mid-nineteenth century as new immigrant populations from Germany and elsewhere brought a strong culture of beer that infringed on cider's dominance, and as the early stirrings of the temperance movement, along with continuing western immigration, made many farmers abandon or destroy their cider orchards.

Whereas early Americans equated apples with cider, their twentieth-century counterparts regarded them as a healthful snack. L. H. Bailey, one of the nation's leading horticulturists in the early twentieth century, once quipped, "The gradual change in customs, whereby the eating of the apple (rather than the drinking of it) has come to be paramount, is a significant development."

But even as a food the apple slowly lost much of its character. In the early twentieth century, the U.S. Department of Agriculture identified more than seventeen thousand varieties of apples in its *Nomenclature of the Apple*. Many of these still exist, preserved in heirloom and research orchards like the government-run Plant Genetic Resources Unit in Geneva, New York. But for most Americans, apples mean one of a dozen or so commercially produced varieties, like the Granny Smith or Red Delicious, pretty but ineffectual fruits that would have horrified horticulturists like Washington and Jefferson and been an abomination to that great patron saint of apples, John Chapman.

## The Backwoodsman

Serene, not sullen, were the solitudes
Of this unsighing people of the woods.

—Lord Byron, *Eulogy on Colonel Boon*

F ROM THE EARLIEST DAYS of colonization, the prevalence of forests and trees caused settlers to face situations unknown to them in Europe. In response, these emigrants developed a new vocabulary to express their culture, an American vocabulary. The word "backlog," for example, which now means unused excess supply, was originally a seventeenth-century term for the large log that sat in the rear of a fireplace. Its first written reference appeared in a 1684 work by the influential Puritan minister Increase Mather: "The spit was carried up [the] chimney, and came down with the point forward, and stuck in the back-log." "Log-rolling," a political term for trading favors to advance legislation, derived from the practice of neighbors teaming together to roll logs off of newly cut land. The "stump speech," another staple of American politics, was once a campaign oration literally delivered from atop a tree stump, a widespread practice when ever-present stumps formed natural platforms.

One of the most interesting American neologisms, largely forgotten now, was the word "backwoodsman." The concept emerged comparatively late. Its root, "backwoods," first appeared in the 1742 *Calendar of Virginia State Papers* when several frontier explorers petitioned the governor for official recognition: "[S]ettling ye back parts of Virginia which was a veri Great Hassirt [hazard] & Dengrous, . . . has proved hortfull to severil of ous that were ye first settlers of these back woods." "Backwoods," then, specifically meant the uncleared forested area to the west of the early settlements, beyond the Alleghenies, a type of woods so broad and remote that no geographical equivalent existed in England. Most of territorial early America, in effect, was backwoods, the domain of savages, wild animals, and mighty trees. And for the first 150 years of settlement, this wilderness saw few visitors aside from fur trappers, traders, and perhaps the occasional botanist. The term "backwoodsman" itself only appeared in 1784, after the Revolutionary War had already concluded.

Few Americans at this point had any idea who or what a backwoodsman was. Culture in this period was oriented decidedly toward the inhabited settlements of the seaboard. Washington was the great hero, relations between the thirteen colonies the order of the day. The connection between western expansion and the American idea, subsequently made famous by such historians as

Frederick Jackson Turner, was in its infancy—Michaux's proposed trip was ten years away; Lewis and Clark's a decade beyond. While the majority of people lived in and around forests, they were not the unknown forests of the interior. The waves of settlers that poured across the Alleghenies only gained momentum around the turn of the century, the same period when Johnny Appleseed was roaming Ohio. To the extent that Americans thought of men living at the forested frontier it was generally with disdain. Crèvecoeur, for example, described such people as "no better than carnivorous animals of a superior rank," who, "remote from the power of example, and check of shame, . . . exhibit the most hideous parts of our society."

The hazy idea of the backwoodsman first received a face when Daniel Boone arrived on the national scene in 1784. That year a version of his "autobiography" appeared in a fifteen-page appendix to John Filson's well-known work *The Discovery, Settlement and Present State of Kentucke*. The narrator—ostensibly a fifty-year-old Boone, but likely Filson, who had used Boone as a guide while traveling through Kentucky—recounted a series of battles that he fought with the Indians while attempting to settle the new territory. It was a bloody narration, though told almost dispassionately: "[They] cut his head off, while [the] little daughter shut the door." The image of Boone that emerged was of a man predisposed to exist exclusively in the great interior forests, who loved hunting above all else and fought valiantly when circumstances demanded. Reflecting back on his life, the Boone of this history wrote,

> Many dark and sleepless nights have I been a companion for owls, separated from the cheerful society of men, scorched by the summer's sun, and pinched by the winter's cold, an instrument ordained to settle the wilderness: but now the scene is changed; peace crowns the sylvan shade.

Although Filson's Boone never called himself a "backwoodsman," he set forth many of the elements that later defined the archetype. He was savage enough to both kill Indians and live among them, not a Native American but an American Native. Unlike earlier settlers, he preferred the forest and its trees, which offered him a respite from civilization and fertile hunting grounds. He was self-reliant and a preternaturally good shot. The rifle, not the ax, was his most trusted tool, for his concern was not in taming the woods but in exploiting the habitat without changing it. He was as much a creature of the forest as the bears, bucks, and raccoons whose skin he wore as clothing.

The real Daniel Boone, it will come as no surprise, was more complex than the figure Filson portrayed. He was born on October 22, 1734, in western Pennsylvania to Quaker parents (though he was not religious). During his twenties, he served in both the French and Indian War and the Cherokee Uprising, and when he wasn't soldiering he earned money as a market hunter, making expeditions into the wilderness that lasted weeks or months. In 1767, one of these long hunts took him to Kentucky for the first time.

Boone was not, as some legends claimed, the first pioneer to explore Kentucky, but he was instrumental in its development, largely as a pawn in the chaotic chess game of land speculation. Boone's family was among the roughly fifty British settlers who attempted in September 1773 to form the territory's first permanent settlement. Later he fought with the Virginia militia in Dunmore's War, a conflict that ended when the Shawnee Indians relinquished their claims to Kentucky. Shortly thereafter, a prominent land speculator hired Boone to lead a survey mission across the territory, and in this capacity Boone literally blazed a famous trail, later known as the Wilderness Road, and also founded the settlement of Boonesborough.

These Kentucky adventures had been the entirety of Boone's story in the Filson biography, but the historical figure actually lived until September 26, 1820, often in contravention of his own growing mythology as a backwoodsman. He fought in the Revolution, mostly to defend his community from Native American attacks, and was court-martialed for treason but acquitted. After the hostilities ceased, he served three stints in the Virginia state assembly (which included the settled portions of Kentucky) and achieved fleeting prosperity as a speculator, even owning seven slaves at one point. Mounting debts eventually caught up to him, and the already renowned Boone fled from America to Spanish-controlled Missouri in 1799. Of course, by the turn of the century, the veneer of the Boone mythology had already peeled away from the actual man and taken on a life of its own.

Throughout the early decades of the nineteenth century, his legend swelled. An 1816 article asserted that he was "the first settler of Kentucky" and had "taken part in all the wars of America." Willfully ignorant of Boone's fleeing from his debts, the author wrote, "he might have accumulated riches as readily as any man in Kentucky; but he *prefers the woods*."

The popular Boone myth was actually only one of a number of social and political factors that were pushing the backwoodsman character upward from the lowest rung of society. The western migration that was sustaining Johnny Appleseed's work had brought millions into the backwoods—the population of the trans-Appalachian West, the supposed domain of the backwoodsman, grew from 0.1 million in 1790 to 3.7 million by 1830. Additionally, Jefferson's ideals of rural democracy had taken root and championed these yeoman farmers, who were perceived to follow in the literal footsteps of the backwoodsmen.

The frontier hunters became known as the trailblazers that opened up the interior for farming. They were no longer the antisocial vagrants of Crèvecoeur, but the embodiment of resourcefulness and bravery, an American original.

The first person to put this newfound national icon to work was an author named James Paulding. He was part of a New York–based community of writers known as the Knickerbocker Group, which was the most influential American literary circle in the early 1800s and included Washington Irving. Irving and Paulding were close friends and collaborators, but had differing views on the direction that American literature should take, with Paulding favoring a more nationalist flavor over the traditional attachment to British culture. Paulding wanted to write literature that captured the ethos of America, reflecting the quality of the landscape and the realities of life in the new country. He once wrote, "[My] object was to indicate to the youthful writers of [my] native country, the rich poetic resources with which it abounds, as well as to call their attention home." And the first work that he produced in this new style was an epic poem titled *The Backwoodsman*.

Published in 1818, *The Backwoodsman* was a landmark in American literature for its patriotic intent, the forefront of the movement to build an artistic style around national tropes, not borrowed European conceits. Unfortunately, the poem hardly survived the barbs of its critics. As Paulding's son wrote in a biography of his father, the intention behind the work was "hardly admissible as an apology for a total lack of any clear plot." The backwoodsman of Paulding's poem was not yet the unflappable hunter of Boone legends, but a poor, landless New Yorker who headed west over the Alleghenies in search of independence and property—someone who settled the backwoods and then devoted himself to farming and clearing trees. (This rival character type, the settler farmer, was also claiming the name "backwoodsman" early on, though the Boone version largely won this logomachy.) Nonetheless, Paulding's work, when not stalled in the treacle of scenery and confused narration, included many elements of "backwoods" life, such as Indian battles and the hero's fearing that society was quickly catching up.

*The Backwoodsman* may have failed as art, but it succeeded in inspiring others, as the author had hoped. One writer in particular, James Fenimore Cooper, took the message to heart. He was the son of William Cooper, the founder of Cooperstown, New York, and a passionate promoter of a domestic maple sugar industry that never took off in New York State. The younger Cooper's first book, *Precaution* (1820), had been set in England and, as he later lamented, had "embraced a crude effort to describe foreign manners." Cooper noted that his friends—Paulding almost certainly among them—reproached him for writing about "a state of society so different from that to which he belonged." The same year that Cooper published *Precaution,* Paulding, in fact, had written a seminal essay on his movement for a national literature. It argued that America was on the cusp of literary greatness, when the country's "early specimens will be sought after with avidity, and that those who led the way in the rugged discouraging path will be honoured, as we begin to honour the adventurous spirits who first sought, explored, and cleared this western wilderness."

Cooper, as though responding to Paulding's challenge, in 1823 published *The Pioneers.* It combined American themes of settling the wilderness with a more realistic approach to his subject matter. The title page featured a quatrain from *The Backwoodsman* as an epigraph, making Cooper's influences unambiguously clear. The novel became a critical and commercial success, selling several thousand copies its first day and establishing the career of America's first great novelist.

In *The Pioneers,* Cooper introduced America to one of the nineteenth century's best-known literary characters, the backwoodsman Nathaniel "Natty" Bumppo. He appeared, fittingly, to the sound of a rifle shot that others heard while passing through the woods:

> There was a peculiarity in the manner of the hunter. . . . He was tall, and so meagre as to make him seem above even the six feet that he actually stood in his stockings. On his head, which was thinly covered with lank, sandy hair, he wore a cap made of fox-skin. . . . His face was skinny, and thin almost to emaciation; but yet it bore no signs of disease; on the contrary, it had every indication of the most robust and enduring health. The cold and the exposure had, together, given it a color of uniform red. . . . On his feet were deerskin moccasins, ornamented with porcupines' quills, after the manner of the Indians, and his limbs were guarded with long leggings of the same material as the moccasins, which, gartering over the knees of his tarnished buckskin breeches, had obtained for him, among the settlers, the nickname of Leather-Stocking.

Bumppo—or Leatherstocking—was the iconic backwoodsman, a part of the forest and its trees, mistrusting of society, dependent on his rifle for survival, noble in his actions. Cooper explored this definitively American character through five novels, known collectively as *The Leatherstocking Tales* and, perhaps, the most influential series of nineteenth-century American literature.

Cooper's backwoodsman, unlike that of Paulding, contrasted sharply with the actual farmers and loggers who inhabited the forests of America. Leatherstocking embraced the woodlands, while the others were fighting it. A prototypical logger was even featured in *The Pioneers* for contrast. He was a friend of Bumppo's but not his peer—Leatherstocking defeated him in a shooting contest. The logger stood in particularly sharp relief to the backwoodsman when the former described his abilities: "I'll turn my back to no man . . . for chopping and logging; for boiling down the maple sap; . . . making potash . . . or hoeing corn." These were the skills of a settler, not a frontier-chasing pioneer who lived free of society.

Leatherstocking shared many qualities with Boone, and this was likely intentional. The myths and legends that started with Filson had inspired Cooper. In *The Last of the Mohicans,* the fourth book in the Leatherstocking series, Bumppo even mounted a daring raid on an Indian encampment, an episode ripped straight from Boone's life when he saved his daughter from the Cherokees. To many ears, the names Nathaniel Bumppo and Daniel Boone also held a slight echo.

Boone may have been source material for Cooper's new universal icon of America, but soon the new Leatherstocking-like archetype overtook and consumed most of the true-to-life substance still left in the Boone mythology. Essentially, the sociohistorical elements of the backwoodsman (pioneer forest hunters; men of quasi-nomadic disposition; blazers of wilderness trails for the incoming waves of settlers) and the fictional-mythological qualities (limitless valor; unrivaled marksmanship; disdain for society; oneness with the forest and its trees) were competing to form a new American hero.

This phenomenon came to fruition in 1833, when Timothy Flint published his biography of Daniel Boone. Much as Washington's biographer had invented the cherry tree story to popularize the first president, Flint embellished Boone to make him a hero for the adventure-loving soul of American settlers. The old Indian-fighting stories remained, but now Boone was battling a bear with his bare hands and swinging from vines to escape danger. Flint's book went through fourteen editions between 1833 and 1868, becoming arguably the most widely read biography of the nineteenth century.

By the mid-1830s, the backwoodsman, whether as the literary archetype, the superhero version of Boone, or some quasi-historical frontiersman, had become the corporeal embodiment of westward expansion. The forest and its trees that had so frightened the earliest settlers now hosted the most rugged American warrior. He represented autonomy, mobility, and enterprise for the burgeoning middle-class population of the Jacksonian and antebellum eras, and he appeared in countless works throughout the nineteenth century.

## Wooden Technology

WHILE THE BACKWOODSMEN captured the imagination of a nation, they represented a small percentage of Americans, and their very existence was somewhat ephemeral—both Boone and Leatherstocking eventually left the forests for less populated territories to the west. By and large, most Americans were small farmers, more concerned with clearing the land than blazing it, dependent on the ax before the rifle. For these men, standing trees were a nuisance to settlement, but their wood was the most useful resource that nature provided, necessary for housing, fuel, fencing, and countless other products. For the urban population as well, wood was paramount, the raw material for artisans and laborers, including carpenters, coopers, tanners, homebuilders, shipbuilders, carriage makers, furniture makers, packing-box makers, cartwrights, and wainwrights.

The historian Lewis Mumford in his landmark work *Technics and Civilization* (1934) identified three phases of technological development: eotechnic, paleotechnic, and neotechnic. One of the key shifts between the eotechnic and paleotechnic periods globally was the move from economies based on wood, stone, and water to those based on iron, coal, and steam, the materials that facilitated capital-intensive production and commoditized labor. In Europe, the transition was well under way by 1700, but America lagged behind, luxuriating in its illimitable supply of wood, which, according to Mumford, "was the universal material of the eotechnic economy." Life in America looked much different from that of the Continent as much due to this difference as to any cultural factors, such as immigration, the Puritan work ethic, or religious pluralism. The preponderance of trees encouraged early Americans to become heavy resource consumers, always happy to save a day or dollar by chopping down another trunk. It was, as historian Brooke Hindle observed, a "society pervasively conditioned by wood."

In terms of sheer quantity, domestic fuel demands accounted for the greatest number of felled trees in the new nation. America, after all, had been a land "of good living for those that love good fires" since the time of the Pilgrims. Settlers built homes with gigantic, inefficient fireplaces that chewed through wood and lost about 90 percent of the heat out the chimney. These hearths were often able to hold logs four feet across—the standard unit for cut wood, the "cord," measured 4 by 4 by 8 feet, or 128 cubic feet. Crèvecoeur, describing his wood use in America, wrote: "One year with another I burn seventy loads, this is, pretty nearly so many cords." Americans collectively burned roughly 1.08 billion cords up through 1810—of these, 268 million cords were spent just between 1800 and 1809.

In 1742, Benjamin Franklin, fearing that wood "will of course grow scarcer and dearer," had attempted to remedy the gross wastefulness through innovation. He invented a self-enclosed iron heating stove that consumed exponentially less wood than a traditional fireplace. But it was slow to catch on. In the countryside, where most Americans lived, few saw any need to increase their fuel-use efficiency. Settlers considered the Franklin stove (and its many derivatives) as an unnecessary capital expense, and one that increased labor to boot—its small opening required that settlers cut fuelwood down from its cord dimensions into fifteen-inch chunks. Franklin's stove was more rapidly adopted in the cities; however, when coal-burning models appeared later, urban Americans hesitated to abandon wood fuel even though coal was often cheaper. Even by the middle of the nineteenth century, coal accounted for less than 10 percent of the nation's aggregate energy consumption.

A similar scenario of wooden resources trumping labor and capital was log cabins, the archetypal symbol of frontier settlement. This housing style likely originated in New Sweden, a short-lived, mid-seventeenth-century colony along the Delaware River. Settlers of all backgrounds quickly co-opted the design as the most pragmatic for a forested environment. The advantage was that it used wood before labor or capital. Each home required about eighty logs between twenty and thirty feet for the main structure and several dozen split logs for gables and the roof. But no costly nails or precision holes were necessary, and the entire process took between one and three days with help from a few neighbors. The subsequent draftiness made roaring fires obligatory day and night, continuing the cycle of wood consumption. These buildings, meant to be temporary shelters, proliferated in the late eighteenth and early nineteenth centuries. As late as 1855, more than thirty-three thousand remained in New York State, housing for about one-fifth of all farm families.

On the commercial side, Americans were equally profligate in the industries that depended on wood. An excellent example of this concerned the sawmills that dotted every waterway across the country. The wider a sawmill's blade (at least before modern metallurgy), the less prone it was to breakage and the better suited it was to high-speed operations. But wide saws made a broad cut, or kerf, which unnecessarily wasted large amounts of wood. To put this in perspective, a kerf one-tenth of one inch converted 10 percent of every one-inch-thick board into sawdust (for lengthwise cuts). When billions of board feet were cut, differences in kerf added up to enormous quantities of wasted lumber. According to one historian, circular saws in England, where wood remained scarce, were half the width on average of their American equivalents until the time of the Civil War.

Similar indifference to efficiency pervaded the naval stores industry of the South. The longleaf pines, an excellent source of pitch, tar, and turpentine, stretched across the coastal plains from Virginia southward all the way to Texas. Southerners extracted the raw materials by "tapping" the pines, cutting a "V" into the bark and leaving a pan to catch the exudate. While it was possible to harvest the sap in a way that left the trees relatively uninjured, destructive practices developed that needlessly killed untold numbers of trees.

Intensive wood use had become a profound part of the national mind-set. Even as the newer technologies of Mumford's paleotechnic era—steam power, railroads, iron, and steel—began to arrive, Americans modified them to suit their wood-centric lifestyle. In the case of iron, for example, nearly all British smelters had shifted by 1800 from charcoal (a wood derivative) to coke (a coal variant). But the first American experiments with coke only took place in 1835. Twenty years later, almost 80 percent of American iron furnaces were still using charcoal. This despite the fact that charcoal was more expensive to produce than coke and less efficient—eight tons of wood were required to produce two tons of charcoal; charcoal was 2.6 times as bulky as coke; and, ultimately, 1.7 tons of coke did the same work as two to three tons of charcoal. In the case of early steam engines, which began appearing in large numbers early in the nineteenth century, wood persisted as the primary fuel well into the 1880s. Up and down the nation's rivercourses, thousands of woodcutters and scavengers, known as woodhawks, mined the land, ready to supply steamboats wherever they stopped. Coal only proliferated once Americans had stripped the lands near the waterways of wood.

From the fireplace to the steam furnace, endless supplies of wood shaped the way that Americans behaved and developed. As late as 1840, roughly 95 percent of the nation's energy needs for heating, lighting, and locomotion still came from trees. Americans on a per capita basis consumed almost six times more lumber than their British counterparts during the opening decades of the nineteenth century. Alexis de Tocqueville, the French essayist, in talking of the way settlers approached their environment, once commented, "It would be difficult to describe the avidity with which the American rushes forward to secure this immense booty that fortune offers." Not until the middle of the nineteenth century would some Americans begin to question their country's attitude toward nature and trees.

# 3

## The Unrivaled Nature of America

Tulip Tree

### The Big Trees of California

THE DRIVE TO EXPAND WESTWARD was a defining characteristic of America in the first half of the nineteenth century. Lewis and Clark, Johnny Appleseed, and Daniel Boone were all contributors to a grand effort that rapidly reoriented America away from its coastal roots. Many felt that it was the nation's fate to stretch across the entire continent, an idea later known as "manifest destiny." This goal finally became a political reality in 1848 after the United States defeated Mexico in the Mexican-American War. As a condition of peace, the nation gained over 1.2 million square miles of territory, an area encompassing nearly all of the greater Southwest and also California, the great and majestic guardian of the Pacific.

The newly claimed Californian territory turned out to be a land of geological and natural wonders. Separated from the rest of the continent by the Sierra Nevada Mountains, it possessed a climate and topography unique in the nation and the world. The earliest American settlers—especially those who flooded the region's forested interior during the Gold Rush of the late 1840s and early 1850s—sent accounts to their eastern relatives of fantastic flora, spectacular scenery, and unknown animals. Often these narratives took the form of "tall tales," mythic yarns that attempted to distill the grandeur and curiosity of this newly claimed land. Mark Twain, the rakish author, satirized this phenomenon in his famous short story "The Celebrated Jumping Frog of Calaveras County." In it, the narrator, who admits to having a "lurking suspicion" that the entire episode is a myth, recounts a California tale of a frog named Dan'l Webster who "could get over more ground at one straddle than any animal of his breed you ever see."

Of course, not all the stories coming out of the territory were fictitious.

In the spring of 1852, Augustus T. Dowd was working for a California mining outfit, Murphy's Camp, located in the Calaveras County of Twain's story. The camp had employed Dowd as a hunter to supply the workmen with fresh meat, and day after day he roamed the western slopes of the Sierra Nevadas in search of game. One afternoon in May, having shot and wounded a bear, Dowd pursued the injured animal through a wilderness of pitch pine, sugar pine, white fir, and incense cedar. Eventually, the chase landed Dowd in an unknown part of the mountains about sixteen miles from his camp, near the headwaters of the Stanislaus and San Antonio Rivers. He looked up and saw before him a tree with dimensions too great to comprehend. According to James Hutchings, a California explorer and promoter who published the best-known account of Dowd's discovery, "All thoughts of hunting, or bear pursuing, were forgotten, or absorbed and lost in the surprising admiration which he felt."

Dowd rushed back to his camp to share the news of what he had found, but the other miners, inured to California's culture of exaggeration and invention, dismissed his entreaties as just another tall tale. A few days later, Dowd once more burst into camp, this time claiming to have shot the largest grizzly bear he'd ever seen. He rounded up a troop of men for assistance, and they set out into the wilderness of the Sierras, hiking deep into the forest, across ridges and ravines, beyond cliffs and canyons, until they arrived at the gargantuan trunk that Dowd had encountered days before. According to Hutchings, Dowd then cried out, "[N]ow, boys, do you believe my big tree story? That is the large grizzly I wanted you to see. Do you still think it a yarn?"

The trees that now surrounded Dowd's men soared heavenward, free of branches for more than one hundred feet. Hundreds of feet higher still hung their ragged, evergreen crowns. But the most overwhelming feature was their massive girth, with some over thirty feet wide at the base, a footprint as large as that of a single-family home. Dowd's big trees made the old-growth forests of

New England look like a collection of twigs—the mighty white pines that had once provided masts for the British navy rarely grew wider than four feet, but a single branch from the big trees could be six feet across! These forest miracles were, quite simply, the largest living objects on earth.

For Dowd, these trees must have appeared almost supernatural, even divine, but botanists and explorers have filled in much of the mystery over the years. Relatives of the big trees once thrived across three continents, but glaciation and climate changes restricted their survival to California alone. Currently, the trees occur naturally along a chain of groves that stretches approximately 260 miles through California's Sierra Nevadas at altitudes between five thousand and seven thousand feet. Mature trees number only in the tens of thousands (about one hundred of which are found in Dowd's Calaveras Grove), a paltry number for any species, and the list of remarkable specimens is below five hundred. While these quantities are minuscule, the lucky trees that have survived several hundred years of nature's wrath to reach maturity are effectively indestructible: They have no serious fungal enemies; a root and trunk system sturdy enough to survive windstorms; and a bark up to three feet thick that withstands the heat of wildfires. The oldest specimens have been measured at thirty-five hundred years old, with the largest trees containing over half a million board feet of lumber, more wood than is typically found in several acres of healthy forest. And yet, this incredible feat of natural engineering sprouts from a seed half a centimeter across.

Dowd was not the first to notice the big trees. Native Americans knew the species well, and most historians agree that the first westerner to document them was Zenas Leonard, who explored California's Yosemite Valley in 1833. His journal, which surfaced only in 1904, described trees that measured "from 16 to 18 fathoms [six feet equal one fathom] round the trunk"—given his Yosemite location, he had likely encountered the Mariposa Grove, a large collection of big trees about one hundred miles south of Calaveras. Dowd's discovery, however, brought the trees to the attention of the general public for the first time. A small California paper, the *Sonora Herald*, published his finding in 1852, and although many questioned the story's validity, accounts of the big trees soon appeared in nearly every major newspaper throughout the country. Within a year, the news reached London.

Enterprising Californians rushed to capitalize on the public's burgeoning interest. Axes in hand, they descended on the Calaveras Grove and cut down the very specimen that had first captivated Dowd. According to Hutchings,

> This tree employed five men for twenty five days in falling it. . . .
> [A]bout two and a half days of the twenty-five were spent in

inserting wedges, and then driving them in with the buts [*sic*] of trees, until, at last, the noble monarch of the forest was forced to tremble and then to fall, after braving "the battle and the breeze" of nearly three thousand winters.

One can only imagine the sound of such a grand tower crashing to the forest floor, the echo of more than a thousand tons reverberating through the mountains. After the tree was leveled, the team stripped off over fifty feet of the bark with the intent of shipping it to the 1853 New York World's Fair for display. One observer was "dreadfully shocked at the vandalism and barbarity of flaying that giant of the woods and depriving California of its greatest growing exponent." Another justified this initial felling on practical grounds: "[I]n taking its proportions to the World's Fair . . . millions of the inhabitants of the earth will see it."

Promoters shipped the initial load of stripped bark, which weighed twelve tons, across the country to the delight of easterners who had refused to believe the newspaper reports. The following year, another Californian entrepreneur removed 116 feet of bark from a different tree. This supposedly required the labor of five men for ninety days. The 8-foot sections were shipped downriver to San Francisco, then around Cape Horn in Chile, en route to New York, but no buildings in America were large enough to hold the reassembled display, which measured 90 feet around at the base. The bark subsequently traveled to England, but even the grand buildings of London were too low to accommodate it. Finally, in April 1857, the display found a permanent home within the massive Crystal Palace of Sydenham, England, but a fire later consumed the building and the tree.

Other pieces of various big trees toured the country throughout the nineteenth century. One noteworthy exhibit was held in Boston in 1871, when a special building was erected for the event. Louis Agassiz, the esteemed Harvard natural historian and one of the most respected scientific minds of the age, was so impressed that he sent an unsolicited endorsement to the exhibit's organizers, which ended up featured in the promotional broadside: "Nobody who has any curiosity to see something of the wonders of nature ought to allow the opportunity of seeing a section of one of the big trees of California to pass unimproved." According to one paper, "The average attendance has not been much less than a thousand a day."

While many experienced the big trees through these traveling displays, others flocked to Calaveras to see them in their natural habitat. A Connecticut traveler, upon first seeing the grove in 1856, wrote, "[I]t really seemed that we had never seen a tree before. And yet they were only medium specimens."

The original site, located far from any settlements and initially accessible only on horseback, developed into one of California's premier early tourist destinations. By 1854, there was an onsite hotel with accommodations for more than fifty guests. Promotional literature encouraged people to take advantage of the grove's excellent hunting and trout fishing. The tree that had been felled in 1853 was incorporated into the convivial scene. An early visitor explained, "The stump has been planed off and . . . used as a ballroom and stage for a theatre." Hutchings added, "[H]owever incredible it may seem, on the 4th of July [1854], 32 persons were engaged in dancing four sets of cotillions at one time [on the stump], without suffering any inconvenience whatever; and, besides these, there were musicians and lookers on."

Over the years, countless American luminaries visited the big trees and shared their impressions in widely read travelogues. Horace Greeley, the editor of the *New York Tribune* and an abolitionist who helped found the Republican Party, visited in the late 1850s and imagined, correctly, that the "forest mastodons" were "a relic of some bygone world." William Cullen Bryant, poet, naturalist, and long-serving editor of the *New York Evening Post,* described them in 1872 as "vast beyond any thing that I had ever seen." Both Theodore Roosevelt and William Howard Taft made tours of the big trees during their presidencies.

The big trees not only testified to the power of nature, but symbolized America and its greatness in the minds of many. Scottish poet James Hedderwick commented in an 1862 article that "it is only a country like America which can produce these mammoth enormities in whole forestfuls." Trees had built the nation, been responsible for its strength and rapid expansion, so it was only fitting that their proudest specimens be found within its shores. Many of the big tree nicknames honored great Americans or national symbols, including George Washington, Uncle Sam, and General Sherman, the decorated Civil War officer whose name was bestowed on the largest tree of all, measuring 275 feet tall and 109 feet in circumference.

In the mid-1850s, the national pride that Americans felt for their mammoth trees triggered a controversy that set scientists aflame on both sides of the Atlantic. Traditionally, botanical naming rights belonged to the first scientist to correctly identify any given species, and this privilege was often used to pay tribute to friends, colleagues, or public figures. In the case of the big trees, an Englishman published the first taxonomic description on December 24, 1853, labeling them with a new genus, *Wellingtonia gigantea,* an homage to the legendary Duke of Wellington, who had defeated Napoleon at the Battle of Waterloo. Few names could have been more offensive to America's scientific community. Renowned American naturalist C. F. Winslow, tossing aside botanical convention, summed up the attitude of the nation's scientists:

[I]t must have been a prominent idea . . . that American Naturalists would regard with surprise and reluctance the application
of a British name, however honored, when a name so worthy of
immortal honor and renown as that of Washington would strike
the mind of the world as far more suitable to the most gigantic
and remarkable vegetable order indigenous to a country where
his name is the most distinguished ornament. As he and his generation declared themselves independent of all English rule and
political dictation, so American Naturalists must, in this case,
express their respectful dissent from all British scientific "stamp
acts." . . . I trust the scientific honor of our country may be vindi-
cated from foreign indelicacy by boldly discarding the name now
applied to it, and by affixing to it that of the man whose memory
we all love and honor, and teach our children to adore.

Before the controversy bubbled over into crisis, scientists in both France
and America determined, somewhat expediently, that the English designation
of *Wellingtonia gigantea* was scientifically invalid. The big trees, they argued,
belonged to the same genus as California's coastal redwoods, the tallest trees
in the world; and the redwood's genus had earlier been classified as *Sequoia,*
a name that honored the Native American who had independently created a
writing system for the Cherokee nation. The big trees were subsequently designated *Sequoia gigantea* or, in layman's terms, the giant sequoia. This common
name stuck in America, but many English people persisted in using the name
*Wellingtonia.* The scientific controversy, meanwhile, simmered deep into the
twentieth century, when the big trees were again recognized as an independent
genus.

The biggest fight over the sequoias, however, concerned not their names but
their protection.

The national government as a matter of policy encouraged the transfer
of federal territories into private hands both to generate revenue and on the
theory that private actors would use such lands most productively. The forests
containing giant sequoias were no exception. Thus, while the big trees were
needlessly difficult to fell and produced mediocre timber, they were nonetheless vulnerable to the ravages of progress and the ax. In a rapidly developing
region like California, their eradication appeared inevitable from the outset.
The editor of an influential newspaper, the *California Farmer,* wrote in 1853:

[M]any a towering mountain, upon whose lofty summit now
stand, in all their pride and glory, those giants of the forests, that

like that wonder of the age, "the Mammoth Tree," the woodman will no longer spare, these too must give place to that onward march of the Anglo-Saxon race, o'er mountain, hill and valley, and marking its progress onward along the Pacific, by civilization, cultivation and Christianization.

Such an attitude was commonplace at midcentury, and would only strengthen as logging activities accelerated.

Admirers of the big trees rallied to their defense. Hutchings considered any cuttings to be "a sacrilegious act" and a "desecration." The trees were part of the natural heritage of America, a treasure that belonged to all citizens. Lands containing sequoias, the protectionists argued, must not be parceled out like any ordinary piece of woodland. An 1854 *New York Herald* editorial expressed a commonly felt sentiment: "[I]t is the duty of the State of California, of Congress, and of all good citizens, to protect and preserve these Californian monuments of the capabilities of our American soil."

Following a decade of lobbying, the defenders of the sequoias won a major battle on June 30, 1864. That day, President Abraham Lincoln signed landmark legislation that forever altered the relationship between the federal government and the nation's natural resources. Known colloquially as "The Yosemite and Big Tree Grant," the act ceded lands containing the sublime Yosemite Valley and the nearby Mariposa Big Tree Grove to the state of California, "for public use, resort, and recreation [to be] inalienable for all time." This was the precursor to every national park in the country: the first time that the federal government stepped in to preserve natural resources (even if done obliquely through state transfer); the first time the government recognized a noncommercial value in land; and the first time that concern for the commons triumphed over private development. The big trees and Yosemite Valley had captured the imagination of a country and, for a moment, reoriented its priorities.

But the 1864 act was ultimately only a small step toward preservation, decades before its time. As late as 1900, a government report noted:

> At the present time the only [sequoia] grove thoroughly safe from destruction is the Mariposa, and this is far from being the most interesting. Most of the other groves are either in process of, or in danger of, being logged. The very finest of all, the Calaveras Grove, with the biggest and tallest trees, the most uncontaminated surroundings, and practically all the literary and scientific associations of the species connected with it, has been purchased recently by a lumberman.

For Dowd's Calaveras Grove, protection finally arrived in 1931 with the creation of the Calaveras Big Trees State Park, but only in 1954 did the park expand to incorporate all the nearby big trees. The process of defending every grove of big trees from logging would extend late into the twentieth century.

## Thoreau's Life in the Woods of Concord

Back East, forests continued to fall in the name of progress. Many of the most forbidding backwoods from the Revolutionary period had yielded to fertile fields in little more than two generations. Even gone were the forests around Cooperstown where Natty Bumppo of *The Leatherstocking Tales* had once supposedly roamed. Bumppo's pure wilderness was little more than a memory for the next generation, which included James Fenimore Cooper's daughter Susan Fenimore Cooper, a writer and amateur naturalist. In 1850, she published *Rural Hours,* a popular work that recorded her daily interactions with the region's landscape:

> Probably there is no part of the earth, within the limits of the temperate climate, which has taken the aspect of an old country so soon as our native land. . . . Whenever we pause to recall what has been done in this secluded valley during the lifetime of one generation, we must needs be struck with new astonishment.

And while she, like most Americans, considered these developments across New York's Otsego County "wonderful changes," she nonetheless worried that such rapid development and deforestation risked leaving the country "bleak and bare" in the future.

Susan Cooper's fears, however, had already been realized across the older settlements in New England. There, the forests that had once covered 95 percent of the land in many places had been reduced to the few areas where husbandry proved impractical because the soil was too poor or the terrain too uneven. Even where scattered forests remained, the individual trees were not the pristine giants that had overwhelmed early explorers, but youthful pines and hardwoods that were three, and sometimes four, generations removed from the forest primeval, the results of hundreds of years spent converting trees into fuel. The largest old-growth region in all of eastern Massachusetts by that point contained a meager four hundred acres, well less than a square mile.

No place better represented the development of New England in the mid-nineteenth century than Concord, Massachusetts. The twenty-six-square-mile town, located about twenty miles east of Boston, was founded in 1635, the first inland settlement of the Massachusetts Bay Colony. When the Revolutionary War broke out, Concord had been part of the initial hostilities, the final stop in a daylong fight that became known as the Battles of Lexington and Concord. In the early nineteenth century, the town thrived thanks in part to its proximity to Boston—one of the nation's earliest railroad lines connected the two locations, allowing for easy transport of goods, including timber. By the 1830s, in addition to the miles of farmland, Concord boasted mills for wood, grist, and cotton, as well as large factories for lead pipes and shoes, and countless smaller manufacturers, who produced everything from clocks to pencils.

All of this economic and social growth had taken its toll on the trees of the local environment. Forests originally covered more than 90 percent of the town, but by 1850 that number had dropped to an incredible 10.5 percent (which, it turned out, represented a historic low for the area). Residents had slowly but inexorably cleared most of the land for agriculture, and remaining trees invariably ended up burning in their hearths or in those of Boston—by midcentury, that city's 135,000 inhabitants were consuming about six hundred thousand cords a year for heat. White pines that had once grown to diameters of four feet or more were rarely found larger than ten or twenty inches. Only four isolated woodlands remained.

Against this denuded backdrop of Concord was born Henry David Thoreau in 1817. He was the son of a pencilmaker, one of the countless local careers dependent on trees, in this case cedars. Thoreau sometimes worked with his family's business, but his primary interests were writing and nature, twin obsessions that defined him. Compared to the standards of the day, he lived an existence while pursuing these two activities that was highly eccentric. He never married; showed little interest in pursuing women; preferred to live alone; assiduously skipped church; refused to pay state taxes; avoided voting; and abstained from strong drink, tobacco, or meat. Thoreau, in short, was an iconoclast.

His appearance was suitably striking. Novelist Nathaniel Hawthorne, after meeting Thoreau, wrote in his journal: "He is as ugly as sin, long-nosed, queer-mouthed, and with uncouth and somewhat rustic, though courteous manners, corresponding very well with such an exterior. But his ugliness is of an honest and agreeable fashion, and becomes him much better than beauty."

While a student at Harvard in 1836, Thoreau read a widely circulated essay, "Nature," which affected him profoundly. The author, the popular Concord-based minister and philosopher Ralph Waldo Emerson, posited that nature—in his words, "essences unchanged by man"—was a force for salvation and restoration. Emerson wrote: "In the presence of nature, a wild delight runs through the man, in spite of real sorrows. . . . In the woods, is perpetual youth. . . . In the woods, we return to reason and faith. . . . In the wilderness, I find something more dear and connate than in streets or villages." Emerson's essay was attempting to reorient the relationship between Americans and their forests: While early settlers had openly feared the woods and later generations had learned to exploit its resources, few, aside from the botanists and back-woodsmen, ever delighted in the restorative, almost divine, powers of the wild. For Thoreau, who found himself naturally drawn to Concord's rapidly dimin-ishing wilderness, the ideas expressed in "Nature" justified and nourished his youthful interest.

Emerson's essay was not a work in isolation, but one of the foundational texts of a major social movement coalescing at the time Thoreau was enter-ing adulthood. Part philosophy, part activism, it was known as transcendental-ism and centered on Concord. The philosophical component was a uniquely American outgrowth of several epistemologies popular in nineteenth-century New England, including Unitarianism, German Idealism, and Swedenbor-gianism, the same creed that Johnny Appleseed had attempted to popularize. (Emerson once called Swedenborg a "man of genius, who has done much for this philosophy of life.") In the broadest terms, the Concord-based movement asserted that an ideal spiritual state transcended the material world and that a correspondence existed between human thoughts and the natural universe, allowing for insight through personal reflection.

Although few could pinpoint exactly what a transcendentalist was (Emer-son bravely attempted the challenge in his 1842 essay "The Transcenden-talist"), many rushed to join in the movement. It became a hub of not only intellectual activity, but of progressive causes and social reform. Transcenden-talists were among the first to articulate seminal concepts like "self-reliance," "civil disobedience," and the restorative powers of nature. They also champi-oned social causes such as abolition, free public libraries, utopian communities, and vegetarianism.

In the late 1830s, Thoreau met Emerson, and the two immediately entered into an informal mentorship. Under Emerson's tutelage, Thoreau began keep-ing a journal and crafting essays for transcendentalist publications such as *The Dial*. But the young writer found no immediate success. For nearly ten years, he bounced from job to job, as teacher, editor, tutor, and repairman. Emerson provided frequent support, offering his home to Thoreau and finding him new sources of employment, but Thoreau seemed plagued with bad luck as well as tragedy. In 1842, his brother, John, contracted a fatal case of tetanus from a shaving cut and died in Thoreau's arms. Two years later, Thoreau accidentally set fire to several hundred acres of Concord's scarce woodland. While he ratio-nalized the damage as equivalent to "if the lightning had done it," he noted in his journal that "some declared behind my back that I was a 'damned rascal.'"

A decade of toiling was leading nowhere for Thoreau, and in 1845 he decided to radically redirect his life. His plan was to abandon all concerns for the community-oriented society of Concord and retreat to the woods, where he could work undisturbed on a book project and, perhaps, find the sort of enlightenment that Emerson had described in "Nature." As Thoreau famously wrote, "I went to the woods because I wished to live deliberately, to front only the essential facts of life, and see if I could not learn what it had to teach, and not, when I came to die, discover that I had not lived."

Of course, finding a forest for this purpose was no easy task in Concord. Thoreau once more turned to Emerson, who happened to control a tract of land in one of the town's four remaining woodlands. It was located a few miles from town on the edge of a body of water known as Walden Pond, which Thoreau considered "a perfect forest mirror." However, the forests around Walden were not the dark and savage woodlands of old, but a collection of young trees, allowed to stand because the underlying soil was too poor to sustain cultivation. The only people who used Walden Woods were woodcutters and the ice harvesters who skimmed the pond in wintertime. Walden was less than an hour's walk from downtown Concord; the train to Boston passed nearby, its whistle echoing among the trees.

In early 1845, Thoreau set out for Walden Pond, ax in hand. He selected for his planned retreat a site by the shore of the pond, an area he described as "in the midst of a young forest of pitch pines and hickories." These surrounding trees became the raw materials for a modest shelter, and he spent the spring consumed in the laborious task of erecting his home. After several months of tiresome work, Thoreau moved into his dwelling on July 4. Walden Pond then became his full-time residence for two years, two months, and two days, until September 6, 1847.

Life in the woods allowed Thoreau to finally focus on his two delights, writing and the contemplation of nature. He passed days recording his thoughts in a journal and drafting a manuscript that described a trip he had taken with his departed brother, later published under the title *A Week on the Concord and Merrimack Rivers*. When he wasn't writing, he explored the surrounding forest, observing and taking notes, interacting with the animals, canoeing along the pond, enjoying the solitude. The trees acted as his new companions. He explained:

> Instead of calling on some scholar, I paid many a visit to particu-
> lar trees . . . such as the black-birch, of which we have some hand-
> some specimens two feet in diameter; its cousin, the yellow-birch,

with its loose golden vest, perfumed like the first; [and] the beech, which has so neat a bole and beautifully lichen-painted, perfect in all its details. . . . These were the shrines I visited both summer and winter.

While Thoreau's spiritual life existed among the trees, his social life was not wholly eliminated. He visited his family often, and his mother frequently provided him lunch. Occasionally, he passed through town, including one famous incident in 1846 when the tax collector briefly imprisoned him for tax evasion, an experience that inspired him to write his famous 1849 essay "Civil Disobedience." He even took a lengthy excursion to Maine in which he ascended Mount Katahdin and described the pristine forests as "something savage and awful, though beautiful." Still, it was within the woods of Walden that Thoreau transformed from a promising talent to one of the most influential voices in the history of America.

In 1854, at the age of thirty-seven, Thoreau published *Walden; or, Life in the Woods,* the work that came to define him as a writer and thinker. In form, it used a series of loosely collected essays that followed the cycle of a single year—for literary effect, Thoreau had shortened his period of residency. In substance, it was a plea for the virtues of simple living and the promise of nature. With the wit of a satirist and the graceful language of a poet, Thoreau challenged his readers to question the values of modern life, insisting, "The mass of men lead lives of quiet desperation."

*Walden* built on the idea from Emerson's "Nature" that renewal awaited in the solitude of wilderness. But unlike Emerson, Thoreau treated the outdoors not from the spiritual perspective of the minister, but from that of a rapt observer, always ready to capture a telling detail and the slightest nuance. The natural world of Concord, limited though it was, came alive in stories of a cagey lark, a stubborn beanfield, or a noble pine, and the forests of Walden provided Thoreau with the fulfillment that he'd been unable to find in the materialistic culture of New England.

While the thrust of *Walden* was not on the need to protect the forests, Thoreau nonetheless stood up to defend them against the wanton tree felling that characterized his time. "Since I left those shores," he wrote,

the woodchoppers have still further laid them waste, and now for many a year there will be no more rambling through the aisles of the wood, with occasional vistas through which you see the water. My Muse may be excused if she is silent henceforth. How can you expect the birds to sing when their groves are cut down?

Thoreau, it should be noted, was not mourning the death of America's pristine forests—such a lament would have been akin to grieving for long-departed ancestors. He was simply requesting the salvation of that tiny fraction of uncultivated land that remained. For him, some semblance of nature was a necessary counterbalance to society: "Our village life would stagnate if it were not for the unexplored forests and meadows which surround it. We need the tonic of the wildness."

Like many great literary works, *Walden* appeared to tepid initial sales, but soon an audience found the book and it has remained in print ever since. Thoreau crafted his thoughts as though projected through a prism, such that each allowed for multiple interpretations. For some, the book was a transcendentalist call to arms against the excesses of modern society. For others, it was a new way to look at nature or a polemic for conservation. Many considered his lucid writing style to represent a break from a then fashionable circumlocution. At one point in the work, Thoreau declared, "How many a man has dated a new era in his life from the reading of a book!" This statement, one of his many quote-ready aphorisms, might as well have been directed at *Walden* itself. Few books have had such a profound impact on American culture.

After publishing *Walden*, Thoreau's fascination with the natural world only deepened. He produced a series of books based on excursions he'd taken to Canada, Cape Cod, and Maine, each landscape inspiring his prose anew. When Thoreau wasn't traveling, he worked as a land surveyor, which allowed him to disappear into the wilderness around Concord, an unlimited source of new discoveries. Emerson once commented, "[Thoreau] loved Nature so well, was so happy in her solitude, that he became very jealous of cities, and the sad work which their refinements and artifices made with man and his dwelling." The observations Thoreau made in the forests and meadows of Concord served as raw material for the journal he had begun on Emerson's suggestion in 1837. Eventually, it contained more than two million words, the majority focused on how different organisms in the natural world interact, a field that later developed into ecology.

Thoreau's health began to fail him in his late thirties, and in these final years the study of trees claimed more and more of his attention. Three of his final essays dealt with the subject exclusively. "Autumnal Tints" was a panegyric to the beauty of New England's fall foliage. "Wild Apples" sang the praises of fruits propagated from seed. Lastly, "The Succession of Forest Trees" attempted to explain why forest compositions changed over time, as when pines repopulated an oak forest and vice versa. This final work was, in many respects, more ecology than transcendentalism. The scientist in Thoreau had overtaken the poet.

One evening in 1859, Thoreau ventured into the forest near Concord during a rainstorm to count the rings on tree stumps. It was slow, tedious work, requiring hours of uncomfortable kneeling and intense concentration, the sort of labor reserved for the fanatical. Thoreau spent that night with his knees digging into the cold earth, pushing down against the wet humus that coated the floor. Soon after returning, he became ill, having aggravated a case of tuberculosis that he'd first contracted in 1835. The disease consumed Thoreau's lungs over the course of the next three years, leaving him bedridden for the final stage of his life. On his deathbed, with insight all that he had left, the man who had turned to the forests to find solace in an ever-developing world said, "I *suppose* that I have not many months to live; but, of course, I know nothing about it. I may add that I am enjoying existence as much as ever, and regret nothing."

## "A Democratic Development of the Highest Significance"

I N 1811, the architects of New York's City Hall, looking to save costs, decided to use brownstone instead of marble on the back walls. Since the building was meant to mark the northernmost boundary of the city, no one should have ever seen the rear side. But New York City was about to expand faster than anyone had predicted. The establishment of the Stock Exchange Board in 1817, the cornering of East Coast steamship trading routes by the 1820s, and the opening of the Erie Canal in 1825, among other things, provided the city with the foundation for almost unlimited economic growth. Immigrants flooded in from countries throughout Europe, while rural Americans and New Englanders moved to New York to capitalize on the new economic promise. The population exploded from approximately sixty thousand in 1800 to more than half a million in 1850. For comparison's sake, Philadelphia, Boston, and Baltimore, which also grew as part of a national trend toward urbanization, each gained only about one hundred thousand residents during this period.

Within a decade of City Hall's completion, the region to the north of its brownstone-clad rear wall, instead of being a tranquil, tree-filled zone outside the urban boundaries, held the nation's first slum, Five Points. Containing a volatile mix of poor European immigrants and African Americans, the neighborhood became a hotbed of civil unrest, with frequent rioting and strikes throughout the 1820s and 1830s. These political struggles, repeated across numerous cities, were, in many respects, a reaction to the deplorable condition of urban life: streets dirtied with trash, human excrement, and horse manure;

foul water; epidemics that ravaged the poor populations every few years; catastrophic cyclical financial crashes; incomprehensible income disparity—by 1845, New York's top 1 percent owned half of the city's wealth, while the top 4 percent controlled four-fifths.

Among the other indignities of urban life was an almost total absence of trees or wilderness. Dynamic growth came at the expense of standing trees—cities, the joke went, were places where you cut down the trees and then named the streets after them. The great metropolises of the Eastern Seaboard lacked anything resembling even the curtailed forest solitude of Walden. The few "parks" that existed in the populated section of Manhattan were rarely larger than a city block, not the type of space that made one feel outside of the urban chaos. And the paucity of trees stretched for miles in every direction. An urban population's insatiable demand for timber and, especially, for fuel wreaked havoc on nearly all the locally accessible woodlands. The unbounded expansion of New York City depended on its access to the nation's biggest logging network, which stretched up the Hudson River, through the Erie Canal, and into the Great Lakes.

The wealthy were able to escape the barrenness of New York and its environs. Some possessed manicured estates outside the city, and many of the well-to-do sought nature in upstate visits to spas and retreats at Saratoga Springs (near Albany) and in the Catskill Mountains—this latter destination became incredibly fashionable during the 1840s, in part due to the landscape paintings of the Hudson River School. Such picturesque refuges, however, were wholly inaccessible to the urban poor, whose ranks continued to swell.

In 1848, a powerful voice finally spoke out against this worsening metropolitan dilemma. Andrew Jackson Downing was a landscape gardener and, by almost all accounts, the most influential personality in American horticulture. In the mid-nineteenth century, when the newly wealthy were designing grand pastoral estates and the majority of the nonurban population still derived their income from husbandry, the national master of horticulture commanded everyone's attention.

Downing's reputation rested on his 1841 book, *A Treatise on the Theory and Practice of Landscape Gardening, Adapted to North America,* the first comprehensive manual on the subject from an American point of view. It drew heavily from the English gardening practices that had developed more than a century earlier and had fueled Bartram's international trade in American trees. The central principle in the English tradition was the creation of a naturalistic setting, one that relied on artifice to imitate an ideal, almost imagined, wilderness. This aesthetic had captivated many wealthy Americans, including Washington and Jefferson early on, but Downing was the first to translate it systemically to American tastes and modify it to suit the nation's more dramatic geography, places like the picturesque Hudson River Valley.

Of especial importance to Downing were trees. He devoted half of the book to them, writing:

> Among all the materials at our disposal for the embellishment of country residences, none are at once so highly ornamental, so indispensable, and so easily managed, as *trees,* or *wood.* We introduce them in every part of the landscape,—in the foreground as well as in the distance, on the tops of the hills and in the depths of the valleys. They are, indeed, like the drapery which covers a somewhat ungainly figure, and while it conceals its defects, communicates to it new interest and expression. A tree, undoubtedly, is one of the most beautiful objects in nature.

During the 1840s, Downing's influence on American society had expanded through *The Horticulturist,* a magazine he founded, edited, and contributed to. While it had a wide readership, its impact was dramatically amplified through the countless periodicals that reproduced its content. Downing used this bully pulpit to advance issues that ran from the pragmatic to the aesthetic and, occasionally, the political, for he was committed to social reform.

In October 1848, *The Horticulturist* published an editorial by Downing titled "A Talk about Public Parks and Gardens." The subject matter, while novel, was not entirely unfamiliar to city dwellers—William Cullen Bryant, for example, had suggested a "pleasure ground" for New York in an 1844 editorial in his *New York Evening Post.* Nonetheless, Downing's editorial, reproduced nationally, marked the beginning of a serious debate on the topic and laid out the reasons that tree-rich public parks were a necessary next step for American democracy.

Downing began his piece with an appeal to national pride, noting that several European countries, while less republican than America in a political sense, were "far more so, in many of the customs of social life." International cities such as Frankfurt, Munich, Paris, and The Hague all hosted elaborate parks, maintained at public expense. Within these communal spaces, Downing argued, citizens of all classes gained "health, good spirits, social enjoyment, and a frank and cordial bearing towards their neighbors, that is totally unknown either in England or America."

In the mid-nineteenth century of Downing's day, however, noncommercial public-works projects were almost unheard of in America, and the idea that public parks could justify the costs (financial and political) associated with their creation and maintenance was suspect. Downing's editorial turned for guidance to the privately funded but publicly accessible rural cemeteries that had recently proliferated, such as Mount Auburn in Boston (1831) and Greenwood in Brooklyn (1836). These landscaped memorials, financed through the selling of lots, had, to the surprise of many, quickly become fashionable recreation spots, filled with carriages and picnicking families on the weekends. Public parks, according to Downing, would be superior to cemeteries for "allay[ing] some of the feverish unrest" of city life. Downing assured that the money could be found either through "voluntary taxation" or an "appeal to public liberality," though he did consider a financing scheme, likely in jest, wherein patrons of the park would be "owners in 'fee simple' of certain fine trees."

In the years following Downing's editorial, plans for a public park in New York City slowly coalesced. The press picked up the debate, hashing out the pros and cons in passionate editorials, with Downing's *Horticulturist* and Bryant's *Evening Post* particularly stalwart proponents. By 1851, both mayoral candidates supported some form of a park, but a battle was raging over its size and location—whatever space was chosen would have an enormous impact on the city's development and the value of all adjacent property. Downing again asserted himself, writing in an 1851 piece titled "The New-York Park":

> *Five hundred acres* is the smallest area that should be reserved for the future wants of such a city, *now*, while it may be obtained. Five hundred acres may be selected between Thirty-ninth-street and the Harlem River, . . . a good deal of which is yet waste area.

Political infighting continued for several more years, until July 21, 1853, when the New York state legislature finally authorized $5 million for the purchase of more than seven hundred acres within the region that Downing had proposed. The designated area, located in the middle of Manhattan island, was half a mile wide and two and a half miles long, bounded by Fifty-Ninth Street in the south, 106th Street in the north, Fifth Avenue in the east, and Eighth Avenue in the west.

Although more space had been allocated for a park than seemed politically possible a few years earlier, the massive rectangle contained some of the poorest-quality land in the entire city. *Harper's New Monthly Magazine* put it bluntly: "Never was a more desolate piece of land chosen for a pleasure-ground." Its barrenness had contributed to its availability, for few politically connected New Yorkers had claims to any of the seventeen thousand plots involved. The southern half, in particular, alternated between marshy lowlands and rocky highlands, with very few trees. But within the landscape still lived more than fifteen hundred poor and marginalized people, including a large African American community, known as Seneca Village—their claims to the land were eventually abrogated through eminent domain, one of the forgotten costs in creating the new park.

With the location settled, organizers needed to determine the park's character and design. Downing's pastoral, tree-rich landscape ideas were but one option among the many European antecedents. The popular Luxembourg Gardens of Paris, for example, were laid out in the older, formal landscaping style of the Continent. They contained straight avenues, smaller plants laid out in geometric patterns, and music and coffee houses. On the other hand, Tsarskoye Selo, the 350-acre residence of the Russian imperial family outside St. Petersburg, demonstrated an eclectic cultural style. Within its grounds were a complete model Chinese village, Egyptian-style pyramids, a Turkish mosque, and countless monuments.

In 1857, after rejecting several designs, the recently created Board of Commissioners for the Central Park decided to hold an open contest. The only requirements were that any proposed plan include four transverse east-west roads as well as a few then fashionable architectural elements. With the fate of the nation's first major park hanging in the balance, the competition drew a large amount of interest, and landscape gardeners submitted entries that ran the gamut of styles. Notably absent from the competition was Downing, who had died tragically in a riverboat accident five years earlier. However, his former apprentice, a talented English landscaping architect named Calvert Vaux, did participate. And before entering the competition, Downing's protégé made the politically savvy decision to team up with the park's newly appointed superintendent, a little-known thirty-five-year-old named Frederick Law Olmsted.

Up to this point in time, Olmsted, whose name soon became synonymous with Central Park, had lived a life of promise without equivalent performance, unable to find a pursuit that used his natural practicality and industriousness. The son of a successful Connecticut merchant, he had received a privileged if haphazard education, but was unable to complete his college degree at Yale due to the lingering effects of severe sumac poisoning. His life following this was a series of jobs and travels whose sum was less than the whole of their parts. He apprenticed with local farmers, clerked for a silk importer, traveled to China as a ship's boy, and ran a farm and orchard on Staten Island. He also authored a number of books based on travels first to England, where he studied parks and drainage projects, and later to the American South, where he strengthened his commitment to social equality. By August 1857, however, Olmsted's life was spiraling downward personally, economically, and professionally: His brother was in the final stages of fatal tuberculosis; and the publishing firm in which he had invested five thousand dollars of his father's money in exchange for a partnership share had collapsed, leaving behind thousands of dollars in debt.

Fate, however, seemed to find him at that moment. He crossed paths with a friend who had just been appointed to the park's board of commissioners. The board, he learned, was searching for a new park superintendent to oversee labor. Olmsted quickly applied for the job, having determined, he explained to his brother, "what else can I do for a living?"

Becoming superintendent of Central Park brought Olmsted's life into new focus. It was as though everything had been leading up to this moment. His peripatetic early life had armed him with a diverse knowledge of agriculture, engineering, and landscape design. His commitment to social justice aligned with the reformist ideas that led to the park's creation—he described it as "a democratic development of the highest significance." And his disposition— pragmatic, industrious, and organized—was perfectly suited to an ambitious project of this scope. He immediately tackled problems created through mismanagement, political favoritism, and a devastating 1857 financial panic. The biggest concern was the park's initial labor force, an undisciplined and often delinquent group that held their jobs through political connections. Within months, Olmsted had remedied the situation, boasting that he had transformed "a mob of lazy, reckless, turbulent and violent loafers [into] a well organized, punctual, sober, industrious and disciplined body."

Olmsted's involvement with the park's landscape design, much like his appointment as superintendent, arose serendipitously. He had been reluctant to participate in the design competition, fearing that he might offend his supervisor, who had submitted a preliminary plan that was discarded in favor of the open contest. "I should have had nothing to do with the design of the Central Park," Olmsted later remarked, "had not Vaux invited me to join him. . . . But for his invitation I should not have been a landscape architect." Ironically, Vaux had sought Olmsted less for his artistry than for his administrative skills and political connections—he was Republican, as was a majority of the board.

Once the two men began collaborating, however, Olmsted's refined artistic sensibility blossomed. His vision for the park broadly followed the teachings of Downing: The goal was a heightened form of nature, one that depended heavily on trees to create a pastoral oasis and exploited natural features of the landscape to achieve the picturesque. The project consumed the two men throughout the winter of 1857–58, and they barely finished in time for the March 31 deadline. Their submission was a highly polished, professional presentation, complete with a ten-foot-long hand-drawn map and a series of tableaux juxtaposing the "present condition" against the "effect proposed." Known as the Greensward Plan, it beat out more than thirty other entries to win the competition, though city politics likely played as large a role as aesthetics.

Regardless of why it was selected, the Greensward Plan was a landmark of innovative design. Olmsted and Vaux started with the premise that Central Park needed to be completely set apart from the bustling city that would soon engulf it. Their submission explained, "For the purpose of concealing the houses . . . from the park, and to insure an umbrageous horizon line, it is proposed . . . to plant a line of trees all around the outer edge of the park." Trees would thus create the illusion of infinite wilderness as soon as a visitor stepped inside the park (the arrival of skyscrapers in the twentieth century put an end to this effect). In order to maintain the illusion within the park, the plan called for the four transverse roads to be sunk below the surface, a radical engineering solution that some worried would be impossible to construct. Additionally, the grounds of the park, especially in the southern half, needed to be terraformed: draining the marshes; shaping the high, rocky outcroppings; pulverizing boulders that served no aesthetic purpose; creating several new bodies of water in the valleys. The landscape that resulted, in places pastoral, in others picturesque, would also contain a host of fashionable constructions that the board required: a broad carriage path; ornate brick and stone arches; a majestic avenue; a grand fountain overlooking one of the newly formed lakes.

Olmsted and Vaux also devoted almost one-third of the Greensward Plan's accompanying description to a proposed American arboretum. While such an artificial feature ran counter to their general design approach, it brought benefits that justified its inclusion. The authors wrote:

> The north-east section of the upper park is shown as an arboretum of American trees, so that every one who wishes to do so may become acquainted with the trees and shrubs. . . . [I]t is proposed to limit this particular collection to American trees, because . . . it will afford an opportunity to show the great advantage that America possesses in this respect. No other extra-tropical country could furnish one quarter the material for such a collection.

On paper, the Greensward Plan appeared ambitious but well thought out. In practice, no one knew if it could work with the troublesome plot of land involved. Up to that point, landscape gardening, according to Olmsted, had been "chiefly directed to the improvement of naturally wooded scenery, and that on a small scale." Olmsted later wrote, "It would have been difficult to find another body of land of six hundred acres upon the island . . . which possessed less of . . . the most desirable characteristics of a park, or upon which more time, labor, and expense would be required to establish them."

The implementation of the Greensward Plan, consequently, was a colossal, almost absurd undertaking, the single largest and most expensive public-works project ever attempted in an urban area. The board promoted Olmsted to architect in chief, responsible for overseeing the entire operation. Vaux, somewhat insultingly, was deputized as a consulting architect. The demands of the project necessitated that the workforce swell first to 2,000 and then to an average of 3,000, with a peak at 3,800—for years it was the largest employer in a city rocked by the unemployment that followed the Panic of 1857. Costs began to spiral, becoming a constant source of tension between Olmsted and the board. By 1860, the total bill was already estimated at $2.5 million, almost $1 million more than the Greensward Plan had estimated. The number grew with each passing year.

Tree planting—as with drainage and the sunken transverses—constituted a major component of the landscaping. The Greensward Plan devoted more than 25 percent of its operating budget to tree purchase, planting, and soil improvement. Olmsted, recognizing the importance that trees had in his vision, advised the board "to select immediately the finest trees which can be found." Later, he issued specific instructions that "No tree or shrub is to be planted under any circumstances except in the best manner." To oversee the planting, Olmsted selected from within the ranks of his staff an Austrian American landscape gardener named Ignaz Pilat, who had trained in Vienna. Pilat proved capable of realizing the most elaborate sylvan effects, even Olmsted's demand that in one section of the park, known as the Ramble, the foliage be planted so densely as to appear tropical. The plans for the American arboretum, meanwhile, became more cosmopolitan, with new instructions to plant "specimens of every tree and shrub which can be grown upon the site in the open air."

Construction of the park was not completed until 1873. Olmsted estimated that the amount of earth and stone transported in the park totaled 4,825,000 cubic yards, "or nearly ten millions of ordinary city one-horse cart-loads, which, in single file, would make a procession thirty thousand miles in length." The amount of imported or redistributed materials, if spread equally throughout the park, would change the elevation by nearly four feet, according to Olmsted. Over 18,500 cubic yards of topsoil alone were imported from New Jersey, as the park's natural soil was too infertile to sustain extensive tree plantings. And the number of trees planted in this re-formed earth reached more than 400,000. An 1873 catalogue listed 1,447 hardy species and varieties.

Even before the construction was completed, the park that Olmsted and Vaux designed proved an instant success. It drew on average more than one hundred thousand visitors per month throughout the warmer seasons. An 1861 article in the *Atlantic Monthly* gushed: "[T]he Central Park in New York,—the most striking evidence yet of the sovereignty of the people yet afforded in the history of free institutions,—the best answer yet given to the doubts and fears which have frowned on the theory of self-government." *Harper's* described it as "the finest work of art ever executed in this country." Olmsted, lauding its salubrious effect for society, proclaimed, "No one . . . can doubt that it exercises a distinctly harmonizing and refining influence upon the most unfortunate and lawless classes of the city."

The park's popularity propelled Olmsted onto the national stage, and he eventually grew weary of the day-to-day budget fights and petty squabbles with the board. Looking for a new challenge and swept up in the bellicose atmosphere of the Civil War, he decided to join the Union army as executive secretary of the United States Sanitary Commission, an agency tasked with improving military sanitary conditions. Olmsted's new priority became sanitary reform. Using the administrative skills he had honed in Central Park, he attacked "slovenliness [as] a national vice," in the estimation of one historian of the period. Following his service in the war, Olmsted accepted a position as superintendent of the Mariposa Mining estates in California, where he encountered the legendary big trees. He joined the cause of sequoia preservation, which he considered, like Central Park, a matter of basic democracy: equal opportunity for all to enjoy the trees. In 1865, the governor of California appointed him commissioner of the new state park comprising Yosemite and the Mariposa Big Tree Grove.

But Olmsted's greatest passion was landscape gardening, and soon he returned to it. In the 1860s, he formed a business partnership with Vaux, and the two men ushered in a new era of public-park creation throughout America. One of their first commissions was in the borough of Brooklyn, where they designed the 585-acre Prospect Park, a triumph of landscape design that Olmsted considered superior in many ways to Central Park. Their subsequent projects, far too numerous to recount in full, ranged from giant citywide initiatives (such as the "Emerald Necklace" system in Boston, which included Harvard's famous Arnold Arboretum) to national landmarks (such as the Niagara Falls State Park). Olmsted's firm also handled private commissions, from Stanford University in California to the Lawrenceville School in New Jersey to his final major project, George Washington Vanderbilt's estate in North Carolina, known as Biltmore.

While Olmsted's style developed over time, it largely stayed true to the sylvan aesthetics that Downing had first set forth. Over the course of a forty-year career in landscape gardening, he had turned the American metropolis green. Sadly, his most famous commission, Central Park, began to decline almost as soon as it was completed, the victim of municipal corruption that endured into the twentieth century.

## Man and Nature

T HE BULK OF Central Park's construction took place against the backdrop of the Civil War, and the bloodiest conflict in the nation's history turned trees, like nearly everything, into a matter of tactics and strategy. Forests provided cover for troop transport and made large-scale infantry engagements impractical. Both sides set fire to the woods, sometimes as an aggressive maneuver to destroy the enemy's property and sometimes as a defensive ploy to impede hostile forces with a wall of fire. Trees also provided the raw materials for innumerable war supplies. According to one contemporary source, "In the first two years of the present civil war in the United States, twenty-eight thousand walnut trees were felled to supply a single European manufactory of gunstocks for the American market."

The year 1864 was perhaps the most violent of the war. In the wake of President Lincoln's Emancipation Proclamation and Gettysburg Address, Union and Confederate forces were fighting with renewed intensity, locked in a winner-take-all struggle for the future of the country. Each passing month produced tens of thousands of casualties.

The height of war was not a likely moment for a shift in attitudes about trees, but in May of that year appeared a book, *Man and Nature,* that historian Lewis Mumford would later label "the fountainhead of the conservation movement." It argued that the nation's forests were much more than zones on a military map or mines for timber and fuel. Trees, the book explained, were essential to the very habitability of the nation.

George Perkins Marsh, the author of *Man and Nature,* was one of the nineteenth century's most capacious thinkers. His personal library included more than twelve thousand volumes, and he reportedly spoke twenty languages comfortably. He belonged to both the American Academy of Arts and Sciences and the American Philosophical Society. His writings prior to *Man and Nature* included a treatise on Icelandic grammar, a history of the English language, and a monograph on the camel. According to one contemporary, "it was the general opinion of his friends that he possessed one of the broadest minds and a most absorptive memory." *Man and Nature* was his crowning achievement, the synthesis of several lifetimes' worth of study and experience.

The ideas that developed into his book traced back to his boyhood observations. He was born in 1801 in Woodstock, Vermont, and, like Susan Fenimore Cooper and Thoreau, grew up watching the surrounding forests fall in the name of progress. "[I] spent my early life almost literally in the woods," he once commented. "I have had occasion both to observe and to feel the effects resulting from an injudicious system of managing woodlands and the products of the forests." Most of his contemporaries thought that the effect of such "injudicious" land management was simply the hastening of man's dominion over nature—the forests were savage places meant to be dominated. But Marsh, despite this mantra that cleared land was superior, saw consequences for the surrounding environment in the disappearance of trees. He wrote to a friend:

> For instance my father had a piece of thick woodland where the ground was always damp. Wild turnips grew there and ginseng, and wild pepper sometimes. Well, sir, he cleared up that lot, and drained and cultivated it, and it became a good deal drier. . . . Now I am going to state this as a *fact* and I defy all you speculators about cause and effect to deny it.

Marsh was not only an observer, but also a busy participant in the rough-and-tumble world of early nineteenth-century America. His list of jobs and business ventures made the peripatetic early careers of Thoreau and Olmsted look focused by comparison. After earning a college degree from Dartmouth at nineteen, Marsh entered the profession of law, but the first twenty years of his career also included stints as a gentleman farmer, lumber dealer, manufacturer, mill operator, newspaper editor, road builder, speculator, and state bureaucrat. Through these manifold activities, Marsh coped with the twin tragedies he suffered in 1833, when he lost his wife and son: "It was well for me [that business] drove me into a constant succession of severe labors of a very engrossing character." Unfortunately, none of these enterprises proved especially fruitful. Partly it was bad luck, and partly it was that Marsh's mind was often lost in intellectual pursuits. By the 1840s, with little to show for his efforts as a businessman, he turned to politics. His father had been a U.S. senator, and in 1842 Marsh was able to win a congressional seat as a Whig representative from Vermont.

The first public record of Marsh's interest in man's effect on the natural environment appeared during his tenure as congressman. In 1847, he delivered an address to an agricultural society in his native Vermont that touched on the subject. The speech was, for the most part, a valedictory to the harmonizing influences that modern life had on the natural world. "The arts of the savage are the arts of destruction," he said. "Civilization, on the contrary, is at once the mother and the fruit of peace." This was standard rhetoric at the time. However, in the middle of the talk, Marsh detoured from this accepted narrative:

> [T]rees are no longer what they were in our fathers' time, an incumbrance. . . . The functions of the forest, besides supplying timber and fuel, are various. . . . [T]he annual deposit of the foliage of deciduous trees, and the decomposition of their decaying trunks, form an accumulation of vegetable mould, which gives the greatest fertility to the often originally barren soils on which they grow, and enriches lower grounds by the wash from rains and the melting of snows. . . . [W]here too large a proportion of the surface is bared of wood, the action of the summer sun and wind scorches the hills which are no longer shaded or sheltered by trees, [and] the springs and rivulets that found their supply in the bibulous soil of the forest disappear.

The thrust of Marsh's argument was twofold. First, deforestation meant not only the elimination of trees, but the alteration of entire ecosystems: drier soils; less regulated temperatures; erosion; uneven water flows. Second, to remove trees risked permanently degrading the land, such that nature alone could not ameliorate the problem. Marsh went so far as to use the word "evil" to describe the "injudicious destruction of the woods." His language drew on the rhetoric of morality, of religious obligation. Traditionally, however, the forests themselves were associated with evil forces. And while backwoods settlement, Hudson River School paintings, and transcendentalism had mitigated this somewhat, the connotation persisted. Marsh was flipping popular sentiment on its head. But at this early stage he still sublimated these concerns to the larger argument that humanity was superior to nature.

In 1849, Marsh's tenure as congressman ended, and for the next dozen years he bounced between public and private life, a period crucial to the intellectual development that led to his writing *Man and Nature*. Of particular importance were two diplomatic turns he made in Europe, first as minister to Turkey in 1849, then as special envoy to Greece in 1852. Marsh used the opportunities to travel through some of the world's most long-settled regions, providing him a valuable counterpoint to the young nation that was his home. The ancient treeless European landscapes and lifeless deserts of Egypt and Arabia struck Marsh as the end result of thousands of years of unchecked deforestation, a glimpse of his own country's future. After completing his diplomatic service in 1855, he returned once more to America, but then headed back to Europe in 1861 when President Lincoln appointed him ambassador to Italy.

By this point, Marsh, who was already sixty years old, felt equipped to begin the most ambitious scholarly project of his life. His intention, according to one of his letters, was to demonstrate "that whereas [many] think that the earth made man, man in fact made the earth." The proposed "little volume" was going to show precisely how the so-called civilizing effects of mankind—the same ones he had praised in 1847—had transformed all the inhabited regions of the earth, more often than not by destroying and compromising a natural world that was otherwise in balance. To prove this assertion, Marsh planned to rely on his own experiences—as a boy in Vermont, as a business-man in diverse affairs, and as a diplomat in Europe—as well as on an enormous array of sources, from different regions and historical epochs, which were only accessible to a man with Marsh's breadth as a scholar and facility as a linguist. What would make *Man and Nature* groundbreaking, therefore, was not sim-ply the boldness of its claims—some of these issues had been floating around since the time of the Romans—but the comprehensiveness of the research. Marsh intended to overwhelm readers with examples until they submitted to the humbling conclusions.

In particular, Marsh hoped that his final product served as a cautionary tale to his countrymen. He wrote to Secretary of State William Seward during the editing phase that he wanted "to show the evils resulting from too much clearing and cultivation, and often so-called improvements in new countries like the United States." For much of Europe, the lessons contained in *Man and Nature* would arrive too late, though some countries had already begun man-aging their forests out of necessity.

The final text of *Man and Nature* showed almost no patience for the status quo American attitude that the forests existed to be exploited in the name of progress. "Man alone," Marsh wrote, "is to be regarded as essentially a destruc-tive power. . . . The destructive agency of man becomes more and more ener-getic and unsparing as he advances in civilization." This assertion cast aside the very premise upon which the country was based: that man stood above nature, permitted by divine right to exert his domain across all the land. Marsh stated: "Man has too long forgotten that the earth was given to him for usu-fruct alone, not for consumption, still less for profligate waste." Here was the root of the idea that human development came coupled with a responsibility to the natural environment.

Although *Man and Nature* addressed many different facets of this natural environment, the book placed deforestation squarely at the center of its analysis. Substantively, the writing was expanding on the ideas Marsh first put forth in his 1847 address, only now, instead of speaking in generalities, Marsh included scores of specific historical examples, which filled hundreds of pages and lengthy footnotes. And all of this evidence pointed Marsh toward one inevitable conclusion: "With the disappearance of the forest, all is changed . . . and thus the earth is rendered no longer fit for the habitation of man."

Though severe in tone, *Man and Nature* did not suggest that humanity's presence led to an inevitable conclusion for the environment. Rather, the future of any given environment rested in the hands of its inhabitants, which was especially important for America. Marsh wrote of his countrymen: "[W]e have not yet bared all the sources of our streams, not yet overthrown all the barriers which nature has erected to restrain her own destructive energies. Let us be wise in time, and profit by the errors of our older brethren!" Earlier reformers had looked to economic consequences as the sole reason to preserve the forests, but Marsh was providing environmental rationales, culled from the annals of history. His book nourished an entirely new line of argument against deforestation, that of environmental degradation.

After months of editing and revising, Marsh's book finally appeared in May 1864. Charles Scribner, the publisher, sold very few copies at the start, and Marsh considered the book's prospects so bleak that he relinquished the copyright (though it was later repurchased for him). However, demand for *Man and Nature* soon increased, and within a few months Scribner had exhausted his initial run.

While the full impact of *Man and Nature* was not felt for several generations, Marsh's ideas quickly began to influence other thinkers. In 1865, the Reverend Frederick Starr of St. Louis, who had read Marsh, wrote an influential article titled "American Forests: Their Destruction and Preservation." The thrust of the piece considered the economic consequences of deforestation, and Starr included a "Warnings from History" section that drew heavily on Marsh. Two years later, Increase Allen Lapham of Wisconsin published a report for his state's legislature that combined both the economic and environmental arguments against deforestation. On the cover of the report, Lapham quoted Marsh's line that "the earth was given to [man] for usufruct alone." The following year, Calvin Chamberlain delivered a lecture to the Maine Board of Agriculture titled "Man a Destructive Power" that quoted extensively from Marsh's prose.

Marsh, meanwhile, spent the remaining years of his life in Italy. He held the post of ambassador until his death in 1882, the longest continuing tenure for a diplomat in American history to that point. He devoted much of his time to revising *Man and Nature*. In 1874, an expanded copy was published, retitled *The Earth as Modified by Human Action*. He was working on another revision when he died.

*Man and Nature*—together with transcendentalism, the parks movement, and the fight to save the big trees—had sown the seeds for a conservation movement that would flourish at the turn of the century. These early stirrings, however, could not hold back the approaching tide of industrialization, an ethos America pursued with relentless vigor as the country emerged from the ravages of the Civil War and remade the landscape once more.

# 4

## Forests of Commerce

American Chestnut

## An Iron Horse Built of Wood

O N THE MORNING of May 10, 1869, a crowd one thousand strong gathered at Promontory Summit in the Utah Territory to witness a feat once thought unachievable. The midwestern-based Union Pacific Railroad and the western-based Central Pacific Railroad, separated five years earlier by almost two thousand miles, now stood one hundred feet apart, about to unite a continent. As noon approached, Irish and Chinese immigrants, working for the two lines, respectively, set down the final tracks. Soon the locomotives from each company were almost touching, their exhaust merging into a black cloud that slowly dissipated into an otherwise splendid blue sky.

As the last rails were laid in place, the crowd closed in to hear the decorated speakers who had come to mark the occasion. One of the most distinguished, Leland Stanford, was both governor of California and president of the Central Pacific Railroad—such was the political power of railroads in the second half of the nineteenth century. He took the orator's platform and presented a final golden spike to become "a part of the great highway which is about to unite [California] in close fellowship with her sisters of the Atlantic." A team of honorees then took turns driving this ultimate spike into the transcontinental railway. Once the final blow was issued, the crowd burst into cheers and the two locomotives cried out with their steam whistles.

Telegraphs relayed the news to cities around the nation, setting off a sequence of spectacular, often spontaneous, celebrations. In San Francisco, business was suspended as people joined in the longest procession the city ever hosted. In Chicago, a parade stretched out four miles long. In New York, the mayor ordered a one-hundred-gun salute. In Philadelphia, the bells of Independence Hall rang with such intensity that uninformed bystanders mistook it for a general alarm of fire. President Ulysses Grant received the official telegraphic dispatch from Stanford at 2:47 p.m. Eastern time: "We have the honor to report the last rail laid, the last spike driven. The Pacific Railroad is finished."

Stanford's message to Grant, like so much of the press across the continent, made it sound as though the railroad were a strictly metal-based technology, the harbinger of an age of iron and steel in America. The multiple speakers at Promontory Summit struck a similar tone, using metaphors like "iron horse" and the "iron chain [that would] marry the Atlantic and Pacific Oceans." These attitudes were, of course, understandable. Trains were a transformative technology ushering America into a new age of industrialization, one defined by increased mechanization, easier transport, and geometric growth in productivity. However, the material that the railroads depended on most, especially during the formative years in the nineteenth century, was neither iron nor steel, but that stalwart of American development: wood. In truth, every aspect of the system relied on forests and their timber in vast quantities.

The concept of using a railed pathway for transport had largely been developed in England during the seventeenth and eighteenth centuries. At that time the British already possessed well-developed iron forges and abundant coal deposits, but wood remained relatively expensive (just as it had in Hakluyt's day during the reign of Queen Elizabeth I). British engineers favored the materials most readily available—as well as the most permanent—and designed a system that used iron rails set in granite or stone pilings.

When railroad technology first reached America in the early nineteenth century, however, the resource situation was almost the opposite of England's. Wood was cheap and plentiful, while iron forging remained costly and primitive. Eager to reduce costs and labor, and unconcerned about the long-term survival of any given railway, American engineers quickly modified the British design to use wood throughout the system, including the tracks.

Most early American railroads used wooden rails with thin straps of iron placed upon them, so-called strap railroads. This design appeared in the nation's first commercial railway, the Granite Railway, a three-mile-long track built in 1826 to haul granite from Quincy, Massachusetts, to nearby Milton during the construction of the Bunker Hill memorial. According to a contemporaneous report, "the rails are of pine timber 6 inches wide and 12 inches deep. . . . On top of the wooden rails there is nailed oak scantling, 2 inches thick and 4 inches wide, on which is fastened a bar of rolled iron 5-16 of an inch thick and from 2½ to 2¾ inches wide." This American style of strap rail construction reduced iron use from ninety-one tons per mile (the British average) to only twenty-five, dropping the cost per mile from $180,000 to between $20,000 and $30,000. By 1840, when the nation had more than three thousand miles of track, fully two-thirds of American railways used some variation of strap rails, with the underlying wood varying based on region and availability.

The strap rail system may have reduced construction costs, but it also created problems that more than offset any savings. The most notorious concern was something known colloquially as "snake heads," when the strap of iron pulled free of the wooden rail and curled upward. One midcentury observer noted, "A twenty-foot bar of iron, wriggling its way through a well filled passenger car, has, on more than one occasion, resulted in the mangling of as many human forms as in some of our first-class 'smash ups.'" Such shortcomings, combined with advancements in iron production and iron-track design, convinced most Americans to abandon wooden tracks. Strap rails fell out of fashion largely before the midcentury construction boom that increased the national network more than twentyfold between 1840 and 1870. Nonetheless, instances of wooden railways persisted throughout the nineteenth century. During the Civil War, for example, cash-strapped and hurried Confederates were compelled to build them in order to move troops and supplies. Wooden railways also proved popular in lower-cost logging operations of the late nineteenth century—in extreme cases, lumberjacks simply lined felled logs in two parallel tracks, and a locomotive outfitted with special, spool-shaped wheels rolled along these so-called pole roads.

While strap rails yielded to pure iron ones relatively early in the development of the nation's train network, wood endured far longer as the primary material for railway bridges. The entire transport system depended on such bridges, for every line inevitably crossed ravines and rivers in the nation's rugged landscape. The English had favored structures of iron and masonry, but Americans again found that they could reduce costs and increase construction speeds by substituting timber. Before the arrival of railroads, American engineers had already developed sophisticated timber bridges that used truss and trestle geometry to give wooden architecture incredible strength. In 1812, for example, a 340-foot-long truss-reinforced timber bridge, appropriately named "Colossus," spanned the Schuylkill River in Philadelphia without any intermediate supports, making it the longest such structure in the world. America's prowess in wood construction prompted a Scottish engineer to write in 1859, "To any engineer about to practice in a new country, the study of the American timber bridges is invaluable, as showing what gigantic and useful works may be constructed with that material."

Nearly every railroad built before 1875 relied on wooden bridges. The Granite Railway, for instance, had used wooden frames to cross several deep ravines. The Baltimore and Ohio Railroad, the nation's first major railroad and the earliest to feature a steam-powered locomotive, erected a 110-foot timber-truss bridge in 1829. The following year, the South Carolina Railroad began constructing a 136-mile-long trestle railroad, in which the entire structure was set atop elevated wooden supports, often ten feet high. The Central Pacific Railroad, as it passed through the Sierra Nevada Mountains en route to Promontory Summit, Utah, built numerous elaborate bridges, some more than one hundred feet high and one thousand feet long.

Eventually, wooden bridges, like wooden railways before them, fell out of favor. While they were cheaper and faster to construct than metal and stone structures, they decayed more rapidly. More permanent materials, such as stone, earth, iron, and steel, started to replace timber, and new major bridges, benefiting from advances in metallurgy, began to feature all-steel designs as early as 1873. Despite this, many wood trestle bridges endured. An 1896 government report estimated that more than two thousand miles of timber trestles remained, valued at $60 million, roughly twice the total capital invested in iron and steel structures to that point. Over the course of the twentieth century surviving trestle bridges grew increasingly scarce.

The era of the timber bridge was also the era of the wood-burning steam engine. Wood remained the cheapest source of fuel in the country until the late nineteenth century. It burned cleanly and evenly, and, most important, was readily available almost everywhere. American engineers adapted the coal-burning engines of British design for the tree-rich landscape; and the wood-burning locomotive, with its proud funnel-shaped smokestack, became the iconic image of the American railroad. It was a voracious, inefficient consumer of fuel that feasted upon trees and required a network of intermediate supply stations to provide fresh loads of wood, keeping farmers along the route busy gathering fuel. By midcentury, these American engines were devouring three to four million cords annually—in comparison, recall that the entire city of Boston required only six hundred thousand cords. The annual amount of cordwood burned in railroad engines likely peaked at seven million cords around 1870.

As with wooden rails and bridges, wood-burning engines were an imperfect technology. Most notably, American locomotives produced a billowing smoke infused with cinders. Charles Dickens, during his initial visit to North America in 1842, described the exhaust as "a whirlwind of bright sparks, which showered about us like a storm of fiery snow." An 1831 traveler on the first American-built passenger train explained how the wood-burners terrorized passengers:

> They used dry pitch-pine for fuel, and . . . a volume of black smoke, strongly impregnated with sparks, coals, and cinders, came pouring back the whole length of the train. Each of the outside passengers who had an umbrella raised it as a protection against the smoke and fire. They were found to be but a momentary protection . . . all having their covers burnt off from the frames, when a general *melee* took place among the deck-passengers, each whipping his neighbor to put out the fire. They presented a very motley appearance on arriving at the first station.

Eventually, engineers created spark arresters and smokestacks that provided some degree of protection for passengers, but the deadly exhaust remained a fire hazard for the surrounding countryside. Wherever the train went, forest blazes followed, often raging unchecked across thousands of acres. This problem continued even after trains converted from wood fuel to coal—by 1880, coal was providing more than 90 percent of engine fuel—and it lessened only with the eventual shift to diesel and electric locomotives.

Aside from locomotives, which featured metal construction from the outset, every other type of railroad car was built almost entirely of wood throughout the nineteenth century. American engineers had modeled the first railway cars in imitation of the popular melon-shaped road carriage, which featured all-wood construction. By 1835, the body design had changed to the more familiar long rectangular body, but the wooden construction remained. Railroad car manufacturers produced thousands of these each year, and they required enormous quantities of high-grade lumber. A major builder like George Pullman could consume 50 million board feet annually. Some reports estimated that 350,000 acres of commercial forests—an area greater than all of Cape Cod, Massachusetts—disappeared each year in the late nineteenth century to meet the needs of the railway car industry. The shift away from wood began in earnest only during the 1890s, when iron and steel became structural necessities for longer coach bodies. Like the trestle bridge, however, the wooden car enjoyed a graceful slide toward obsolescence—in 1920, 60 percent of the passenger cars in service still featured all-wood construction.

The American railroad's largest single use of timber—one that exceeded the combined totals for rails, bridges, cars, snow fences, telegraph poles, and the countless other aspects of train infrastructure—was the crosstie, the lateral beam that rested below the rails. These intermediate supports acted as cushions and shock absorbers, ensuring a smoother and safer ride. British engineers had supported their early rails with stone blocks, the most permanent material available. Americans initially had followed this model, but limitations appeared quickly: New England's harsh climate compromised the integrity of the blocks; laborers could not produce new ones fast enough to keep pace with demand; and high prices made them prohibitively expensive for many train lines. Shortages of stone blocks forced engineers to look for alternatives, and again wood offered a plentiful and cheaper option.

Once railroads began to employ wood ties, engineers discovered that they offered benefits beyond economic expediency. A passenger from the 1830s explained: "The moment of passing from the wooden to the stone [supports] can be at once both heard and felt by the passengers in the car. Upon the wood the sound is less harsh, and the vibration less rapid than upon the unyielding stone, the elasticity of the [wood] rendering it the most pleasant to ride upon."

Not just any slab of timber, however, was suitable for a rail tie. The wood needed to be sturdy enough to withstand the force of a passing train without splitting or wearing down. It also had to hold spikes well and resist decay, though even the best ties succumbed to nature after about ten years. The most coveted varieties were hardwoods such as white oak and chestnut. Railroad men felt that the highest-quality ties came strictly from the heartwood of second-growth trees, and, as an 1874 article noted, they never hesitated to select from "among the very best fine young trees, eight to ten inches in diameter." With average ties having dimensions eight feet long and eight inches square, most trees only produced a single tie, and each mile of track required an average of twenty-five hundred ties.

Initially railroads used ties from the local forests and woodlots, but as the network expanded, demand for ties outstripped local supplies. By midcentury, the need for crossties made railroads the single largest consumer of wood in the country. An 1873 article summarized the situation:

> It is estimated that the number of railroad ties in present use in the United States are 150,000,000. And as young timber is mostly used, a cut of 200 ties to the acre is above rather than under the

average, and it, therefore, has required the product of 750,000 acres of well timbered land to furnish the supply. Railroad ties last about five years, consequently 30,000,000 ties are used annually for repairs, taking the timber from 150,000 acres.

Consumption likely peaked around 1880, when railroads consumed 60 million ties (about 2 billion board feet) for new construction and repairs of worn-out track.

Unlike the other wood-based aspects of the railroads, wooden ties never lost their ground to newer technologies. More than twenty-five hundred different patents for ties were introduced, but none effectively replaced the combination of strength, durability, and cost savings that wood provided. In the late nineteenth century, railroads began to use preservatives such as creosote to extend the life of wooden ties, further enhancing their utility—this practice also tempered the rate of forest depletion.

Even relatively early on in the development of the railroad, the impact that trains had on the nation's trees was difficult for some to ignore. In 1854, Thoreau in *Walden* addressed the situation with typical passion: "That devilish Iron Horse, whose ear-rending neigh is heard throughout the town, has muddied the Boiling Spring with his foot, and he it is that has browsed off all the woods on Walden shore." Within a decade, the scene in Concord was repeated across forests throughout the nation as the railroad expanded its network. Andrew Fuller, one of the earliest voices urging the railroads to remedy their destructive practices, wrote in 1866: "Even where railroads have penetrated regions abundantly supplied, we soon find that all along its track timber soon becomes scarce. For every railroad in the country requires a continued forest from one end to the other of its lines to supply it with ties, fuel, and lumber for building their cars."

Most Americans, however, turned a blind eye to the depletion situation, focusing instead on the new prosperity that railroads seemed to promise. Trains allowed for fast and easy transport of goods and integrated small communities into the trading spheres of large cities. They also opened up new regions for settlement, especially in the Midwest. The laying down of railroad tracks was often the first step toward any region's economic development, and construction booms followed the ever-growing network.

The increased construction rates that railroads brought about also created a more intense demand for lumber generally. No new houses could be built without timber for framing. No new farms begun without wooden storage barns. No animals raised without wooden fences. Progress required billions of board feet, and a quickening pace of life was producing a quickening pace of lumbering.

## The Lumber Baron and Industrial Logging

I N JULY 1852, eighteen-year-old Frederick Weyerhaeuser landed in New
York after a six-week voyage from his hometown of Nieder Saulheim, Germany. Other members of his family had already settled near Erie, Pennsylvania, and Weyerhaeuser joined them there, soon finding work with a local brewer. Though the young immigrant had no formal education past age twelve, he was a fast learner. He mastered the brewing business thoroughly, but abandoned it when, as he later explained, he "saw how often brewers became confirmed drunkards." Vice and indolence were intolerable to Weyerhaeuser, who showed little interest in leisure activities. By age twenty-one, the industrious German had earned enough money to set out on his own and, like many immigrants at midcentury, decided to head further west.

In early March 1856, he arrived at Rock Island, Illinois, a young, bustling town on the banks of the Mississippi River. With access to the nation's most important commercial watercourse and a recently completed railroad to Chicago, Rock Island offered new settlers plenty of opportunities. Germans, in particular, had flocked to the town, and they provided a social community for Weyerhaeuser. But his limited funds, poor education, and heavily accented English forced him to accept whatever work he could find. He began doing mechanical repairs and odd jobs for the railroad, though, in his own words, "the work didn't suit [him]." He wanted to focus instead on the commercial aspects of business.

Several months after Weyerhaeuser arrived in Rock Island, one of his friends offered him a position as the night fireman for a local sawmill. This new job seemed no more promising than the railway work, but Weyerhaeuser still accepted the employment, "expecting to learn to run the engine," he later explained. The work, however, shifted almost immediately from mechanics to lumber counting and sorting, tasks that suited Weyerhaeuser well. He was promoted to lumber salesman after making an unsupervised deal that netted his firm sixty dollars in gold and earned him the mill owner's approval. From there, his position within the firm improved steadily. "The secret of this," Weyerhaeuser wrote with characteristic humility, "lay simply in my readiness to work. I never counted the hours." During this period, Weyerhaeuser supplemented his income from the firm with investments and business arrangements throughout Rock Island and the neighboring towns.

By 1858, he was doing well financially but the sawmill that employed him was not. The Panic of 1857 had greatly weakened its financial position, and it went broke when an unscrupulous lumber dealer fleeced the mill owners of a shipment that they had purchased on credit. Weyerhaeuser, who had mastered the lumber industry's commercial side, decided that the bankrupted mill was a worthwhile investment, and in a move that would be characteristic of his career, he sought out a partner to share the financial burden and spread the risk. The man he selected, F. C. A. Denkmann, was a German immigrant who ran a grocery store in Rock Island and had a reputation as a good machinist, the skill that Weyerhaeuser lacked; additionally, Denkmann was married to the sister of Sarah Elizabeth Bloedel, a woman whom Weyerhaeuser was courting and would later marry. The two men pooled their capital and purchased the mill property for about four thousand dollars. Weyerhaeuser now owned a sawmill, the first piece in an empire that would change the lumber industry, and with it the nation.

I N AMERICA, ESPECIALLY in the North, lumber meant white pine. The same trees that had once provided masts for the British navy also produced a timber that farmers and builders prized above all others. The durable pinewood resisted cracking, decay, shrinking, splintering, and warping. It not only held glue, paint, and varnish well but also gripped nails firmly, even when they'd been removed and replaced in the same hole. And unlike logs cut from hardwoods, those from white pines floated easily upon water, an invaluable quality in a young nation where rivers functioned as commercial highways.

Transporting pine logs downriver generally took one of two forms. In some cases, especially on the more easily navigable rivers, men bound the newly cut wood into rafts. Skilled pilots guided these cumbersome objects through a river's eddies, islands, and shallows, under its bridges and over its rapids until they reached the mill. In other cases, logs were dumped directly into the rivers, a practice that became popular during the nineteenth century and was known as log driving. Here, loggers waited for the arrival of the spring, when the freshets swelled every stream, and they pushed the entire winter season's cutting into the flow. Countless thousands of logs, typically branded with a unique mark to distinguish them, tumbled and crashed over one another as they wound their way toward the local sawmills. The processing centers then stopped the logs with booms (floating barriers that could be employed to divert the wood from its downriver course). The term "logjam" originated with these drives: Occasionally, logs got trapped or wedged against objects in the river, setting off a chain reaction that could pile up fresh lumber for miles.

The nation's logging industry originated in the forests of Maine and New Hampshire, where some of the densest commercial white pine stands surrounded mighty rivers like the Piscataqua. New England's network of rivers carried logs toward Portsmouth, New Hampshire, and other coastal outlets, destined for colonial cities or for export.

As the population moved deeper into the nation's interior forests, so did the North's logging network, following a patchy distribution of white pines that extended across much of New York State and northern Pennsylvania. The pioneers carving new lives from the backwoods in these regions were also shipping timbers downriver to cities whose wood-hungry populations were booming in the early nineteenth century. Logs followed the Hudson River to New York City, the Delaware River to Philadelphia, the Susquehanna system all the way to Baltimore, and the Allegheny and Ohio Rivers, which flowed westward, to Pittsburgh and Cincinnati.

Eventually, New York State supplanted Maine as the nation's premier supplier of timber. By 1839, it accounted for 30 percent of the nation's total lumber production by value, with much of it passing through Albany, the country's largest wholesale distribution center. Maine followed New York with about 14 percent, while the other New England states boasted 10 percent and Pennsylvania added roughly 9 percent. Thus, this northeastern white pine belt composed almost two-thirds of the commercial lumber produced in the entire nation that year, an estimated 1.6 billion board feet—this number, however, ignored much of the noncommercial output that farmers generated in clearing their land for agriculture.

Around this time, lumber production rates started to rise rapidly, largely in response to new technologies and improved techniques. In the mills, steam-powered engines began to replace waterwheels, and engineers improved the power and efficiency of the innumerable waterwheels that remained. Cutting saws also benefited from advances in engineering, as well as in metallurgy. The most powerful saw in the first half of the nineteenth century was the muley, a long, stiff blade held by clamps and guided by rails that cut between 5,000 and 8,000 board feet per day. By midcentury, mills began shifting to both steam-powered circular saws (toothed disks that spun rapidly) and gang saws (multiple blades that cut a single board instantaneously into inch-thick planks). Each of these was capable of producing more than 40,000 board feet a day. The sawmills slowly grew from one- or two-man operations to large factories that employed up to one hundred men.

The nation's annual timber cut—which, over the first forty years of the nineteenth century, had gradually grown by one billion board feet—started to increase that amount or more almost every year after 1840. By midcentury, lumbering was the nation's second-largest manufacturing industry, trailing flour and grist, but besting cotton, cloth, wools, leather, liquor, and slaughtering.

The industry's turn to higher production also coincided with a shift toward midwestern markets. Though demand in the East remained high, it was growing exponentially along the Mississippi River and across the prairies. Waves of immigrants and new settlers flooded these regions in search of inexpensive, fertile land. This new terrain lacked the dense forests that blanketed much of the eastern United States, which meant that farming could begin immediately but that there were no nearby woodlots to provide material for houses, barns, fences, and tools. Timber ceased being a resource free for the cutting and became a commodity imported from afar. Adding to this demand were the enormous requirements of the railroad network that was making much of this westward expansion possible. The viability of towns like Rock Island depended upon a steady supply of trees that the local environment lacked.

The solution to this geographical imbalance lay far to the north of Rock Island and the countless other towns that dotted the Mississippi River and the prairies. Some of the richest white pine forests in the nation occupied a vast, pristine swath of forest that stretched over much of Michigan, northern Wisconsin, and parts of Minnesota. These three states, known collectively as the Lake States, also contained a high proportion of navigable rivers and lakes for bringing the white pine logs to market. As a sanguine congressman explained in 1852, "Upon the rivers which are tributary to the Mississippi, and also those which empty themselves into Lake Michigan, there are interminable forests of pine, sufficient to supply all the wants of the citizens . . . for all time to come." The amount of commercial pine available totaled hundreds of billions of board feet.

Lumbermen from the East began to resettle in the Lake States, bringing with them the techniques of commercial logging. The exodus was, perhaps, most noticeable in Maine, where many of the choicest pine stands that had once seemed infinite were nearing exhaustion. A congressman from that state in 1852 lamented "the stalwart sons of Maine marching away by the scores and hundreds to the piny [*sic*] woods of the Northwest."

Lake States pine typically followed two paths to market. Trees growing along streams that emptied out into Lakes Michigan and Superior—an area that included most of Michigan, northeastern Wisconsin, and northern Minnesota—wound up in Milwaukee or, more likely, Chicago. From there, logs could travel eastward through a recently completed canal system and ultimately reach the Atlantic Ocean. In 1856, Chicago, which had sprung up seemingly overnight as a center for both railroad traffic and lumber distribution, displaced Albany as the nation's largest wholesale processing center. The other main artery of Lake States commerce was the Mississippi River. Streams originating far north in Wisconsin and Minnesota wandered southward and eventually emptied into the great river. Upon reaching the Mississippi, logs floating on giant rafts, each containing hundreds of thousands of board feet, could travel as far south as New Orleans and the Gulf of Mexico, passing towns like Rock Island en route.

By 1860, the Lake States lumber trade was supplanting the northeastern pine belt as the nation's largest supply region, but the real growth was only beginning.

WEYERHAEUSER HAD SPENT much of the 1860s working with Denkmann to improve their sawmill. They invested in the new technologies that had begun to appear around midcentury, and their mill's capacity, which was initially between 6,000 and 10,000 board feet a day, doubled within two years and jumped to more than 200,000 feet of lumber per week by the late 1860s. The local paper described it in 1869 as "one of the best lumbering establishments on the river" that contained "a perfect wilderness of saws." Over sixty employees worked in the mills and in the various lumberyards that Weyerhaeuser and Denkmann owned or rented. Their clients included the Union Pacific Railway Company, which once placed a single order for 950,000 feet of bridge lumber, likely related to the construction of the transcontinental railroad.

Weyerhaeuser's increased production capacity required enormous quantities of raw timber, but the supply system along the Mississippi River was a logistical nightmare. The lumber industry's rapid growth had created a disorganized and segmented transportation network that included lumberjacks, landowners, log drivers, boom operators, raft pilots, upriver mill owners, and downriver Mississippi mill owners like Weyerhaeuser. Most of these components of the lumber industry operated independently of one another, held together through a series of contracts and uneasy relationships. Adding to this chaos were the vicissitudes of mother nature: Droughts impeded log driving; logjams slowed down supply; floods pushed logs outside the normal flow of a river, scattering them along the banks and surrounding forests for hundreds of miles. Weyerhaeuser, like all the Mississippi mill owners, was one of the final links in this concatenation of pine dealers and, consequently, had no means to guarantee his supply. As his capital investments and output capacity increased, his need to secure delivery of white pines from the great forests of the Lake States grew increasingly urgent.

The key to controlling the Mississippi River section of the region's lumber trade was the 285-mile-long Chippewa River, which rose in northwestern Wisconsin some 30 miles south of Lake Superior. Of the four major watercourses that flowed southward through Wisconsin and emptied into the Mississippi, the Chippewa possessed the greatest commercial supply of white pine, an estimated 46.6 billion board feet in the forests that surrounded its headwaters. Geologists calculated that the river and its tributaries drained 34 percent of the entire timber region in Wisconsin. One contemporary expert in the lumber industry, in comparing the Chippewa to other parts of the Lake States, commented: "The Chippewa valley might be called a logger's paradise, a very large part of its area being heavily forested with the finest quality of white pine timber, while rivers, streams, and lakes offered a network of excellent transportation facilities."

In 1868, Weyerhaeuser traveled into the Chippewa Valley for the first time. After spending countless seasons contracting with every raft pilot and shady contractor along the Mississippi, he had decided to visit the source of his precious logs. Unlike most millmen, he enjoyed the spartan life that the logging camps provided, always happy to spend a night in a plank bed or fight off the morning frost as he surveyed the woods. This comfort allowed him to venture deeply into the magnificent stands of pine along the Chippewa and gain a true appreciation of his industry's potential. For the business to thrive, he realized, the increasingly well-capitalized mill owners needed to extend their reach all the way upriver into the source of the white pine, bypassing the chaos of middlemen that made sustained growth and consistent investment returns a near impossibility.

He started to experimentally purchase logs directly from contractors inside the Chippewa district. This allowed for enormous profits when the logs arrived, but the problems along the rivercourse continued to disrupt his supply. In particular, upriver mill owners—men operating in towns like Eau Claire and Chippewa Falls, Wisconsin—trapped Weyerhaeuser's logs in their sorting booms, meaning his inventory might not arrive for several years, if at all. As Matthew Norton, a Mississippi mill owner and contemporary of Weyerhaeuser, explained: "For a mill man to have his capital tied up for that length of time meant certain ruin or disaster. Mr. Weyerhaeuser, however, was not inclined to give up an undertaking which seemed to him to have merit."

The challenge was figuring out how to get logs purchased from the Chippewa forests through the chaos of the river, especially the obstructionist upriver mill owners. For Weyerhaeuser, the first step toward implementing order was to align his Mississippi colleagues, all of whom faced similar problems in log delivery. Unfortunately, these men tended to trust one another no more than their upriver antagonists. As Weyerhaeuser's son later explained, "Many members of the Mississippi valley group were ready to fight one another upon the slightest pretext."

Weyerhaeuser set his eyes on control of Beef Slough, a fifteen-mile-long spur channel that connected the Chippewa and Mississippi Rivers. It was an ideal site for all the Mississippi millmen to organize the millions of driven logs that made it through the upriver gauntlet. While a boom was already in place, few downriver men capitalized on it: The company that operated this boom was nearly insolvent after years of poor management, continued upriver obstruction, and insufficient capital reserves. Weyerhaeuser and Denkmann seized on this opportunity and in 1870 leased the boom for a two-year term, hoping that others would join them in the massive operation. They soon extended partnership offers to all the major Mississippi mill owners, and by year-end nearly every substantial player as far south as St. Louis had invested in Weyerhaeuser's franchise.

On December 29, 1870, this group of downriver lumbermen, putting aside their former hostilities and rivalries, met in Chicago to form a new company for the purpose of purchasing and running the Beef Slough Boom. They named the new venture the Mississippi River Logging Company (MRLC) and authorized capital of one million dollars, making it one of the largest logging ventures in the nation. The members reputedly represented three-fourths of the sawmilling interests from the top of the Mississippi down through St. Louis. In 1872, Weyerhaeuser, who was widely recognized as the inspiration for the idea, was elected president, a position he would hold for almost forty years.

The MRLC's great size did not initially translate into authority over the Chippewa River. During the first year, upriver obstruction prevented almost three-quarters of the members' logs from reaching Beef Slough. According to Norton, who was an original member of the MRLC:

> This was enough to discourage almost anybody, yet, stimulated by Mr. Weyerhaeuser's faith in ultimate success, the parties engaged in the enterprise expressed a willingness to go on the second year.... [I]t was decided that the only way to make the Chippewa River a success was to put in so many logs that [the upriver millmen] could not detain them all without filling their own booms with logs that did not belong to them, thus interfering with their own supply for the season.

MRLC members pooled their resources and increased the number of driven logs from 40 million board feet to more than 100 million board feet in a single season. The Chippewa River was choked its whole length with pine, and Weyerhaeuser's strategy soon succeeded. In 1874, for example, 133 million feet of logs reached Beef Slough despite the best efforts of the millmen at Eau Claire and Chippewa Falls.

The measures required to gain de facto control of Chippewa navigation created a new challenge for Weyerhaeuser. As Norton explained, "He could see from the amount the Company was putting in [each year that] the timber owned by the loggers from whom it was getting logs would soon be exhausted; and to make its business more permanent and give it a standing on the river, pinelands would have to be purchased so far as means were available to do so." The new target, therefore, were the pine trees themselves. Most remained under the control of either the federal government, a handful of speculators, or, somewhat curiously, Cornell University—the school's founder, Ezra Cornell, who made his original fortune laying down telegraph poles, had recognized that Lake States pinelands were a valuable commodity and in 1868 endowed his eponymous institution with a $250,000 investment in five hundred thousand acres of prime tracts along the Chippewa.

During the early 1870s Weyerhaeuser quietly began to purchase several lots along the Chippewa. He then made his first major acquisition in 1875 on behalf of the MRLC: fifty thousand acres from Cornell at ten dollars an acre (a twentyfold increase on what Cornell had paid seven years before), with payment to be made over a ten-year span at 7 percent interest. The purchase contained more than five hundred million board feet of white pine, and the financing structure encouraged members to log the land as quickly as possible to cover the annual payments. Profits rolled in, and Weyerhaeuser's colleagues began to imitate his actions. By the end of the 1870s MRLC members had acquired more than three hundred thousand acres of prime Chippewa pineland under terms similar to this first Cornell purchase.

With these land purchases, the Lake States industry officially entered the era of industrial capitalism. Mill owners now controlled every step of the lumbering process, from tree felling straight through to distribution. This was the same sort of vertical integration that was happening in major industries across the nation. Weyerhaeuser had helped accomplish the same feat as John D. Rockefeller in the oil industry or Andrew Carnegie with steel. The main difference was that lumbering was such a massive industry, present in so many jurisdictions, that it was impossible to forge a national monopoly on the scale of Rockefeller's Standard Oil. The most that was possible was complete control of a region, and this was Weyerhaeuser's new goal.

In the spring of 1880 a great flood roared through the Chippewa Valley. The surge swept millions of board feet downriver that belonged to the upriver Wisconsin sawmills. Much of their product ended up floating in the Beef Slough Boom, presenting the downriver mill owners a potential opportunity to exact revenge on their longtime antagonists. Weyerhaeuser, however, was convinced that infighting ultimately harmed everyone's bottom line—in Norton's words, he "saw the importance of a unity of interest of all who were operating on the Chippewa." Relying on his reputation for sound judgment, honesty, and insightfulness, Weyerhaeuser engineered a log exchange between the two factions. Downriver men kept the logs already in the boom, while the upriver men gained the rights to logs that the MRLC had not yet driven. The following year, building on the goodwill he'd amassed through the log exchange, Weyerhaeuser led an effort to purchase an enormous upriver boom using a coalition of firms that included six upriver sawmills.

In the fall of 1881, Weyerhaeuser finally managed to link all rival mill owners together through a new corporation. Members of the MRLC and most of the upriver mill owners jointly formed the Chippewa Logging Company, a comprehensive enterprise "to cover and govern in the ownership of such timberlands, improvements and franchises . . . [thereafter purchased] for the use and benefit of such united interests." This new organization became known as the "pool," though some referred to it as the Weyerhaeuser syndicate, for he was the undisputed leader. A letter sent to the *Milwaukee Sentinel* in 1887 from Eau Claire, formerly a hotbed of upriver resistance, explained: "[H]is associates place him at the forefront of all the lumber corporations in which he is interested. They have the utmost faith in his experience and abilities, and his word is law. They believe that no other man in America knows so much about pine as he does."

With Weyerhaeuser at the helm, all the members of the pool benefited from increased security and economies of scale. This new company drove an annual average of a billion feet of logs down the Chippewa throughout much of the 1880s. In its peak year, it sent one and a half billion feet of logs, an amount effectively equal to the national total from 1839—Norton suggested that this quantity "can hardly be comprehended by one not acquainted with lumbering." Weyerhaeuser's pool soon became the largest lumbering concern in the entire country, and Weyerhaeuser became the nation's greatest lumber baron, overseeing an empire worth an estimated $70 million—for comparison, this amount equaled the 1882 capitalization of the Standard Oil Trust. In the words of an 1888 *New York Times* article, "[Weyerhaeuser] has at last, it seems, become powerful enough to practically monopolize the great industry of [the Lake States]."

The Lake States logging industry that Weyerhaeuser helped build, however, was already approaching the limits of its growth. Production peaked in 1892. The rapacious logging of thirty years was beginning to take its toll on many of the best stands of white pine on the Chippewa and other rivers. The industry also started to face increasing competition from railroads, which could reach the commercial trees far away from any rivercourses. Furthermore, new logging frontiers were starting to open in the South and the West. Lumbermen, including Weyerhaeuser (whose story was far from completed), shifted their energies and capital toward these virgin forests. The Lake States region was no longer leading the nation in production at the close of the nineteenth century.

Nonetheless, during the thirty years that followed the Civil War, the Lake States lumber industry had ushered in an era of industrial capitalism and provided the raw materials for the infrastructure boom that reshaped much of the nation. The region produced between eight and ten billion board feet annually throughout the 1880s. The first historian of lumbering in the Old Northwest estimated in 1898 that Lake States loggers, in total, had "enriched the nation" by over $4 billion, an amount almost twice what the North spent on the Civil War and more than triple the value of all the gold from the first fifty years of California's gold rush.

This development, however, did not come without a price. The thirty-year assault on the forests of the Lake States had forever corrupted the landscape. Lumber barons, responding to financial and tax structures that incentivized rapid clear-cutting, favored a policy of "cut out and get out." Few worried about the environmental impact of their actions, especially since the government provided no forms of regulation. Industrial logging ultimately left millions of acres denuded. Much of the Chippewa pinelands that so impressed Weyerhaeuser during his 1868 visit, once cut over, proved inadequate for agriculture, and large tracts remained unrehabilitated for generations, unlikely to ever regain their former glory.

While the saw and ax bore much of the responsibility for this destruction, they did not act alone. The single greatest source of devastation for the nation's trees in the age of industry was actually forest fire, the new scourge of a nation increasingly dependent on its vast woodlands.

## The Great Peshtigo Fire

THE LUMBER TOWN of Peshtigo, Wisconsin, was a tiny island of commerce in a wooded ocean. In the words of the local priest, Peter Pernin: "Trees, trees everywhere, nothing else but trees as far as you can travel . . . valleys overgrown with cedars and spruce trees, sandy hills covered with evergreens, and large tracts of rich land filled with the different varieties of hard wood, oak, maple, beech, ash, elm, and birch." While the town was relatively isolated, it had excellent access to the Chicago-based half of the Lake States distribution networks. The swift-flowing Peshtigo River, which bisected the town, emptied into Lake Michigan's Green Bay six miles to the southeast, and a narrow-gauge railroad connected Peshtigo to a port on the bay. From there, vessels shipped goods from Peshtigo directly to Chicago for dispersal across the nation.

Commercial life in Peshtigo revolved around a diversified lumber business known as the Peshtigo Company. The enterprise belonged to William Butler Ogden, a Chicago industrialist who had made his fortune in land speculation and the railroads—he was, among other things, the first president of the Union Pacific Railroad Company and the first mayor of Chicago. "To my mind," wrote Isaac Stephenson, a lumber baron who was a partner in the Peshtigo Company, "[Ogden] was one of the dominating figures of the Middle West during this period and had as much if not more to do with its development than any other man." The centerpiece of Ogden's Peshtigo investment was an enormous woodenware factory, rumored to be the largest in the world. The main building was 341 feet long and, in some places, four stories tall. Every working day this massive operation produced 45,000 shingles, 5,000 broom handles, 1,500 pails, 170 tubs, 92 barrelheads, and 50 boxes of clothespins. Other properties in the Peshtigo Company included two sawmills and a second factory that manufactured sashes, blinds, and doors. The entire operation employed roughly eight hundred men, about half the total population of the town.

By 1871, Peshtigo was developing into a bustling and vibrant community, enjoying the prosperity that the lumber boom years were providing. Along sawdust streets and wood-plank sidewalks stood countless small shops, two boardinghouses, a fancy hotel, and a school. A Congregational church rested on the eastern side of town and a Catholic church, run by Father Pernin, claimed the western side. The first issue of a local paper, the *Marinette and Peshtigo Eagle,* appeared that June. To top it off, a new railroad was about to connect Peshtigo directly with Chicago.

Despite all these positive signs, the summer of 1871 brought trouble in the form of a severe drought. Laborers working on the new railroad at times laid down their tools and refused to work in protest over insufficient amounts of drinking water. The region's swamps grew so dry that one could walk freely along the surface. According to Stephenson, "the forests and brush were reduced to tinder." As the season wore on and the rains refused to arrive, the threat of fire began to grow.

Fire had always been part of forest life, but industrialization had heralded a new age of deadly forest burns across the nation. When loggers cleared an area of its commercial trees or railroad workers forged a new path through the woods, they left behind all the small trees, stripped branches, and undergrowth. This accumulated refuse dried out over time, becoming increasingly combustible. As the scale of industrial logging and railroads increased, whole forests were turned into tinderboxes waiting to explode. All that was lacking was a necessary spark, and the same industrialized activities that created the situation often provided one. One of the worst offenders, as noted earlier, was the cinder-filled exhaust from wood-burning trains. Loggers also contributed their fair portion to the problem through careless behavior, especially the failure to extinguish the smoldering embers from campfires.

As summer drifted into fall in Peshtigo, the threat of catastrophic fire began to close in. A conflagration broke out to the northeast of the town during the second week of September but burned out before reaching the village. Then, on Saturday, September 23, fire arrived for the first time. An observer of that initial scare wrote, "It is as though you attempted to resist the approach of an avalanche of fire hurled against you. . . . [B]uildings were covered with wet blankets and all under the scorching heat and in blinding suffocating smoke that was enough to strangle one. . . . Strange to say not a building was burned—the town was saved." The townspeople had avoided an outright disaster, but the underlying threat remained. A correspondent for the local paper wrote on October 7, "Unless we have rain soon, God only knows how soon a conflagration may sweep this town." He spoke with chilling prescience.

The morning of October 8, like most mornings that fall, started without any clouds that might offer potential respite. The air hung mercilessly still, full of trapped summer heat. Far above a dense mass of smoke hovered in the sky. The small train that connected Peshtigo to Green Bay rolled into town as though everything were normal, carrying a cargo of two hundred laborers fresh from Chicago to help lay rails for the new train. Father Pernin tried to leave for Marinette, a nearby village where he also said Mass, but villagers begged him to stay. He explained, "There seemed to be a vague fear of some impending though unknown evil haunting the minds of many, nor was I myself entirely free from this unusual feeling." As morning wore on, villagers noticed flocks of birds behaving strangely, forming and flying away without making a sound. By noon, the sun disappeared completely, in its place an eerie yellow half-light, which came from no visible source and cast a ghastly pallor over the town.

This yellowish light turned to a sullen red as the day wore on. The morning's smoke continued to thicken, building from the west. Around 9:00 p.m., villagers started to notice a terrifying sound coming from the same direction as the smoke. According to Pernin, "This sound resembled . . . the rumbling of thunder, with the difference that it never ceased, but deepened in intensity each moment more and more." Suddenly, a whirling slab of fire, seemingly from nowhere, flew through the air and crashed into the street. In an instant the sawdust streets and wood-plank sidewalks of Peshtigo were ablaze. Winds as powerful as tornadoes ripped through the town and spread the fire from building to building. Within thirty minutes the flames had penetrated every structure.

Villagers ran chaotically through the streets, trying to escape the inferno surrounding them. Forty people, disoriented from the opening blast of fire, rushed into the Peshtigo Company's boardinghouse, praying that the building might withstand the assault. The flames roasted every one of them alive.

The only hope to escape this fiery hell lay in the Peshtigo River, and the villagers who had avoided the worst ravages of the opening firestorm raced toward possible safety in its waters. Father Pernin was among the people who reached its shore. "As far as the eye could reach," he wrote,

> [the banks] were covered with people standing there, motionless as statues, some with eyes staring, upturned towards heaven, and tongues protruded. The greater number seemed to have no idea of taking any steps to procure their safety, imagining, as many afterwards acknowledged to me, that the end of the world had arrived and that there was nothing for them but silent submission to their fate.

The sky above raged with brilliant flashes of orange. The heat grew so intense that logs in the nearby millpond started to smoke and burst into flames. Hundreds of desperate villagers and imported laborers struggled to survive in the river, their bodies in the chilly flow, their heads in the searing atmosphere. Father Pernin remained immersed until 3:30 a.m., an excruciating five and a half hours.

The fire had consumed Peshtigo but its hunger remained. Flames devoured trees for miles around, feeding on the dry debris that littered the forest floor, wiping out thousands of acres of marketable trees. The logging towns of Marinette and Menominee to the northeast appeared to be next in line for nature's fury. Town leaders packed the women and children on steamers, which headed out into the safety of Lake Michigan. Most of the men stayed behind. According to Isaacson, who was in Marinette when the fire struck, "we struggled all night in the blinding smoke and intense heat, not knowing how soon the seething fringes of fire would close in upon us." The flames burned through about half the city, but shifted course as if by miracle. Other settlements were not as lucky, and several smaller communities fell before rain finally began to fall on October 9.

When the fire finally died and a new day dawned, those in Peshtigo who survived opened their eyes to "a scene with whose horror and ruin none were as yet fully acquainted," according to Pernin. The charred bodies of people and animals lay everywhere. "In many cases," wrote Stephenson, "there was nothing left of human beings other than a streak of light ashes which would scarcely have filled a thimble." Thick, dark ash covered every surface. Almost nothing remained beyond a few stone foundations, some iron tools, and the boilers of the locomotives. A correspondent from the *New York Tribune,* upon visiting the village the following week, wrote: "In the glory of this Indian Summer afternoon I look out on the ghastliest clearing that ever lay before mortal eyes. The sandy streets glisten with a frightful smoothness, and calcined fragments are all that remain of imposing edifices and hundreds of peaceful homes." As for the trees that had once filled these broad forests, in the words of Stephenson, "[W]here the forest had been, gaunt disfigured tree trunks stood like sentinels of death under the low-hanging pall of smoke." In total, the fire had destroyed 1,280,000 acres, roughly 2,000 square miles, an area 33 percent larger than Rhode Island.

News of the disaster was slow to reach the outside world. Earlier in the summer fires had destroyed the telegraph poles that connected the lumber settlements to Chicago. The morning after the blaze, Stephenson sent an emissary to the city of Green Bay, where telegraph lines still functioned, to issue a distress message to Governor Lucius Fairchild. This initial message arrived on the morning of October 10, two days after the fire began.

Fairchild tried to disseminate the news quickly, but the world's attention was already focused on a different disaster: The same night that Peshtigo burned, an unrelated fire swept through Chicago, leaving much of the city in ashes. News outlets focused primarily on the "Great Chicago Fire," which destroyed hundreds of millions of dollars of property overnight and eviscerated the center of the entire midwestern economy. The magnitude of this story left little news space available for the tragedy just to the north.

In the weeks following the Peshtigo firestorm, survivors began the arduous task of counting the dead. The numbers seemed to climb indefinitely. Peshtigo, by far the heaviest hit, conservatively claimed six hundred victims. The total number, given the hundreds of transient laborers passing through the town, might have been much higher. No other towns sustained more than one hundred casualties, but several reported more than fifty deaths, and hundreds of other people perished in isolated locations scattered throughout the forest: fur trappers, homesteaders, lumberjacks, timber surveyors. The final death toll stood somewhere between eleven hundred and twelve hundred people, roughly five times greater than that of the Great Chicago Fire, making Peshtigo the deadliest forest blaze in the history of the nation, if not the world. Even into

the twentieth century, reports still surfaced occasionally of charred bodies discovered in nearby swamps and bogs.

The town of Peshtigo had been demolished but was not defeated. Governor Fairchild came to the aid of the survivors and broadcast appeals for
donations. Contributions poured in from all over the state, the nation, and
even overseas, amounting to $166,789 in total. The federal government also
provided surplus army supplies: 4,000 woolen blankets, 1,500 pairs of trou-
sers and overcoats, 100 wagons, and thousands of rations of foodstuffs. The
railroad company completed the line from Chicago, though only after threat
of lawsuit over damages—Stephenson, like many, argued that "the fire [was]
directly due to the carelessness of the contractors." William Butler Ogden,
who had lost approximately $3 million in the twin fires of October 8, ordered
that his woodenware factory be rebuilt. Others followed his lead and the local
economy slowly recovered. When the new governor of Wisconsin visited the
town in 1873, he noted: "I was pleased to find that the majority of the survivors had returned to their clearings; many had raised fair crops, and were
hopeful of the future. I found nearly all very grateful for the relief that had
been extended to them, but for which, they declared, they could not have
survived."

Incredibly, the Peshtigo tragedy had almost no impact on the practices of
the lumber industry or the way that new settlers approached life in the forests.
In the ensuing decades, as the rate of industrial logging increased, the problem
of forest fires actually worsened throughout the country. Wisconsin alone suffered major fires in 1880, 1891, 1894, 1897, 1908, 1910, 1923, 1931, and 1936.
Losing half a million acres in a year was almost commonplace. Many considered any year that lost fewer than one hundred thousand acres to be a relative
success. The demand for trees outpaced the means of arresting their greatest
threat, and man-made fires would remain the main scourge of the nation's forests for another eighty years.

## From Rags to Riches

A S DEPENDENT AS Americans had become on the wood from their
trees, at the time of the Peshtigo Fire in 1871 they were only using it
for timber and fuel. A revolution, however, was brewing. Trees, the nation was
about to discover, could provide not only wood but wood pulp, the raw material for cheap paper, something as important to America's development as the
railroads, if not more so.

The process of making paper is, at its most basic level, fairly straightforward. The main ingredient is cellulose, a carbohydrate that forms the chief

component of all leafy green plants. Cellulose fibers are separated from the rest of the organic matter using mechanical or chemical means. The cellulose-rich pulp that remains is spread out in a thin layer along a screen, which is drained, pressed, and dried, leaving behind a solid sheet of paper. The earliest papers were made of papyrus and began to appear in roughly 1800 BCE. Over time, other fibers like cotton, flax, and linen displaced papyrus.

In America, before the late nineteenth century, virtually all paper was made from cloth rags. The process of textile manufacture reduced cotton and linen to almost a pure cellulose. Worn-out fabrics thus provided an excellent source of raw-paper fiber—the practice of calling newspapers "rags" arose from this relationship. Supplies were inherently limited, but demand remained low throughout the colonial period, for paper was a luxury good: Most of it was hand-crafted and expensive. On occasions when papermakers needed to increase their supplies, they often took to the streets in search of collections. The following advertisement appeared in the *Boston News-Letter* in 1769:

> The BellCart will go through Boston before the End of next Month, to collect Rags for the Paper Mill at Milton, when all people that will encourage the Paper Manufactury may dispose of them. . . .

> > *Rags are as Beauties, which concealed lie,*
> > *But when in Paper, how it charms the Eye:*
> > *Pray save Rags, new Beauties to discover,*
> > *For Paper truly, every one's a lover:*
> > *By th' Pen and Press such Knowledge is display'd*
> > *As wou'dn't exist if Paper was not made.*
> > *Wisdom of Things, mysterious, divine,*
> > *Illustriously doth on Paper shine.*

During the first half of the nineteenth century, several factors converged to drive up the demand for paper and rags. Populations swelled and literacy rates grew. Residents of the ever-expanding metropolitan zones wanted to read about the events of the day in their local newspapers, which increased in size and number. At the same time, the old-fashioned papermakers slowly yielded to the paper mills. These hungered insatiably for raw materials, especially as new technologies improved their efficiency: A machine appeared in 1817 that spooled paper onto a cylinder; ten years later a paper mill imported from France the foudrinier, a device that created an endless sheet of paper.

To meet the surging demand America was purchasing 2 million pounds of foreign rags annually by 1843. This number ballooned more than twenty times in less than a generation. In 1857 alone, America imported 44,582,080 pounds of rags, primarily from distant trading partners like Alexandria (in present-day Egypt), Smyrna (in present-day Turkey), and Trieste (in present-day Italy).

The rag situation bubbled over into crisis during the Civil War. Trade restrictions and the collapse of the cotton crop produced something of a rag famine, while the growth of the political bureaucracy and the proliferation of newspapers heightened the demand. "Who shall write the lyric of the great Rag Hunt of the last four years?" asked the *New York Tribune* in 1866, adding, "[T]imid men began to fear that a return to vellum and palimpsest was all that remained."

The price of paper, especially newsprint, skyrocketed, and newspapers took dramatic actions to avoid bankruptcy. The *New York Evening Post* reduced its page dimensions by four columns. Other papers, like the *New York Tribune* and the *Philadelphia Daily Evening Register,* similarly cut back their sizes. Some papers raised prices or lowered circulation to offset their mounting supply costs. A frustrated editor of the *New England Farmer* commented, "Paper is too high. These high prices operate as a tax upon education. They greatly abridge the circulation of books, newspapers and letter-writing."

Desperate publishers and paper mill owners began searching frantically for rag substitutes to help lower the costs of production. They experimented with a dizzying array of potential replacements from across the plant kingdom: agave of Cuba, bamboo, corn husks, esparto grass, forest leaves, hemp, hops, jute, white moss from Scandinavia, yucca, and countless others. Many of these had merit, but none matched rags for quality nor offered a supply stream sufficient to meet demand and curtail the price spiral. As an article in the *Tribune* lamented, "Industry and science had found an ingenious mechanism capable of printing all the books of the world over again—where was the paper?"

Those searching for a rag replacement also auditioned innumerable types of trees. The *Boston Journal* managed to print one 1863 edition on basswood, and other isolated attempts occurred during the 1850s and 1860s. The problem with trees was the same one that doomed all the other substitutes: papermakers lacked cost-effective technologies to separate the cellulose from the extraneous materials. The situation, however, was about to change.

In the 1850s a German inventor had discovered a simple process to convert wood into pulp. His machine used an iron weight to force a piece of wood against a spinning grindstone. A stream of water ran constantly at the point where the wood met the stone, and it carried the resulting pulp away and onto a series of sieves and rollers. The final product was a sheet of thick, coarse drawing paper. In 1866, two American brothers, who had acquired the patent rights, brought this novel machine to Curtisville, Massachusetts. They ground their first batch of pulp in early March 1867, and a nearby paper mill produced a finished product several days later.

A second wood-pulp process, known as soda pulp, was evolving contemporaneously. The inventor, Hugh Burgess, was an Englishman, and his technique employed a bath of alkalis (caustic soda) to separate out the fibers from the wood. This soda pulp process produced stronger, more uniform paper than groundwood pulp. Burgess took out an American patent and began production at Manayunk, Pennsylvania, in 1854. Output remained meager for the better part of a decade, but it began to rise following the formation of the American Wood Paper Company in 1863. One reporter who visited the works in 1866 wrote, "[I]f [the owners] succeed in making paper as perfect and useful as that upon which I am now writing (and which came from their mill), they will revolutionize the art of paper-making, and greatly lessen the cost of knowledge."

The early manufacturers of both forms of wood pulp almost universally favored poplar, a tree with few commercial uses up to that point. "Poplar wood," wrote a reporter in 1868, "is by nature so pure and white that no chemicals or bleaches are required to make a fit material for manufacturing printing paper." The wood's suitability, however, did not translate to availability, since no distribution network existed to ship it from the forests to the pulp manufacturers. In 1866, for example, the *Philadelphia Inquirer* appealed directly to its readership for supplies: "Poplar wood wanted, from 100 to 10,000 cords of White Poplar Wanted, to be delivered at The Philadelphia 'Inquirer' Paper Mills and Wood Pulp Works." During the industry's formative years, it relied largely on local farmers cutting poplar trees from their woodlots and delivering them to nearby railroads. The distribution system formalized over time, especially as growing demand outstripped local supplies. Occasionally, poplar lumber even followed pines downriver during the springtime log drives.

The wood-pulp industry expanded throughout the 1870s, and major newspapers began to embrace the new product. The *New York World* first featured wood-pulp paper in 1870. The *Providence Journal* and *Brooklyn Eagle* followed a year later. The *New York Times* first tried wood-pulp stock in late August 1873, and by year-end they had changed over completely. In 1877, an article noted, "In our own country the use of wood in making paper has increased, so that almost all paper for newspapers is one-half wood pulp." This assertion was somewhat premature, but only by a few years. Nearly every large-circulation paper had shifted to wood pulp by 1882, avoiding the apocalyptic predictions of a worldwide rag shortage.

The main appeal of wood-pulp paper was not its quality—which was far inferior to that of rag paper—but its price. At the end of the Civil War, newsprint paper sold for between thirteen or fourteen cents per pound on average. The earliest wood-pulp papers, in contrast, cost around eight cents per pound, and this price dropped steadily thanks to increased competition, improved technologies, and economies of scale. At one point, mills offered paper for an astonishing one cent per pound. These decreases were even more remarkable in light of the period's inflation. In 1894, a newspaper article noted,

> With the rapidly increasing output, prices have as rapidly declined, until to-day a grade of newsprint paper worth 25 years ago, 13 cents or 14 cents per pound, is now sold at 2½ to 3 cents— a decline in price unequalled in the history of any other industry. This enormous decrease in the cost of paper is due especially to the introduction of wood as paper stock. To-day it is the principal material used in the manufacture of paper for all but the highest grades of book and writing paper.

This unprecedented drop in paper prices eventually resulted in cheaper periodicals. Newspapers that had sold for four, then five, then six cents in the 1860s and 1870s reversed the trend in the two decades that followed. The *New York Herald* dropped from four cents to three in 1876, and shaved another penny off the price in 1883. The *New York World,* which had cost five cents in 1866, sold for two cents in 1882, even though it doubled its size that same year.

The advent of cheap wood-pulp paper changed not only the cost of periodicals but the structure of the entire newspaper industry. Historically, many publishers had opposed circulation increases on the theory that increased paper consumption made such moves unprofitable. This attitude began to change when Joseph Pulitzer purchased the *New York World* in 1883. He introduced features designed to drive up readership: large headlines, comic strips, strong editorials, and sensational journalism. Buoyed by a two-cent price tag, the paper expanded its circulation from 20,000 to 250,000 in four years and generated enormous profits thanks to the reduced production costs that wood pulp provided. Other publishers followed Pulitzer's example, and soon every major city had mass-circulating penny papers—between 1880 and 1890 the total amount of paper used by American newspapers rose from 106,874,792 pounds to 670,929,492 pounds. This new business model facilitated the rise of newspaper titans like Pulitzer and William Randolph Hearst.

The shift to wood pulp, as much as any single economic, political, or social phenomenon, helped to democratize information in the late nineteenth century. Inexpensive periodicals allowed information to flow more freely, contributing to a more informed body politic. Cheap books encouraged literacy. And low-cost paper allowed all classes of people to write one another letters for the first time. One newspaperman wrote in 1881: "The invention of wood pulp . . . has brought good books, good newspapers, and writing paper within the means of thousands of common people who could never have afforded such luxuries had rags remained the only available material for papers of good quality." As another reporter, reflecting on America's newfound appreciation for paper, observed in 1894: "Some philosopher has said that the civilization and property of a country may be measured by its consumption of paper."

The more Americans grew accustomed to cheap paper, the more they clamored to see it used everywhere, and a veritable paper craze emerged in the closing decades of the nineteenth century. In Atlanta, promoters constructed a store made entirely from paper. The ceiling of New York's state assembly chamber was made of paper. A journalist wrote in 1891:

> At first, wood pulp was used entirely in the manufacture of newspapers, but now it is employed for manifold purposes. Its use bids fair to be large for mouldings, and it is being made into barrels, tubs, pails, washboards, water pipes, doors, caskets, carriage bodies, floor coverings and furniture, imitations of leather cloth and silk have been made from it. . . . Thus we see the uses to which wood pulp can be put are almost unlimited.

The wood-pulp industry, meanwhile, had made great strides from its modest beginnings in the 1860s. Daily output had grown from the 13 tons that the American Wood Paper Company produced in 1866 to 100 tons in 1877, 410 tons in 1884, and 2,000 in 1891. By the mid-1880s, the booming industry had run through all the economical sources of poplar, and companies began to shift toward spruce and fir, which grew abundantly throughout the Northeast, often on lands that the lumber industry had already cleared of white pines. Pulp manufacturers constructed massive factories in the woods of Maine, New Hampshire, and New York, and began to purchase enormous tracts of timber throughout these states. Fifty thousand people were working in the industry at the turn of the century.

Like the lumber and newspaper businesses, the wood-pulp industry quickly started to consolidate. Smaller firms could not compete with the increasingly complex enterprises that invested enormous amounts of capital in machinery and timberlands. And as newspapers grew in size, they sought out these larger firms, whose massive reserves guaranteed timely supply. Congress hastened this trend toward consolidation with the 1897 passage of the Dingley Tariff, which placed a duty on imported Canadian wood pulp, knocking out the only serious competition to the American firms.

In late January 1898, twenty mills from across the Northeast merged together to form the International Paper Company. The initial capitalization totaled $45 million, and the company's assets reportedly included 1 million acres of American timberland and 1.6 million acres in Canada. The company's president declared in his first annual report that International Paper controlled 90 percent of eastern newsprint production. However, other great combinations, like the Great Northern Paper Company, followed on its heels.

By 1906, the papermaking and allied printing trade ranked sixth in national importance, but this number failed to capture how important the new industry was becoming to American society. Newspapers and books offered the primary form of information exchange in the years before radio and television. Cheap paper facilitated record keeping and permitted the growth of businesses and government. The introduction of such products as paper towels, sanitary napkins, tissue paper, and toilet paper transformed domestic life. Later, new papermaking techniques produced stronger, cheaper materials that revolutionized the shipping and container industries, everything from cardboard boxes to milk cartons. Americans began living in a brave new world of paper thanks to trees.

The growth of the paper industry, however, placed further stress on America's forest resources, already straining under the weight of commercial logging, rampant forest fires, and agricultural clearing. Paper companies were cutting down 625 square miles of spruce land annually. A government official noted in 1898: "[T]he original forests cannot long suffice to supply the increasing demands for spruce which are made upon them. . . . Cutting for pulp does far more harm than cutting for lumber, because it takes a vastly greater number of trees."

WOOD-PULP MANUFACTURING was not the only sector exploiting the nation's forests for nontimber resources during the last half of the nineteenth century. Many essential American industries depended on such forest products, though the finished goods often bore no signs of their dependence on trees.

One of the largest consumers of forest resources was the leather industry. Though this material had long been integral to American life, it gained new importance in the late nineteenth century. Factories relied on leather belts to turn their equipment; farmers and ranchers depended on leather harnesses and saddles; furniture featured leather as upscale upholstery; it was the main material of countless fashion articles. By 1910, the Central Leather Company was one of the ten largest businesses in the nation.

The key to making leather was a compound known as tannin (hence the term "leather tanner"). Heavy hides were soaked in tannin for twelve to fifteen months, yielding a finished product that was tough, flexible, and decay resistant. In the nineteenth century, the best source of tannin was tree bark, especially from black oaks and hemlocks, which grew abundantly in New York and Pennsylvania. The lumber industry had already opened up these forests to commerce by the 1840s but they had taken only the white pines. Leather producers, who required two and a half cords of bark to produce sufficient tannin for one hundred hides, soon began to strip these forests of the hemlocks that remained. At the industry's peak around the turn of the century, hemlock was being cut on over a million acres annually.

The iron industry also owed a debt to the nation's forests. While the majority of the metal came from coal-powered forges, a significant percentage depended on charcoal, a type of fuel formed by burning trees in an oxygen-deprived environment. Charcoal-forged iron, though not the most popular, had unique physical attributes that made it particularly well-suited for several industrial uses, most notably railroad wheels. Thus, the countless millions of wooden railroad cars produced in the nineteenth century were sitting above countless millions of wheels equally dependent on American trees.

The process of manufacturing charcoal also generated volatile chemicals. Initially, these were considered worthless, but they gained value as the nineteenth century progressed and scientists made advances in industrial chemistry. Most large charcoal furnaces started to include retort facilities that separated the chemicals into useful by-products including tar, methanol, acetone, and acetate of lime. For a number of years trees were producing more industrial chemicals than any other source.

Perhaps the most valuable tree-derived compound was the solvent turpentine. Its uses in the nineteenth century were countless: varnish; cleaning materials; naval stores; a thinner for oil-based paints; a cheap alternative to whale oil, the most popular source of lamp fuel. The turpentine industry flourished in the long-leaf pine forests that ranged across the South and had been providing the nation with naval stores since colonial times. Scraping trees for turpentine was dangerous work—the vapors harmed many major systems in the body, including the central nervous system; they were also flammable. Few free laborers wanted to risk the work, and in the years after the Civil War, the industry gained a reputation for using convict labor, a practice permitted in every southern state after 1876.

It seemed as though hardly any industry in the nation did not rely on trees during the late nineteenth century. Forests were no longer regions to be cleared for settlement but regions to be cleared for commerce. As the U.S. Commissioner of Agriculture's Report of 1883 noted:

> There is scarcely a comfort or convenience of life with which the forests are not intimately connected. We depend upon them, to an important extent, for food, shelter, and clothing, the prime necessities of life. . . . The[re] would not be either precious or useful metals, if we had not the forests with which to make them such. Our [rail] cars and ships are the products of the forests. The thousand tools of our various handicrafts, the machineries of our factories, the conveniences of our warehouse, and the comfort and adornments of our dwellings are the product largely of the forests. Behind all the varied industries and conveniences of life stand the forests as their chief source and support.

Of course, this prolonged period of industrial exploitation was leaving the forests more vulnerable than ever. Lumbermen were cutting out the white pines at breakneck speeds, while other industries followed to exploit the manifold tree species that remained. The forests that had once seemed endless began to reveal their limitations, and attitudes toward the nation's trees started to shift. Some people advocated better treatment of the forests on moral grounds. Others warned that the day of reckoning was coming and that soon the nation would run out of timber. Out of these concerns emerged new structures and institutions that would forever change the nation, and forever alter the relationship that Americans had with their trees.

# 5

## A Changing Consciousness

Douglas Fir

## Shading the Prairie

FOR MOST OF THE NATION'S first century, the average American showed little interest in planting and cultivating trees. Men like George Washington were notable exceptions in a country populated by utilitarian-minded farmers and, increasingly, by wood-hungry industries. Tree planting required capital, labor, and several decades' worth of patience, but the American style of productivity minimized these factors in favor of resource exploitation whenever possible. With forests abundant throughout the East, few outside the wealthiest classes, the cider orchardists, or the occasional town father, saw the merit in growing something that nature seemed to provide inexhaustibly.

Attitudes began to change noticeably during the mid-nineteenth century's demographic shift toward the Midwest. While the enormous Lake States logging industry provided timber to the region, the operations of men like Weyerhaeuser, Ogden, and Stephenson could not entirely supplant the needs, both economic and cultural, of a people conditioned to life in the tree-rich eastern states. By the mid-1860s midwestern states started to implement small-scale legislation to encourage tree planting. An 1868 Kansas act offered a bounty of two dollars per acre to anyone successfully cultivating timber for three years. Similar-themed laws appeared over the next several years in Iowa, Kansas, Minnesota, Missouri, and Nebraska. At the same time, midwestern railroads, desperate for cheap supplies of ties, began experimentally planting trees. The Kansas Pacific Railroad created three tree stations in 1870, and the idea quickly spread to other train lines.

Almost all of these new laws and programs, however, were limited in scope, short-lived, and generally unsuccessful. Few individuals knew anything about the methods of propagating trees—the nascent study of tree care, known as arboriculture, had not yet reached America—and the local climate, more arid than back East and susceptible to severe winter frosts, inhibited growth. Farmers and railroads planted countless acres of trees only to watch them wither and die. The anticipated economic and cultural benefits failed to materialize.

While these early efforts were largely unremarkable, they foreshadowed a much wider embrace of tree planting. The idea that trees were not simply a natural resource to be exploited but also a civilizing agent to be stewarded was about to capture the collective imagination of the nation. This movement would involve millions of people and evolve over several decades, though it began, like so many things, with the vision of a single person.

J. Sterling Morton was born on April 22, 1832, in New York State. His family had deep roots in American soil, with some ancestors arriving on the ship that followed the *Mayflower*—one of his relatives was secretary of Plymouth Colony. When Morton was two years old, his parents moved to Michigan, and he spent most of his early years there, attending the state university at Ann Arbor and working briefly as a journalist for the *Detroit Free Press* and the *Chicago Times*.

After marrying in 1854, the ambitious Morton decided to seek out new opportunities farther west. The area that now comprises the state of Nebraska was just beginning to open: The Indian title to the Omaha and Otoe lands had been extinguished in the spring of 1854, and, shortly thereafter, Congress passed the Kansas-Nebraska Act, which created the Kansas and Nebraska territories and also declared that settlers would have the right to determine if slavery would be permissible (known as "popular sovereignty," this aspect of the act was a key catalyst in the formation of the Republican Party, which fervently opposed any expansion of slavery). In November 1854, Morton arrived at the eastern edge of the Nebraska territory with the very first wave of settlers, few of whom had a chance to plant crops. He explained, "I remember that we commenced the winter of 1854–5, a little colony of hopeful boarders, purchasing everything that we ate, and even feed for our horses and cattle." The following year he and his wife settled in Nebraska City, a small community on the fertile western bank of the Missouri River.

Morton began working as editor of the local paper, the *Nebraska City News,* and used this platform to help establish his reputation. His biographer explained that over time people got to know him "as a vigorous and colorful writer, a forceful and entertaining speaker, [and] a Democrat who clung tenaciously to the traditions of the party." His politics were notably conservative: He vehemently defended the expansion of slavery into Nebraska, and he described Indians as a race of people who "must die, and a few years hence only be known through their history as it was recorded by the Anglo-Saxon." But these issues were not necessarily his paramount concerns. Rather, Morton primarily preached the virtues of an agriculture-based society and also spent much of his early career fulminating against the excesses of the "wildcat" banks that sprung up in his territory, encouraged speculation, and, in his words, "defrauded [Nebraskans] of some hundred thousands of dollars worth of capital and labor."

Before long, influential Democrats recruited Morton into public service. President James Buchanan appointed him secretary of the Nebraska Territory in July 1858, and Morton held this position for three years—he spent six months of this time doing double duty as the acting governor. For the rest of his career he was a frequent Democratic candidate for a wide range of political offices, though he never served in an elected position (as Nebraska leaned Republican).

Outside of his life in newspapers and politics, Morton displayed a passion for horticulture, particularly as it related to trees. When he and his wife settled in Nebraska City, they had acquired a farm of 160 acres—this was the standard size for homesteader plots, which were known as quarter sections since they constituted one-fourth of a square mile. Much of this land he devoted to tree planting, constantly experimenting to see what varieties of forest and fruit trees might thrive on the plains. One of his contemporaries commented in 1871, "his farm . . . is one of the best improved places in Nebraska. He has an orchard of some two thousand fruit trees, with all the best varieties of apples, peaches, plum, &c., which are as prolific as in any state in the Union. In his horticultural capacity he has performed a commendable work in dispelling the old fallacy that 'fruit will not grow in Nebraska.'"

Morton not only grew trees, but also encouraged tree planting in speeches and through his newspaper. Their propagation, he believed, was an essential component in civilizing the young state and in promoting it as a new destination for potential settlers, many of whom worried about restarting life in a treeless region, even if there was cheap land for the taking.

Morton's passionate advocacy on this topic led to the State Horticultural Society asking him in 1871 "to prepare and publish an address to the people of the State setting forth all important facts relative to fruit growing in Nebraska." Morton delivered this speech in early January 1872 at the society's annual meeting. He argued, in one of his most eloquent appeals for tree planting:

> There is comfort in a good orchard, in that it makes the new home more like the "old home in the East." . . . Orchards are missionaries of culture and refinement. They make the people among whom they grow a better and more thoughtful people. If every farmer in Nebraska will plant out and cultivate an orchard and a flower garden, together with a few forest trees, this will become mentally and morally the best agricultural State, the grandest community of producers in the American Union. . . . If I had the power I would compel every man in the State who had a home of his own, to plant out and cultivate fruit trees.

On the day of this speech, however, Morton did more than just talk about the need to grow trees. Concurrently with the Horticultural Society gathering, the State Board of Agriculture was holding its annual meeting, and Morton attended both events. During the board's discussions, he presented the following fateful resolution: "Resolved, That, Wednesday the 10th day of April, 1872, be and the same is hereby especially set apart and consecrated for tree planting in the State of Nebraska, and the State Board of Agriculture, hereby name it 'Arbor Day.'"

Members of the board reacted warmly to Morton's novel suggestion for raising awareness about tree planting. They had already tried offering small cash prizes for tree planting, and Arbor Day seemed like a creative way to get more Nebraskans involved in an activity that they all agreed was vital to the state's future. The only concern that some raised dealt with the proposal's name. Several members preferred "Sylvan Day." Morton countered that this would wrongly imply an emphasis on forest trees ("sylva" typically connoted woodlands, as in the word "Pennsylvania," which literally meant "Penn's Woods"). Morton's vision included both forest and fruit trees, and he ultimately used his prestige and authority to coerce the board into accepting the name "Arbor Day." Little did any of them appreciate how famous this term would become.

The original resolution passed unanimously. One of its strongest backers on the board was its president, Robert Furnas, a staunch Republican and Morton's bitter political rival. The two men stood on opposite sides of the slavery question and nearly everything else, but tree planting was an issue where they found common ground. They put their differences aside to promote the proposed holiday and petitioned media outlets throughout the state to rally behind the event in order to drum up interest. Furnas later explained, "The newspapers of the State were generous, and kept Arbor Day well before the people."

By the time April 10 finally arrived the entire state was abuzz with talk of trees. According to Furnas, more than one million trees were planted during that inaugural celebration. Morton was unable to participate because the eight hundred trees that he ordered failed to arrive. He did, however, submit an article to the *Omaha Daily Herald* to commemorate the occasion and, once again, argue for the importance of tree planting in producing a strong society: "There is a true triumph in the unswerving integrity and genuine democracy of trees, for they refuse to be influenced by money or social position and thus tower morally, as well as physically, high above Congressmen and many other patriots of this dollaring age."

With each passing year, the status of Arbor Day in Nebraska grew. In 1874 Furnas, now governor, issued an executive proclamation urging "the whole people of the state to observe it, by planting forest, fruit, or ornamental trees." The legislature formally designated it a legal holiday in 1885, selecting as the official date April 22, Morton's birthday. Ten years later it resolved that the state "shall hereafter, in a popular sense, be known and referred to as the 'Tree Planter's State'"—this moniker lasted until 1945, when it was changed to the "Cornhusker State," reflecting the state's shift in priorities.

As word of Arbor Day spread beyond Nebraska, others rushed to emulate the holiday. The earliest adopters were similarly situated states that wanted to promote tree culture to encourage agriculture and settlement. Iowa's horticultural society instituted an Arbor Day later in 1872, and other states across the interior followed soon thereafter. By the mid-1880s, however, some form of Arbor Day had spread to nearly every state in the nation. The holiday became especially popular in public schools throughout the country, the result of a campaign that several advocacy groups began in 1882 to help raise awareness of the importance of trees to the nation. Arbor Day even proved to have resonance beyond America's borders, with countless nations rushing to adopt the practice. Furnas commented in the 1890s, "No observance ever sprang into existence so rapidly, favorably, permanently, and now so near universally throughout the whole civilized world as that of 'Arbor Day.'"

Morton had a theory to explain the worldwide resonance of a day devoted to tree planting: "'Arbor Day' . . . is not like other holidays. Each of those reposes upon the past, while Arbor Day proposes for the future. It contemplates, not the good and the beautiful of past generations, but it sketches, outlines, establishes the useful and the beautiful for the ages yet to come."

While Arbor Day became the defining legacy of Morton's life, it was far from his only accomplishment. He continued to promote agriculture throughout Nebraska for another three decades, and in 1893 President Grover Cleveland appointed him to his cabinet as the secretary of agriculture, a post Morton held for four years. After this he began to edit the multivolume *Illustrated History of Nebraska,* a project he was still working on when he died on April 27, 1902. Following Morton's death, his family home in Nebraska City was turned into a state park, the Arbor Lodge State Historical Park and Arboretum. Known throughout his life as a devoted family man, Morton also had several sons who went on to earn great renown. One served as the secretary of the navy under President Theodore Roosevelt. Another founded the Morton Salt Company and devoted part of his fortune to erecting a massive arboretum in Illinois, testament to a love for tree planting instilled by his father.

THE EASTERN PART of Nebraska where J. Sterling Morton lived may have lacked trees, but the land was relatively fertile. Annual rainfall averaged around thirty inches, a paltry amount compared to the eastern states, but enough to sustain traditional agriculture techniques and, with care, tree cultivation. As Nebraska extended toward the West, however, the situation changed. Beyond the ninety-eighth meridian—a latitude demarcation roughly one-third of the way across the state—annual rainfall decreased to less than twenty inches, making conventional agriculture and tree raising near impossible. This arid region expanded far beyond western Nebraska, stretching from the ninety-eighth meridian in the east to the Rocky Mountains in the west, from the Canadian border in the north to almost the Mexican border in the south. Known in the nineteenth century as "The Great American Desert," it included about one-fifth of the land in the continental United States.

Conditions in this region inhibited the traditional forms of agriculture-based permanent settlement that Americans had practiced since colonial times. The area's primary inhabitants were Native Americans and ranchers who moved herds of grazing animals along these endless plains.

Many pioneering Americans refused to accept the fact that an enormous portion of the nation's geography resisted domestication. Various theories appeared explaining how the land might be forced to yield to the entreaties of settlers. One school of thought suggested that the key was to increase rainfall, and over the years a belief developed that a possible way to accomplish this was through widespread tree planting. Exactly how trees might bring the rains remained vague, but the logic was compelling enough to win over many men of science.

Among the theory's most influential proponents was Ferdinand V. Hayden, director of the United States Geological and Geographical Survey of the Territories from 1867 to 1879. He had come across Marsh's *Man and Nature* shortly after it was published and, like a number of readers, found compelling meteorological proof that forests increased rainfall. (While Marsh had quoted some favorable statements on the matter, he did this only to criticize them and assiduously avoided reaching any positive conclusions himself.) Hayden first expressed his belief that trees increased rainfall in an 1867 report on Nebraska. It read:

> I do not believe that the prairies proper will ever become covered with timber except by artificial means. . . . It is believed, also, that the planting of ten or fifteen acres of forest trees on each quarter section will have a most important effect on the climate, equalizing and increasing the moisture and adding greatly to the fertility of the soil. The settlement of the country and the increase of the timber has already changed for the better the climate of that portion of Nebraska lying along the Missouri . . . [and] I am confident this change will continue to extend across the dry belt to the foot of the Rocky mountains as the settlements extend and the forest trees are planted in proper quantities.

Hayden's report (and its follow-ups) not only bolstered the increased rainfall theory by adding the government's imprimatur, it also injected the supposed authority of geographical expertise through the inclusion of passages paraphrased or directly reproduced from *Man and Nature*—Hayden discarded Marsh's skeptical rejoinders and selectively inserted the positive assertions without sufficient context.

The increased rainfall theory gained force in the ensuing years. Horticultural societies throughout the Midwest debated its merits, while Hayden and other federal officials touted it as a potential solution to the challenge of the Great American Desert. To complicate matters, the entire prairie region was experiencing an upturn in annual rainfall. This eventually proved to be part of a cyclical weather pattern that oscillated between high rainfall and drought, but many saw it as evidence for the impact of settler tree plantings and as a rationale to expand the practice. The prevalence of the increased rainfall theory likely contributed to Arbor Day's popularity across the Midwest—Morton himself hadn't initially discussed this rationale, but in later years claimed that one of his several motivations was, in fact, "to improve the climatic conditions." Some, like Major John Wesley Powell, director of the United States Geological Survey (a successor to Hayden's survey), contested the increased rainfall crowd, but such dissents were largely drowned out.

As increasing numbers of people accepted that forests brought the rains, they began to demand that the federal government take action to hasten this vital natural phenomenon. The matter finally reached the United States Senate floor during the same winter that Morton had introduced Arbor Day. Its champion was Phineas Hitchcock, a senator from Nebraska who, like many midwestern politicians, showed almost unshakable faith in the region's agricultural potential. He proposed a bill in February 1872 "to encourage the growth of timber on western prairies." It would grant any settler a free quarter section in the plains states so long as he planted forty acres with forest trees and cultivated them for ten years—the bill resembled the famous Homestead Act of 1862, but essentially substituted tree planting for the residency requirements. Hitchcock's proposal echoed the suggestions that Hayden had offered five years earlier. And while there were many reasons to encourage tree planting on the plains, Hitchcock took pains to make his belief in the increased rainfall theory clear: "The object of this bill is to encourage the growth of timber, not merely for the benefit of the soil, not merely for the value of the timber itself, but for its influence upon the climate."

On March 3, 1873, President Ulysses Grant signed Hitchcock's bill into law as the Timber Culture Act. Suddenly Americans were entitled to claim land simply by demonstrating a willingness to plant and tend trees. The nation had shifted 180 degrees from the days when land was free for the taking so long as a settler was willing to clear the trees away.

Problems with the Timber Culture Act, however, surfaced almost immediately. For starters, the requirement proved more onerous than the government had likely intended. Trees, in many cases, simply refused to grow in such arid conditions or died in winter frosts. A government land officer noted in 1884, "I have never seen any instances of . . . success, except in the eastern portion of Nebraska and southeastern Dakota [two regions east of the ninety-eighth meridian]." But the larger issue was the act's susceptibility to abuse and fraud. Many were less concerned with bringing rains to the plains than with gaining title to cheap lands, and the act became a favorite vehicle for speculators. Morton expressed the frustration that many felt in an 1885 article: "[B]y the timber-culture act we pay bounties in millions of acres of the public domain every year for the sham planting of counterfeit forests,—forests which no more resemble in value, in beauty, and in sanitary influences the primeval pines and oaks which we tariff to their destruction than a five-cent nickel resembles a twenty-dollar gold piece." Ultimately, the Timber Culture Act turned out to be one of numerous late-nineteenth-century laws designed to encourage settlement but ripe for manipulation. Congress finally repealed the Timber Culture Act in 1891.

By the closing years of the nineteenth century, the increased rainfall theory began to be dismissed as junk science. Several severe droughts convinced even die-hard adherents that the trees planted across the plains had had no effect on the general climate. Some settlers who had emigrated to the Great American Desert fled back toward more fertile lands back East. Others began to develop techniques of dry-land farming and learned to survive in a region with little rainfall, though some of the more arid regions remained the exclusive province of ranchers or simply remained unpopulated. Eventually the increased rainfall claim landed in the trash heap with that other great canard of prairie development, "Rain follows the plow."

For twenty years, however, the idea that tree planting might bring rains to the Great American Desert had shaped policies in states and territories throughout the high plains. And this was far from the only tree-based political movement coalescing in the late nineteenth century. In New York State, voices were starting to speak up on the need to protect forests, an idea whose time had finally arrived.

## "A Central Park for the World"

FAR TO THE NORTH of New York City, beyond the state capital of Albany, up where the proud Hudson River takes it first breath, sits the broad Adirondack plateau. It lies between Lake Champlain in the east and the valley of the Black River in the west, extending toward the fertile plains of the St. Lawrence River to the north and the dells of the Mohawk River to the south, in total an area greater than the state of Vermont. Four hilly ranges run southeasterly across the Adirondack plateau, including a chain of mountains that climb above five thousand feet and contain Mount Marcy, the state's highest peak. Nearly all of this land is blanketed in a dense forest, endless acres of sugar maples, beeches, and yellow birches with clumps of white pines, spruces, and hemlocks sprinkled throughout. Since colonial times, countless settlers had attempted to conquer these forests, but the soil is poor and withstood nearly all attempts at agriculture. For most of the nation's history the land remained uninhabited save for some isolated hamlets and a small tourist section around Saranac Lake.

The Adirondack forests, however, captured the public's imagination in 1869. That year the Reverend William H. H. Murray published *Adventures in the Wilderness; or Camp-Life in the Adirondacks*. Murray, who tended a congregation in Boston, was probably the nation's second-most prominent preacher, trailing only the formidable Henry Ward Beecher. The book, he explained, was written "to encourage manly exercise in the open air, and familiarity with Nature in her wildest and grandest aspects." It was not only a panegyric to the majesty of wilderness but something of a practical guide for recreation, explaining the best ways to reach the Adirondacks, providing the names of reputable guides, and even suggesting the best clothing for a woman to wear in the forests. The work seemed to tap a latent fervency of the general population for the outdoors and became a runaway success.

Thousands descended on the Adirondacks in the wake of *Adventures in the Wilderness*. The region quickly transformed into the most fashionable summer retreat for well-to-do easterners. Fancy "wilderness" hotels sprang up to meet this new demand, offering everything from hunting to gambling to horseback riding. One establishment built in 1882 was the first hotel in the world to outfit each room with electric lights; another boasted a guest list that eventually included four current or future presidents: Grover Cleveland, Calvin Coolidge, Benjamin Harrison, and Theodore Roosevelt. In addition to tourism the Adirondack forests began to serve as the nation's premier retreat for those suffering from tuberculosis, a disease of the lungs that was the nation's greatest killer for much of the late nineteenth century. Countless victims of this "White Plague" booked rooms in the sanitoriums that populated the mountains, hoping to benefit from an environment with air much purer than that of the cities.

So great was the flow of people toward the Adirondacks that as early as 1872 an opinion piece in the *New York Times* lamented: "[The Adirondack] region is now ruined for the lover of solitude and nature. . . . [T]hat once imposing forest solitude is now rather more crowded and decidedly gayer, than the Central Park on a summer's Saturday afternoon."

In truth, however, the more serious threat to the forests of the Adirondacks was not the tourist or consumptive, but the men eager to cut down the trees for profit. Tanners destroyed the hemlock trees for their bark; charcoal furnaces clear-cut the surrounding forests for fuel; and loggers felled every merchantable white pine within easy distance of a river. As in the Lake States forests, the threat from industry was not simply the trees that workers destroyed directly but the heightened risk of forest fire from the brush and slash that was left behind. The region's long-term prospects were no better than those of any other commercial woodlands in the nation.

The earliest call for protection of the Adirondacks arose partly in reaction to these manifold threats. On August 9, 1864, the *New York Times* published a lone editorial, which historians suspect was written by a close friend of Frederick Law Olmsted:

> Within an easy day's ride of our great City, as steam teaches us to measure distance, is a tract of country fitted to make a Central Park for the world. . . . [L]et [our citizens] form combinations, and, seizing upon the choicest of the Adirondack Mountains, before they are despoiled of their forests, make of them grand parks. . . . In spite of all the din and dust of furnaces and foundries, the Adirondacks, thus husbanded, will furnish abundant seclusion for all time to come.

This proposal, however, was years ahead of its time: The nation was still in the throes of war; Marsh's *Man and Nature* had only just arrived, and few Americans had absorbed its message; Murray's *Adventures in the Wilderness* would not appear for another five years.

Practically the only person who heeded the *Times* message initially was a young man named Verplanck Colvin. His father had encouraged him to practice law but Colvin fell in love with the Adirondack mountains and forests. He began to survey them in 1865 and three years later started promoting the idea of a park. Among his many concerns was a fear—similar to the argument from *Man and Nature* that had been misappropriated by the increased rainfall crowd—that if the trees were destroyed then the land would no longer adequately regulate the water supply, causing havoc on the rivers that originated in the Adirondacks, including the Hudson. He submitted a report to the state legislature in 1870 that argued: "The interests of commerce and navigation demand that these forests should be preserved, and for posterity should be set aside."

By the early 1870s others began to join in Colvin's one-man show. Not only had many at this point discovered the Adirondack region through tourism, but circumstances had changed since the *Times* editorial. The fires of 1871, especially in Peshtigo, had awoken some to the potential threat of forest destruction back East—a drought that was ravaging New York State in 1872 stoked this fear. Additionally, a very public effort was under way (with Ferdinand Hayden at the helm) to preserve the scenic Yellowstone region in Wyoming with its fabulous geysers, wildlife, and vistas; this advocacy culminated in President Grant's creation on March 1, 1872, of the Yellowstone National Park, the first such federally protected park in the nation or the world.

Shortly after Grant authorized Yellowstone, the New York State legislature finally took some action on the Adirondack question to placate the preservation crowd. It established a Commission of State Parks even though no actual parks yet existed. The commission's mandate was simply "to inquire into the expediency of providing for vesting in the State the title to the timbered

regions . . . [of the Adirondacks] and converting the same into a public park."
This directive nonetheless represented a significant first step in a long process
toward the radical idea of placing forested lands within the hands of the people. The seven-person commission included Colvin, the most vocal champion
for a park, as well as Horatio Seymour, a former governor whose participation
added a degree of gravitas.

The following year the commission produced its inaugural annual report,
the first serious study of the park question. It determined that protecting the
forests from "wanton destruction" was "absolutely and immediately required."
The foremost concern—testament to Colvin's influence on the commission—
was the need to regulate the water supply. "Without a *steady, constant* supply
of water from these streams of the wilderness, our canals would be dry, and a
great portion of the grain and other produce of the western part of the State
would be unable to find cheap transportation to the markets of the Hudson
river valley." (Interestingly, the report, which appeared two months after Congress enacted the Timber Culture Act, specifically refuted the claim that forests could increase rainfall.)

The outcome of the report, however, seemed to prove the old adage: When
you want nothing to get done, appoint a committee. Following its release, the
Adirondack issue languished for the better part of a decade with practically no
public activity aside from Colvin's continuing geographical surveys.

Nonetheless, the report's arguments about watershed protection resonated
with some of the state's more influential downriver residents. Businessmen
in New York City depended on the trade in goods along the Hudson River,
and some grew anxious as the destruction of Adirondack forests continued
unabated in the early 1880s. A *New York Tribune* article from 1883 noted: "The
matter is reduced to a simple business issue. Is the [Hudson] river worth to
the City and the state as much as it will cost to save the woods?" By the end of
1883 the powerful New York Chamber of Commerce had appointed a forestry
committee to advocate on this issue. The committee's president was Morris
K. Jesup, a businessman who had made a fortune in the railroad business and
then retired to pursue projects in the public interest—among other things, he
helped found the YMCA and presided over both the American Museum of
Natural History and the Audubon Society of New York State. The indefatigable Jesup recruited other organizations, like the New York Board of Trade
and Transportation and the Brooklyn Constitution Club, to the cause, and his
Forestry Committee pressured the state legislature to start purchasing lands
within the Adirondack forest, going so far as to draft a model bill.

The legislative leadership in Albany, many of whom did not share the concerns of New York City businessmen, took up the issue once more but moved

cautiously. They failed to authorize any funds to buy lands, but did withdraw the approximately seven hundred thousand acres' worth of state holdings within the Adirondacks from future sale—most of this territory had reverted to the state through tax sales after commercial operators stripped the land of all the useful timber and abandoned it. The legislature also authorized another committee, this time tasked with outlining a policy of state control of the withdrawn forests.

This new group was placed under the leadership of Charles Sprague Sargent, perhaps the nation's most respected voice on all tree-related issues. Born in 1841, Sargent had attended Harvard and served in the Union army before developing an interest in horticulture during his late twenties. In 1873 his alma mater appointed him the first director of its recently completed Arnold Arboretum (which had been designed by Frederick Law Olmsted). Under Sargent's half century of leadership, the arboretum would blossom into the national center for the study of trees. The industrious Sargent, however, extended his reach far beyond its confines. In 1880, for example, he took charge of the U.S. Census's new section on forests. This culminated in his 1884 *Report on the Forests of North America*, a masterful study of 412 tree species that quickly became a standard reference work—the report also emphasized the need to conserve the nation's timber resources; Sargent, like many, had read and been influenced by *Man and Nature*.

The Sargent committee issued a lengthy report on the Adirondacks in January 1885. It confirmed much of the analysis from the earlier 1873 report, particularly the need to preserve the forests for their role in regulating rivers. However, to many people's surprise, the committee opposed the state purchase of land on practical grounds: "There is nothing in the past management of its wild land by the State to justify their increase by purchase at this time. Little attention has ever been paid to the care of these lands." The report instead advocated both the creation of a new, powerful forestry commission to actively manage the land and the modification of existing tax laws to discourage the rapid destruction of property. Only through these measures, it argued, would the actual risk of forest fire be reduced and the trees spared from the timber thieves, lumbermen, and railroads. Attached to the report, the Sargent commission included three draft bills addressing these proposals.

Sargent's suggested legislation, however, seemed to please no one. Legislators chafed at the creation of a new, semiautonomous state Forest Commission, which would have been the first of its kind in the nation. People living in and around the Adirondack zone opposed any effort to ramp up regulatory activity—the report likely won few admirers when it stated, "it is an open boast that the population live almost entirely upon the products of State lands." The anxious business community in New York City disagreed with the report's central conclusion against the state's purchase of lands and further objected to aspects of the proposed bills that allowed for controlled logging.

With Sargent's legislation foundering in Albany and the need for Adirondack management growing more urgent as tax-delinquent lands continued to revert to the state, the secretary of the New York Board of Trade and Transportation, Frank Gardner, stepped in to break the logjam. He called for a conference in New York City at which all the major players could hammer out a resolution. Attendees included Jesup, Sargent, and the two friendly legislators who had sponsored the Sargent bills. No one kept minutes of this gathering, but when it concluded there was a new draft bill that everyone approved.

In May 1885, Governor David B. Hill signed this new measure into law. It designated as a "Forest Preserve" all lands that the state owned or acquired within the Adirondack and Catskill regions (while this act combined the two areas, subsequent legislation treated them separately). The heart of the act was Section 8: "The lands now or hereafter constituting the forest preserve shall be forever kept as wild forest lands. They shall not be sold, nor shall they be leased or taken by any corporation, public or private." This language marked the first time—other than Lincoln's 1864 protection of the Mariposa Grove of giant sequoias—that a government, at the state or federal level, took concrete measures to protect forests from the threats of commercial life. In addition to Section 8, the act introduced penalties for the intentional burning of public land; required railroads to manage, cut, and remove flammable materials and outfit their locomotives with spark arresters; and, most notably, created a three-member Forest Commission to oversee fire-management activities.

While the act represented a decisive victory—the largest in a thirteen-year struggle to protect the state's threatened tree resources—it was not without its limitations. The language of "forever wild" proved more plastic than the drafters likely intended. The newly appointed Forest Commission, which included a prominent lumberman among its three members, interpreted Section 8 to allow for managed timber cutting. Soon cutting rights were being sold to private companies and individuals, including, most controversially, the lumberman on the commission. Additionally, the act had failed to allocate funds either for the future purchase of lands or, more problematically, for the enforcement of its very provisions. The activity of timber thieves—and the fire threat they created—thus continued unabated. Even when government officials caught them, the consequences were insignificant. As one lumberman explained to the *New York Times* in 1889: "We are not responsible if the State fails to run strings around their lots. We can't always tell which is State and which is our timber. So the Forester inquires what the market price is of logs we cut, and we pay him, and everybody is satisfied."

Newspapers and public-minded citizens railed against these injustices, pushing public sentiment toward even greater protection for the Adirondacks. A forest preserve no longer seemed sufficient; the Adirondack constituency was starting to call for the establishment of a state park, a clearly defined region in which the state could concentrate its holdings and more easily protect the trees. Governor Hill addressed these concerns on January 22, 1890, with a special message to the legislature that asked for further action. In response, state politicians finally allocated twenty-five thousand dollars to the Forest Commission and requested that it prepare a report addressing the proposed park idea. The resulting publication included a map of the Adirondack region encircled by two lines, an outer boundary in red denoting the Forest Preserve area and an inner boundary in blue marking the hypothetical dimensions of a park zone.

Several private lobbying groups, frustrated by the legislature's continually slow pace, drafted new bills themselves creating an Adirondack park. One of the leading organizations was the New York State Forestry Association, whose president was the redoubtable Jesup.

The various draft bills that began to appear grappled with two main issues of contention. The first considered whether to allow timber activities within the proposed park. Hard-line park proponents, especially the downriver businessmen, wanted no lumbering activities whatsoever. Upstate voices countered that this would deprive local residents of jobs simply to ensure a pleasure ground for wealthy urbanites. The second provision concerned the possibility of the government exchanging public lands outside the park's boundaries for private lands within. This seemed to be the only mechanism through which the government might consolidate its holdings to form a park without allocating monies; however, a version of an exchange system had been put in place in 1887 and was widely condemned, with many fearing that the lumber lobby pushed this solution as a way to upgrade their holdings at no cost. The *New York Times* warned that loggers "sought in every possible way" to exchange worthless tracts for "such of the State lands as lie along streams or lakes [and] which are extremely valuable."

A compromise piece of legislation began to work its way through the New York legislature. And in May 1892, Governor Roswell P. Flower signed the Adirondack Park Enabling Act, which declared that the region falling inside the Forest Commission's proposed Blue Line would be a state park. The total land area was 2,807,760 acres, of which 551,093 acres (roughly 860 square miles) already belonged to the state.

While this new legislation formally created an Adirondack park, it failed to resolve the two main points of debate that went to the heart of what a state park was to be. The timber-cutting issue remained ambiguous—the act simply listed "a future timber supply" as one of three main purposes, along with recreation and watershed protection. And the legislature allocated no funds for future land purchases, leaving the suspect land exchange system as the only avenue toward further consolidation. On this point, the governor simply assured the many skeptics that "all revenues from the sale of the so-called 'outside' lands will be devoted to the purchase of new lands better adapted for the purposes of a forest preserve."

The new governor, however, quickly lost what credibility he had among the park's proponents. The following year he signed another bill that authorized timber sales within the park. Ostensibly passed as a revenue-generating measure to cover maintenance fees, this new "cutting bill" enraged downstate groups like the Board of Trade and Transportation. Enormous wood-cutting operations were quickly projected, with some contracts entered into by the Forest Commission itself.

Advocates of forest protection concluded that the park's future was unsafe in the hands of the commission, the legislature, or the governor. As an article in *Garden and Forest*, a journal edited by Sargent, quipped: "It would seem that the time has already come when the Park ought to be preserved from its preservers." Gardner, the secretary of the Board of Trade and Transportation, said, "I am convinced that the forests will never be made safe until they are put into the State Constitution."

It so happened that the following year was the state's fourth Constitutional Convention (unlike the federal government, some states hold new constitutional conventions from time to time). Gardner's offhand remark quickly became the subject of serious talks at the Board of Trade and Transportation. A committee began working on a draft amendment to fully protect the trees in the Adirondacks—the language was based on Section 8 of the 1885 law. The board, in advance of the formal convention, presented its amendment to the convention's president, who said: "You have brought here the most important question before this assembly. In fact, it is the only question that warrants the existence of this convention." Delegates revised the amendment's language until settling upon the following:

> The lands of the State, now owned or hereafter acquired, constituting the forest preserve as fixed by law, shall be forever kept as wild forest lands. They shall not be leased, sold, or exchanged, or be taken by any corporations, public or private, nor shall the timber thereon be sold, removed, or destroyed.

The amendment's ultimate clause, absent from the earlier 1885 act, would ensure that no legislature or government agency could ever authorize timber sales.

When the amendment reached the convention floor on September 13, 1894, it was approved by a unanimous vote of 122 to 0, the only amendment so honored (not only at the 1894 convention but in all previous ones as well). The general population voted it into the constitution two months later, and on January 1, 1895, the amendment finally went into effect, the culmination of a quarter century's struggle for adequate protection of the state's tree resources.

Over the years the Adirondack park proved incredibly popular with the citizens of New York, and the constitutional amendment withstood countless challenges. The park's dimensions have more than doubled, and state holdings have increased more than fivefold, to 2.7 million acres, an area over 50 percent larger than the state of Delaware. The Adirondacks now contain the largest protected forested zone, state or federal, in the continental United States.

The movement to create the park also served as a template for many subsequent state and federal initiatives to create parks and forest reserves. But it was not the only such movement. Far to the west, a new voice appeared, focusing less on trees' importance to the climate or economy, and more on their spiritual value to the nation.

## "God's First Temples"

IN THE SPRING OF 1871, Ralph Waldo Emerson, the transcendentalist minister from Concord, now sixty-eight years old and one of the country's most famous individuals, headed to California for a speaking tour. Among his many stops was a visit to the legendary Yosemite Valley and the nearby Mariposa big trees. He arrived at the valley on May 5 and, shortly thereafter, received an admiring and enthusiastic letter from a little-known thirty-three-year-old who lived nearby, named John Muir. The missive pleaded for the Concord sage to take a break from his schedule and join Muir "in a month's worship with Nature in the high temples of the great Sierra Crown beyond our holy Yosemite."

Emerson, intrigued by the letter and by accounts that some locals provided about Muir's knowledge of the California wilderness, decided to pay him a visit. The following day he and a friend, James Bradley Thayer, traveled to the address provided. Upon arrival they were greeted with great eagerness by Muir, a thin man, shorter than average, but possessing the poise and strength of one tempered through toil and the trials of nature. Muir appeared to be, in many respects, the embodiment of self-reliance, that powerful, American creed that

Emerson had first postulated in a famous essay years earlier. According to Thayer, Muir worked to impress Emerson by bringing out "a great many dried specimens of plants . . . and hundreds of his own graceful pencil-sketches of the mountain peaks and forest trees," which he discussed "with enthusiastic interest."

The aged transcendentalist and the young naturalist forged a kinship around their love of nature. Emerson invited Muir to join him for a scheduled visit to the big trees and, once in the forests of the Sierra, Muir acted as his guide. Thayer explained that as they walked toward the Mariposa Grove, Muir "talked of the trees; and we grew learned." The party spent a day admiring the sequoias—Emerson was even asked to name one, an honor rarely extended to visitors. As the group prepared to leave, Muir once again pleaded with Emerson to stay with him: "You are yourself a sequoia. . . . Stop and get acquainted with your big brethren." But Emerson's companions, fearful of the effects such an outing might have on his health, forbade him to accept Muir's offer, and the two soon parted ways.

After this legendary encounter, they continued to correspond until Emerson's death the following year. Emerson even included Muir's name on a list composed shortly before his passing titled "My Men"—it included only eighteen names in total, a veritable catalogue of nineteenth-century titans, including Henry David Thoreau and William Butler Ogden. According to many sources, Emerson went so far as to claim, "[Muir] is more wonderful than Thoreau." No higher praise could the Concord minister have offered. It was as though Emerson had foreseen the role that Muir was about to play in reshaping America's understanding of the wilderness and, consequently, its relationship to trees.

John Muir was born in 1838 in Dunbar, Scotland, one of eight children in a strict Presbyterian family. As a boy, he was, in his own words, "fond of everything that was wild." This innate curiosity, however, landed him in frequent trouble with his father, who felt that any activities distracting from Bible study were frivolous. Much of Muir's childhood was thus spent studying scripture, and by eleven the bright child could recite from memory all of the New Testament and much of the Old Testament.

In 1849, Muir's family emigrated to the United States, settling in the wilderness near Portage, Wisconsin, about seventy miles northwest of Milwaukee. The years that followed were difficult ones as the family attempted, like so many new Americans, to carve a farm from the forest. Muir's stern father compelled him to spend long days clearing trees and laboring in the fields, leaving little time for study, exploration, or a budding interest in mechanical invention. The indomitable teenager took to rising at 1:00 a.m., training himself to exist on five hours' sleep. Of this predawn time, Muir wrote, "Fire was not allowed, so to escape the frost I went down cellar, and there read some favorite book or marked out some invention that haunted me." With little more than a pocket-knife and wood, the gifted Muir created countless ingenious devices, including an "early-rising machine," doubtless to assist him in maintaining his morning study regime. He eventually entered some of his contraptions in a state fair, and they earned him praise as a "genius" and encouragement to pursue further studies, something his father had strongly opposed.

Muir finally left home at the age of twenty-two and spent the next seven years pursuing opportunities as they came, living a somewhat peripatetic lifestyle (not entirely dissimilar from the experience of a young Thoreau and Olmsted). He spent several semesters enrolled at the University of Wisconsin–Madison, but lack of funds compelled him to suspend his education—his college tenure did, however, introduce him to botany and geology, two lifelong passions. In 1864, fearful of getting drafted into the Union army, he trekked into Canada, spending several months on an unplanned tramp in the forests around Lake Huron and several more months working with his brother, another Civil War draft dodger, in a woodworking factory. Muir's skill with mechanical equipment helped him to find factory work wherever he wandered, and by 1867 he had settled in Indianapolis, employed as a sawyer for a company that made wagon parts.

One night in early March that year, while working late to improve the factory's belt system, Muir lost his grip on a file. The tool flew upward and pierced his right eye, rendering it temporarily blind. "I felt neither pain nor faintness," Muir explained, "the thought was so tremendous that my right eye was gone—that I should never look at a flower again." He was compelled to spend several weeks lying in a dark room as he healed (though his right eye remained forever weak). This period of convalescence gave him a chance to reflect on his life thus far, his years of toiling in factory work away from his beloved forests. He determined to break free from the shackles of his mechanical labor and set out to explore the world. He wrote: "This affliction has driven me to the sweet fields. . . . God has to nearly kill us sometimes, to teach us lessons." That September Muir, now "joyful and free," began his first major ramble, a thousand-mile walk to the Gulf of Mexico.

In the spring of 1868, Muir's travels brought him to San Francisco, California. He intended to remain there only a few months before heading to South America, but then he discovered the nearby Sierra Nevada Mountains, a place that he later named the "Range of Light." And at the heart of the Sierras was the Yosemite, a sprawling area of sheer rock walls, spectacular waterfalls, and fantastic geological formations. (Yosemite State Park, created with the same

1864 law that protected the Mariposa Grove of big trees, covered only a small portion of the region, the main Yosemite Valley, home to such natural wonders as Yosemite Falls, Cathedral Rock, El Capitan, and Sentinel Rock.) The entire Sierra region captivated Muir like nothing before. He had finally found his home:

> We are now in the mountains and they are in us, kindling enthusiasm, making every nerve quiver, filling every pore and cell of us. Our flesh-and-bone tabernacle seems transparent as glass to the beauty about us, as if truly an inseparable part of it . . . a part of all nature, neither old nor young, sick nor well, but immortal. . . . How glorious a conversion, so complete and wholesome it is, scarce memory enough of old bondage days left as a standpoint to view it from!

It was not, however, simply the remarkable geography that attracted Muir, but also the Sierra's trees. Muir, by all accounts, was a self-professed tree lover. Charles Sprague Sargent, the don of American trees, who later became Muir's close friend, said of him: "Few men whom I have known loved trees as deeply and intelligently as John Muir." And the forests of the Sierra were something of a tree utopia. Muir, over the course of his life, would fill countless pages and write dozens of articles explaining their character. His descriptions remain unmatched in their elegance:

> No other coniferous forest in the world contains so many species or so many large and beautiful trees,—Sequoia gigantean, king of conifers, "the noblest of a noble race," as Sir Joseph Hooker well says; the sugar pine, king of all the world's pines, living or extinct; the yellow pine, next in rank, which here reaches most perfect development, forming noble towers of verdure two hundred feet high; the mountain pine, which braves the coldest blasts far up the mountains on grim, rocky slopes; and five others, flourishing each in its place, making eight species of pine in one forest, which is still further enriched by the great Douglas spruce, libocedrus, two species of silver fir, large trees and exquisitely beautiful, the Paton hemlock, the most graceful of evergreens, the curious tumion, oaks of many species, maples, alders, poplars, and flowering dogwood, all fringed with flowery underbrush, manzanita, ceanothus, wild rose, cherry, chestnut, and rhododendron.

Though Muir preferred to devote all his time to exploring the region's natural wonders and its trees, he nonetheless needed some employment to support his minimal wants. During his first eighteen months he took a series of odd jobs, including two stints as a sheepherder in the Sierra Nevada Mountains—these experiences convinced him that sheep, which ate all the young forest growth, were "hoofed locusts" destined to destroy the trees if left unregulated. In the fall of 1869, Muir finally received an offer of permanent work from James Hutchings, the same California pioneer and promoter who had published the best-known account of the giant sequoia discovery. Hutchings contracted with Muir to construct and operate a local sawmill, in which he would be free to reside as well. Muir, sensitive to the frailty of his new habitat and unwilling to kill any living trees, agreed on the condition that the operation only cut downed wood. This sawmill was where Muir first met Emerson, in 1871. It was also where Muir began his career as a writer—his first published piece, "Yosemite Glaciers," appeared in the *New York Tribune* in December 1871 and argued that the Yosemite Valley was formed through glacier movement, a controversial though largely correct theory that clashed with the prevailing view that the magnificent natural features had resulted from earthquakes.

In 1876 Muir first lent his voice publicly to the cause of forest preservation. The *Sacramento Daily Record-Union*, a newspaper in Northern California, published an editorial of his on February 5 of that year calling for government protection of all the forests of the Sierra Nevada's giant sequoia belt. The article was called "God's First Temples: How Shall We Preserve Our Forests." The provocative title was an allusion to a well-known 1825 blank-verse poem, "A Forest Hymn," written by the famed poet and nature lover William Cullen Bryant—it began, "The groves were God's first temples." This literary reference reflected Muir's belief that the nation's trees possessed a dynamic, spiritual dimension worthy of protection for its own sake. His philosophy of preservation thus differed from that of many other early voices, including those who fought for the Adirondack park primarily out of concerns over the Hudson River. A subsequent article made this distinction clear: "Thousands of tired, nerve-shaken, over-civilized people are beginning to find out that going to the mountains is going home; that wilderness is a necessity; and that mountain parks and reservations are useful not only as fountains of timber and irrigating rivers, but as fountains of life."

In some respects, Muir's philosophy echoed transcendentalism, the movement founded by Emerson, but the Californian also broke from the views of his New England predecessors. Nature was wild, uncertain, vast, dynamic, and sublime, divine for its own sake, not its reflection of the afterlife. While Muir greatly admired Thoreau, he occasionally scoffed at what his intellectual fore-bear accepted as "wilderness." One of his articles chafed at those who "[l]ike Thoreau . . . see forests in orchards and patches of huckleberry brush, and oceans in ponds and drops of dew."

By the time the "God's First Temples" editorial appeared in 1876, Muir was thirty-eight years old, already the preeminent expert on the California mountains and widely respected for his writings. But he had yet to settle down, and a life of solitude was beginning to weigh on him. Two years earlier he had met Louie Wanda Strentzel, the twenty-seven-year-old daughter of a prosperous immigrant orchardist. She shared Muir's love of botany, and they formed a close bond, culminating in their marriage in April 1880, when Muir was forty-two. His first daughter was born the following spring and a second appeared five years later. Throughout the 1880s, the responsibilities of supporting a family consumed much of his time, but Muir's wife, sensing her husband's need for wilderness, urged him to return to his travels and writing.

Up to this point, Muir, aside from his appeals in "God's First Temples," had largely remained outside politics. But he was about to be thrust into the center of a national movement for forest preservation.

In May 1889, he met Robert Underwood Johnson, the well-connected associate editor of the influential *Century Magazine*. Johnson was in San Francisco for a story on gold hunting and had called on Muir to accompany him for a side trip into the Sierra Nevada—Muir supposedly got lost in the corridors of Johnson's hotel and cried out, "I can't make my way through these confounded artificial cañons." While in the mountains, Johnson noticed that the spectacular waterfalls and verdant meadows he'd read about in Muir's articles seemed to disappear outside the confines of the limited area within the Yosemite State Park. Muir explained to his companion—in an argument that seemed ripped from the pages of *Man and Nature*—how unrestricted sheep grazing had destroyed the underbrush and trees, leaving nothing to hold the winter snows and regulate the summer water flow. Johnson responded, "Obviously the thing to do is to make a Yosemite National Park around the Valley on the plan of the Yellowstone." (Johnson, here, was using the term "Yosemite" to describe the much larger area of intense geological formations.) This proposal initially failed to impress Muir, who doubted that there was sufficient political will. But the editor persisted: If Muir was willing to write two articles for the *Century Magazine* describing a proposed park, Johnson would spearhead a lobbying effort in Washington, D.C. By the time the two men descended from the Sierras, Muir had agreed to the plan.

The obstacles, however, were enormous. The sheepmen and lumbermen, who made their living exploiting the forests, sharply opposed any efforts to curb their operations. Many Californians also objected to any encroachments by the federal government as a matter of principle. But the largest hurdle was the federal government itself. Though it owned hundreds of millions of acres throughout the West, official policy was to alienate the lands as quickly as possible. Partly this was a revenue-generating issue and partly it was a reflection of the laissez-faire policies that dominated nineteenth-century thinking. The federal government's only prior direct effort to reserve land with the main purpose of protecting trees had been for naval purposes—starting in 1799, the government had purchased or set aside certain southern lands covered in live oak, a tree considered especially useful in ship construction, but this practice was abandoned with the shift to metal hulls in the 1860s. The only federal land that had ever been preserved for its own sake (not for economic or security reasons) was in Yellowstone almost twenty years earlier, but this was, in many respects, a poor analog: That land had less commercial potential than the Yosemite forests, and the Yellowstone National Park had been sponsored in part as a tourism ploy for a major railroad with a right of way through the region.

While attitudes about the regulation of public lands were beginning to soften—especially among eastern congressmen—it would take a powerful voice to persuade the general population and the federal government of the need for a new national park.

The Yosemite campaign began in earnest the following summer. Muir drafted a "proposed boundary" for the national park, and Johnson set about persuading his contacts at the Committee of Public Lands of the House of Representatives. Then, in August 1890, Muir's first article appeared. Titled "Treasures of the Yosemite," it included the "proposed boundary" map and discussed Muir's lifetime of experiences with the region's innumerable geological wonders and its unrivaled conifer forests. Interestingly, the article's only explicit rationale for preservation involved the sequoia forests: "These king trees, all that there are of their kind in the world, are surely worth saving." As a naturalist, Muir wanted all the land preserved for its own sake; as a pragmatist, he understood that trees, more than rocks, required actual protection and might spur the public to action.

With Muir's first article as a propaganda piece, Johnson was able to cajole some sympathetic legislators into producing a National Parks Bill. The following month appeared Muir's second article, "Features of the Proposed Yosemite National Park." This one focused exclusively on the natural wonders located outside the state park, particularly the Hetch Hetchy Valley, a rival in grandeur to the Yosemite Valley itself. Once again, Muir used the region's trees as the main reason to encourage protection: "[T]he bill cannot too quickly become law. Unless reserved or protected the whole region will soon or late be devastated by lumbermen and sheepmen, and so of course be made unfit for use as a pleasure ground. . . . [W]hen the region shall be stripped of its forests the ruin will be complete."

The fight to protect Yosemite achieved its desired end in early October 1890 with the passage of the National Parks Bill. The new act not only carved out a park that corresponded generally to Muir's map, it also preserved two other nearby stands of giant sequoias, designating them General Grant National Park and Sequoia National Park. Johnson appreciatively wrote to Muir on October 3, "[T]he Yosemite bill is of course the result of your very outspoken reference to the depredations in that region, and practically to your sketch of the limits." Thanks in great part to Muir's pen, trees for the first time enjoyed federal protection for more than just their economic value.

After the Yosemite victory, Muir devoted much of his remaining twenty-five years to the cause of forest protection. He authored countless books and articles on the subject, his name a frequent byline in *Harper's*, the *Atlantic*, and the *Century*. In 1892 he helped found the Sierra Club, an organization devoted to the preservation cause, and was elected its president, a post that he held for twenty-two years. Under Muir's leadership, this organization championed an expansion of the national park system, winning major victories in 1899 with the creation of King's Canyon National Park in California and in 1905 when the poorly administered Yosemite State Park was transferred to the federal government. And among all of this preservation activity Muir interspersed voyages to Alaska, South America, and Africa, including a world tour of trees that he undertook with Sargent.

On Christmas Eve 1914, at the age of seventy-six, Muir died as a titan of the country's intellectual and political life. The day after his passing, the *New York Times* ran an editorial to accompany his obituary that aptly summarized his impact on the nation: "To John Muir more than to any other man or body of men the citizens of the United States owe the preservation of their great natural parks in the Far West." But Muir's ultimate legacy was much greater than this: He would become the guiding spirit of environmental movements throughout the twentieth century, a visionary for a new balance between nature and Americans.

Nonetheless, Muir's ideas about preservation were not the only ones of importance for Americans concerned about the fate of the nation's trees. Many considered them too radical and impractical for a nation dependent on timber. The best solution, some argued, was not to lock up trees from the threats of man, but to teach Americans how to exploit the forests without destroying them. This new mantra would explode onto the national consciousness around the turn of the century.

## "How Would You Like to Be a Forester?"

ONE MORNING IN late August 1885, as twenty-year-old Gifford Pinchot was making the final preparations for his freshman year at Yale University, his father, James, pulled him aside and offered a curious suggestion: "How would you like to be a forester?" The younger Pinchot did not realize it at that time, but this simple question would guide much of his life. In turn, it would set off a chain of events that forever altered America as well as the fate of its trees.

The Pinchots were among the most prominent and influential families in the eastern United States. Gifford's maternal grandfather, Amos Eno, had made a fortune in New York City land speculation and had become one of the wealthiest Americans, his Manhattan real estate holdings alone reaching $25 million. Pinchot's father, James, was a prosperous businessman in his own right. While not possessing wealth on the scale of Eno's, he had been so successful as a merchant in New York City that he was able to retire in 1865, the same year that Pinchot was born. As for Pinchot's mother, Mary, she was not only a well-connected socialite who moved in the highest New York circles but also a woman with a strong social conscience—her influence would help usher her son toward a life of public service.

Gifford, scion of this esteemed family, was a natural leader. Bright, talented, and fiercely independent, he carried himself with a patrician demeanor and an innate air of authority. He stood six feet two, with a trim but sturdy frame, handsome features, and an ever-present mustache, which he had already cultivated by the time he was readying himself for Yale.

James's proposal that his son take up forestry, while unexpected, was not wholly without antecedents. The elder Pinchot had been the son of a minor Pennsylvania lumber baron and, likely in reaction to this, had developed an appreciation for the importance of protecting America's trees. His son's first name, in fact, had been chosen to honor Sanford Gifford, a famous Hudson River School painter—the artist's renowned work *Hunter Mountain, Twilight* (1866), which conveyed the devastation that the tanning industry had brought to the Catskill region, hung in the Pinchot family home. James's interest in the well-being of the nation's forests exerted a profound influence on Gifford. "I loved the woods and everything about them," he wrote. "As a boy it was my firm intention to be a naturalist." In 1882, seeking to foster this interest, Pinchot's parents even presented him a copy of Marsh's *Man and Nature*. Nonetheless, it was very atypical that a wealthy, influential New York merchant might urge his son to abandon commerce for nature.

But James's suggestion of forestry as a career was radical in a second, more profound sense. What truly made it, in Pinchot's words, "an amazing question for that day and generation" had little to do with the family's elevated social and financial position. Professional forestry—the ideas of treating timber as a crop, harvesting trees without destroying the underlying environment, and managing forests to encourage sustainable-yield practices and to minimize waste—existed exclusively in European countries, where limits in forest resources had necessitated its development. In America, by contrast, the concept of managing forests was, according to Pinchot, "something far outside the field of practical affairs." There was, at the time, not a single American forester to be found anywhere, nor a single acre of trees administered according to the tenets of forestry. Pinchot's father was thus coaxing his son toward a field that he would need to create largely from the ground up.

This was not to say that no one in America was talking of forestry before Pinchot. Fears about rapacious lumbering and unchecked forest fires had convinced some that the nation needed to rethink the way it handled its tree resources. As early as 1875, the U.S. Department of Agriculture had noted in its annual report: "Forestry has excited much attention in the United States in recent years in consequence of the rapid deforesting of large areas, and the expression of fears of a timber famine at no distant day." That same year a group of private citizens formed the American Forestry Association—one of the founders and early leaders was James Pinchot. The federal government soon took up the issue as well, allocating funds in 1876 to the study of the topic and formally creating a Division of Forestry five years later. Then, in 1882, the city of Cincinnati hosted the first American Forestry Congress, an event that lasted for several days, brought together the most knowledgeable voices on trees, and even included a citywide parade that culminated with an Arbor Day–inspired tree planting.

The problem with this early American forestry movement, at least in Gifford Pinchot's view, was that those involved "thought only of forest preservation, forest influences, and tree planting." In other words, "forestry" functioned as something of a catchall term to describe almost any late-nineteenth-century activities concerned with tree protection or propagation. Arbor Day was thus an aspect of forestry. The campaign to create the Adirondack park was another. Muir's advocacy of saving the trees of the Sierras also counted. The subjects that received the least discussion were forest management and continuous timber production, the mainstays of the actual profession in Europe.

When Pinchot arrived at Yale, he attempted to study forestry, but the school offered few relevant classes besides botany and natural history. It was just as well, since his collegiate interests were more social than academic. Pinchot wrote, "What I learned outside the classroom was worth at least as much as what I learned inside it." He threw himself into the vibrant extracurricular scene, eventually earning membership in Skull and Bones, the legendary secret society. At commencement, he was even given the honor of addressing his class. Though he had carefully prepared a talk, he abandoned it at the last moment in favor of an impromptu discussion of forestry. He explained: "[M]y future profession welled up inside of me and took its place, and I made to the exalted graduates of Yale . . . my first public statement on the importance of Forestry to the United States—and my first public declaration that I had chosen it as my lifework."

Not everyone was thrilled to learn of Pinchot's intentions. His maternal grandfather, for example, wanted Pinchot to become a businessman—he would go so far as to offer Pinchot a twenty-five-hundred-dollar salary as inducement to abandon his plans. Even those at the forefront of America's proto-forestry movement found Pinchot's proposal suspect. Charles Sprague Sargent, dean of American trees and a family friend, dismissed it as tomfoolery. George Loring, former U.S. commissioner of agriculture, was equally skeptical. No less an authority than the director of the federal government's Division of Forestry, a German-born forester named Bernhard Fernow, cautioned Pinchot that true forestry was simply impractical in America and that any effort in that direction was largely a waste of time. About the only people who supported him were his parents, but in the end that was enough, and the headstrong Pinchot went forward with his plans.

He traveled to Europe shortly after graduation to begin training as a forester. Armed with letters of introduction and the mystique of being the first American to study the profession seriously, Pinchot received a warm reception from many of the Continent's greatest authorities. His formal studies took place at L'Ecole Nationale Forestière in Nancy, France, one of the most prestigious forestry academies in Europe. This was where he gained an initial understanding of the profession, learning the basics of forest economics, law, and science. It was also where Pinchot first encountered a professionally managed forest:

> [The French forests] were divided at regular intervals by perfectly straight paths and roads at right angles to each other, and they were protected to a degree we in America know nothing about. There was, for example, a serious penalty for building any fire in the woods for any purpose. . . . This was the kind of forest I had read about, where peasants carried away every scrap of dead wood, and where branches down to the size of a pencil could be made into fagots and actually sold.

In addition to his training at Nancy, Pinchot spent extensive time with Sir Dietrich Brandis, a Prussian-trained forester who had famously introduced the profession to British-controlled Burma and India in the 1850s. Pinchot immediately felt a kinship with Brandis and treated him as a mentor, noting that "he had accomplished on the other side of the world what I might hope to have a hand in doing in America."

Pinchot decided to return to America after thirteen months, before completing his curriculum. Both Brandis and the forestry professors at Nancy cautioned him that it was too soon, that his training was incomplete. Of this there was little doubt, but the cocksure Pinchot felt that additional training was excessive. In his view the technical aspects of European forestry were ultimately of limited applicability in America. What mattered was getting the new profession started, and for that further study was unnecessary.

He returned home in late 1890, eager to put his training to use. Fernow, head of the Division of Forestry, made him an offer to serve as the division's assistant chief, but Pinchot demurred. His mentor, Brandis, had advised him that the best way to introduce forestry was not to work for the government, but to find a forest and start. No such opportunities, however, were forthcoming. For much of the first year, he worked in a series of consulting jobs. The pay was often nonexistent, but the work, which required extensive travel, allowed him to discover the nation's diverse forests and their seemingly innumerable varieties of trees.

In early 1892, the opportunity that Pinchot had been awaiting finally materialized. George W. Vanderbilt, heir to one of the nation's greatest family fortunes, was constructing near Asheville, North Carolina, a grand estate—the Baedeker Company, then the world's authority on travel, would soon call it "the finest private residence in America." Known as Biltmore, it stretched out across eighty-eight hundred acres, half of which were forest. Frederick Law Olmsted, the venerable landscape architect who was rapidly approaching the end of his career, was commissioned to oversee the project and, ever the innovator, recommended that the woodlands of Biltmore be devoted to practical forestry. When Vanderbilt agreed to this plan, Olmsted, who was an old friend of Pinchot's father, offered the job to Gifford.

At twenty-six years old, Pinchot finally had a chance to practice his new profession and realize the goal that his father had first suggested seven years earlier. Under his guidance, the woods around Biltmore were transformed from an unmanaged oak forest to a center of lumber production where trees were carefully chosen and selectively cut. Timber was treated like a crop to be grown, not a resource to be mined, and Vanderbilt's property quickly became, in Pinchot's words, "the beginning of practical Forestry in America." Pinchot's venture even generated a profit, at least on paper—this was vital, since one of the strongest critiques of forestry in America was that it fundamentally cost more than traditional "cut out and get out" lumbering.

Pinchot's twenty-five-hundred-dollar Biltmore contract stipulated that he prepare an exhibit on forestry for the upcoming 1893 World Columbian Exposition in Chicago, a grand gathering to honor the 400th anniversary of Christopher Columbus's discovery of America. More than 26 million people would attend the celebration. Attractions included the original Ferris wheel, the world's first commercial movie theater, and Buffalo Bill Cody's Wild West Show. Alongside these unforgettable exhibits, Pinchot presented the first public display of practical forestry in America.

W HILE PINCHOT WAS BUSY launching his professional forestry career, others in the nation's proto-forestry movement were concentrating on a different initiative. The federal government, despite its policy of distributing lands as quickly as practicable, still possessed hundreds of millions of forested acres throughout the West. Nearly all of these public wooded lands faced direct threats from logging, grazing, or the forest fires that such activities helped bring about. The fate of these forests up to this point had been largely ignored, but various groups started lobbying to change this. The most vocal faction, taking a page from the Adirondack park movement, wanted the public's tree resources protected because of their role in regulating watersheds—this was especially important throughout the West, where water was relatively scarce. Others felt that tighter control over the nation's trees was the only way to stave off the impending timber famine, a concern that swelled following the declaration by the superintendent of the 1890 census that the nation's frontier was effectively closed. A small faction of activists also wanted to expand Muir's ideas of preservation throughout the public domain. From these diverse viewpoints arose the idea of forest reserves, areas carved from the extensive western public domain where settlement would be forbidden and commercial activities, such as lumbering, would be limited if not restricted entirely.

Initial efforts to win over Congress failed under heavy resistance from westerners. Then, in early 1891, a landmark piece of forest legislation, in Pinchot's words, "slipped through Congress without question and without debate" when a last-minute amendment was added to a bill whose main purpose was to repeal the disastrous Timber Culture Act. Known as Section 24, or the Forest Reserve Act, the amendment stated: "That the President of the United States may, from time to time, set apart and reserve, in any State or Territory having public land bearing forests, . . . public reservations." At its most basic, Section 24 simply transferred power to create reserves from the legislature to the executive, but this proved crucial. Shortly after the act's passage, President Benjamin Harrison set aside the first reserve, an area adjacent to Yellowstone National Park that contained more than one million acres. By the end of 1892 he had created fifteen reservations that totaled over thirteen million acres, mostly with the stated purpose of protecting water supplies.

While the Forest Reserve Act marked the beginning of a system of national forests, problems with the new reserves quickly surfaced. Section 24, reflecting the general confusion over just what the reserves were for, had failed to provide any mechanism for administration. Consequently, once a reserve was declared it signaled the end of any commercial activities whatsoever, a fact that pleased the more hard-line forest defenders but enraged westerners used to unencumbered use of public lands. At the same time, the absence of any effective administration meant that the federal government had no way to enforce its stated policies. Thus, timber theft, grazing, and forest fires continued unabated regardless of presidential decree. By 1893 President Grover Cleveland, recognizing the inherent flaws in Section 24, decided to temporarily suspend the creation of any additional reserves.

The need for a solution to this reserve situation preoccupied many in the proto-forestry movement. Sargent's *Garden and Forest* journal began advocating a high-level, expert commission to study the issue fully. Soon others joined this chorus. By 1895 Robert Underwood Johnson's influential *Century Magazine* was also calling for "a commission composed of men of sufficient reputation to make their recommendations heeded." Action was finally taken the following year, when the secretary of the interior asked the National Academy of Sciences (NAS) to appoint a committee to investigate the matter and prepare a report for Congress and the president. To lead the seven-person committee the NAS selected Sargent. He, in turn, appointed Pinchot, bringing the young forester into national politics for the first time.

The NAS committee headed west in July 1896 to study the forest situation firsthand. When the men eventually arrived in California, they met with John Muir, who had been invited to act as an advisor. Muir's inclusion in the committee reflected the eclectic nature of the early forest reserve movement; differences over policy—specifically about whether to preserve forests or put them to productive use through professional forestry—had not yet calcified as they would during the twentieth century. Pinchot and Muir, who had met several years earlier and corresponded, used the trip to solidify their friendship. They bonded over their appreciation of nature and their interest in trees. Pinchot especially impressed Muir through his ruggedness when facing the elements. Describing an August excursion to Crater Lake in Oregon, Muir wrote: "Heavy rain during the night. All slept in the tent except Pinchot." The two men were kindred spirits on the trail.

The trip west left the committee divided over the question of whether to open the reserves to use, but a strong majority felt that the reserve system, despite its flaws, warranted expansion even before this issue was resolved. In January 1897, Sargent sent a preliminary report to the NAS calling for the creation of thirteen new reserves totaling more than 21 million acres. The report landed on President Cleveland's desk in a matter of days, with an additional note from the secretary of the interior: "[T]he birth of the Father of our Country could be no more appropriately commemorated than by the promulgation by yourself of proclamations establishing these grand forest reservations." Cleveland took this suggestion to heart and on February 22, 1897, ten days before his presidential term concluded, he authorized all of the proposed reserves, more than doubling the national system in a single stroke.

This proclamation, however, triggered another firestorm, one that far exceeded any earlier furor over forest reserves. Voices across the West complained that the federal government had finally gone too far and that this presidential power to lock up huge swaths of forests without any legislative approval was simply intolerable—one could almost hear echoes of the colonial loggers protesting the King's Broad Arrow policy. Sympathetic western congressmen rushed to appease their irate constituents. Their solution was to revoke Cleveland's actions through an amendment to the 1897 Sundry Civil Bill, an omnibus legislation that provided government funding for the upcoming year. The modified bill reached the president for signature the day that he was leaving office, and when he learned that his forest reserve proclamation had been undone, he threw the measure on the floor in disgust. According to Robert Underwood Johnson, who was involved with the reserves, the president declared, "I will veto the whole damned Sundry Civil Bill!" The fight over the nation's forests had, for the moment, paralyzed Washington.

Cleveland's pocket veto of the Sundry Civil Bill forced his successor, President William McKinley, to call an extra session of Congress on March 15, 1897. Those who supported the forest reserves used this window to lobby for alternative legislation. The situation seemed to favor the western-based opposition, but then the proponents of reserves scored a coup with the conversion of South Dakota senator Richard Pettigrew, a powerful member of the Public Lands Committee. He soon sponsored a new, compromise amendment allowing the Cleveland reserves (and any future reserves) to stand, but granting the secretary of the interior administration rights, including for the purpose of logging. This so-called Pettigrew Amendment, by opening the government forests to use, diffused the core of western opposition, and a new Sundry Civil Bill was signed into law in early June 1897.

While the more preservationist-minded members of the nation's forestry community were upset with the outcome, believing that it was a capitulation to the lumber industry, Pinchot was thrilled. The new legislation opened up a path for professional forestry to be practiced across tens of millions of acres, on a scale unknown anywhere in the world. He later commented, "Except for the Act of 1891, the Pettigrew Amendment . . . was and still is the most important Federal forest legislation ever enacted."

Nonetheless, many obstacles stood in the path to effective administration of the government's forests. The new administrative power rested with the Department of the Interior, a hotbed of cronyism and petty corruption. The government's purported experts on forestry, meanwhile, worked for the Division of Forestry, which was part of the Department of Agriculture. A bureaucratic wall effectively kept the division separated from the new timber reserves. And even if this hurdle could be overcome, the division was poorly equipped to provide assistance—it had placed little emphasis on forest management out of the conviction that professional forestry was impractical in the United States.

I N MID-1898, thirty-two-year-old Pinchot was offered the chance to run the Division of Forestry after Fernow, the former director, resigned to take over a new forestry school at Cornell. Upon learning that he'd been selected, Pinchot's first reaction was to refuse the job. His private-sector responsibilities kept him busy, and he remained skeptical of the division as ineffectual. However, as Pinchot later explained, "[E]verybody I consulted in Washington said I ought to pitch in and have a try at bringing the Government's forest work to life. So did my Father. . . . In a week I threw off my prejudice, came to my senses, and realized that here was the chance of a lifetime."

Pinchot's arrival as chief forester marked a new era for the fledgling division. The top priority was now the expansion of professional forestry in America, and Pinchot brought seemingly inexhaustible energy to the task. He began to spread the word that his division was prepared to offer free assistance to any timberland owners interested in applying the principles of practical forestry. Then, on October 15, barely three months after his arrival, the division issued Circular 21, a short pamphlet that publicized these free services. The effect was nearly immediate: Applications poured in, and soon Pinchot was using much of his meager twenty-nine-thousand-dollar budget and his small staff of ten to handle the Circular 21 program. Early beneficiaries included lumber baron

Frederick Weyerhaeuser, the Great Northern Paper Company, and the Northern Pacific Railroad.

As demand for forestry services grew, the dearth of qualified American foresters quickly became a problem. By 1900, Pinchot had grown his division from 10 to 123, but many of his employees lacked any meaningful forestry education. The nation's only training facilities at the turn of the century were Fernow's program at Cornell and one at Biltmore. Both of these, however, were struggling with administrative and financial difficulties that would soon prove their undoing. Pinchot appealed to his parents, proposing that they endow a new forestry school at his alma mater. Ever supportive, they agreed and provided an initial $150,000 endowment for the Yale School of Forestry, which opened in the fall of 1900 with an entering class of seven. That same year Pinchot also founded the Society of American Foresters, an organization designed to bolster his inchoate profession.

In hindsight, the first three years of Pinchot's reign at the division, though unprecedented in terms of impact, were merely a warm-up for what was to follow. His true political career did not begin until September 14, 1901. That day, President McKinley died as a result of a gunshot wound he suffered from an assassination attempt the week before. McKinley's replacement was his vice president, forty-two-year-old Theodore Roosevelt, an unflappable politician who had built his reputation with the "Rough Riders," a U.S. Cavalry regiment, during the Spanish-American War. Roosevelt quickly demonstrated that he was committed to reform and happy to use his office as a bully pulpit. Near the top of his agenda were the country's long-neglected natural resources, and the person he would rely on most to shape his policy was Pinchot.

The two men were already close friends at the time of McKinley's assassination. Roosevelt had first won Pinchot's affection in 1897 by sponsoring his election to the Boone and Crockett Club, an exclusive society of big-game hunters that Roosevelt cofounded. This was but one of the manly pursuits that united the two men, who both reveled in contests of strength and athletic prowess. Once, during a get-together in 1899, Roosevelt, who had recently been elected governor of New York, challenged Pinchot to a wrestling match. The stockily built politician won handily, but Pinchot exacted his revenge during a round of boxing that followed. He proudly noted, "I had the honor of knocking the future President of the United States off his very solid pins." Their friendship, however, was equally grounded in a shared sensibility about the proper role of government. Each felt that it was an engine of reform, a tool to curb the excesses of corporations and expand equality. And both were willing to stretch the limits of their mandate to garner results they felt achieved this. When Roosevelt ascended to the presidency, he informally elevated

Pinchot from a midlevel bureaucrat to one of his chief advisors, a member of his "Tennis Cabinet," the new center of power in Washington.

Pinchot's priorities became Roosevelt's priorities. And near the top of the list, at least initially, was the expansion of practical forestry. Pinchot considered this essentially a matter of principle, the only rational approach between the extremes of wanton forest destruction and strict preservation. And the surest way to achieve this was through transfer of the western forest reserves from the Department of the Interior to Pinchot's bureau (recently elevated from division status). Roosevelt, the forester's new champion, stressed these points in his first message to Congress, delivered in early December 1901. Like many of the president's future speeches, it bore Pinchot's fingerprints:

> Public opinion throughout the United States has moved steadily toward a just appreciation of the value of forests. . . . The great part played by them in the creation and maintenance of the national wealth is now more fully realized than ever before. Wise forest protection does not mean the withdrawal of forest resources . . . from contributing their full share to the welfare of the people, but, on the contrary, gives the assurance of larger and more certain supplies. The fundamental idea of forestry is the perpetuation of forests by use. Forest protection is not an end of itself; it is a means to increase and sustain the resources of our country and the industries which depend upon them. . . . [Usefulness of the forest reserves] should be increased by a thoroughly business-like management. . . . [Responsibility for the reserves] should be united in the Bureau of Forestry, to which they properly belong. The present diffusion of responsibility is bad from every standpoint.

Roosevelt's December message was but the opening salvo in a multiyear campaign that Pinchot spearheaded to elevate the status of practical forestry and gain control of the reserves. The chief forester turned his bureau into a propaganda machine, churning out endless reams of proforestry literature. This was necessary, since his plan was initially under attack from all sides: The Department of the Interior did not want to cede control; the lumber industry and countless western interests staunchly opposed any government actions that would bring tougher regulations; and the preservationist strain of the forest lobby, a group that included Sargent and Muir, worried that Pinchot's plan, intentionally or not, would undo the protectionist measures that they had fought so hard to enact. To make matters worse, many charged that Pinchot's aggressive lobbying was a misuse of government funds. The president, however, offered his full support, writing, "It is doubtful whether there has ever been elsewhere under the Government such effective publicity—publicity purely in the interest of the people—at so low a cost."

Pinchot's offensive culminated with the American Forest Congress, a five-day event held in Washington in early January 1905. Sponsored by the president, it brought together the leading voices from all sides of the forest debate, almost four hundred delegates in total. The agenda was broad, with more than fifty featured speakers, but for Pinchot and Roosevelt the primary objective was to build a final consensus about transferring the reserves.

The congress served as a showcase for the effectiveness of Pinchot's proforestry propaganda. Several years earlier it had been commonplace to dismiss the profession as impractical and misguided, a European concern with no place in tree-rich America. Now many industry leaders embraced it wholeheartedly, at least in public. N. W. McLeod, president of the National Lumber Manufacturers' Association, said during his address, "The Bureau has in a large measure succeeded in convincing the lumbermen that forestry is not antagonistic to the lumbermen's interest, but in line with it." Frederick Weyerhaeuser, who wasn't able to attend, conveyed a similar message through his son: "Mr. Weyerhaeuser wishes me to say that he sincerely regrets his inability to be here, and further to assure those present that he and his associates in the lumber business are thoroughly in sympathy with the work and plans of the Association and the Bureau of Forestry, and stand ready to do whatever is in their power to cooperate in them." Railroad magnate James Hill added his voice to the chorus: "Irrigation and forestry are the two subjects which are to have a greater effect on the future prosperity of the United States than any other public questions, either within or without Congress."

At the conclusion of the five days, the delegates passed a resolution calling for the transfer of the reserves. The legislature responded almost immediately, and Roosevelt signed the Transfer Act into law on February 1, 1905. The new legislation finally gave Pinchot control of the reserves, and in its wake came two important symbolic changes. First, the reserves were renamed as "national forests," something Pinchot felt cleared up any confusion over their purpose as a public resource to be used. Second, the Bureau of Forestry became the United States Forest Service, reflecting its new role as steward of these national forests.

Passage of the Transfer Act signaled a new era for America. Congress had given Pinchot a mandate to implement the ideas of practical forestry on a scale unknown anywhere in the world—by the time of the transfer, the reserves, which Roosevelt and Pinchot were constantly expanding, had reached 86 million acres, an area roughly the size of New York, New Jersey, and Pennsylvania combined. Pinchot explained:

For us in the Forest Service the transfer meant a revolutionary change. Before the Forest Reserves came into our hands, all
we could say to whoever controlled a forest, public or private,
was "Please." . . . After the transfer the situation was radically
changed. . . . We had the power, as we had the duty, to protect the
Reserves for the use of the people.

Shortly after gaining control, Pinchot set forth his philosophy on management in a letter to the secretary of agriculture. The centerpiece of this was a
modified version of a utilitarian maxim: Questions would "always be decided
from the standpoint of the greatest good of the greatest number in the long
run." Thus, the national forests would be fully open to meet the needs of the
people, with an eye to sustainability. The details of administration were soon
spelled out in a publication aptly dubbed the *Use Book,* which every forest
ranger carried with him. It assured, "Forest reserves are open to all persons
for all lawful purposes." The early administration efforts were thus a far cry
from the punctiliously curated forests in Nancy, France, but they did finally
put qualified public servants in charge of grazing rights, logging activities, fire
prevention, and a raft of other issues.

While Pinchot attempted to placate the westerners who used the national
forests, the constituency could not be appeased. The battle was more ideological than pragmatic, rooted in a fundamental difference over the meaning of
public land and the role of the government. One westerner wrote: "In a word,
the Federal Government must constitute itself a gigantic feudal landlord, ruling over unwilling tenants by the agency of irresponsible bureaus; traversing
every local right, meddling with every private enterprise." Another critic color-
fully added: "The poor sawmills! They have borne more abuse than the early
Christians." As the Forest Service expanded the scope of its programs and
Roosevelt continued to proclaim new national forests, these voices of opposition gained strength throughout the West. They finally won a victory in 1907,
when a caucus of western congressmen pushed through the legislation that
Pettigrew had foiled ten years earlier, terminating the president's right to create new national forests across most of the West.

Never one to be bullied, Roosevelt declared 16 million acres of new national
forests in the period before the law took effect. Known as the "midnight forests," these were the last pieces in an unprecedented six-year-long expansion
of federal authority to protect the nation's trees. Pinchot and Roosevelt, in
the final tally, had increased national forests almost fivefold, from just over 40
million acres to nearly 200 million. The president proudly noted in his autobiography that this represented a greater increase "than during all previous

and succeeding years put together"—this statement remains as true today as when it was first written in 1913. But more than simply expanding the network of national forests, they had finally provided a foundation for their effective administration, ensuring some degree of protection from the threats of an industrialized society.

The legacy of this early forestry movement, however, reached far beyond the nation's trees. From it grew the idea of "conservation," an overarching philosophy that all natural resources ought to be managed with an eye to sustainability and efficient use. Roosevelt, a major exponent of this new ethic, described it as "nothing more than the application to our other natural resources of the principles which had been worked out in connection with the forests." The goal of conservation was soon applied to everything from water and soil to minerals and coal. It became one of the pillars of Progressivism, the movement that brought sweeping reforms to many aspects of life in the early twentieth century. Pinchot, who was widely credited with first articulating conservation in 1907, was perhaps its greatest champion. He explained, "In its broad sense conservation applies to the handling of almost every human problem."

The potential scope of conservationist projects seemed to ensure Pinchot a bright future in the federal government, but in reality his days were numbered. The countdown clock began ticking when Roosevelt, his great advocate and defender, decided not to run for a third term and chose as his successor William Howard Taft, who handily won the election of 1908. The incoming president had shown little patience for Pinchot's tendency to operate with more authority than the post of chief forester technically allowed. Worse, Taft simply mistrusted him, once stating: "Pinchot is a socialist and a spiritualist, a strange combination and one that is capable of any extreme act."

Serious tensions between Taft and Pinchot first surfaced when the new president, shortly after taking office, selected Richard Ballinger as secretary of the interior. Pinchot, like many, felt that Ballinger was anticonservationist and viewed his appointment as a betrayal of Taft's promise to continue Roosevelt's policies. In July 1909, Pinchot's suspicions appeared confirmed when charges surfaced that Ballinger had used his office to obstruct a government investigation into the illegal selling of mining rights in Alaska. Taft, however, soon exonerated Ballinger of any wrongdoing. This only inflamed Pinchot, who suspected that the president had acted out of fealty to corporate interests and in opposition to conservation principles. The chief forester called for congressional hearings on the matter and publicly rebuked the president. This action proved his undoing. Taft fired Pinchot for insubordination, putting a swift and inglorious end to one of the most celebrated government careers of the early twentieth century.

The dismissal, however, had a silver lining for Pinchot. Details of the Ballinger-Pinchot Affair, as it became known, dominated national headlines for months and familiarized the populace with both conservation and Pinchot's impressive record at the Forest Service. Many came to view him as a martyr for the Progressive cause. Roosevelt was among this group; the Ballinger-Pinchot Affair precipitated Roosevelt's 1912 presidential campaign as a Bull Moose Progressive, which split the Republican Party and delivered the White House to the Democrats. Pinchot had lost control of his beloved Forest Service, but he'd become the nation's foremost voice for conservation.

Shortly after the Ballinger-Pinchot Affair subsided, Pinchot found himself embroiled in another major conservation fight. But this time the tables were turned. The enemy was not the resource exploiters, but the preservationists. The conflict had arisen when the city of San Francisco, seeking to increase its power supply, began lobbying Congress for the right to place a hydropower dam across the Tuolumne River, which flowed through the Hetch Hetchy Valley, the original centerpiece of the lobbying effort to create the Yosemite National Park.

The debate over Hetch Hetchy pitted Pinchot against his old friend and mentor John Muir, the very man who had helped to save the valley from destruction in 1890, now a white-bearded sage of seventy-five years. Both men's positions had hardened since the halcyon days they'd spent together in the summer of 1896. While Pinchot was sympathetic to the valley's sacrosanct status, he believed that the principles of conservation required the building of a dam that would provide cheap power to such a large population. Muir found this argument unconvincing: "Dam Hetch Hetchy! As well dam for water-tanks the people's cathedrals and churches, for no holier temple has ever been consecrated by the heart of man." The controversy raged for months, but ultimately Pinchot triumphed. Muir's beloved valley was soon buried beneath the retaining reservoir of the O'Shaughnessy Dam. But as with the Ballinger-Pinchot Affair, there was a consolation for the losing side: The preservationists' furor was an impetus for the creation in 1916 of the National Park Service.

While the Hetch Hetchy affair was the last great episode of Muir's life, it was far from the end for Pinchot. He remained involved in the cause of forestry, serving as something of an éminence grise to the next generation of foresters. He finally married in 1914 at the age of forty-nine and fathered a son the following year. And while he never returned to federal office—despite several attempts, including an abortive presidential run—he remained in politics, serving twice as governor of Pennsylvania and jumping to the forefront of countless conservationist causes. He died at age eighty-one of leukemia on October 4, 1946.

Notwithstanding the continuous years of public service, Pinchot's greatest contributions to his country were the changes he brought to forestry and the resulting changes in conservation policy. He had overseen the transition from proto-forestry to actual forestry, the creation of the great majority of the national forests, and the beginnings of the regulatory state. He had abandoned an easy life of material wealth for an endless series of political battles. Perhaps Roosevelt summed up his contributions best:

> Gifford Pinchot is the man to whom the nation owes most for what has been accomplished as regards the preservation of the natural resources of our country. He led, and indeed during its most vital period embodied, the fight for the preservation through use of our forests. . . . I believe it is but just to say that among the many, many public officials who under my administration rendered literally invaluable service to the people of the United States, he, on the whole, stood first.

WHILE PINCHOT DESERVEDLY stood first with Roosevelt, he was but one of the main players, along with Morton, Muir, Sargent, and numerous others, in the nation's dramatic reorientation of its relationship to trees around the turn of the century. Thanks to their collective efforts, the forty-year period starting around 1870 hosted a wave of innovative programs and policies unthinkable when Marsh published *Man and Nature* in 1864. Trees were no longer an enemy to be chopped down or an infinite resource to be exploited without consequence. They were the protectors of watersheds, the stock for a dwindling timber supply, the promise for future generations, the site of God's first temples.

Of course, this new consciousness butted up against the reality that trees remained central to the economic life of America. And the early twentieth century would witness the emergence of new tree-based industries and the expansion of established ones.

# 6

# New Frontiers

Wild Orange Tree

## Orange Empires

As Christmas approached in 1894, Henry Flagler, the preeminent developer and promoter of eastern Florida, sat in his St. Augustine home, shivering, praying that the temperature fell no further. But the mercury plunged mercilessly lower, flirting with the freezing point, and it finally dipped below thirty-two degrees on December 24. In most parts of temperate North America this news might not have meant catastrophe, but Florida was different. It possessed a semitropical climate, one especially friendly to oranges, a fruit of tropical origin that grew on trees highly susceptible to frost. The impending freeze meant the likely ruin of countless thousands of these trees, a devastating blow to the state's economy. James Ingraham, Flagler's business associate and confidant, explained: "As the orange industry was the principal [one] at that time in Florida, it seemed as if this freeze was a fatal thing and could not be overcome, and in almost every family dependent upon the orange industry it seemed as if death and disaster were in their daily lives."

Flagler was one of the few Floridians not directly reliant on the actual selling of oranges. He had amassed a fortune as a young man through Standard Oil, the company he cofounded with John D. Rockefeller. (When asked if he'd originated the plan for what became the largest company in America, Rockefeller supposedly replied, "No, sir. I wish I'd had the brains to think of it. It was Henry M. Flagler.") Flagler's interest in Florida began in the 1870s, when he first visited the state hoping that the salubrious climate might restore his ailing wife. The warm temperatures failed to save her, but they nonetheless appealed greatly to Flagler. By the mid-1880s he had removed himself from the day-to-day operations of Standard Oil and relocated permanently to St. Augustine, the oldest continuously occupied city in America, founded in 1565 by a Spanish explorer and located on the state's northeastern coast.

In spite of St. Augustine's rich history, Florida—especially its southern and eastern portions—remained one of the last frontiers in continental America, certainly among the eastern states. The civilization that had denuded much of the East Coast and the interior forests had made little impact here. William Cullen Bryant visited the state in 1873 and wrote: "East Florida still remains, for the most part, a forest." He considered outposts like St. Augustine "merely stations in the great forest, which, . . . where it is not swamp, is a sandy plain covered with the trees of the long-leaved pine."

Americans had only begun to encroach on this expansive forest in significant numbers during the decades following the Civil War. Unlike earlier pursuers of the frontier, these settlers were often not seeking cheap lands, but solace and health. Their ranks included many well-to-do and notable Americans, including Harriet Beecher Stowe, whose antislavery novel *Uncle Tom's Cabin* was perhaps the most influential book of the nineteenth century. For these northern transplants, orange groves—signifiers of both cultivation and tropicality—were a defining criterion. Bryant observed, "On the more fertile of [the marshy] spots grow lofty live oaks and magnolias, and here the settler makes his openings, and builds his dwelling, and plants his orchard of orange trees." Nearly all of this preliminary settlement activity and orange tree planting occurred in the northern part of the state. The numbers dwindled dramatically as one headed south, due largely to an almost complete lack of infrastructure.

When Flagler relocated to St. Augustine in the 1880s, he did not approach the state as a typical pioneer agriculturist. Rather, he wanted to exploit Florida's potential as a new hub of eastern tourism, and thus began building hotels in places like Jacksonville and St. Augustine. His investment portfolio quickly expanded to include local railroads, the main mechanism for bringing in tourists. Eventually, he gained outright control over the Florida East Coast

Railway, giving him a monopoly on regional rail construction, the key to commercial development.

By the time of the first great freeze in 1894, Flagler's train network extended as far as Palm Beach, making it the state's de facto terminus. Here he built one of his most impressive projects, the Royal Poinciana, a five-hundred-room hotel modeled on the popular retreats of the Catskills. The attractions of Palm Beach were not merely the climate or Flagler's hotel, but the distinctive trees for which the town was named. They conveyed splendor, exoticism, and the feel of the tropics—variations of palm trees would become a staple plant in almost all of the nation's warmer climes. (Palm Beach's landmark trees were not in fact native but had appeared somewhat serendipitously: Twenty years earlier, a Spanish vessel had foundered offshore and local salvagers had raided its cargo of coconuts and planted them across the barrier island that is present-day Palm Beach.) The palm was only one of the plants used to reinforce the area's tropical feel. Others included agaves, bananas, cacti, poincianas, and, of course, the ubiquitous orange tree.

While Palm Beach was almost 250 miles south of St. Augustine, this distance was not great enough to spare it from the devastating Christmas freeze of 1894. Even here, the temperature dropped far below thirty-two degrees several times that winter. It seemed, for the moment, that no orange tree in the state was safe. Thousands of disappointed settlers began returning north. The situation greatly distressed Flagler, not only because of the money he would lose but because he felt a paternal affection for the state and its inhabitants— at one point, he turned to his associate Ingraham and ordered: "You can use $50,000, or $100,000, or $200,000. I would rather lose it all, and more, than that one man, woman, or child should starve."

In the midst of this crisis, Flagler received a most welcome package, a bundle containing healthy orange blossoms. They had come from lands farther south, where the state was still almost wholly undeveloped. In the most commonly accepted version of the story, the package came from Julia Tuttle, a northern transplant who owned massive holdings in the area of present-day Miami. She had been pressuring Flagler for years to extend his railroad, but he had rebuffed all such entreaties. The reason she was now sending this package, according to her daughter-in-law, was "to prove [Tuttle's] point that the disaster had not touched Miami." Along with the orange blossoms, Tuttle gave Flagler an assurance: If he delivered her a train, he could have a portion of her land holdings.

Tuttle's surprise package proved even more persuasive to the state's great developer than she could have hoped. Upon receiving the blossoms, Flagler turned to his agent Ingraham and asked, "How soon can you arrange for me to go to Miami?" Plans to extend his rail line the seventy miles from Palm

Beach to Miami commenced almost immediately. By April 1896, barely fifteen months later, the final tracks were being laid to connect Tuttle's small, isolated outpost with the rest of the nation. That July, 502 voters incorporated the city—the local council pressed to name it "Flagler," but the target of this honor urged them to keep the original Indian name—and Miami was born.

Bolstered by the orange industry and tourism, the new city grew rapidly. Ingraham recalled, "There were hundreds of people who had come into this territory to engage in trucking, vegetable gardening, putting out nurseries of young trees, who had been brought in by the railroad and encouraged to settle this community." Flagler constructed new hotels and hired laborers to improve the overall infrastructure. By the time the great developer died in 1913, the young city's population had swelled to nearly twenty thousand. It eventually became the nation's sixth-largest metropolis, after New York, Los Angeles, Chicago, Dallas, and Philadelphia.

The orange tree was, in many respects, the key component in the founding and early growth of this vibrant American city as well as all of Florida. But the story of Flagler, Tuttle, and the great freeze was merely a small chapter in a larger tale, one that was unfolding three thousand miles away in the foothills of Southern California.

L IKE THE APPLE, the orange had a long history before it arrived in the New World. It was initially cultivated several thousand years ago as a hybrid of two citrus varieties thought to have originated in the Malay–East Indian Archipelago. References to the fruit first appeared in the second book of the Five Classics, a Chinese work from roughly 500 BCE. The orange reached the Western Hemisphere in 1493 as part of Columbus's second voyage and then spread throughout the Americas in parallel with the growth of the Spanish Empire.

When Franciscan missionaries first reached present-day California in the mid-eighteenth century, they brought orange trees with them. It was common for each mission to feature a few of the trees with their fragrant white blossoms and dark green leaves. In 1804, the padres of the San Gabriel Mission outside the pueblo of Los Angeles planted four hundred seedlings in a six-acre grove, the largest in the region to that point.

The first person to appreciate the fruit's commercial potential in Southern California was William Wolfskill, a trapper from Boonesborough, Kentucky, who emigrated to Los Angeles in 1831. Ten years after his arrival, he planted a two-acre orchard within the tiny city's confines. An 1858 report from the

California State Agricultural Society sang the praises of Wolfskill's produce: "The oranges . . . were of superior size and excellence, showing conclusively that these tropical fruits can be raised in Southern California perfection."

While Wolfskill had confirmed the region's potential for commercially grown citrus, seemingly countless obstacles stood in the way of significant production. For starters, much of the Southern California land with the best soil and temperature for growing—the foothills of the San Gabriel and San Bernardino Mountains, for example—was arid and thus inhospitable to the water-loving trees. Even if the land were irrigated, no transport network existed to ship the products to the lucrative markets back East. And in addition to these logistical quandaries was the problem that no demand yet existed. Most Americans in the northeastern population centers had never actually seen the fruit and knew little about the trees it grew on.

Despite these challenges, some intrepid Americans, hearing tales of Southern California's agricultural potential, began to stake out towns along a fifty-mile-long stretch of land that began at Los Angeles and extended eastward. This region would soon be known across the state and the nation as the Citrus Belt.

No town within this zone embodied the burgeoning citrus culture better than Riverside, located near the Santa Ana River. It had begun in 1870 with an appeal from Judge J. W. North, a man whose advocacy of racial equality had made him a pariah in his hometown of Knoxville, Tennessee. His initial announcement declared, with great optimism: "We wish to form a colony of intelligent, industrious and enterprising people, so that each one's industry will help to promote his neighbor's interests." Twenty-five like-minded middle-class families from the East—few of whom had any agricultural experience—signed on as members of what became the Southern California Colony Association. The group purchased the Riverside site in 1871 for $3.50 an acre; nearly everyone set out a grove of orange seedlings.

In addition to planting trees, the early Riverside settlers devoted their capital, skill, and labor to improving the surrounding infrastructure, particularly the irrigation. In 1881, two men constructed a series of concrete pipes to channel water from streams in the nearby San Gabriel Mountains toward the town. Several years later another colonist financed a $175,000 canal to siphon part of the Santa Ana River and irrigate four thousand acres in the region. A contemporary account marveled, "Its course is eleven miles long, and runs around the edge of a mountain, across high aqueducts, and through sixteen tunnels, one of which is seven hundred feet in length." This project, the largest waterwork of its time, paved the way for the countless irrigation ventures that soon helped establish the citrus industry.

Initially, Riverside families experimented with a wide variety of orange trees, as it was commonplace to propagate different seeds and hope for the best. But this practice was about to change—forever reshaping the citrus industry— thanks to the actions of one of Riverside's founding families (as well as a fair bit of chance).

Luther and Eliza Tibbets were an odd couple: fiercely progressive, intolerably quarrelsome, and intensely devoted to spiritualism, a belief in supernatural communication popular at the turn of the century (no less than Gifford Pinchot was an adherent). Before settling in Riverside, the Tibbetses had lived in Washington, D.C., next door to William Saunders, the superintendent of gardens and grounds for the U.S. Department of Agriculture (USDA). Saunders, who was also in charge of plant importation for the fledgling USDA, had recently acquired a dozen orange cuttings from a consul stationed in Bahia, Brazil. They were unique in having come from a mutated tree that produced seedless oranges; moreover, each fruit contained an embryonic orange within, giving it the appearance of possessing a navel. Eliza Tibbets likely knew nothing about these novel navels, but she was aware that Saunders was a horticulturist and wrote asking for any samples. Saunders explained, "[She] was anxious to get some of these plants for her place, and I sent . . . them by mail."

The Tibbetses lacked irrigation (a by-product of one of Luther's countless petty squabbles), and Eliza, according to legend, resorted to using dirty dishwater to nurture the newly received cuttings. Unsurprisingly, not all the Brazilian samples survived, but two managed to thrive and produced fruit after several seasons. In the winter of 1878–79, Mrs. Tibbets submitted several of her oranges, which she called Washington Navels, to the annual Riverside Citrus Fair. They immediately caused a sensation. One of the first men to taste them said, "We . . . sampled the fruit, and wondered how it could be. Larger and juicier and more pungent fruit we had never known."

The new variety quickly became the standard bearer for California citrus, accounting for more than 50 percent of the marketplace. Less than a decade after they first appeared, one grower was already able to assert, "The Washington Navel stands to-day the peer of any orange known in the market, and is really the autocrat of the price list." More than one million Washington Navel orange trees were planted across the Citrus Belt during the 1880s, all grafted from the two Tibbets trees. Following the Washington Navel in popularity was the Valencia, a variety the Wolfskill family likely brought to Los Angeles in 1876. Together these two types accounted for nearly all of Southern California's oranges moving forward, and since the Navel ripened in winter and the Valencia in the summer, the region suddenly had a crop that could be available all year round. But the question remained: How would the product reach the East?

The original transcontinental railroad of 1869 ran only to Northern California, leaving the southern half of the state with no easy way to move freight to eastern markets. But this problem was about to be remedied, almost in parallel with the rise of the orange industry. An extension of the Central Pacific first reached Los Angeles in 1876; five years later, a second transcontinental railroad, the Southern Pacific (SP), provided Southern California with a direct line to New Orleans; and in 1885 the Atchison, Topeka, and Santa Fe line arrived to give the SP competition for eastern commerce. The Wolfskill family held the honor of sending the first full carload of oranges east, a monthlong journey to St. Louis in 1876. A decade later the first special train packed exclusively with oranges departed River Station in Los Angeles.

The railroads, especially the SP, promoted the nascent orange industry out of self-interest. They were able to fill westbound trains with tourists and eager settlers looking to exploit one-way teaser transport rates, but they needed freight to help make the return trips profitable. Oranges, of course, were not the only possible crop, but they represented a high-growth industry at the same time that wheat, one of the biggest Southern California agricultural products from the 1860s to 1880s, was entering a pricing freefall.

SP's desire to build up the California market was so strong that it almost single-handedly sponsored the state's exhibit at the New Orleans World's Fair in the winters of 1884–85 and 1885–86. The display included a three-acre outdoor "California Park" replete with transplanted flowers, shrubs, and fruit-bearing trees, especially oranges. It was at this World's Fair that fruits from Southern California swept the overall gold medal for oranges, defeating the heavily favored products from Florida. According to E. J. Wickson, author of one of the most influential late-nineteenth-century books on California fruits, "The premiums won by California oranges at the New Orleans World's Fair gave us a name [in] the East." Demand for the fruit skyrocketed, launching a new California "gold rush" in the late 1880s—*Sunset,* the official publication of the SP, quipped: "Los Angeles and the southern part of the Golden State had no yellow metal, but around 1885 some eastern prospectors discovered an inexhaustible supply of twenty-two karat climate."

With rapid growth, however, came new challenges. Settlers now scrambled to grab any land that they could find. Prices for orchards shot up, sometimes fivefold in a single year. The clamoring for oranges grew so intense that, according to Wickson, "With all the trees to be had in Southern California nurseries, and all that were brought from Florida, the demand for planting in the spring of 1888 could not be supplied." The established parts of the citrus industry had other problems on their hands. A pest, known as the cottony cushion scale, began to wreak havoc among the fruits. And the monthlong journey to eastern markets often turned healthy fruit into spoiled mush.

But as the decade progressed the industry learned to handle these manifold issues. Increased irrigation efforts opened up more lands to settlers. The growers combated the cottony cushion scale by importing Australian ladybird beetles, the pest's natural predator. And the railroads worked steadfastly to address the spoilage problem, developing increasingly elaborate refrigeration systems.

By the early 1890s, the glory days of orange trees had arrived in Southern California. As one grower observed, "The cultivation of the orange in favorable localities, is probably the most profitable business to which an acre of ground can be devoted for horticultural and agricultural purposes." Riverside was per capita the richest town in the nation by 1895—one of the original Tibbets trees, the source of these riches, was triumphantly transplanted to a prominent location in 1903 during a ceremony that featured President Roosevelt. Pasadena, another town in the heart of the Citrus Belt, boasted a Millionaires' Row. Residents of these Citrus Belt towns used their wealth to transform their environments into veritable earthly paradises. Not only were their orange orchards immaculately tended, but their properties were lavishly landscaped with ornamental trees, rare flowers, and semitropical plants. To many, California was a new Garden of Eden, with unlimited horticultural potential.

The citrus industry began enthusiastically exporting this sensibility to the populations back East. At the 1893 World's Columbia Exhibition at Chicago, for instance, the California exhibit included a globe and Liberty Bell constructed from sixty-five hundred fresh oranges. And during that fair's California Day, some 230,000 attendees received an orange. Even the industry's packaging was used as a vessel for these Edenic values: the orange crate, originally a nondescript, utilitarian box for protecting fruit during transport, began to feature colorful labels during the 1890s; soon these evolved into fantastic depictions of idealized California scenery. Some labels portrayed groves of orange trees basking on a sun-soaked plain, with snow-covered mountain peaks in the background. Others employed images from Yosemite, like Half Dome or El Capitan. Almost all used a distinctive color palette of pastels. Kevin Starr, a historian of California, explained that the message these labels conveyed "was largely believed in by an entire generation of Americans." The orange, in many respects, was more than a refreshing snack, it embodied ideas of fecundity and earthly perfection.

The view from inside the California horticultural industry, however, was not quite so idyllic. From the outset, the production of oranges (like nearly all of the state's fruits and vegetables) and the planting and cultivation of the trees they grew on required massive infusions of inexpensive labor. Carey McWilliams, author of *Factories in the Field,* an influential 1939 polemic against conditions in the fruit industry written in the wake of John Steinbeck's seminal novel *The Grapes of Wrath,* provided the following explanation:

> If specialized farming [i.e., fruit growing] was to compete with mechanized and extensive farming [i.e., wheat growing], the latter of which could cheapen production by the application of machinery, then specialized farming, which had to rely on labor to so much greater an extent, could do so only by cheapening the labor which it required in its own field.

Initially, the orange industry depended on Chinese labor, but over the years it exploited numerous groups, including Japanese, Filipinos, native Californians, and Mexicans, who became the dominant force in the labor supply after about 1914. The orange tree thus helped create the so-called farm labor problem that still endures in California.

This exploitive treatment of immigrants was an issue that nearly all early commentators overlooked in evaluating the industry. By most accounts, orange growers were among the most enlightened and forward-thinking group of men. J. Eliot Coit, who wrote about the citrus industry in 1915, observed: "California citrus culture, among all horticultural industries, is peculiar in that the people who have built it up have been, in many cases, retired business men or professional men from the New England and Central states. . . . Citrus culture appeals to people of intelligence and refinement." The growers were considered responsible stewards of the land, who invested in their local communities and treated one another with a spirit of cooperation. At the same time, they were comfortable with the mechanics of late-nineteenth-century corporate industrial capitalism—in this respect they differed from farmers in the South and Midwest, many of whom had endorsed a form of populism that was hostile toward railroads, banks, and economic elites.

Beginning in the 1890s, orange growers began to form cooperative associations to better spread risk and to coordinate the marketing and selling of their product. The first, not surprisingly, appeared in Riverside, the Pachappa Orange Growers' Association, created in 1892. Three years later, roughly one-third of the region's growers joined together to form the Southern California Fruit Exchange. This organization flourished for a decade until it was reorganized in 1905 as the California Fruit Growers' Exchange (the Exchange), a name that quickly became synonymous with the state's oranges.

The Exchange, which controlled about 40 percent of the state's citrus at the time of its founding, developed into the nation's most sophisticated agricultural entity. Though it had been organized to coordinate fruit sales, it exceeded this mandate almost immediately in the pursuit of corporate capitalism. It sought to eliminate waste, improve efficiency, boost the size of operations, and apply scientific techniques to growing, managing, and marketing. Any problem that affected the industry seemed to fall within its ambit. In 1907, for instance, it created the Fruit Growers Supply Company to provide materials at cost to the fruit packers, who went through 40 million board feet of wood per year making crates. Eventually, the Exchange simply purchased forestland in Northern California to ensure the delivery of its timber.

Improved production mechanisms generated a new problem for the Exchange: Supply began to outstrip demand. For the older generation of growers this came as something of a shock. The common attitude in the late nineteenth century, according to one prominent orangeman, was that "the demand for choice fruit at high prices will always remain in advance of the supply."

While the efficiencies of corporate capitalism had produced the crisis, these same economic forces offered a solution: mass-market advertising, a new industry that was blossoming around the turn of the century. Advertising theory argued that oversupplies were not due to overproduction but to underconsumption. All that the growers needed to do was inflate demand for their product through publicity. Traditionally, agriculturists had opposed any form of advertising as a waste of money, feeling that the value in their goods resulted from labor inputs, but the orange growers were more willing to experiment.

In 1907, the Exchange commissioned Lord & Thomas, one of the nation's most prominent advertising firms, to coordinate a publicity campaign. It would be the first time that perishable fruits were advertised and, according to some, the first consumer-product saturation marketing effort in history. The Lord & Thomas proposal called for a special Orange Train that would travel through Iowa, chosen as a test state, and champion the slogan "Oranges for Health—California for Wealth." The intent was to persuade consumers that the fruit was not merely an exotic luxury good for special occasions, but an essential part of the diet that ought to be consumed daily.

This initial campaign appeared a success, and the following year Lord & Thomas coined a new name that would transform the Exchange into one of the world's most famous brands: Sunkist. In the wake of this development, as the Exchange increased its advertising budget dramatically, the Sunkist name began appearing everywhere. Lord & Thomas took out full-page ads in mass-circulating periodicals like *Ladies' Home Journal* and *Good Housekeeping*. A Sunkist billboard would eventually appear in New York's Times Square, where countless thousands of people saw it each day. Another massive sign would be placed at Coney Island with "Sunkist" spelled in giant, neon-orange letters that glowed day and night. Soon every American knew that Sunkist meant delicious California oranges. The head of advertising for the Exchange wrote in 1917: "Sunkist has been advertised for eight years and the popularity of the fruit bearing this label is too generally recognized to need discussion. That one word 'Sunkist' is a business asset worth millions of dollars to the Exchange shippers."

As successful as the saturation advertising campaigns had been, there was still much more revenue for the Exchange to extract from its oranges and trees. Sometime after 1910, the cooperative began to experiment with the idea of marketing oranges not only as food but also as juice. This innovation was almost wholly uncharted territory, and the corporate citrus apparatus would need to direct all the tools it had mastered in selling its fruit to the new endeavor. The Exchange began by developing electronic juice extractors. It then started to distribute the machines at cost to soda fountain operators. Finally, in 1916, it launched a massive new advertising campaign: "Drink an Orange." The concept was nothing short of revolutionary. *Simmons' Spice Mill,* a trade journal for the tea and coffee industries, ran a piece in January 1916 that summed up popular sentiment. The title read "Drink an Orange!" and the opening line simply read "What?" The Exchange's relentless campaign ensured that this question soon had an answer. "If the liver is sluggish or you feel 'out of tune,' drink an orange or two daily," advised an ad in *Good Housekeeping.* "Try it for ten days, for better digestion. The results are almost certain if the practice is made a habit."

Sales of orange juice shot up in the years after World War I. The worldwide epidemic of influenza in 1918 that killed 675,000 Americans had made many people more health conscious. Consumers thus bought into the Sunkist rhetoric that orange juice promoted good health. This belief became sacrosanct in the 1920s, following the discovery of vitamin C. Sales of orange juice also grew thanks to Prohibition, which started in 1920 and opened the door for the success of nonalcoholic beverages. Within barely a decade, fresh-squeezed orange juice went from literally unheard of to the second-best-selling drink at cafés and soda fountains, trailing only Coca-Cola. More than seven million boxes of Sunkist oranges, one in every five, were consumed as juice during the mid-1930s.

The remarkable growth of the orange market and its trees in the early twentieth century suggested that the industry would forever reign as the king of Southern California. But soon the region's iconic orange groves would be little more than a memory. The Great Depression collapsed demand for oranges like everything else, and some growers were forced to sell their cherished lands to investors at absurd discounts. Additionally, the city of Los Angeles was growing exponentially, buoyed by both the entertainment industry and, after World War II, defense contractors. The push for real estate began to crowd out the orange trees. By 1970, citrus acreage in Southern California had decreased over 96 percent, replaced with tract houses and exurbs. Riverside lost most of its legendary groves, the legacy of its golden era a small park that still contains one of Eliza Tibbets's original navel orange trees.

The growers who once populated Riverside, Pasadena, and dozens of other towns across the Citrus Belt eventually turned their attention to the state's Central Valley, a region more than four hundred miles long between the coastal range and the Sierras. It had formerly been too arid to support citriculture, but the Central Valley Project, one of the most ambitious programs in President Franklin Delano Roosevelt's New Deal, had developed irrigation across much of this land.

As for America's love affair with the orange, it hasn't disappeared entirely, but much of the juice has been squeezed out. When John McPhee, the Pulitzer Prize–winning author, wrote his book *Oranges* in 1967, he lamented: "People in the United States used to consume more fresh oranges than all other fresh fruits combined, but in less than twenty years the per-capita consumption has gone down seventy-five per cent, as appearances of actual oranges in most of the United States have become steadily less frequent." Long gone are the days when the embodiment of the American Dream was to own a grove of orange trees near Los Angeles, and every piece of fruit offered a little taste of that aspiration.

## The Big Mill at Bogalusa

THE SOUTHERN CALIFORNIA citrus industry had arisen in response to new social, economic, and cultural forces converging around the turn of the century. These same forces were also radically reshaping established tree-related industries, including one of the nation's oldest: logging.

When Charles Sprague Sargent released his hugely influential *Report on the Forests of North America* in 1884, he not only catalogued the nation's tree resources, but speculated on the future of their commercial exploitation. In his view, the unprecedented efficiency of lumber barons like Weyerhaeuser and Stephenson ensured the "extinction of the forests of the lake region," and this meant the inevitable end of its dominance as a timber zone. He then offered a prediction about the industry's future that would have surprised all but the most knowledgeable lumbermen:

> The country between the Mississippi river and the Rocky mountains, now largely supplied with lumber from Michigan, Wisconsin, and Minnesota, must for building material soon depend upon the more remote pine forests of the Gulf region. . . . [T]he pine of Mississippi, Louisiana, and Arkansas will reach Kansas, Nebraska, and the whole country now tributary to Chicago. Western Texas and northern Mexico will be supplied by rail with the pine of eastern Texas.

The South, the Deep South in particular, contained an enormous, nearly untapped forest whose commercial potential dwarfed that of New England or the Lake States. This was not the interior hardwood forest that Daniel Boone had famously tackled, but instead a gigantic maritime pine belt, varying between one hundred and two hundred miles in width, that blanketed the southeastern and Gulf coastlines. It began near the lower boundary of Virginia, stretched down the southern states of the Atlantic coast, enveloped part of the Florida peninsula, and then broadened to cover much of Alabama, Mississippi, Louisiana, southern Arkansas, and eastern Texas. Sargent's *Report* estimated that this region, some 250 million acres in total, contained 237 billion board feet of pine timber, three times the quantity in the Lake States—eastern Texas alone nearly equaled the combined wealth of Michigan, Minnesota, and Wisconsin, a supply that some thought "will last 250 years."

If this massive forest had a monarch, it was the longleaf pine. These trees were a regal sight, often dominating their landscape. One southern writer explained, "The stately trunks rise forty to sixty feet and then spread out their dense foliage, which joins above like the arches of a cathedral. There is little or no undergrowth, and the view fades into a maze of the column-like tree trunks." These longleafs were not only abundant, but the most commercially promising of the area's pines, a group that also included the loblobby, shortleaf, and slash varieties. Longleaf lumber was straight-grained and sturdy, relatively free of defects, and durable when facing the elements, overall an ideal structural timber. As one government report noted in 1884, "It is to the extreme South what the white pine is to the extreme North."

Nonetheless, lumbermen who had been raised singing the praises of white pine were slow to embrace its southern cousin, for reasons based mostly in tradition. Only as the commercial white pines grew scarce did attitudes begin to soften. By 1887, an influential tome on the South could assure, "Southern pine is rapidly winning its way into popular favor in nearly all parts of the United States and also in foreign countries."

The long-standing discrimination against longleafs was only one of the reasons that the southern pine forests had survived the nation's first century largely intact. Much of the responsibility rested with the region's overall lack of economic development, attributable in large part to a system built around cotton and slave labor. When the Civil War arrived, it devastated the area's economy, setting back any incipient industries that might have increased lumber use. The radical Reconstruction era that followed did little to facilitate new economic growth. There were local lumbering activities and a thriving turpentine business, but neither of these affected the forests quite like industrialized logging. Other factors contributed to forest preservation as well. Pines tended to grow on gravelly, relatively infertile soil, which was unproductive even when cleared, meaning that few chopped down the forests for agricultural reasons. The South's warmer climate also meant that settlers felled fewer trees as a source of fuel for domestic heating. Finally, there was the transportation problem: Most of the area's rivers flowed south, away from the main eastern markets, and the nation's train network had been slow to develop in an area of low growth and little industry.

Change within the pine forests arrived in the form of northern capital. Beginning in 1876, largely at the behest of southern politicians desperate for economic growth, federal and state timberlands across much of the South were made available at rates bordering on the absurd, pennies an acre for pristine pinelands as well as for swamps rich with ancient bald cypresses, another valuable timber species. These land sales formed part of a larger strategy among some southerners, known as the "New South" movement, to reconstruct the regional economy with industry instead of agriculture. Northern speculators moved cautiously at first, but as the train network expanded and after Sargent's 1884 *Report* raised the region's profile, lumbermen rushed to take advantage of the situation. From there, things quickly got out of hand. Tens of millions of acres fell into the hands of northern capitalists, especially the lumber barons from the Lake States—they accounted for 69 percent of purchases for lots five thousand acres or greater. By the mid-1880s, a government report warned: "English and Northern capitalists are fast purchasing our magnificent pine forests. The avarice of capitalists, and the great number of saw-mill men, if not in some way checked, will ere long destroy the grand pine forests of this section." Southern politicians moved to stem the tide during the late 1880s, but it was already too late. The South had lost control of its forests, perhaps the region's greatest natural resource.

The new industry that arose in the wake of this land grab differed greatly from what had preceded it in the North. Rivers and lakes gave way to railroads as the primary mode of transporting both felled trees to the mills and processed lumber to the population centers. The absence of serious winters transformed logging from a seasonal occupation into a perpetual one. Mills also grew in size and sophistication. Finally, the laborers were no longer the descendents of New England loggers or immigrants from Northern Europe. Southern loggers comprised a mix of poor white farmers in need of higher-paying work and freed slaves who typically came to the forests from a life of sharecropping.

Together, these factors combined to produce a new dynamic: the industrial company town, an efficient and often ruthless form of production that became commonplace in many extractive industries during the late nineteenth and early twentieth centuries. There were hundreds of these towns spread across the South's pine belt. They sprang up overnight, exhausted the surrounding longleaf pines over the course of ten or twenty years, and then disappeared, their names often lost to history.

Of course, not all the towns were forgotten. Some were simply too ambitious to fade away entirely. Such was the case with a lumber town that suddenly appeared in 1906 at the eastern edge of Louisiana. Rumors quickly spread that it contained the largest mill ever constructed, a sight that needed to be seen to be believed. Its name would soon be known wherever southern pine trees grew.

O N   A N   E A R L Y September morning in 1905, a small band of men on horseback departed Mandeville, Louisiana, a town thirty miles from New Orleans on the upper bank of Lake Pontchartrain. They headed northeast, into the state's vast eastern pine forest. This was land that had originally belonged to the Choctaw Indians, before they were relocated to Oklahoma. Now it was simply the backwoods, a region sparsely populated and barely integrated into any trading networks. The group's ride across this undeveloped land lasted for the better part of the day, through bald cypress swamps and endless stretches of longleaf pines. Eventually the men arrived at a spot near the Pearl River along a creek that the Choctaws had named Bogue Lusa, meaning "dark waters." Here they dismounted and set up tents for the night.

The leaders of this scouting party were Charles and Frank Goodyear, two middle-aged brothers. They hailed from Buffalo, New York, and moved in that city's highest social circles. Charles had begun his career as a lawyer at the same firm where Grover Cleveland, the future president, was a senior partner—Cleveland once described Charles as "one of my best and most intimate friends." Frank's social circle included men whose names are now most often seen on buildings, museums, and colleges: Pierpont Morgan, W. K. Vanderbilt, James J. Hill. But unlike these magnates of banking and railroads, the Goodyears had built their fortune in lumbering. They controlled a small empire of fifteen sawmills that spread across New York and northwestern Pennsylvania.

Their specialty was hemlock, a species bountiful throughout the region—its tannin-rich bark was coveted by the leather industry and its timber became increasingly valuable as white pine supplies shrank.

When the commercial hemlock stands themselves began to dwindle toward the turn of the century, the brothers started to look for new investment opportunities. The talk among many northern capitalists at that time was of the southern pine bonanza, and while much of the best lands had already been purchased and some restrictive legislation had been instituted, millions of acres remained. The Goodyears decided that this offered the best possible return on their capital, especially if they could use their extensive contacts to arrange for a new railroad into the region. In January 1902, they chartered a new enterprise, the Great Southern Lumber Company, and soon thereafter hired as their agent James Lacey, the most famous timber surveyor of the time. He subsequently engineered land purchases in eastern Louisiana and southern Mississippi worth $1,250,000.

The trip to the Bogue Lusa Creek in September 1905 was the final step in the formation of the Great Southern Lumber Company: the selection of a site for the construction of their new mill town. The brothers had initially considered locating their operations in Mississippi, but that state had passed a law limiting real property holdings to $1 million, a pittance compared to the $15 million they intended to invest. This colossal sum dwarfed most of the fly-by-night operations, and the proposed town was correspondingly ambitious. According to a Goodyear family history, when Louisiana locals pressed the scouting party about just what they intended, William Sullivan, the brothers' longtime head of logging operations, jumped up and declared:

> We're going to build the biggest sawmill in the world right here. It'll have a capacity of a million feet of lumber every twenty-four hours. It'll run day and night for twenty-five maybe thirty years. The logs will be skidded by machinery and then hauled by the trainload to the sawmill. This means we'll be building a mile of railroad track every day. . . . The town we build will be one of the largest in Louisiana. There'll be modern homes and schools. There'll be a hospital and banks. There'll be jobs for everyone in Washington Parish. Why, this wilderness will be turned into one of the most prosperous parts of Louisiana before you know it.

Five months after this pronouncement, to the surprise of the skeptical locals, construction on the new town began in earnest. Four-yoke oxen teams delivered supplies from the surrounding settlements, and laborers were brought in to erect a temporary sawmill to handle all the building lumber. The design scheme was one of the most extensive programs of municipal planning ever attempted in America at that point: hundreds of houses, enough for a population expected to reach eight thousand; dozens of public facilities; a twenty-seven-acre log pond excavated from the gravelly soil; a powerhouse with enough generating capacity for the logging operations as well as for the homes of the residents. The Goodyears had also arranged for a new 150-mile train line, running from Jackson, Mississippi, to Slidell, Louisiana, by way of the new town; this was no mere logging railroad, but a new interstate line, the sixth major railway to penetrate the Deep South. Construction activities continued nonstop for more than eighteen months, until November 1, 1907, when the project's completion was announced. Sullivan's predictions had come true. The new town was named Bogalusa, but it quickly earned the nickname "The Magic City."

The centerpiece of Bogalusa was the new sawmill, a marvel of modern construction. The complex, counting the lumberyard, stretched out over 160 acres. Its operation required about 1,750 men, a number that omitted the countless thousands involved in felling the longleaf pines. Each component had to be specially constructed, since they were pushing the limits of contemporary industrial design. The mill's main drive belts, for example, each required the leather from 540 hides—Sullivan supposedly once proclaimed, "A belt of this size has never been made before, you say. And you are right." The General Electric Company, which had provided many of the structure's components, boasted in a 1908 article, "This is at present the largest electrically operated lumber manufacturing plant in the world, and has an annual production of 175,000,000 feet of lumber." But these claims were actually too modest. Bogalusa possessed the largest mill of any kind, and its capacity far exceeded 175 million annual board feet. In 1915, it would set a record for cutting 1 million board feet in a single day, an amount that most mills of the period rarely cut in a month. Production would peak in 1916, when Bogalusa churned out almost a quarter billion board feet of lumber—for comparison's sake, annual production for the entire Weyerhaeuser syndicate in the 1880s was only four times greater.

Once production got under way, Bogalusa quickly earned a reputation not only as the greatest producer of lumber throughout the Deep South but also as a model company town. It was considered the first in America built along truly modern lines, where every home had electricity. Residents were assured basic public services, including a state-of-the-art hospital that opened in 1909. It also earned distinction for its progressive treatment of black laborers, who composed 60 percent of the workforce. The company provided schools for both whites and blacks, and paid its teachers the best rates in all of Louisiana.

Bogalusa even featured YMCAs and YWCAs for each race, something no other Louisiana mill town could claim.

The lumber industry, by and large, treated labor as expendable, blacks especially so. To serve in a lumber town often meant signing on for a new form of indentured servitude, where payment came in the form of company scrip and living expenses quickly exceeded wages. "Big" Bill Haywood, the charismatic and controversial one-eyed leader of the Industrial Workers of the World (IWW) labor union, wrote of the southern logging companies with disgust and anger:

> For miserable shacks [workers are] compelled to pay exorbitant rents; sewerage there is none; there is no pretense at sanitation; the outhouses are open vaults. . . . Insurance fees are arbitrarily collected from every worker, for which he received practically nothing in return, but whether his time be long or short—one day or a month—with the company, the fee is deducted. The same is true of the doctor fee and the hospital fee, which, in all places, is an imaginary institution.

Some laborers began to respond to these squalid conditions using the only leverage available: unions. Organizations such as the IWW and the Brotherhood of Timber Workers (the Brotherhood) began to appear at company towns starting in the early twentieth century—in most instances, whites and blacks were both invited to join, though they were arranged in separate locals. Logging companies, including the Great Southern, responded unequivocally, refusing employment to union members and often threatening the organizers. In 1906, the owners banded together to form the Southern Lumber Operators' Association (the Association) specifically to combat the union menace. In his article "Timber Workers and Timber Wolves," Haywood predicted, "The fight will be a long one and a bitter one. The struggle will be intense. Members and their families will suffer keen heart pangs, as the lumber barons will not loosen the stranglehold on their ill-gotten profits until they have exhausted every weapon that Capitalism has armed them with."

Tensions first boiled over in August 1911. In an attempt to eradicate the Brotherhood, the Association decided to lock out union members at more than forty lumber mills across western Louisiana and eastern Texas. As part of the campaign, the Association also tried to divide the Brotherhood against itself, ridiculing the union for its acceptance of blacks, but this strategy failed to split the movement. Both sides soon armed themselves and prepared for a violent clash that seemed increasingly unavoidable. In July 1912, at Grabow,

Louisiana, the inevitable finally arrived: Men from each side fought a ten-minute gun battle that left four dead, three from the union and one from the companies. The gunfight resolved little, but the trial of fifty-eight union men that followed drained the Brotherhood's resources. The Association, consequently, largely triumphed in what historians have labeled "the Louisiana-Texas Lumber War of 1911–1913." As for Bogalusa, its position in the far east of Louisiana had insulated it from most of the activity, but it was only a matter of time before similar problems would reach the Magic City.

In the wake of World War I, several factors converged to renew the momentum of the union movement across the southern pine forests. The requirements of total war had forced the federal government to intervene broadly in the nation's labor affairs to prevent shortages, bringing new energy and resources to the union movement. Additionally, the Woodrow Wilson administration showed deference to the American Federation of Labor (AFL), the country's largest and most influential union. National union enrollment jumped almost 50 percent between 1916 and 1919, from 2.8 million to 4 million. Furthermore, southern lumberers gained increased leverage both because new regional industries provided wage competition and because large numbers of blacks moved north, a demographic shift known as the Great Migration, which decreased the available labor pool.

In early 1919, the AFL began a campaign to organize southern loggers inside the region that encompassed Bogalusa. The Great Southern Lumber Company flatly refused to allow any union activity, especially among blacks. Lum Williams, a thirty-year-old placed in charge of the union campaign at Bogalusa, wrote to Samuel Gompers, the head of the AFL, that "[t]he success of the entire labor movement of the South depends on this fight," since the town contained the largest mill and owners looked to it as a regional leader.

As the summer arrived, the company initiated "a reign of terror," in the words of the AFL national secretary. Union men were viciously beaten and expelled from the town. Like the Association in 1911, the Great Southern tried to exploit race-based antagonisms. One Bogalusa lumberman recalled that the plan "was to turn the Black men against the whites and then smash the white union." Tensions between the races were already high—in late August a mob lynched a black veteran for allegedly trying to rape a white woman—but the lumber workers stood together in spite of this. They even marched side by side in a Labor Day parade.

In late November, the situation deteriorated further. Problems began when a company-directed mob attempted to kill the leader of the town's black unionists, Sol Dacus. He escaped into the nearby swamps, and, while hiding among the bald cypress trees, encountered two white unionists out for a hunt.

They offered to escort him to Lum Williams's house, where an official report could be filed. The three men marched through the streets of Bogalusa, two white men protecting a black man, an unprecedented sight. Shortly after they reached Williams's garage, a posse seventy-five strong arrived. Accounts differed about precisely what happened, but when the guns stopped firing, three union men were dead, including Williams and one of Dacus's white escorts (his second escort died the following week).

The Bogalusa shoot-out was perhaps the only time that southern whites took up arms and laid down their lives to defend blacks in the first half of the twentieth century. Nothing equivalent would be seen until the civil rights era. Nevertheless, the legendary gunfight also killed union resistance in Bogalusa. The entire southern logging industry followed Bogalusa's lead in this matter, just as Williams had earlier predicted.

With the labor issue handled decisively, the Great Southern turned its attention to a new challenge, but one long familiar to the lumber industry. The trees that once seemed inexhaustible were disappearing, the cathedral-like longleaf pine forests replaced with stump-filled fields. The company's big mill consumed forty to sixty acres of virgin pine every day, roughly twenty thousand acres per year. Bogalusa's management first reacted to this impending crisis in 1917 by opening a pulp and paper mill, which took advantage of new techniques that allowed for the conversion of non-timber quality southern pines into coarse grades of paper known as kraft. But the company also displayed a more enlightened view of forestry policy than any of its peers, and began to replant its cut-over lands in 1920. Soon it was running ads saying, "you can practically insure the complete satisfaction of your trade during the life of your business . . ." because Bogalusa timber was "assured to you IN PERPETUITY by our far-reaching reforestation operations." Their man-made forest would expand by the early 1960s to more than two hundred thousand acres, the largest privately owned hand-planted forest on earth.

The industry as a whole, however, showed little interest in such reforestation efforts. As one southern logger with fifty years' experience explained, "real forest management didn't come along [in the region] until the late thirties." But by then it was too late to preserve most of the forests. The process set in motion with the 1870s land grab reached its inexorable conclusion after northern capitalists stripped the South's forests bare. They left behind millions of acres of cut-over land whose nitrogen-poor soil was worth peanuts, literally, as that was one of the few nitrogen-fixing crops that thrived under such conditions. Bogalusa was among the few mill towns that survived, a lonely reminder of an industry that once reshaped the South and provided much of the nation's building materials.

In the 1930s, the southern pine region would witness a broad resurgence as a producer of kraft paper, the product that the Great Southern had anticipated. This new industry would depend mainly on fifteen- to twenty-year-old second-growth trees, mostly from lands the earlier lumber business had denuded. While these young trees made excellent pulp, they were far too small for timber. But by then the logging industry had found a new source of suitable trees, thousands of miles away, in the far corner of the nation.

## "A Shrewd Deal"

THE LAND AGENT for the Northern Pacific Railway Company laid the final contract on the table the morning of January 3, 1900. Across from him sat Frederick Weyerhaeuser, the lord of the lumber barons, now sixty-five years old, his beard gone white but his intensity undiminished. The man who had built the Lake States logging industry looked over the terms placed before him carefully, studiously, knowing the scope of the purchase and the amount of capital and the number of men involved. Finally, each man at the table grabbed a pen and made the terms official, a transfer of nine hundred thousand acres of Pacific Northwest timberland at six dollars an acre. It was one of the largest private land transfers in American history and—as the years stacked up and more facts surfaced—one of the most controversial.

The property Weyerhaeuser had just acquired sat in the heart of the nation's last and perhaps greatest forest, one that exceeded even the longleaf pine belt of the South. It ranged across Oregon, Washington, and much of Northern California, a region known collectively as the Pacific Northwest. Here, in the far corner of the nation, was a storehouse of timber not only practically untouched but also richer than anything previously encountered. Stewart Holbrook, the preeminent chronicler of the region's lumber industry, observed: "[O]ne acre of [this forest] contains more timber than did five acres of the biggest, thickest stuff Maine or Michigan could offer." The tree resources were so abundant, so capacious, that although they covered a mere one-eighth of the nation's total forest acreage, they contained between one-half and two-thirds of America's commercial standing timber resources in the early twentieth century.

The region possessed a great diversity of tree species, but the most commercially important one was unquestionably the Douglas fir. It was a massive conifer, like the giant sequoias or coastal redwoods of California. Many grew to 250 feet or higher, their dark-gray, arrow-straight trunks often 8 to 10 feet thick. Sargent observed in 1898: "No other American tree of the first magnitude is so widely distributed or can now afford so much timber, and the rapidity of its growth and its power of reproduction under favorable circumstances make it the most valuable inhabitant of the great coniferous forest of the northwest, which it ennobles with its majestic port and splendid vigor." The species, which ranged widely across the western United States, reached its maximum capacity and densest growth within a fifty-five-thousand-square-mile territory that ran north-south from Puget Sound (at the border between the United States and Canada) to Northern California, starting on the Pacific coast and stretching into the western slopes of the Cascade Range.

On the interior side of the Cascades, the stands of Douglas fir petered out but the forest continued, transforming into an equally productive region of mixed conifers. Here the most notable species was the ponderosa pine. Many considered this tree to produce lumber as fine as any eastern white pine. And these western pines were especially easy for loggers to fell. Holbrook explained, "A stand of ponderosa is more like a park than like a jungle. It prefers relatively level ground. There is little underbrush; loggers do not, as in the [Douglas] fir region, have to clear a path to get close to a pine." This pine forest, at its densest in the Pacific Northwest states, extended north and south for the better part of a thousand miles.

Commercial exploitation of these marvelous forests of the Pacific Northwest had begun long before Weyerhaeuser made his famous purchase. The logging industry traced its roots at least as far back as a primitive mill built at Fort Vancouver in 1827. Serious production started around midcentury, when the California gold rush and the growth of San Francisco spurred demand for construction materials. The industry that subsequently developed relied on capital from California, expertise from New England loggers, and markets based on the West Coast or overseas, primarily in Latin America and eastern Asia. Most of the lumber was handled in oceangoing vessels. The scope of operations, however, hardly compared with that of the other lumber-producing regions of the country. For the most part, the Pacific Northwest trade was undercapitalized, limited in scale, and completely isolated from the lucrative markets back East. The majority of forest acreage was simply untouched, pristine.

As the nineteenth century folded to a close, circumstances began to develop that would facilitate a rush of capital in the region's woodlands. The first major factor was, not surprisingly, the arrival of the transcontinental railroads. The Northern Pacific reached Tacoma, Washington, in 1883; the Union Pacific arrived at Portland, Oregon, in 1884; and three years later the Southern Pacific gave Portland a second line. Rates remained high for the first decade, but in 1893, James J. Hill, president of the Northern Pacific, slashed his freight charges low enough to stimulate an eastern trade. At the same time, demand for lumber in the Pacific Northwest started to grow rapidly, largely due to the Klondike gold rush of 1897 and the building boom in Seattle.

The lumber barons of the Lake States watched these developments eagerly. They had been eyeing the region's timber prizes since at least 1884, when Sargent declared in his seminal *Report*: "[T]he prairies . . . must draw their lumber by rail, not as at present from the pine forests covering the shores of lake Superior, but from the fir and redwood forests of the Pacific coast." The desire to purchase Pacific Northwest acreage increased with each year as the supply of white pine dwindled. To make matters seem even more urgent, the federal government was aggressively taking control of these virgin timber resources through presidential proclamation of forest reserves.

What had happened in the southern longleaf forests was about to be repeated, but on an even larger scale.

Most of the valuable acreage was either part of the public domain or had been gifted to the railroads through several highly controversial land grants in the 1860s and 1870s. Lumbermen began to claim this terrain through a combination of shady business deals, strained interpretations of federal law, and outright fraud. Weyerhaeuser led this buying binge with his purchase of nine hundred thousand acres, a deal arranged through James J. Hill, who was not only president of the Northern Pacific but also Weyerhaeuser's next-door neighbor. A 1907 *Cosmopolitan* magazine exposé on the lumber baron explained the impact of his purchase:

> The shrewd deal, whereby Weyerhaeuser got the richest timber lands in the world at practically no cost and without the slightest danger to anyone, turned the attention of the syndicate to the Northwest, and having gobbled up everything in the Mississippi River district, the same machinery that had worked so effectively there was put in operation in the West.

By 1914, 50 percent of the region's timber was controlled by thirty-eight owners—Weyerhaeuser's company holdings alone totaled 90 billion board feet. Weyerhaeuser himself seemed to avoid accusations of illegal land grabbing, but his affiliates and partners did not. They became constant foils for such conservationist crusaders as Roosevelt and Pinchot, their suspicious acquisitions exposed through a series of land fraud litigations. In 1908, an influential polemic addressing the crisis was simply called *Looters of the Public Domain*.

The industry that arose on the back of this land grab diverged from its prior iterations in the Lake States or Deep South. Giant trees and steep mountain slopes created unique challenges that encouraged the development of new technologies. One of the earliest innovations was the skid road, a chute that ran down mountainsides and allowed loggers to slide trees toward a collection point. Then, in 1881, a Northern California logger invented the Dolbeer steam donkey, a powerful engine with a winch capable of pulling felled trees toward a central point, often the skid road. The donkey engine quickly replaced oxen as the main source of motive power, and the system of dragging logs by cables became one of the industry's most widespread techniques. As the twentieth century progressed, Pacific Northwest loggers would lead the way nationally in adopting diesel engines, trucks, bulldozers, and chainsaws, all mainstays of the modern profession.

It wasn't merely technology that defined lumbering in the region. Pacific Northwest loggers themselves differed from their contemporaries in the long-leaf pine forests. In the romanticized version, one not wholly unjustified, these men were seen as travelers from the earlier lumber regions, inheritors of a tradition that extended back to the nation's first tree fellers in Maine and New Hampshire. In fact, it was in the Pacific Northwest at this time that the nation's prototypical lumberjack hero, Paul Bunyan, was given formal life. Legends of his exploits by most accounts had been circulating around lumber camps at least since the 1840s, but it was only in 1914 that he was finally given a face as part of an advertising campaign for the Red River Lumber Company of Westwood, California. According to William B. Laughead, the artist behind the original image, the idea was born when his boss said: "Say, you've heard a lot of this Paul Bunyan stuff in the camps, haven't you? . . . There must be an angle there. . . . You go ahead and write something up and let me see it." The character—with his ax and boots, checked coat, and thick mustache—soon began to appear in advertisements placed in lumber trade magazines across the country. And the legend—once confined to the occasional logging campfire— quickly grew into one of the most important folk heroes in America. Within twenty-five years, there had been at least seventeen full-length books written about his exploits, each grander than the next. He could fell whole forests with a single swing. One account suggested that "when he was but three weeks old [he] became restless in his sleep and rolling over destroyed three-four acres of standing timber." He made logging seem like the domain of heroes, men of unlimited capacity.

But reality in the Pacific Northwest was often far less inspired. Many of the loggers there were not simply eastern transplants, but immigrants, wayfarers, and poor young men with few options. In 1920, Rexford G. Tugwell, who later became one of President Franklin Roosevelt's top advisors, described them through the eyes of a Progressive witnessing a scene of social breakdown:

> Picture a bent and, to me, a rather pathetic figure, plodding along
> a woods-trail in the astonishing Northwest forest. . . . Perhaps he

drags along a frayed old imitation-leather suit-case; more likely everything in the world he can call his own is wrapped in a filthy blanket-roll that hangs upon his back. His eyes are dull and reddened; his joints are stiff with the rheumatism almost universal in the wettest climate in the world; his teeth are rotting; he is racked with strange diseases and tortured by unrealized dreams that haunt his soul.

The life of a Pacific Northwest logger, as Tugwell suggested, was a difficult one. The pay was bad, the work unsteady, the owners unsympathetic. In Tugwell's words, "As a community, a lumber camp is a sad travesty at best."

The main solace for many of these destitute and shiftless laborers came at the end of the logging season or between jobs, when they could blow their paychecks on the vices of nearby cities. There, they lived a life that would make a sailor blush. The parts of town where loggers gathered became known as "skid roads," a term (along with the bastardized version, "skid row") that eventually came to denote the worst sections of an urban area. Holbrook vividly described these as "block upon block of rooming houses, houses of easy virtue, beer joints, pool halls, tattoo parlors, burlesque theaters, an I.W.W. or wobbly hall, and the kind of store that has a pile of paper suitcases on openhanded display near the entrance, with every one chained down."

The arrival of industrial logging in the Pacific Northwest brought not only this new logging culture, but an increased threat from serious forest fires. The same circumstances that had set the Lake States forests ablaze—accumulated slash and debris, sparks from railroads, abandoned campfires—now shook the region. The first of the major conflagrations struck in September 1902. Known as the "Yacolt Burn," it ripped through more than six hundred thousand acres in Washington and Oregon, killing thirty-five and destroying more than seven billion board feet of timber. One of the hardest hit was Weyerhaeuser, whose purchase of nine hundred thousand acres had overlapped with the affected region.

Up until now, lumber barons had generally been unwilling to invest in forest fire protection, but their attitudes were beginning to change. The Pacific Northwest was the last sanctum of virgin forest on the continent. If the trees disappeared here, there would be no new frontier to chase. Furthermore, lumbermen better appreciated the inherent value of stumpage (land already containing mature timber); there was more money to be made through stumpage appreciation than through lumber manufacturing, and every acre lost through fire was money literally gone up in smoke. While the industry had a long way to go before embracing most of the tenets of professional forestry, it was ready to start tackling this central element of timber preservation.

Leading the charge was George S. Long, the man Weyerhaeuser had personally selected to oversee his mushrooming Pacific Northwest holdings. He was among the first to appreciate the value that professional forestry techniques offered the lumber industry and, following the Yacolt Burn, began to discreetly lobby the state legislatures of Washington and Oregon concerning forest fire prevention. In 1903, Washington became the first state in the country to enact such a law. Two years later, Long helped arrange for the industry to get involved directly through formal patrol agreements. The first of these saw Weyerhaeuser's company join with two others to monitor a heavily forested portion of Oregon. This patrol agreement system proved so popular that within a decade forty similar organizations had formed throughout the country. Of course, despite increased vigilance, fire remained a constant menace in the region, punctuated by the Big Burn of 1910, which destroyed more than five thousand square miles along the Idaho/Montana border (an area roughly equal to Connecticut in size), and by the Tillamook blowup of 1933, an Oregon fire that, in the public imagination, rivaled the Dust Bowl as a symbol of environmental degradation.

The industry's early fire-prevention activities eventually opened the door for it to embrace more extensive forestry practices. George Long again led the way, at one point writing, "I am a Pinchot man in every respect pertaining to forestry matters." He directed a series of internal industry discussions that resulted in the formation of the Western Forestry and Conservation Association in 1910. This group augmented many of the activities that the Forest Service was undertaking simultaneously. The industry, while still guilty of widespread wasteful practices, had come a long way from the days of "cut out and get out" logging, when forestry was practically a four-letter word. Perhaps the change in attitude resulted from a generational shift: The old lumber barons were dying and in their place came men influenced by the writings of Muir and Pinchot.

The greatest baron of all, Weyerhaeuser, passed away in May 1914. He had given more than fifty years to the industry, built from nothing a fortune once thought to "overshadow that of John D. Rockefeller," and brought the techniques of modern capitalism to one of the country's oldest and most important economic sectors. When he died, he sat upon an empire of trees that comprised more than 2 million acres in the Pacific Northwest, along with countless thousands more in the Lake States and the South. Certain estimates suggested that the full extent of his control—including all his partnership deals and minority stakes—reached 50 million acres in the Pacific Northwest alone (an area larger than the entire state of Wisconsin, where he'd first begun to purchase stumpage a few thousand acres at a time). Upon hearing of Weyerhaeuser's passing, his friend James J. Hill declared, "The entire Northwest has no man whose death will be felt so keenly as that of Mr. Weyerhaeuser. His place can not be filled. He was a national force among men who have helped to build up the country, and his loss truly reaches far beyond the limits of his family and business associates." Not everyone was so kind in their assessment. Pulitzer Prize–winning muckraker Charles Edward Russell wrote in 1912: "This great domain [in the Pacific Northwest] once belonged to the people; . . . it was filched from them by the railroads; and . . . the spoilers being despoiled, it is now a part of the empire that is dominated by Frederick Weyerhaeuser."

The lumber baron's death did not mark the end of his empire. Shortly after making his legendary nine-hundred-thousand-acre purchase, he had incorporated the Weyerhaeuser Timber Company, an entity that lives on into the present as the Weyerhaeuser Company, one of the world's foremost producers of lumber and other forest products.

The same year that Weyerhaeuser died, the United States completed the Panama Canal, one of the largest governmental initiatives of the twentieth century. Practically overnight the canal revolutionized transcontinental shipping by making it cost effective to send goods, including lumber, to eastern markets using ocean transport. This development marked the beginning of a new era for the Pacific Northwest logging industry. Up to this point, much of the focus had been on acquiring stumpage, but now production started to move toward its eventual position of national dominance. The first few years of this transition were rocky, as the industry dealt with complications brought on by World War I as well as the brief economic contraction that followed. But when the boom of the twenties arrived, the region's lumber mills were prepared to meet the demand. Pacific Northwest production soon accounted for 30 percent of the national total, nearly equaling that of the Deep South. And by the end of the 1920s, the region finally emerged as the new king of American logging, displacing the Deep South, which had held the title for much of the early twentieth century. In 1929 alone, the mills of Oregon, Washington, and Northern California manufactured a remarkable 14.1 billion board feet, equivalent to the national total as late as 1870.

Here, among the great forests of Douglas fir and ponderosa pine, the logging industry finally settled. The combination of incredible timber resources and improved practices offered a degree of sustainability. Moreover, the huge stumps that remained after logging made cut-over lands difficult to convert into fields for agriculture, meaning that forests tended to regrow if protected from fire. As Holbrook once noted, "I've heard professional foresters say that four out of five acres of forest land in western Oregon and Washington are fit to grow trees and nothing else. . . . You could hardly turn your back on a newly cleared field" without "the firs, hemlocks, and cedars" reappearing. The region has accounted for 50 percent or more of the nation's timber for over fifty years. And, consequently, the economy of the Pacific Northwest owed more to trees than almost anywhere else in twentieth-century America. Holbrook wrote in 1952: "The forest . . . is still the most important single fact in the Northwest. Our statisticians publish figures every little while to say that sixty-five cents of every dollar in our region derives from the forest."

## The Forest Products Laboratory

FOR ALL THE advances that industrial capitalism had brought to lumbering, in several key respects the profession remained fairly primitive at the beginning of the twentieth century. While lumber barons knew plenty about how to get timber from the forest to the market, they understood surprisingly little about what their product was in any scientific or technical sense. Most knowledge about trees was simply the accretion of tradition and experience, with little hard evidence for support. Loggers, with few exceptions, lacked real information about the structure, strength, quality, or durability of their products. To cite one example: The widespread prejudice against longleaf pine as a structural timber stemmed in part from the belief that these trees were weakened through the process of turpentine harvesting, which often preceded the timber haul; but no one had ever bothered to investigate the truth of this claim.

Related to the issue of insufficient technical information was the industry's failure to use trees efficiently during the manufacturing process. While twentieth-century lumberers were less profligate than their predecessors, they still discarded the majority of their raw material, as very few processes had been developed to use a timber tree's by-products. Nearly everything that was not serviceable as finished timber ended up in the waste pile. Emanuel Philipp, the governor of Wisconsin in the late 1910s, once quipped: "[N]ature would have been a great conservator of forest products if she had permitted trees to grow square rather than round." An early Forest Service report attached numbers to this trenchant observation. It estimated that of the total volume of trees cut for lumber in the United States, 25 percent was wasted in slabs, trimmings, edgings, and other unusable pieces; 10.5 percent ended up as sawdust; and 9.8 percent was bark; in total, more than 45 percent of the original material (and that wasn't counting the stumps).

But what was lost in the lumbering process was only a portion of the problem. Decay claimed untold millions of rail ties, fence posts, and utility poles. Aggressive turpentine-harvesting techniques cut short the lives of yellow pines across the southern forests. Inefficient designs for countless types of wooden crates and other forms of packaging frittered away enormous quantities of timber. Irrational prejudices led loggers to ignore whole species of useful trees. The list went on and on, and the sum total of all this inefficiency, ignorance, and waste was billions of board feet per year.

The private sector, for the most part, lacked incentives to address these shortcomings. They were simply a cost of doing business; the amount of capital necessary to investigate any of these questions was prohibitive. The various tree-related industries would have liked better information and cost-saving innovations, they just didn't want to pay for the privilege.

The members of the emerging Forest Service, however, took a different view. For them, these problems were almost as important as the need to protect the nation's trees directly. Increased information and efficiency, after all, offered a second, indirect method to conserve vital tree resources. William Greeley, the third head of the Forest Service, explained,

> To make the most of our forest resources Mr. Pinchot and his associates foresaw that knowledge of the use of wood must progress hand in hand with the national movement to assure a sufficient supply of this essential raw material. Each had an integral part in forest conservation. It was not enough to create National Forests in which the Federal Government might embark on the business of timber production and to assist the private owner in keeping his woodlands productive. It was equally necessary to build up a practical science of wood use.

The federal government's interest in tree research actually predated Pinchot and his acolytes. Throughout the late nineteenth century, Bernhard Fernow, Pinchot's predecessor at the Division of Forestry, had championed the issue personally. In 1887, he wrote, "The properties upon which the use of wood, its technology, is based, should be well known. . . . Our ignorance in this direction has been most fruitful in fostering a wasteful use of our natural forests. . . . Crude 'experience' has been our guide, and 'crude' has remained our knowledge." Under Fernow's direction, the early Division of Forestry devoted much of its resources to the study of "timber physics," as the field was then known. These investigations flourished for the better part of a decade until the program was terminated in 1896 as "not germane to the subject of the Division"—the man who gave this order, ironically, was J. Sterling Morton, the founder of Arbor Day, then serving as secretary of agriculture.

While Pinchot, after taking control of the Division of Forestry, did not initially make wood research a priority, he reintroduced some testing in 1901 as part of his general program of expansion. It began with small investigations into wood preservation and turpentine production techniques. Then, in 1902, the division organized its first timber-testing laboratory in Washington, D.C., and it quickly expanded the testing program through affiliations with Purdue University, Yale University, and the universities of California, Oregon, and Washington. Early payoffs from this work included studies proving that both the longleaf pine and the Douglas fir produced superior timber for structural uses. The Forest Service's head of forest products observed that this resulted "in bringing in to use a lot of timbers which before were considered absolutely worthless."

These testing laboratories initially operated independently, with no coordination in methodology. But such variability became a hindrance as more tests poured forth. In 1906, the task of promulgating a system of standards was given to McGarvey Cline, a young engineer who worked for the Forest Service. He visited each of the testing facilities over the course of a year and determined that uniform practices alone would not be sufficient to meet the Forest Service's growing research requirements. What was needed, he explained, was "the consolidation of these laboratories . . . into one overall laboratory where central supervision could be carried on."

The idea of a centralized research facility proved popular not only among the Forest Service higher-ups but also with the wood-using industries. They had already benefited enormously from the initial round of timber testing and were eager to capitalize on further government-subsidized investigations. In November 1906, the Forest Service hosted a conference to discuss the issue and invited delegates from major industry players, such as the National Lumber Manufacturers' Association. The conference concluded with a unanimously approved resolution: "[T]hat a laboratory for testing the strength and other characteristics of wood, and for solving problems connected with its economic use, is absolutely essential to the manufacturers and users of forest products of this country."

The matter quickly ended up before Congress. The Forest Service's proposal was a onetime two-hundred-thousand-dollar allocation for the construction of a building and the purchasing of specialized testing equipment. At the congressional hearing, however, things quickly deteriorated. A recalcitrant (and very uninformed) committee chair asserted: "It can not take you more than a few years longer to thoroughly test these woods and give the public the results. There is no use in building a permanent building." Pinchot, exasperated, attempted to convince the committee that the proposed laboratory "will save many, many times its cost every year," but no one budged and, for the moment, the project was dead.

McGarvey Cline, the man who first conceived the plan, was not so easily defeated. Congressional funding was only one solution; surely other avenues existed. For nearly a year he struggled without any progress, but then he stumbled upon a possible answer. As Howard Weiss, another member of the Forest Service, explained, "Cline conceived a brilliant idea. It was to secure the cooperation of some university." This was simply an extension of the earlier model of testing laboratories, but on a grander, unprecedented scale: The university would need to commit hundreds of thousands of dollars up front and then provide an annual facilities budget indefinitely.

When Cline's idea reached Pinchot, the chief forester dismissed it as impractical. Nevertheless, the young engineer persisted, and in October 1908 Pinchot sent out an appeal to a list of schools that Cline had preselected.

Pinchot's request proved more popular than he had anticipated. Nearly every school contacted was interested, and the universities of both Michigan and Wisconsin—two states with long histories of dependence on forest products—submitted detailed proposals. Cline suggested that the Wisconsin proposal was superior and Pinchot concurred, but when the Forest Service sent out its official answer, a senior Michigan congressman nearly flew into a rage. Suddenly, both states were vigorously competing against each other. A Wisconsin delegation that included the inimitable Senator Robert La Follette and all the state's congressmen supposedly confronted Pinchot personally to ensure that he stayed true to his word. In early 1909, the chief forester reaffirmed the initial determination, declaring in a subsequent press release: "I have had few decisions to make which were so difficult or which have had such prolonged and careful consideration."

Construction began almost immediately on a fifty-five-thousand-dollar facility, and on June 4, 1910, the doors were formally opened to the Forest Products Laboratory (FPL). It was the first institution in the world to conduct generalized research into the nature of wood and its use, a major step forward in understanding trees and their role in society. The facilities were state of the art, with much of the equipment built specifically for use at the FPL. Highlights in the early years would include a machine capable of exerting one million pounds of pressure as well as a special fungus room used to study decay.

At the head of the FPL was McGarvey Cline, whose tenacity had allowed for the organization's creation. He hired an original staff of fifty-five, thirty-three of whom were technical men, primarily from the professions of chemistry, engineering, and forestry. Their work was much broader than the timber tests of the predecessor laboratories and was initially divided among six departments: timber physics; timber tests; wood preservation; wood distillation;

wood pulp; and chemistry. The idea was to address every aspect of industrial wood use. Experiments rapidly stacked up by the tens of thousands.

As Pinchot had earlier assured Congress, the benefits of the FPL arrived with little delay. Early discoveries (far too numerous to cover adequately) included: improving hardwood distillation from the refuse of lumber manufacturing; finding new species of trees besides spruce for groundwood pulp; refining a process that allowed for the production of high-quality kraft paper using southern pines; crafting more efficient turpentine collection processes; identifying the molecular structure of wood; designing shipping containers that required less wood but possessed greater strength; and developing new kiln drying techniques to better season lumber. In 1920, Carlisle "Cap" Winslow, the third director of the FPL, attempted to translate a few of the laboratory's accomplishments into concrete figures and determined conservatively "a combined annual increase in production and decrease in waste aggregating $30,000,000."

While the FPL was founded primarily to increase knowledge and eliminate waste, it also produced a stream of discoveries allowing for the use of wood in ways never before recognized. For instance, researchers identified ever-expanding roles for cellulose, the most abundant component in wood and the basis of pulp and paper production—cellulose-based products included cellophane, gunpowder, photographic films, and rayon. Additionally, experiments with sawdust processed under heat generated an inexpensive, sheetlike material usable as floor tiles and wallboards. FPL chemists also learned ways to derive sugar from wood and turn sawdust into cattle feed. These types of discoveries were welcome news to a host of tree-dependent industries facing competition from newer industrial materials like steel and plastic.

The FPL led the way in these investigations but it was not acting wholly alone. For example, masonite, a type of hardboard composed of sawmill refuse from southern pines, was patented in the 1920s by William H. Mason, an independent inventor. The Weyerhaeuser Timber Company founded its own research arm in 1920, and numerous large companies soon followed. Several other nations also began to fund copycat institutions.

By the mid-1920s, Congress finally awoke to the benefits of wood research as well. In May 1928, it passed the McSweeney-McNary Act, a landmark law that identified research as an essential component of the national forestry program. The law even made a special provision for the FPL, more than twenty years after the chair of the congressional committee on agriculture had declared that wood research couldn't possibly justify a building. The FPL still exists in Madison, Wisconsin, center of a national network of tree research.

While the facility's early research program was remarkably broad, it was not, in fact, comprehensive. In particular, the laboratory paid relatively little attention to issues of tree diseases. This aspect of tree culture had traditionally generated much less concern than the risk of forest fires or the dangers of profligate waste. But in some ways it was more powerful than either of those. Diseases could wipe out entire species, changing the forest forever. Up until the twentieth century, the nation had largely avoided such catastrophes, but luck was fast running out.

# 7

# Under Attack

American Elm

## The Saga of the Sakura

IN LATE JANUARY 1910, President Taft received an unusual communication from the U.S. Department of Agriculture. His direct authorization was sought for an action never before taken in American history: the wholesale destruction of an imported plant shipment. The request had come from the USDA's top scientists. They had identified a score of insects and other hostile pests that, according to their report, presented an "extreme danger" to the ecological safety of the United States. Their reluctant conclusion was "that the entire shipment be burned as soon as possible."

Normally, this matter might have remained within the USDA, but this was no routine overseas delivery. The intended recipient was the president's wife, First Lady Helen "Nellie" Taft. And the sender was the mayor of Tokyo, acting on behalf of Japan, the fast-rising Eastern power with imperial ambitions. The shipment at issue contained two thousand hand-selected flowering cherry trees, also known as sakuras, the most venerated trees of Japan, meant to serve as "a perpetual reminder of the friendship of the two people." Any decision to burn the trees thus carried diplomatic consequences, a potential international incident that few wished to see materialize. But there was even more at stake than that, more than Taft likely realized. The question of what to do with these Japanese imports stood at the center of a bitter fight within the USDA over the ecological future of the nation—would it have open borders or not? And beyond that issue, there was also a personal crusade to bring sakuras to America's capital, a struggle with roots that reached back over twenty-five years.

By most accounts, the effort to introduce flowering cherry trees to Washington, D.C., began with Eliza Scidmore, one of America's foremost travel writers during the late nineteenth and early twentieth centuries. She had first traveled to Japan in 1884, when she was twenty-eight years old and still little known. Much about that country's culture impressed her, but nothing captivated her quite like the flower festivals that took place during the spring months. In *Jinrikisha Days in Japan,* a book she later wrote describing this first trip, Scidmore proclaimed, "The miracles of Japanese floriculture presently exhaust the capacity of wonder."

For Scidmore, one flower outshone all others: the sakura, blossom of the Japanese cherry tree. It was a marvel of horticultural wizardry, each bloom a universe built from hundreds of smaller flowers, all bundled together in delicate harmony, swollen rosettes that ranged in color from pure white to deep crimson. Sakura trees had been bred over countless generations to devote all their energy to flower production—unlike most cherry trees, their fruit was either tiny or absent altogether. The beauty of these blossoms made sakuras one of the most popular tree species in Japan, planted widely in public spaces and sacred sites.

Scidmore quickly learned that sakuras were not merely objects of aesthetic perfection for the Japanese, but also symbols rife with meaning and power. In an article that she subsequently wrote for the *Century Magazine,* she attempted to explain the importance of sakuras to an American audience:

> It is not only the national flower, but the symbol of purity, the emblem of chivalry and knightly honor, the crest of a cult the vernal celebration of which has been observed with unflagging zeal for at least two thousand years. . . . Except Fuji-yama [Mount Fuji] and the moon, no other object has been theme and inspiration of so many millions of Japanese poems as the cherry blossom.

When Scidmore returned from Japan in 1885, she brought with her visions of an American sakura grove. It seemed like the perfect tree to adorn the parks and pleasure grounds that were proliferating during the late nineteenth century. Her specific plan was for a field of sakuras in Washington, D.C., where she resided. She thought that they would be an ideal adornment for a stretch of swampland along the Potomac River that had been recently reclaimed and rehabilitated through an Army Corps of Engineers project. As she later argued, "[S]ince they had to plant something, they might as well plant trees that would afford an annual flower-show at the season when . . . the city receives its greatest number of visitors and sight-seers." Scidmore quickly brought her proposal to the superintendent of public buildings and grounds for Washington, D.C., but was summarily rebuffed. She pressed her case anew with each successive superintendent, but always with the same result. It appeared hopeless, and would remain that way for more than twenty years.

At the time Scidmore began her sakura campaign, David Fairchild, her future partner in the fight, was still a teenager, unaware of the remarkable direction his life would soon take. Born in 1869 and raised in Michigan and Kansas, Fairchild described himself as "a prairie boy who had never seen the waves of the sea." He was a gifted student, scion of a family that had long prized education—his grandfather helped found Oberlin College; his father served as the president of the Kansas State College of Agriculture. As an undergraduate at Kansas State, Fairchild first discovered a love of botany, which he called "a turning point in my life." His particular interest was the incipient field of plant diseases, soon to be known as plant pathology.

In 1893, Fairchild encountered Barbour Lathrop, a wealthy world traveler in his midforties who, in Fairchild's words, "was to 'direct my destiny.'" For the next several years, the two men roamed around the world by steamship with Lathrop footing the bill. And it was during one of these voyages, on New Year's Eve 1897, that Fairchild experienced the second turning point in his life (one that would eventually lead him to the sakuras). As he later wrote,

> [Lathrop] began to lay before me his ideas of what a botanist could do if he were given an opportunity to travel and collect the native vegetables, fruits, drug plants, grains and all the other types of useful plants as yet unknown in America.

By the time midnight struck and the New Year began, Fairchild had decided to abandon plant pathology in favor of plant exploration. He was now committed to what he described as a "philosophy of a free exchange of plant varieties between different nations of the world."

Fairchild's newfound philosophy was, in most respects, nothing revolutionary in American thought. The idea of open commerce in flora had helped to fuel the colonial-era trade between John Bartram in Philadelphia and Peter

Collinson in London. Thomas Jefferson once claimed, "The greatest service which can be rendered any country is, to add [a] useful plant to its culture." And this attitude persisted among many botanists and horticulturists throughout the nineteenth century. Recall that the Washington Navel orange, linchpin of the California citrus industry, was introduced from trees discovered by an American living in Brazil.

But Fairchild's vision differed from these antecedents in a crucial way. Like his contemporaries Gifford Pinchot and Teddy Roosevelt, Fairchild possessed a turn-of-the-century faith in the power of the federal government to address large challenges, specifically through the use of agencies. Thus he wanted to build a federal institution to formalize his philosophy regarding botanical exploration and exchange. In 1898, upon returning to the States after four years abroad, he helped convince the USDA to create a new Office of Foreign Seed and Plant Introduction (FSPI). Its job was to coordinate and manage nonnative plant introductions and to support a roster of plant explorers, foremost among them Fairchild himself.

It was in his new capacity as official government plant explorer that Fairchild first encountered the sakura. He had journeyed to Japan in 1902 as part of a collecting mission. Travel delays had forced him to miss the legendary springtime festivals, but he nonetheless arranged to meet a Japanese horticulturist and artist renowned for his work both in raising and in drawing sakuras. Upon seeing this man's depictions of the famous trees, Fairchild experienced a level of wonder reminiscent of Scidmore's a generation earlier. He wrote, "I have rarely been so thrilled, for I had had no idea of the wealth of beauty, form, and color of the flowering cherries."

Fairchild and Scidmore almost certainly knew each other before this point. Both of them were active members of the prestigious National Geographic Society (NGS) in Washington, D.C. Scidmore, for her part, had been appointed the organization's first female board member. Fairchild, meanwhile, was a favorite of the NGS's ex-president, Alexander Graham Bell, the world-famous inventor of the telephone—Bell's youngest daughter, Marian, would soon marry the plant explorer. In the wake of Fairchild's trip to Japan, he and Scidmore likely began to discuss their mutual love of sakura trees and to talk about the possibilities of bringing them to America.

In 1905, Fairchild took the first major step. He and his new wife purchased a forty-acre property in Maryland with plans to turn the grounds into the nation's first sakura grove. It was, according to Fairchild, "one of our chief preoccupations." He used his influence as head of the FSPI and his connections from his earlier trip to arrange for the importation of 125 trees representing 25 varieties. Some questioned whether the specimens would be hardy enough to survive American winters, but proof came the following spring: a brilliant display of cherry flowers, the likes of which had never been witnessed in the United States.

After concluding that sakuras could survive in the region, Fairchild and his wife determined "to do something towards making them better known in Washington." They devised a plan to provide every public school in the city with one sakura, all to be planted on Arbor Day 1908. Funds were raised from among their social circle, and Fairchild placed a new order for three hundred trees.

On the day before the proposed plantings, an energized Scidmore met with Fairchild and spoke at length about a potential next step: creating a grand field of cherry trees along the Speedway (what is now the corridor of Independence Avenue in West Potomac Park). This idea impressed Fairchild, and he invited Scidmore as a distinguished guest to the ceremonial planting being held the next day. During his keynote speech, he told the large audience about the need for a sakura field on the Speedway, the first time someone had publicly advocated Scidmore's plan. The *Washington Star*, which covered the event, wrote that he further "aroused the enthusiasm of his audience by telling them that Washington would one day be famous for its flowering cherry trees." Fairchild's prediction was bold and, for the most part, unsupported by evidence, but circumstances were about to shift in his favor.

The 1908 election that gave the country President William Howard Taft had also produced a new First Lady. Nellie Taft was strong-willed, intelligent, outgoing, and unconventional, the sort of sure-footed person who openly opposed Prohibition at a time when the nation was tottering toward teetotaling. The arc of President Taft's political ascent had turned Nellie, like Scidmore and Fairchild, into a traveler and admirer of Asia. She had first spent several years in the Philippines—a territory the United States acquired during the Spanish-American War—after her husband took charge of its civil government in 1900. During that time, Mrs. Taft grew to admire the Luneta, a tree-lined riverside park that overlooked Manila Bay. A subsequent diplomatic trip to Japan introduced her to the sakuras.

Shortly after Nellie arrived at the White House, she began to receive appeals from both Fairchild and Scidmore regarding the plan to bring sakura trees to the Speedway. Their requests seemed to dovetail with ideas that the First Lady had already been considering—as she later explained, "I [had] determined, if possible, to convert Potomac Park into a glorified Luneta where all Washington could meet." The indomitable First Lady moved quickly to advance the Scidmore/Fairchild plan, pushing through the bureaucratic red tape and opposition that had tripped up Scidmore for more than twenty years.

By April 7, 1909, barely one month after the inauguration celebration, she was able to write to Scidmore, "I have taken the matter up and am promised the trees."

The plan then seemed to grow of its own momentum. The week after Nellie sent her letter to Scidmore, a Japanese delegation arrived at the White House as part of a celebration of Japanese-American relations. Among the delegates was Dr. Jokichi Takamine, a chemist best known for the discovery of adrenaline. When he learned of Mrs. Taft's plan, he offered to supplement the project with a gift of two thousand additional sakuras. Other Japanese diplomats endorsed Takamine's gesture but preferred that the trees be offered through public channels. The deal was quickly repackaged as coming directly from the city of Tokyo, and everyone found this plan satisfactory. The State Department confirmed the arrangement with Japanese diplomats over the summer months. By November President Taft was personally working to direct the removal from Potomac Park of recently planted elms in order to make room for the sakuras.

For many of those involved, the importance of the sakura project expanded far beyond a straightforward cultural bequest. The political overtones were difficult to avoid. Japan had recently established itself as a serious international power through its victory in the Russo-Japanese War (1904–5). The U.S. government under Roosevelt had helped to negotiate that war's peace treaty and hosted a conference in Portsmouth, New Hampshire, where the final documents were signed. However, the attitude of many Americans toward the Japanese was far from cordial. In the West, especially in cities like San Francisco, people were agitating for legislation to exclude the Japanese (as had already occurred with the Chinese through a set of Exclusion Acts in the 1880s). The newly empowered Empire of Japan felt that such an outcome would be an intolerable offense. This issue became so incendiary that Roosevelt, who held a positive view of Japan, was forced in 1907 to accept an informal arrangement, known as the Gentlemen's Agreement, whereby the United States promised not to impose any immigration restrictions and Japan agreed to curb further emigration. Seen in this light, the proposed gift of sakuras was an informal diplomatic action that offered an avenue to help strengthen tense bilateral relations.

The shipment of two thousand flowering cherry trees departed on a steamer from Japan in mid-November 1909 and reached Seattle, Washington, on December 10. The sakuras were then loaded onto refrigerated railcars and transported across the country. On January 6, the trees arrived at the capital, where Fairchild received them. The plan was for a ceremonial planting that would receive national media attention. But before any of that could happen, the project hit an unforeseen snag. The same U.S. government that had arranged for the sakuras' importation suddenly proclaimed that the trees represented an unacceptable threat to national safety.

F AIRCHILD'S PHILOSOPHY OF open and frequent plant exchanges represented only one perspective. The same flora that he felt offered economic opportunity also could threaten the ecological stability of established species or could harbor harmful pests. Investigations early in the twentieth century had shown that at least 50 percent of the insects classified as injurious to American flora originated in other countries. And some estimated that imported pests were costing the United States up to one billion dollars annually.

European nations had been the first to take up the issue of plant control. The need for such legislation had arisen largely in reaction to an American pest that had arrived during the mid-nineteenth century and proceeded to devastate vineyards across the Continent. In 1881, an international conference to address the matter was finally convened at Bern, Switzerland, and this produced a wave of plant quarantine restrictions.

Around the same time as the Bern conference, some individual states within America started moving to implement stronger controls. California fruit growers, for instance, had lobbied successfully for statewide quarantine legislation in 1881.

The federal government, however, only started to address the matter seriously in the early twentieth century. The USDA, as an initial step, developed inspection protocols by 1906 for materials that its own agents, such as Fairchild, arranged to import—the sakura shipment would fall within this category.

The most zealous proponent for stricter federal plant controls in this period was Charles Marlatt, then assistant chief of the Bureau of Entomology at the USDA. Though he held views diametrically opposed to those of Fairchild, the two men were, remarkably, the closest of friends. They had both grown up in Kansas and had a similar fascination with plant diseases. Marlatt had even been the best man at Fairchild's wedding. But such amity did little to dissuade Marlatt.

In 1909, he took control of the USDA's campaign to tighten plant importation. His initial strategy was to quietly shepherd a bill through Congress that gave the USDA a general quarantine power as well as the right to wage campaigns against emerging pest menaces. Marlatt's effort, however, collapsed when the American Association of Nursery Men learned about the proposed bill and marshaled resources to slow its progress. According to historian Philip Pauly, Marlatt in reaction "determined to raise the consciousness of both influential elements of the public and forces in the government about the danger posed by infested nursery stock."

At roughly that moment arrived the celebrated shipment of two thousand flowering cherry trees from Japan. The USDA's inspection team, with Marlatt overseeing, determined that the sakuras were a hotbed of potential threats. According to the findings, nearly every tree hosted a scale insect pest known as Chinese Diaspis; several specimens were infested with San Jose scale, an insect that had already wreaked havoc in the western states; others contained wood-boring Lepidopterous larvae, hitherto unknown in America and flagged by Marlatt as potentially "a source of tremendous loss in later years to fruit interests"; more than 70 percent of the trees displayed root gall worm and 45 percent crown gall. Marlatt, temporarily serving as chief of the Bureau of Entomology, wrote to the secretary of agriculture on January 19 that "[t]he recommendation for the destruction of these trees is thoroughly merited." He pegged much of the problem on "the fact that very old stock ha[d] been sent, the object being to give large, showy trees."

While the scientific findings seemed sound, some questioned their validity. The *New York Times* issued a sharp editorial when the news became public, writing: "We have been importing ornamental plants from Japan for years, and by the shipload, and it is remarkable that this particular invoice should have contained any new infections—or any at all, for that matter." Fairchild raised concerns as well. Reflecting on the situation years later, he described the inspection process with a tinge of incredulity: "[A]lmost every sort of pest imaginable was discovered." But even Fairchild conceded that the size and condition of the trees meant that "the greater number of them would have perished in the raw soil of the Speedway."

The inspection team's uncomfortable findings rattled their way upward through the political and diplomatic ranks in the closing weeks of January. By the time the news reached Taft, it was all but a foregone conclusion that the trees would be destroyed. And on January 28, a team of USDA technicians, with presidential authorization in hand, set the entire shipment of sakuras on fire, the symbol of friendship suddenly nothing more than a pile of ashes.

Stoking the flames of bilateral tension was Colonel Richmond Hobson, a U.S. congressman from Alabama and one of the nation's premier anti-Japanese agitators. He had recently taken to the floor of Congress to rail against the Japanese threat, declaring, "[T]he only way to solve the race problem of the Pacific coast is to segregate all the yellow people there." His incendiary comments were almost certainly unrelated to the sakuras, but the timing couldn't be worse.

Top American diplomats scrambled to smooth over the embarrassing but seemingly unavoidable destruction of Japan's prized trees. Members of the State Department, including Secretary of State Philander Knox, reached out to their various analogues in Japan. Colonel Spencer Cosby, the superintendent for public buildings and grounds in Washington, D.C., wrote to Mayor Ozaki of Tokyo personally to express his regret and attached to his letter a copy of the USDA's final report. The awkwardness extended beyond international relations: the March issue of the *Century Magazine* ran a lead article by Scidmore celebrating the arrival of the sakuras. A footnote on the first page of the issue declared: "As this paper goes to press it is announced that the experts in Washington have found it necessary to destroy the cherry-trees which have arrived, as a protection against certain kinds of infection attaching to them. This disappointment, which will be national in extent, does not impair the graciousness of the gift."

To everyone's relief, Japanese officials reacted, for lack of a better term, diplomatically. Mayor Ozaki, who had overseen the delivery, quipped: "To be honest about it, it has been an American tradition to destroy cherry trees ever since your first president, George Washington! So there's nothing to worry about. In fact you should be feeling proud!" He added, on a more sincere note, "[W]e are more than satisfied that you dealt with them as you did; for it would have pained us endlessly to have them remain a permanent source of trouble." Ozaki proposed that his city undertake whatever actions were necessary to rectify the situation. New sakura scions were quickly selected and propagated under the strictest conditions of sterility. By late January 1912, they were ready for shipment to America. This time, when the trees arrived, they passed Marlatt's inspection.

On March 27, a small group of people, carrying a solitary shovel, walked into Potomac Park. There were no media, no cameras, no fanfare, only the First Lady, Eliza Scidmore, Spencer Cosby, and the Japanese ambassador and his wife. (Fairchild was unable to attend.) In the time since Mrs. Taft had first orchestrated plans for the sakura grove, she had suffered a stroke and now moved with greater difficulty. Nonetheless, she took hold of the shovel and planted the first of some three thousand sakura seedlings. Scidmore looked on, watching the realization of a vision almost thirty years in the making.

What Fairchild had proclaimed on Arbor Day 1908 soon came to pass: The capital became "famous for its flowering cherry trees." The city's inaugural "Cherry Blossom Festival," which numerous civic groups cosponsored, took place in 1935—it has continued every year since, bolstering the stature of the sakuras as one of Washington's premier attractions. By 1938, barely twenty-five years after the first planting, the flowering cherry trees had become so beloved that, when rumors swirled that some would be destroyed to make space for the Jefferson Memorial, a group of women chained themselves together among the trees in protest and received national media coverage—a compromise was eventually reached. Today, to the delight of thousands of locals and tourists, the sakuras in Potomac Park continue to make their grand displays every spring, though all but two of the original plantings have needed to be replaced.

The triumph of the cherry trees, however, was something of a Pyrrhic victory, at least for Fairchild. The same year that the second shipment arrived, Marlatt successfully guided a legislative effort that produced the Plant Quarantine Act. This new law tracked his earlier effort from 1909 and gave the USDA broad powers to inspect plant importations, target suspected threats, and issue quarantines as needed. Marlatt's bureau subsequently gained increasing power over the nation's trade in plants, hampering the work of cosmopolitan plant explorers. When Fairchild retired from the Office of Foreign Seed and Plant Introduction in 1928, he was fighting a losing battle against the expansion of quarantines.

But the world's pests proved much tougher foes for Marlatt than his old friend Fairchild. The quickening pace of global and domestic trade hastened the opportunities for new threats to pierce the control system. And the USDA's inspection protocols themselves often came up short. This was, predictably, the situation with the second shipment of sakuras that Marlatt had personally approved—in 1919, during hearings before the House Committee on Agriculture, he lamented, "This second sending . . . looked perfectly clean, but years afterwards these trees proved to be infested with a borer. . . . The insect brought in with this importation has spread from the District into Maryland and into Virginia."

Marlatt also had to contend with countless dangers that had traversed the nation's borders and established residence long before any federal controls had been implemented. The worst of these was already well known to plant pathologists by the time the initial quarantine legislation took effect. Soon it would be familiar to almost all Americans, for this invader was systematically and ruthlessly eliminating one of the country's most important trees.

## "The Most Deadly Plant Parasite Known"

A MATURE AMERICAN CHESTNUT tree was a marvel of the forest, one that distinguished itself from other woody plants during all seasons. In the winter, when its branches were bare, it stood out on size alone, its columnar trunk soaring upward, its silhouette, often one hundred feet tall, shadowing nearly all other hardwoods. In the springtime appeared its distinctive leaves, long and canoe-shaped, punctuated with sharp points along the sides—botanists focused on this last feature when selecting a name for the species: *Castanea dentata,* the second part being derived from the Latin word for "tooth." In the summer, usually in mid-July, long after most forest trees had flowered, the American chestnut finally set forth its blooms, a brilliant display that added a burst of color to the landscape—President Theodore Roosevelt, in his autobiography, fondly recalled that time each year "when the blossoming of the chestnut trees patche[d] the woodland with frothy greenish-yellow." Of course, most Americans who thought about these trees thought about the fall months, when the species came into fruit. Each autumn, the branches grew heavy with an abundance of spiny green burrs, and inside of these, coddled in tan velvet, was one of the treasures of the forest, the American chestnut, whose sweetness and rich flavor were admired far and wide. Thoreau, in describing these nuts, once wrote, "They are plump and tender. I love to gather them, if only for the sense of the bountifulness of nature they give me."

The American chestnut tree originally dominated much of the forestland in the eastern United States. Its natural range stretched north-south from central Maine to lower Alabama and east-west from the Atlantic seaboard to the far shore of the Mississippi River. Nearly everywhere within this massive territory, the tree appeared in substantial numbers—by some accounts it constituted 20 percent of all trees east of the Mississippi. Legend claimed that at one point a squirrel could bounce along the chestnut canopy from Georgia to New England without ever hitting the ground.

The finest region for chestnuts was the southern Appalachian Mountains, an area that included parts of North Carolina, Tennessee, Virginia, and West Virginia. There, individual specimens could reach prodigious sizes, sometimes 120 feet tall and 12 feet in diameter. And in certain parts of the Appalachians, chestnuts grew in almost pure stands for miles on end. The nut production of these regions was remarkable—the chestnut mast could be more than a foot deep by late fall. Frederick Law Olmsted, who traveled through the southern Appalachians in the years before his appointment as superintendent of Central Park, observed, "[T]he chestnut mast is remarkably fine. The swine at large in the mountains, look much better than I saw them anywhere else at the South. It is said that they will fatten on the mast alone."

Early American colonists needed little time to recognize the importance of chestnut trees to daily life. The nuts, a favored food source for many Native American tribes, offered easy sustenance in a foreign environment. But settlers also found special value in the tree's timber. Chestnut wood, though weaker and softer than oak, was nonetheless lightweight, rot resistant, plentiful, and easily split, qualities that made it ideal for many construction tasks. The wood's most widespread use was for fencing, a ubiquitous feature across the colonial landscape, necessary both to denote property ownership and to keep animals out of the homestead and away from the crops. Most colonists favored the snake fence, in which logs were stacked several feet high in an interlocking zigzag pattern—the technique required minimal skill but demanded immense quantities of wood, most often chestnut.

The heavy demand for chestnut trees only increased the species' predominance across the eastern forests. As soon as a mature tree was felled, new shoots sprang up from the stump and grew vigorously—other hardwoods possessed this sprouting ability but rarely on the same scale. Farmers exploited this quality, turning chestnut groves into woodlots that could be harvested periodically and repeatedly, a technique known as coppicing.

During the nineteenth century, the emerging technologies of the Industrial Revolution brought additional uses for the American chestnut. The fast-growing train network required millions of rail ties, and the chestnut's abundance and durability made it one of the most popular sources across the East. In the 1840s, the introduction of the telegraph created a new demand for tall poles to support transmission wires. Chestnuts filled this role as well, especially east of the Mississippi River—the number of chestnuts used for poles only increased with the arrival of telephones, electricity, and streetcars, all of which used high-strung cables. But it was not just the structural value of chestnut timber that made it a darling of the new industries. Its wood, like the bark of the hemlock, contained high concentrations of tannin, an essential ingredient in producing leather (and also the chemical that made chestnut so rot resistant). Thus, in many parts of the East, laborers harvested chestnut for tannin as well. P. L. Buttrick, an early-twentieth-century forester and professor who wrote about the tree's role in industry, concluded that it had "a greater variety of uses than almost any other American hardwood."

But the impact of the chestnut on the nation's industrial system formed only part of the story. The tree also proved indispensable to domestic life. Chestnut, in addition to being durable, looked attractive when given a natural finish and could hold paint well. Decorators preferred it for a host of features inside middle- and upper-class homes: trims, casings, panelings, ceilings, almost anything other than floors, as chestnut was too soft to withstand excessive wear. And few woods played as large a role in the manufacture of American furniture. This was especially true from the early nineteenth century onward, after the forests had been stripped of prized species like black walnut and white oak. Less-expensive furniture was often constructed wholly from chestnut, while more-costly pieces frequently used it as core stock, upon which was glued veneers from fancier woods like black walnut, black cherry, white oak, curly maple, burl elm, mahogany, and rosewood.

In southern Appalachia, chestnut trees took on yet one more responsibility. The heart of chestnut territory was one of the most economically underdeveloped parts of the East throughout the nineteenth century. Many inhabitants continued to live in log cabins—constructed of chestnuts—long after the rest of the nation transitioned to more modern and elaborate home designs. Though the region hosted a thriving lumber industry, practically none of the wealth reached the people who populated the mountains. Most were poor, isolated from the outside world, and remarkably dependent on their forest trees. The annual chestnut harvest provided not only a bountiful source of food for families and their animals, but also an income stream—each fall, Appalachian residents gathered up the inexhaustible supply of chestnuts and hauled them to the local general store, which paid a nominal fee and then sold them to traders. As one Appalachian phrased it, "[C]hestnuts were like the manna that God sent to feed the Israelites."

The seemingly endless utility of the American chestnut made it perhaps the nation's most important tree species by the beginning of the twentieth century. The lumber industry was cutting above half a billion feet of chestnut timber per year, the highest amount of any single hardwood species. Americans rode on chestnut-paneled trains running along chestnut rail ties to reach jobs behind chestnut desks to receive messages transmitted over chestnut utility poles. They dined on chestnut stuffing at chestnut tables while wearing leather clothes tanned with chestnut. In 1915, Buttrick noted: "At last when the tree can serve us no longer in any other way it forms the basic wood onto which oak and other woods are veneered to make our coffins." From the cradle to the grave, then, the chestnut tree affected almost every phase of life. If something were to happen to this inimitable species, America would be forever altered.

I N THE SUMMER of 1904, Herman Merkel, chief forester of the New York Zoological Park (now known as the Bronx Zoo), was strolling along the grounds when he noticed something troubling. Some of the leaves on one of the park's American chestnut trees had withered and turned brown. Merkel moved to inspect the tree and discovered that the infected branches displayed a ring of dry bark and were peppered with tiny orange dots. It looked like a fungus, but nothing he'd observed before. As Merkel continued walking through the park, he spotted other chestnuts with brown leaves as well. He decided to treat all the diseased trees with a fungicide, hoping that the problem would stop there. But by the following spring it was evident that this initial approach had failed completely. Nearly every chestnut tree in the park was now infected.

Merkel was desperate for a solution. The park, barely five years old, was drawing more than a million visitors annually and the chestnuts formed an integral part of its landscape. Their eradication would be a calamity. He determined to send samples of the diseased bark to the USDA with a plea for assistance. His urgent package landed in the hands of Flora Patterson, a government mycologist (who later served on the inspection team that rejected the 1910 delivery of sakuras from Tokyo). She suggested that it was a common fungus, *Cytospora*, and recommended that Merkel aggressively prune infected branches and spray the trees with "Bordeaux mixture," a chemical cocktail originally developed to fight the grape blight that had terrorized much of Europe in the mid-nineteenth century. Merkel followed Patterson's instructions, but, skeptical of her conclusions, contacted William Alphonso Murrill, the recently appointed mycologist at the nearby New York Botanical Garden.

Murrill rushed over to the park, looked over the infected trees, and concluded that Merkel had been correct to doubt the USDA's conclusion. It was definitely not a *Cytospora*, he assured, but what it was he couldn't say. Murrill began to collect specimens and then spent much of the next year growing fungus cultures and studying their behavior under laboratory conditions.

In June 1906, Murrill published his findings in the *Journal of the New York Botanical Garden*. It was the first article to address the topic and, with minor exceptions, remarkably accurate in its conclusions. Murrill warned, "[T]his fungus may be classed with the most destructive parasites." Once it infected a tree, it destroyed the host branch or trunk through a modified form of girdling, the process of removing a strip of bark all the way around a tree to interrupt the flow of water and nutrients. In the case of the fungus, this girdling occurred when the mycelium—the long, wispy, vegetative growth of the fungus—encircled a tree's inner bark or cambium. Murrill found that mycelia injected directly into healthy trees caused the death of small branches within six weeks, a phenomenal speed. As the fungus killed its host, it also produced a huge quantity of spores. Murrill was uncertain exactly how these spores reached new chestnut trees, but speculated, correctly, that they were "liable to fall into even the slightest abrasions of the bark and germinate." The article concluded that little could be done to save the trees already affected.

Reports soon began to appear of sightings beyond New York City. The fungus was spreading rapidly to surrounding counties in Connecticut, New Jersey, and New York. By the spring of 1907 infected trees had been recorded as far north as Poughkeepsie, New York, and as far south as Trenton, New Jersey. Two credible observers claimed that they had seen a similar fungus as early as 1893, suggesting that the threat had deeper and broader roots than initially thought. The issue finally gained coverage in the *New York Times* in May 1908 (though the front page was reserved for more important stories, like the birth of a Rocky Mountain goat at the Zoological Park). "Chestnut Trees Face Destruction," read the headline: "Thousands of trees, amounting to millions of dollars in value, are dying, the victims of the most deadly plant parasite known, the chestnut canker, for which there is no known remedy."

The potential scope of the threat put the fungus back on the radar of the USDA. Department scientists accepted that their initial analysis had been wrong and marshaled resources toward further study. Much of the initial work fell to the Bureau of Plant Industry, which had been created in 1901 to oversee a range of issues—it housed Fairchild's Office of Seed and Plant Introduction but also would help to administer the Plant Quarantine Act after its passage in 1912. The bureau reached conclusions dishearteningly similar to Murrill's, but took the attitude that the spread of the disease must be checked at all costs. In 1911, scientists at the bureau issued a report on methods to control the disease. Much of the advice was technical, but some language reflected the fight then raging over the passage of the Plant Quarantine Act and the need to strengthen federal control: "[I]t is essentially a national issue, but there is no law whereby the Federal Government can attempt to cope with the emergency. Each State must act on its own initiative and control the disease . . . [but] will be seriously handicapped if neighboring States do not."

By the time this somewhat unhelpful pronouncement was made, the state of Pennsylvania had already heeded its message. The year before, the Main Line Citizens' Association, a group of concerned and influential Philadelphians, had directed a campaign that ultimately produced state-level legislation to provide "efficient and practical means for the prevention, control, and eradication of a disease affecting chestnut trees, commonly called the chestnut-tree blight." The new law created a Chestnut Blight Commission and formed the basis for a grant from the state legislature of $275,000, an enormous sum that almost equaled the amount provided for all other state forestry activities. Agents of the commission subsequently began traveling across the state inspecting trees and destroying any suspicious specimens. The law authorized them to proceed even if the property owners protested.

In early 1912, the Chestnut Blight Commission hosted a conference at Harrisburg, Pennsylvania, to bring together the leading minds in the field for the first time. The sentiment among many of the participants was Pollyannaish, patriotic, and contemptuous of anyone who questioned the Pennsylvania program. The state's deputy commissioner of forestry declared to rousing applause: "The mere fact that somebody believes that something cannot be done is going to have mighty little weight in the work of this Commission. . . . [W]e do not care to join hands with those who see simply gloom and failure." A participant from New York accused naysayers of being "un-American." Murrill, who had spent more years studying the blight than anyone else, struggled to be heard above this dominant can-do spirit: "I do not believe in . . . wasting the public money uselessly. . . . I should say, keep in touch with the disease in every stage [but not] with reference to eradication, because I deem that impossible. Devote this year, at least, to scientific investigation."

One of the most pressing scientific mysteries at the time of the conference concerned the disease's origin. Some argued that knowing this information would help researchers devise strategies to limit its spread or possibly find a natural enemy to wipe it out altogether. The leading theory among pathologists at the Bureau of Plant Industry posited that it had come from somewhere in eastern Asia—the rationale was that Japanese and Chinese chestnut trees planted in America demonstrated resistance to the blight. In 1913, bureau researchers approached the nation's preeminent plant explorer, David Fairchild, with a request for assistance. He quickly assigned the task to Frank Meyer, an FSPI agent already on a mission in China. Meyer's skills in the field were legendary. He lived like an ascetic, covered incredible distances on foot, and helped introduce thousands of new plants to America (his name lives on in grocery stores across America with the Meyer lemon). Of the chestnut assignment, Fairchild explained, "Meyer was not a trained pathologist, but I felt confident that he would find the disease if it were common on the Chinese trees." Meyer didn't disappoint. Barely a month after receiving a sample of infected bark, he sent Fairchild a cablegram to announce his discovery of an identical fungus growing on Chinese trees. Bureau scientists analyzed a bark sample that Meyer sent soon thereafter and confirmed his claim. This discovery allowed agents to trace the likely source of the disease to Asian nursery stock imported in the late nineteenth century.

For a brief moment, it appeared to some that American scientists and forestry agents might get the upper hand on the outbreak. But the reality was stark. Discovering the source of the blight ultimately failed to produce new solutions. The existing control techniques continued to stumble along without slowing the spread of the disease. Federal quarantines, once they were introduced, did little to impede the blight's progress. Each year the zone of infection swelled, sometimes by as much as thirty miles, an incomprehensible rate of expansion.

When the Pennsylvania Chestnut Blight Commission issued a new report in 1914, the confidence of two years before had faded. The earlier optimistic language had been replaced with the type of circumspection that formerly

Trees have long been used as political symbols in America. *Above left,* a 1652 pine tree shilling from the Massachusetts Bay Colony. During the colonial era, certain trees also served as reminders of British control. *Above right,* in a nineteenth-century print, a royal timber surveyor places the King's Broad Arrow on a pine tree. When the colonies finally moved to break away from England, revolutionaries gathered beneath Boston's famous Liberty Tree to spread their message. *Below,* a Royal Stamp Act officer gets tarred and feathered beneath the boughs of the Liberty Tree.

The log cabin and cider barrel symbolized the spread of small freeholders and the settling of the forested landscape. *Above,* both symbols were featured prominently in ephemera from the 1840 presidential campaign of William Henry Harrison. In the cities, projects such as New York's Central Park, begun in 1857, brought nature and trees back into the landscape. *Below,* an 1859 architect's rendering of how trees would transform a stretch of Central Park.

As industrial logging developed, logs followed many different paths to market.
*Top,* two horses haul a massive cargo of timber from Michigan to the 1893 World's
Columbian Exposition in Chicago. *Middle,* an enormous raft of logs travels to market
along the Columbia River in Oregon. *Bottom,* a wood-burning train carries logs across
a timber-trestle bridge in the Cascade Mountains in the Pacific Northwest.

Millions of Americans have worked in industries dependent on trees. *Top,* Pacific Northwest loggers sit on the stump of a giant fir tree. *Middle,* laborers harvest turpentine from Southern pines. *Bottom,* workers pick oranges in California.

Teddy Roosevelt and Gifford Pinchot (seen above in a photo taken in 1907), who worked together to dramatically expand the national forest system, advocated for the wise use of natural resources through conservation. Others, like John Muir and John Burroughs (seen below in a photo taken in 1912), felt that nature deserved protection for its own sake and not just to ensure a long-term supply of resources.

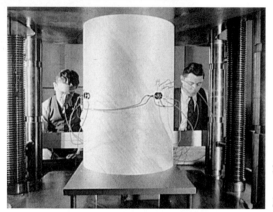

Numerous government agencies have appeared since the late nineteenth century to oversee the nation's tree resources. *Top,* a Forest Service ranger patrols for fire. *Middle,* two scientists at the Forest Products Laboratory in Madison, Wisconsin, run an experiment on a veneer cylinder. *Bottom,* agents from the Bureau of Plant Industry reject a gift of cherry trees from Japan after discovering infections in 1910.

Efforts to raise public awareness about trees have taken many forms. *Top left*, the 1932 Arbor Day stamp to celebrate the holiday's sixtieth anniversary. *Top right*, a 1938 advertisement in *American Forests* after the arrival of Dutch elm disease. *Bottom left*, a poster promoting the Shelterbelt, a pet project implemented by FDR during the New Deal. *Bottom right*, a government poster from World War II encouraging forest fire prevention as a military tactic.

Getty Images

*Above*, a tree being planted in Levittown in Long Island, New York, the archetypal post-WWII suburb, where each plot featured a similar wood-framed home. *Below*, Mayor Michael Bloomberg of New York City in 2010 at the 9/11 memorial site in downtown Manhattan dedicating the Survivor Tree, a Callery pear tree found alive among the wreckage at Ground Zero.

Getty Images

belonged to naysayers like Murrill. The report included a statement from the commission chairman that declared: "[I]t seems necessary to call sharp attention to the real lesson to be learned from the chestnut blight epidemic—viz: the necessity of more scientific research upon problems of this character; to be undertaken early enough to be of some value in comprehending, if not controlling, the situation."

Americans used to a life dependent on chestnuts were slow to accept the idea of total defeat. It simply seemed impossible that a tree so central to American ecology and culture could actually disappear. There was no precedent for such a change. In 1920, Gifford Pinchot, still one of the nation's leading authorities on forestry issues, said, "What happens as a rule is what I expect will happen in the case of the chestnut, . . . the plague itself will ultimately weaken, grow scarce, and disappear."

Across the South, the nation's great storehouse of chestnuts, residents hoped and prayed that Pinchot's prediction was proved correct, that the fungus would peter out naturally before destroying their natural environment. But this was no less naïve than the early attitude of the Pennsylvania commission. The first sign of trouble for the southern chestnuts had come in 1912, when the disease crossed the Potomac River, which historian Susan Freinkel described as "a botanical Maginot line." From there the fungus moved inexorably downward, infiltrating the Appalachians in the late 1920s and blanketing the entire region within fifteen years. The sight of dead chestnuts stretching off into the horizon was overwhelming. Fairchild wrote in 1938, "Last summer when I saw the hillsides in the Appalachians dotted with the tragic dead crowns of what had once been magnificent forest trees, . . . I regretted any feelings of impatience I may have had towards their quarantines and inspections."

By midcentury, the disease's triumph over the American chestnut was effectively complete, the scope of the damage difficult to comprehend. The merciless fungus had traversed some 200 million acres, wiping out virtually every mature specimen along the way. Scientists estimated that it killed between three and four billion American chestnut trees. When every mature tree had fallen, all that remained were the ever-persistent stump sprouts, which would grow for several years until the blight inevitably struck, a cycle that continued until the rootstock was finally exhausted. The American chestnut became, in effect, an understory shrub. The regal species that once lorded over the eastern forests had all but disappeared, gone from the mountains, gone from the woodlots, gone from the parks and gardens, gone from the life of a nation.

America slowly adjusted to this new reality. Industries turned to new tree species or new materials altogether. The same was true of residential construction and furniture making. The Appalachian inhabitants that had depended on their once-glorious trees were thrust further into poverty, and the chestnut vendors who once sold the Appalachian harvests switched to other varieties, many imported from overseas, none quite as flavorful. The eastern forests adapted to the incommensurable loss as well. Much of the chestnut territory yielded to oaks and a mix of other hardwoods that varied by region. But none of these trees could match the chestnut for mast or timber production. And none could offer the same midsummer blossom display that had once so enthralled President Roosevelt.

The destructiveness of chestnut blight marked it as one of the worst ecological disasters in the nation's history. But in the popular consciousness, it was not necessarily the most devastating tree plague. That honor belonged to a disease that first appeared in America at the height of the chestnut rampage. This time the concern was the eradication of a species prized not for its remarkable utility, but for its unmatched beauty.

## "The Most Magnificent Vegetable of the Temperate Zone"

UNLIKE THE AMERICAN CHESTNUT, the American elm was never prized for its wood. If anything, the situation was the precise opposite. A letter published in the *Atlantic Monthly* once declared, "[American elms] are the most useless piece of vegetation in our forests." It went on to explain, "They cannot be used for firewood because they cannot be split. The wood cannot be burned because it is full of water. It cannot be used for posts because it rots in a short time. It can be sawed into lumber but it warps and twists into corkscrews."

With all of these shortcomings, the species should have been little more than an afterthought in the national catalogue of trees. But what the American elm lacked in utility it overcame with elegance and grace. Charles Sprague Sargent once described the tree as follows: "[It] suggests a fountain in its manner of growth. . . . The massive shaft bursts into a sheaf of springing boughs, which again break into a shower of branches, with a spray of twigs. . . . [It] produces at all seasons an architectural effect of permanent beauty by the arched interlacings of the great bending boughs." The botanist François André Michaux (son of the French botanist André Michaux, who had collected American plants for France in the 1780s and 1790s) was more direct than Sargent in his praise. He simply dubbed the species "the most magnificent vegetable of the temperate zone."

This magnificent vegetable tended to grow along river bottoms and on low fertile hills. Though the trees were less abundant than chestnuts, their native range was much broader. With the exception of southern Florida, American elms covered the entire eastern United States, as far west as the region once known as the Great American Desert.

When the early British colonists arrived in America, they already possessed a special fondness for elms—many Massachusetts Bay settlers had emigrated from parts of England where English elms, a close relative of the American variety, had been a popular fixture of hedgerows and village greens since the late Middle Ages. According to Sargent, the colonists' "remembrance of the Elm-trees" hastened their embrace of the magnificent new species that they discovered along the moist bottomlands of New England forests. American elms were thus quickly cultivated as house trees—Sargent asserted that they were "the oldest and noblest trees . . . planted by man in North America." Many of these initial plantings developed into grand monarchs of the landscape, subjects of legend and veneration. One of these mighty specimens would mature into the famous Liberty Tree of Boston.

By the time of the Revolution, some wealthy individuals in larger Yankee communities, especially along the Connecticut River Valley, started to fund expansive elm plantings in their respective downtowns as a philanthropic gesture. Foremost among this group was James Hillhouse of New Haven, Connecticut, an officer in the Revolutionary War and later a U.S. senator. In 1786, he orchestrated a subscription campaign to bring a "Row of Elms" to a street that passed through his city's central green (and, conveniently, also through undeveloped property that he controlled). The Hillhouse trees were planted in double rows, spaced out at forty-foot intervals, creating the effect of an outdoor cathedral. Hillhouse worked tirelessly throughout his life to increase his city's elm canopy. When Charles Dickens passed through Connecticut during his famous 1842 trip to America, he marveled at the results of Hillhouse's labors, writing,

> New Haven, known also as the City of Elms, is a fine town. Many of its streets . . . are planted with rows of grand old elm-trees. . . . The effect is very like that of an old cathedral yard in England. . . . [The trees] seem to bring about a kind of compromise between town and country; as if each had met the other halfway, and shaken hands upon it; which is at once novel and pleasant.

The elm canopy that so enchanted Dickens soon expanded across most of New England. Towns and villages throughout the region, following the example set by population centers like New Haven, lined their greens and streets with endless rows of lofty elms. The plantings increased dramatically in the 1840s with the arrival of what one historian described as "a new longing for spatial beauty" that swept the region. Yankees seeking improved townscapes subsequently began to form village improvement societies, most of which placed their emphasis on encouraging elm introductions—the first such organization, founded in Sheffield, Massachusetts, was simply called the Elm Tree Association. The rows of elms springing up across these countless towns helped to counteract the denuded landscape that centuries of deforestation had produced, the same ecological degradation that had driven Thoreau to his seclusion in Walden Woods. In some respects, the widespread planting of American elms was a Yankee response to similar proto-environmentalist forces that helped inspire the novels of James Fenimore Cooper, the painters of the Hudson River School, the landscaped cemeteries of eastern cities, and the wilderness resorts of the Catskills and Saratoga.

The elm's popularity in this period owed a further debt to a new, fervent nationalism that was sweeping through Jacksonian America. Native trees were in vogue. Foreign trees, like the previously favored Lombardy poplar and Chinese ailanthus, were out. Andrew Jackson Downing, the famed landscape architect and tireless promoter of street-tree plantings, routinely cursed the ailanthus tree but described the elm in 1841 as "one of the most generally esteemed of our native trees for ornamental purposes, . . . for planting in public squares, and along the highways."

By the second half of the nineteenth century, the elm had completely colonized New England. In the popular consciousness the tree and the region were inseparable. "The peculiar glory of New England—its Elm-trees!" wrote Henry Ward Beecher, the esteemed Yankee preacher, in his 1867 novel *Norwood; or, Village Life in New England*. He continued: "The Elms of New England! They are as much a part of her beauty as the columns of the Parthenon were the glory of its architecture."

The Yankee region, however, did not control a monopoly on American elms. As eastern settlers relocated west during the nineteenth century, the trees began to appear in homesteads across the country. Thoreau, in comparing the species' expansion to that of the abolitionist movement, once described elms as "free-soilers in their own broad sense [that] send their roots north and south and east and west into many a conservative's Kansas and Carolina." One can imagine that lofty elms might have stood guard over the home of Frederick Weyerhaeuser in Rock Island, Illinois, or of J. Sterling Morton in Nebraska City, Nebraska, or of a teenage David Fairchild in Manhattan, Kansas.

Almost anywhere that a settler planted an American elm, the tree seemed to thrive. This was part of its charm—it was among the hardiest of species. Drought, salt, ice, mild flooding, heavy foot traffic, inconsiderate horses, none of it seemed to trouble the unflappable trees. Elms also endured air pollution, including the particulate matter that coal-burning factories were generating in ever-rising quantities. As a *New Yorker* article once observed, "It can live in almost any filth of smoke and soot and noxious fumes that man himself can tolerate."

During the late nineteenth century, as progressive reformers nation-wide began to agitate for wider metropolitan tree planting, the resilient elm expanded its dominion into many of the nation's burgeoning cities. Urban areas from coast to coast were soon filled with broad avenues shaded by elms. The streets of Minneapolis featured 600,000 specimens. Detroit and Cincinnati each hosted 400,000 trees. Dallas added another 150,000. Sacramento, California, possessed as many elms as New Haven. There were clusters of 10,000 or more ornamental elms in every state. The total number planted nationally by the 1930s exceeded 25 million—according to one contemporary report, "$650,000,000 would be a nominal estimate of what their owners think the trees are worth."

America's urban regions, like all of New England, were now bound by a great, unbroken chain of American elms, a remarkable canopy that shaded an ever-growing percentage of the nation's populace. But this sylvan situation, so central to American culture, was far more vulnerable than anyone had realized.

T HE CRISIS FIRST APPEARED in Europe during the closing months of World War I. Elm trees near Rotterdam, Holland, were exhibiting leaf browning and bark die-back at an epidemic rate. Similar problems were soon reported in parts of France and the other Low Countries. No one had any idea what was going on or where the problem had come from. A preliminary theory blamed the war: Since all of the affected regions had fallen in the conflict's destructive path, it seemed possible that the mysterious plague was nothing more than the aftereffects of nerve gas and extensive artillery fire. But the trouble continued to spread, radiating outward in all directions, ruining thousands of trees. The European scientific community began to suspect that something else was to blame, but no one was sure what.

The answer came in 1922 from a young Dutch graduate student named Maria Beatrice Schwarz. She determined—in a manner similar to Murrill's 1906 identification of the chestnut blight—that a fungus unknown to science, *Ophiostoma ulmi* (then called *Graphium ulmi*), was behind the rampaging elm plague. It entered the trees through wounds, expanded into the water-conducting tissues, plugged and poisoned these channels, and finally killed the host. Subsequent studies determined that the fungus was spread by the elm-bark beetle, a tiny, tree-boring insect—this distinguished the fungus from chestnut blight, whose spores traveled by air and infected new trees directly. Schwarz's discovery was eventually dubbed Dutch elm disease (DED).

Europeans were slow to accept Schwarz's conclusions (in part because of a prejudice against female scientists). This delayed control efforts for nearly a decade. In the meantime, the fungus marched along through Europe like an invincible army. It appeared in Germany in 1921; shortly thereafter it surfaced in Scandinavia; and in 1926 it finally hopped the Channel into England. The ancestral elms of the British countryside began to fall like so many dominoes.

American plant pathologists watched this scene with horror. They were already fighting a losing battle against the relentless chestnut blight. The thought of waging a new war against an equally merciless enemy was terrifying. There was, however, a defense shield in place: In 1918, partly in reaction to the chestnut blight, the USDA—under the guidance of Marlatt—had enacted a general quarantine on the importation of all nursery stock. This decree had dramatically curtailed the introduction of new plant pests (and, to Fairchild's consternation, new flora) from abroad, but most American scientists feared that it was only a matter of time before DED crossed the Atlantic and penetrated the quarantine.

The first scare came in the summer of 1930 when an arborist noticed a strange disease on an American elm in Cleveland. He brought his concern to an Ohio plant pathologist, Dr. Curtis May, who identified the problem as DED. Upon learning of this incident, the USDA's Division of Forest Pathology authorized funds to search for, identify, and destroy any additional cases. Eight infected trees were discovered over the next three years. They were all destroyed, and the outbreak seemed contained.

But many plant pathologists worried that the worst was yet to come. After all, if the disease had reached Ohio, it should have also surfaced along the East Coast, the entry point for commerce from Europe.

In June 1933, a park foreman in Maplewood, New Jersey, found several trees suffering from what appeared to be DED. This quickly proved to be a much broader infestation than the earlier scare in Cleveland. Within weeks the number of infected trees in New Jersey spiraled up to 361. Laboratory tests simultaneously confirmed thirteen cases scattered across southeastern New York. The nation now had a full-scale outbreak on its hands, but without knowing how the fungus was crossing the quarantine it was difficult to design a counteroffensive.

In August, a federal plant inspector at the port of Baltimore finally discovered the breach. A French shipment of elm burls—fancy-grained growths used for furniture veneers—contained both the elm-bark beetle and the deadly fungus. These burls had fallen outside the blanket quarantine. Further investigation determined that infected shipments had been entering America since 1926. The prized elm wood was routinely transported to furniture manufacturers located far inland—this helped explain the mysterious initial DED outbreak in Cleveland.

Now that the disease had established a beachhead in America, the federal government faced a difficult choice: Should DED be allowed to run its course and replicate the devastation in Europe or should resources be marshaled to combat the threat? The backdrop to this debate was, of course, the doomed operation against chestnut blight, a campaign that many felt had wasted large sums of money with few results. But the American elm was too integral to national life for authorities to fold their hands. According to George Hepting, former chief plant pathologist for the U.S. Forest Service, "There was a general agreement that the values at stake were worth the try."

The USDA's authority and jurisdiction had greatly increased since the days of the sakura shipment or the chestnut blight. In late October 1933, the department used its power under the Plant Quarantine Act to institute a supplemental quarantine on all European burl elm logs, largely stanching the flow of new infections. A DED laboratory was then established in Morristown, New Jersey, under the direction of Curtis May, the scientist who had first identified the disease in Cleveland. By early 1934, more than three hundred thousand dollars in federal funds had been issued to finance an eradication campaign.

For many of the people who had tried and failed to save the American chestnut, this initial federal action was reassuring but dangerously insufficient. An editorial in *American Forests* from November 1934 declared, "A half a million dollars is immediately needed and another half million next spring. For want of a million dollars, the American elm may be sacrificed on the altar of chance and official complacency." The American Forestry Association (AFA), which published *American Forests*, worked tirelessly to generate public pressure for greater funding. In December 1934, their campaign finally paid dividends: The federal government issued a grant of $527,000 from the Public Works Administration (PWA), a massive New Deal program tasked with directing funds toward worthy public initiatives. This grant, along with supplemental funds from the federal government and from the governments of New Jersey, New York, and Connecticut (the three affected states), brought the total amount of resources for 1935 above $900,000, more than three times the initial amount.

The eradication program, in response to this infusion of resources, expanded dramatically. Several thousand DED agents fanned out across the tristate region in search of infected trees. They marched through town and city and forest, authorized to destroy all trees that already harbored the infection as well as any whose decrepit condition made them susceptible. By the spring of 1935, *American Forests* was able to proudly declare, "The first phase of the fight against the Dutch elm disease was concluded . . . with the destruction of the last of 7,786 trees known to have been infected." That July, President Roosevelt supplemented the initial PWA allotment with a further commitment of $2.5 million.

The fight against DED, however, was much broader than the USDA-led eradication campaign. The American elm had become an integral part of towns and cities throughout the nation. The dappled shade under an elm canopy was the defining feature of New England, of many downtowns, and of the nation's innumerable Elm Streets. Communities depended on their elms, and many joined in the fight, not necessarily in order to curb the spread of the disease but simply to preserve the trees already in place—well-cared-for elms had a much greater chance of enduring. The soldiers on this front of the DED battle were not only government agents but arborists, men whose full-time job was to take care of trees. The DED epidemic happened to arrive in America just as the profession of arboriculture was coming into its own after years of growing in conjunction with America's increasing preference for shade and ornamental tree plantings—the profession's 1928 National Shade Tree Conference, according to historian Richard Campana, had marked "the formal beginning of a new era in the history of arboriculture."

The early results of everyone's combined effort to combat DED seemed promising. Elms in the cities remained under constant surveillance, while those in the deepest parts of the forests had little time to develop an infection before emergency workers reacted. By December 1937, over five thousand workers had eradicated more than four million trees, and the disease was spreading more slowly than some initial models had predicted. A pamphlet from the AFA declared, "Federal and state officials believe that if $15,000,000 is forthcoming during the next five year period this infection can be cleared up." This sounded like a large sum of money, but was comparable to the almost $11 million that had already been expended or pledged. The campaign seemed to be working. It was hoped that the USDA could contain the disease in the Northeast, just as it had done in Ohio. It would be an incredible triumph for the federal government and for plant pathologists, retribution for the failures of the American chestnut campaign.

But not everyone shared this confidence. For some, the lesson of the chestnut blight was that control efforts were futile against such a powerful pathogen. In early 1936, the chairman of the House Subcommittee on Agricultural

Appropriations had gone on record to declare, "We have been told that there was no hope of eradicating this disease." Part of the skepticism related to the deteriorating situation in Europe, where all initiatives to counter DED had failed utterly. In 1937, the USDA's representative in England explained: "After eighteen years of unsuccessful efforts to fight the disease which threatened her elms, Europe has decided to give it up as an aggressive campaign as far as eradication is concerned. . . . It can be only a few years until all the elms of England and the Continent are gone." If the disease had so thoroughly conquered Europe, the skeptics asked, what hope was there for America?

The answer to this question was demoralizing, but for reasons that no one could have foreseen. In the summer of 1938, a devastating storm struck the Northeast with a fury unknown before or since. Known as the Great Hurricane, it made landfall in New Haven, the Elm City, then on the outer edge of the infected zone. The powerful winds of the Great Hurricane tore down more than one million large shade trees, and the most affected species was, unsurprisingly, the American elm. When the storm receded, millions of board feet of downed elm wood were transported to junkyards and woodlots, creating ideal breeding grounds for the elm-bark beetle. The pest population subsequently swelled, accelerating the pace of DED transmission—the infected region, which had expanded roughly 47 percent in the four years preceding the storm, would balloon 258 percent in the four years that followed. As historian Thomas Campanella observed, "Dutch elm disease and the Great Hurricane converged with remarkable precision, as if an unseen hand had guided each to a fateful rendezvous."

The hurricane meant that more eradication agents were needed, but the political will was not where it had been previously. Congress began to curtail funding, partly out of defeatism and partly out of necessity—the concern for many was the increasing likelihood of America's entry into World War II. Resources would be needed to contain the spread of Nazism and the Axis powers. This trumped the need to contain the spread of DED. By 1940, the flow of federal dollars was essentially stopped. An exasperated AFA railed against this shift:

> It is true that in the light of national defense needs, there are many federal activities that can and should be set aside for the time being, but stopping the elm disease is not one of them. . . . Abandon the battle for even one season and most certainly all will be lost. . . . [A]ll the money spent to date—some $25,000,000— will have been spent in vain, the American elm will be marked for death.

But these protests fell on deaf ears. The needs of total war were simply too great, the odds of containing DED too long.

As America geared up to enter the conflict, DED inched ever deeper into New England, center of elm culture. In 1941, it appeared in Massachusetts for the first time. The state was blanketed during the course of the war. Elms that had stood for hundreds of years, mighty giants that dated back to the days of the first colonists, now started to fall. Soon DED swarmed across the rest of the Yankee districts: Vermont in 1945; Rhode Island the following year; New Hampshire and Maine shortly thereafter. As the AFA feared, the restriction of funds had opened the door for much more aggressive expansion. The elms of New England, subjects of so much poetry, ended up indirect casualties of the nation's effort to defeat the Axis powers.

World War II, nonetheless, introduced a promising new tool to help save the millions of American elms that remained: dichloro-diphenyl-trichloroethane, also known as DDT. In 1939, scientists had discovered that this chemical compound, first synthesized in 1874, possessed potent insecticidal properties. During the latter half of the war, DDT was employed to great effect in combating malaria and typhus. Researchers soon realized that it might also be employed to kill the elm-bark beetle that spread the deadly elm fungus. The first official experiment, which used a high-powered spray to coat elms in the compound, took place at Englewood, New Jersey, in May 1947. According to the *New York Times,* a local official assured that "the spray would be of minimum danger to bird and animal life." The practice of treating elms with DDT quickly spread to other cities and townships, especially in the Midwest, where DED had not yet made serious inroads. In the years that followed, more than a billion pounds of the supposedly safe chemical were dispersed. No one could state definitively that the spraying impeded the spread of DED, but it appeared to be the best tactic available.

As time wore on, however, the claims that DDT was benign received increasing scrutiny. In 1958, a scientific study alleged that the spraying of elms directly led to bird deaths across the Midwest—the theory was that DDT remained on the leaves, which were eaten by earthworms, which were in turn eaten by birds. This study attracted relatively little attention until 1962, when it was referenced in a series of *New Yorker* articles written by Rachel Carson, a well-regarded environmentalist and author. She inveighed against pesticides, particularly DDT, and used elm spraying as one of her core examples. Her article argued that DDT was not only responsible for killing birds and poisoning the environment, but that its benefits against Dutch elm disease had been largely exaggerated. As she explained: "To the public, the choice may easily appear to be one of stark simplicity: Shall we have birds or shall we have elms? But it is not as simple as that. . . . Spraying is killing the birds but is not saving the elms. The theory that the survival of the elms lies in spraying is a dangerous illusion." Carson soon turned her articles into a book, *Silent Spring*, which almost single-handedly revolutionized the way that Americans thought about pesticides. The American elm had found itself at the center of a new national campaign against toxic chemicals, one of the most swift and powerful social movements of the 1960s. By 1972, the practice of DDT spraying was banned. This was, in some respects, the final blow—symbolically if not actually—to the long-standing fight to neutralize the impact of Dutch elm disease.

Attitudes over time shifted to what one forest pathologist called "learning to live with the disease." As Europe had accepted in 1937, there was no possibility of containing the fungus. It was better simply to focus on preserving the elms that remained. Thanks to advances in arboriculture, parks and cities across the country have managed to preserve some of their elm specimens, at least for the time being. Of course, part of the reason these trees survive is the high percentage of elms that have already succumbed, reducing the potential number of host sites for the elm-bark beetle. By the 1980s, DED had claimed the lives of more than 77 million trees.

As with the death of the American chestnut, the decline of the American elm forced society to adapt. No tree could match its unique aesthetic appeal. Even if such a tree existed, it is unlikely that it would ever be planted so expansively out of fear of another plague. The culture that once defined New England and many cities simply disappeared. But it wasn't all bad news: The DED catastrophe led to a strengthening of the urban forestry movement, stimulated new education and research, and promoted tree-planting initiatives.

The decline of two beloved tree species and the rise of a new federal plant control apparatus were far from the only forces affecting the nation's relationship to its trees during the first half of the twentieth century. World War I, the Great Depression, the New Deal, and World War II all influenced the way that Americans understood and interacted with their woody resources. It was an era of ambitious government programs, of wartime sacrifice, of economic necessity. The efforts made to save the American elm and American chestnut, expansive as they were, paled in comparison to some of the other initiatives that would emerge around trees during this time.

# 8

## Trees as Good Soldiers and Citizens

Norway Spruce

## The Wooden Wings of War

O N MAY 7, 1917, Brice Disque, a thirty-eight-year-old retired army captain, received an urgent telegram demanding his presence at the War Department in Washington, D.C. America had declared war on Germany the month before, and the nation was scrambling to institute the largest overseas military mobilization in its history. At the head of this chaotic and disorganized effort sat General John J. Pershing, known to his men as "Black Jack." And it was Pershing's chief of staff who had sent the telegram to Disque.

Disque hurried over to the War Department, assuming that the telegram was a response to his recent offer to reenlist. Perhaps, Disque thought, he was being considered for a coveted position to serve directly alongside Pershing.

But when Disque arrived, he learned that the general had other plans for him. Pershing explained that he wanted Disque to remain a civilian but needed him to carry out a secret mission, one too delicate for official army involvement. "Black Jack" needed a military man he could depend on, and Disque was someone whom he knew and held in high regard. The task was simple: Keep an eye on the situation in the Pacific Northwest lumber industry.

This request struck Disque as odd. In his own words, he knew "not the slightest" thing about logging. He was certainly no forester. He was, rather, a soldier through and through, the sort of man who seemed born to wear a military uniform. As one newspaper report described him, "Equipped with a splendid physique and a fine personality he has been a student of military science to such good effect that few officers of his years can equal him."

His career had been spent almost entirely in the service of his country, much of it in the Philippines, a territory that the United States had acquired during the Spanish-American War (1898). There, he had participated in efforts to suppress the Filipino insurrection, and in that campaign his path had first intersected with Pershing, who was then a fast-rising general. Disque earned praise for his administrative leadership in turning around an underperforming U.S. Army logistics unit in the Philippines. His reputation was that of a man who got things done that others couldn't, even if it cost him friends along the way. Since resigning from the military in late 1916—a decision that had been made largely out of consideration for the needs of his growing family but one that Disque immediately regretted—he had been working as the warden of a state penitentiary in Michigan. It had been a life, in sum, that hardly seemed to qualify him to secretly report on trees for the army.

But Pershing was adamant. He insisted that this covert assignment was far more important than overseas service with the American Expeditionary Force that was then being assembled. The nation's trees, quite possibly, held the key to winning the war.

Pershing's pronouncement was curious, to say the least. But over the course of their meeting, Disque would come to understand the complicated chain of logic that underlay much of the general's concern.

It was, in the most basic strategic terms, a question of air supremacy. Though the war had arrived barely a decade after the Wright brothers' first successful flight at Kitty Hawk, North Carolina, in 1903, the airplane was quickly developing into a military tool of almost unlimited potential. It allowed for overhead spying; it made possible bomb deployments from outside the range of artillery fire; and, of course, there was the new class of flying aces, like Germany's Manfred von Richthofen, the lethal Red Baron, or America's Eddie Rickenbacker, whose exploits would capture the imagination of a generation of young boys. Whoever controlled the skies, many felt, could dictate the terms of ground combat. The need for air supremacy was so essential to U.S. strategic planners that Congress was already in the process of allocating $1 billion toward a wartime airplane program, the largest single government expenditure in American history to that point.

To a remarkable extent, this all-important military technology depended on trees. The most popular aircraft construction material from the outset had been wood, which was plentiful, easy to work, and in possession of a high strength-to-weight ratio. Aviation pioneers, in consequence, had designed planes that depended on wood's unique properties. Most notably, they had exploited the capacity of wooden structures to flex—the first successful airplanes, including those of the Wright brothers, had controls that literally twisted the spars (the wooden beams that supported the wings); this technique, known as "wing warping," allowed for lateral control, a key to the success of early aircraft.

Of course, not just any wood would do. Most hardwoods (such as oak or maple) were simply too heavy, while most softwoods (such as pine or cedar) were too weak. Through trial and error, aviation pioneers had determined that spruce lumber—often disfavored in construction for its susceptibility to decay and insect damage—possessed an ideal combination of lightness, strength, and durability. An article in *American Forests* noted that spruce was "stronger ounce for ounce than high-tensile steel." According to Wilbur Wright, the plane that he and his brother used in 1903 for their first successful flight was constructed primarily from "the very best straight-grained spruce." This type of wood quickly became the standard for almost all early models, including military ones.

But airplane-quality spruce wood was difficult to find. Timber that was warped or knotty or that contained twisted grain was often too weak to survive the strains of a rocky landing or the pressures of takeoff. And short timbers were equally problematic: Much like the ship masts of an earlier era, airplane spars—the all-important backbones in the wings—were strongest when hewn from a single length of lumber.

The northeastern forests, though they supplied some 70 percent of the nation's commercial spruce at the time, were incapable of meeting aircraft demand. The region's dominant spruce species, commonly known as red spruce, typically did not grow large enough to satisfy the construction requirements. Moreover, by the turn of the century, papermakers had already chopped down many of the old-growth spruce stands in the race to acquire pulpwood. The Wright brothers, based in Dayton, Ohio, often butted up against this eastern supply problem. In a 1904 letter, they complained, "We have found it impossible to obtain [spruce] lumber in our local yards."

The answer to this dilemma lay out West. The far corner of the nation was home to the Sitka spruce, the world's largest species of spruce. It was one of the western giants, taller than all but the coastal redwoods and the Douglas fir, its height sometimes exceeding three hundred feet. John Muir described it as "a very beautiful and majestic tree," adding, "I have seen logs of this species a hundred feet long and two feet in diameter at the upper end."

The newly important species grew all along the West's coastal forests, from southern Oregon straight through to Alaska. From the perspective of airplane construction, however, the best stands, in terms of both quality and accessibility, resided exclusively within the Pacific Northwest. As historian Harold Hyman noted, "the Northwest had a virtual monopoly of the world's remaining supply of this suddenly invaluable resource." There were some 11 billion board feet in total, enough to meet the wartime needs of both the United States and the Allies, who were equally dependent on the nation's Sitka spruce trees. One of the representatives of the French Aviation Service observed, "Your spruce will prove the decisive factor in the big European conflict."

The problem—and this explained Pershing's urgent telegram to Disque—was the labor situation in the region. A combination of miserable work conditions, a young, rootless labor force, and intransigent management had turned the forests of the Pacific Northwest into a breeding ground for the radical, syndicalist union known as the Industrial Workers of the World. Conflicts were growing increasingly frequent and violent between IWW members, known as "wobblies," and lumbermen (a broad term that could include the mill owners, timberland speculators, management, and foremen). In the most serious incident up to that point, which occurred in the fall of 1916 at Everett, Washington, some thirty-one wobblies were gunned down by special deputies in an event known as "Bloody Sunday." If the situation continued to worsen, it threatened to shut down lumber production across the region, which would, among other things, cripple airplane production and, consequently, the war effort.

Pershing explained to Disque that he had discussed these concerns earlier with Secretary of War Newton Baker. The two men had agreed that Pershing ought to have someone with a military outlook monitoring the situation, but Baker had insisted that the individual remain unofficial and civilian. Organized labor was a powerful force at that time in America and one that had helped reelect President Woodrow Wilson. If news leaked out of Pershing's interest in the labor situation of the Pacific Northwest forests—and its implication of direct army involvement—it might set off a storm of protest in the nation's reform and labor press, further inflaming the already precarious situation in the forests. Disque, who was technically a civilian, offered a way around this dilemma for the moment.

Even after Pershing finished presenting all of this to Disque, the former army captain remained unconvinced. Accepting the assignment meant delaying his enlistment, which made little sense to a career soldier. Furthermore, Disque had decided that he wanted to remain in the army after the war, and everyone knew that promotions would go first to the men who saw overseas service. Pershing acknowledged that the secret assignment would mean a personal sacrifice, but ultimately it was what the nation needed from Disque most. Eventually, the pressure from America's most powerful military commander proved too much, and Disque, who was patriotic to a fault, reluctantly agreed. He would remain a civilian and become an unofficial watchdog.

As spring turned to summer, and with Disque observing from afar, the labor situation deteriorated further, just as Pershing had feared. The wobblies were demanding improved camp conditions and, most important, the eight-hour workday, which had become something of a signal issue for labor groups around the nation. While these requests were far less radical than the wobblies' heated anticapitalist rhetoric, the lumbermen still refused to budge. Most had no interest in recognizing the wobblies or in ceding bargaining power to unions. And the eight-hour day was an especially problematic demand, one that many lumbermen felt could not be conceded at any cost. As Disque observed, "Being mostly men who had risen from the ranks, who had worked 12 to 14 hours a day in order to attain their present efficiency, they had never considered any work too hard for themselves and they did not consider any work too hard for those whom they employed."

Tensions continued to build until early July, when wobblies throughout the forests began to walk off the job. The strikes quickly "spread through the region like a contagion." By the height of summer, some 40 percent of the workers had laid down their axes, and spruce shipments, which needed to meet monthly orders of 10 million board feet, temporarily dropped to almost nothing. The lumbermen, meanwhile, met the wobbly challenge head-on. At the height of the strike, they banded together to form the Lumbermen's Protective Association, an organization dedicated to holding a hard line against any labor demands. This move took a page from the southern lumbermen, who had earlier formed a similar organization to brutally repress unions, including the famous and bloody incident with the labor activist Sol Dacus in Bogalusa, Louisiana.

By early fall, the labor situation in the Pacific Northwest seemed utterly hopeless. The wobblies who were still working had begun to employ a tactic known as a strike-on-the-job. They idled about during their shifts, sabotaged campsites, and laid down their tools after eight hours. Lumbermen remained largely uncompromising. President Wilson had transmitted a personal message to all involved in the labor conflict, asking for them to cooperate in a "conciliatory spirit," but it had done little to relieve the animosity. To make matters worse, many of the least radicalized loggers had volunteered for the war effort, shrinking the overall labor pool and concentrating the power of the wobblies. Spruce shipments, by this point, were hovering around 2.5 million board feet per month, barely a quarter of what the United States and the Allies needed. But more troubling than all of this was a rumor that had reached all the way up to Secretary of Labor William Wilson: "[U]nless present conditions are changed a complete strike will occur in the spring." If that happened, Allied air power would be doomed.

Disque had been quietly observing all of this for six months, still hoping for an opportunity to join the American Expeditionary Force in Europe, when he was once again summoned to the War Department in early October 1917. This time the call had come from Secretary of War Baker. Upon arrival, Disque learned that Baker had finally reached the same conclusion as Pershing: The army would likely need to get involved in the Pacific Northwest forests. The situation had simply grown too volatile to allow either the lumber industry itself or nonmilitary government agencies to find a workable solution. Everyone involved was tainted or compromised. A central authority figure was needed, someone who "wakes up and thoroughly organizes the work," in the words of one of Baker's staff.

The secretary of war then turned to Disque and made an unusual request: Could he become a soldier once more and take charge of the spruce production problem? It would be uncharted territory, the first time in the nation's history that the army intervened in labor unrest and the first time that it directly took over a civilian means of production. But the outcome of the war just might depend on it.

Once more, Disque felt torn. He desperately wanted to head to the front and had even lined up a potential assignment. But Baker, like Pershing earlier, asked him to put his country first. As Disque later explained, they "presented the thing to me in such a manner . . . that it looked like a national necessity to have the spruce during this winter period [of 1917–18], so that the material could get into the airplanes and be on the west front by the time of the spring drive." They "made it a matter of cold-blooded duty for me to accept it, and finally I agreed."

On October 10, Disque arrived in Seattle. His instructions were to spend two weeks touring the region and then report back to Baker. It was a limited mandate for the moment, but Disque carried himself with a soldier's confidence: shoulders back, chin up, boots polished to a gloss. He didn't hesitate to imply that his authority over the woods was unchecked. And for all that the feuding lumbermen and laborers knew, this was the truth.

But in reality Disque was simply trying to find his bearings in a strange environment where it was almost impossible to determine how to increase spruce production. To help him navigate these issues, the Council of Defense—the nation's civilian wartime advisory board, which Baker chaired—had arranged for a team of local experts to serve as his escorts. This group included Carleton Parker, an academic who had been working on behalf of the government to mediate the western strikes. Parker believed that most wobblies were less radical than their literature suggested and were simply out for improved labor conditions: "The I.W.W. . . . is but a phenomenon of revolt" against "a certain distressing state of [economic] affairs."

Disque initially held a competing view: Wobblies were an inherent threat, a seditious group that needed to be eradicated. This was a relatively commonplace attitude in America, one that had underlain Pershing's original concerns and which he'd expressed during the secret meeting back in May. But when Disque saw the deplorable conditions of the logging camps, he quickly came around to Parker's philosophy. There was no way, he felt, that the labor problem could be mitigated without improving camp life and meeting the wobblies' basic demands. But he would need to carve out some solution that could allow this without alienating the lumbermen.

Working with Parker, Disque began to sketch out plans for an unusual two-pronged solution. First, the army would create a new division, the Spruce Production Division (SPD), tasked with getting the spruce out of the forest. It would include a force of several thousand enlisted men, ideally with logging experience, who could help to supplement the tumultuous labor pool. And, in a worst-case scenario, these soldiers, armed with rifles as well as axes, could intervene to suppress the wobblies. Disque described this proposal—the idea of using soldiers as a workforce in private industry—as "a radical departure from a custom as old as the nation."

But the second prong of his plan was, in many respects, an even stranger departure: a paramilitary labor organization that Disque would lead to be known as the Legion of Loyal Loggers and Lumbermen (4L). It would seek to bring all the interested groups—the lumbermen, wobblies, unaffiliated workers, and SPD soldiers—into a single body built around the idea of patriotism. This meant abandoning most traditional union tactics—namely, the right to strike—but Disque and Parker felt that it was the best chance for a mediated outcome. All members would need to sign a pledge that tracked something of a middle ground between the two sides. Thus, each 4L inductee would promise both to "improve the living environment in camps and mills" and "to stamp out anarchy and sabotage wherever I may find it." Notably absent from the pledge, however, was any mention of the eight-hour workday, which remained the most contentious issue.

Disque soon returned to Washington to sell the odd-sounding plan. Many at the War Department endorsed the proposal, but strong opposition came from Samuel Gompers, who was both the head of the American Federation of Labor union and the representative for organized labor on Baker's Council for National Defense. Gompers was dead-set against allowing a paramilitary labor organization of any sort, partly on principled grounds and partly because it undermined the credibility of his own AFL, which was trying to increase its presence in the Pacific Northwest. Disque tried to push back against Gompers, but ultimately agreed to abandon the 4L in order to gain approval for the SPD.

However, when Disque arrived back in the forests of the Pacific Northwest, he discovered that the 4L idea—which he and Parker had already discussed with industry representatives—had taken on something of a life of its own. The lumbermen now appeared eager to sign up in large numbers. A confidential memo written by George S. Long, the influential manager of Weyerhaeuser's western timber holdings, suggested that Disque's cocksure presence had made the owners fearful of full army takeover if they didn't get behind the new organization. He wrote: "[Disque] has full authority to go to any extreme that may be necessary to bring about [spruce] production. . . . To do this, of course, means some kind of a mutual harmonious solving of the labor problem." It was also possible, as some historians have argued, that the lumbermen were only backing the 4L out of the hope that Disque would crush the wobblies and then disappear once the war concluded.

Regardless of the motivation, the lumbermen's endorsement gave the 4L new momentum. Disque soon found himself unable to contain its expansion and, being a pragmatist, began devoting SPD resources to organizing activities—this despite the promises he had made to Gompers, a man it was never wise to cross. Over the next several months, SPD soldiers spread out through the forests as recruiters. The 4L membership rolls quickly swelled into the tens of thousands. By early spring it was the dominant labor force in the forests, with Disque at its helm. Many workers seemed to have signed up out of a sense of patriotism and a belief that the 4L might bring real relief to camp conditions. However, the army's coercive presence unquestionably helped. As one wobbly wrote, "Its sole hold on its membership is through intimidation and the fact that in some cases it promises more security of position to join it than not to."

The combined growth of the 4L and the SPD suddenly gave Disque unprecedented power over the lumber industry and the trees of the Pacific Northwest. His reach exceeded that of any of the lumber barons in the dominant cabal that controlled production. Even the mighty Weyerhaeuser, who died three years before Disque's arrival, had never possessed as broad an influence (at least over labor conditions and production quotas). Disque had used the promise of providing SPD soldiers—who were considered to be both the most reliable laborers and a sharp influence against radicalism—to gain leverage over the lumbermen: The condition of receiving these soldiers was typically the improvement of camp conditions, such that they rose to a level equal with that of army life. And by early 1918, Disque had fundamentally restructured many of the work conditions in the industry.

However, one challenge still remained, the stickiest issue of all, the eight-hour workday. This point of contention had lain relatively dormant during the initial growth of the 4L. The reason for this was that the reduced daylight hours of the winter months had kept work hours limited naturally. But as the days lengthened, the problem reemerged.

Only now, unlike the situation the previous summer, Disque was in charge. His authority, by this point, arose from not only the army and the 4L, but even from the hard-line lumbermen, whose Protective Association had recently agreed to abide by Disque's conclusions on the eight-hour question. Whatever choice Disque made would be the final word.

But he was himself torn. On the one hand, as he explained: "I can't understand any man who would want to cut his work off on 8 hours during the war period." On the other hand, he feared that "the industry would probably be wrecked for months to come if we didn't announce for the eight-hour day."

Ultimately, pragmatism trumped his principled sense of patriotism. In late February Disque declared that the entire Pacific Northwest lumber industry would shift to an eight-hour workday beginning March 1, 1918. To strengthen this pronouncement, he added that SPD soldiers would only be assigned to camps that complied. Remarkably, his orders were followed practically to the letter. The labor situation finally appeared under control, almost one year after Pershing initially reached out to Disque.

However, it turned out that Pershing's focus on the labor situation had dangerously oversimplified the spruce production challenge. Disque had discovered that while labor unrest was the central problem, it was far from the only one. The industry as a whole was simply not organized around producing airplane-grade Sitka spruce. Lumber companies in the coastal forests historically had designed their operations around access to Douglas fir trees, the region's primary commercial species, and not Sitka spruces. Consequently, many of the best spruce stands remained functionally unreachable, lacking road or rail access. Furthermore, and perhaps more important, most mills could not actually produce airplane-quality Sitka spruce. The tree's grain tended to twist in the outer part of the logs, where the clearest cuts of lumber were found. Traditional mills that tried to cut spruce thus frequently produced cross-grained timbers that airplane manufacturers could not use. In the estimation of one observer, this problem alone had rendered nine-tenths of pre-SPD spruce production useless to the Allies.

Disque determined that the only way to resolve this problem was for the SPD to build its own spruce mill. The government, however, had no more practice at building logging facilities than it did building labor organizations. Plus, given the scale of military requirements, an ordinary-sized mill would barely make a dent in the production orders. But Disque let none of this dissuade him. He devoted much of late 1917 to designing a massive spruce production center, one whose capacity would exceed even that of the big mill at Bogalusa—1.5 million board feet a day, 50 percent greater than the highest day of production at the Louisiana factory. Ordinarily, construction of such an operation would take a year or more, but using SPD labor Disque managed to have it built in roughly forty-five days. And it opened just in time, less than a month before Disque's eight-hour workday pronouncement.

By the spring of 1918, with the labor and mill issues under control, spruce production finally reached the desired 10 million monthly board feet level. This remarkable turnaround staved off an Allied air power crisis. And Disque's success emboldened military planners to make great demands. As he explained, "[T]he Director of Aircraft Production notified me [in mid-1918] that . . . he wanted thirty million feet of lumber monthly, and that the requirement might [go] up to fifty million feet."

Before Disque's arrival in the Pacific Northwest, these amounts would have been inconceivable, but the SPD was now ready for this new challenge. Under Disque's guidance, 4L members constructed hundreds of miles of railroad, opening up billions of feet of timber located in remote stands—an article in *American Forestry* declared this "the most ambitious transportation project ever attempted in one year in the Pacific Northwest." The SPD also initiated construction on several new massive cutting facilities, two of which were equal in size to Bogalusa. And Disque instituted a policy of selective logging, which forced loggers to fell only aircraft-quality spruce and few of the surrounding Douglas firs.

With each passing month, the spruce totals climbed steadily upward. By November, SPD production had jumped to 22 million feet, more than enough for the needs of the United States and the Allies. However, that would be as high as the production totals rose. For on November 11, 1918, armistice was declared. The war was suddenly over, twenty months after the United States had entered the fray.

The end arrived barely a year after Disque had first traveled to the Pacific

Northwest forests, but in that short time he had managed to alter the course of the war and the lumber industry. Pershing and Baker had been correct that the nation needed him in the woods more than at the front. By the time of the armistice, Disque's staff had grown to nearly 30,000 SPD soldiers. The 4L, which he oversaw, counted more than 125,000 members, many of them former wobblies. Disque himself had recently been promoted to the rank of brigadier general, a title that rarely went to those working on the home front.

But the most important measurement of Disque's impact was, in many respects, neither troop levels, nor 4L rosters, nor ranks. It was Sitka spruce production. His programs had managed to raise output levels 1,700 percent, for a total of 143 million board feet during the life of the SPD.

This unprecedented increase in production led directly to a surge in Allied air power. As Disque explained, "Before America entered the war the airplane issue between the two groups of contestants was even. America swung that issue in favor of the Allies. Ten thousand Allied planes were built of American spruce and other American products." At the time of the armistice, the Allies possessed six times as many planes as Germany. The head of the nation's Aircraft Production Board later claimed, "[Disque's] operation, in my opinion, was the most important thing that confronted us. I mean, we could have fallen down anywhere else, and the Allies might have carried on, but if we fell down in the spruce production the Allies went down with us, because they were depending on us for their spruce, and they had no substitute."

For his efforts, Disque might have been remembered as a war hero. But such was not to be his fate. While the SPD had achieved its mission of supplying spruce, the nation's broader aircraft production program had developed into a costly disaster. No U.S.-manufactured aircraft ever saw action at the front, and politicians wanted to find someone accountable. Eventually, a congressional spotlight landed on Disque.

In hearings before the House Subcommittee on Aviation, his activities were picked apart for days on end. Many voices sought to defend Disque—George Long, for instance, noted in a telegram "that without [Disque's] efforts the entire problem of getting out lumber would not have been solved" and that he believed "in the former chief's ability and integrity." But the congressional committee's chairman would have little of it. He and other hostile congressmen (mostly Republicans looking to capitalize on a weakening Democratic Party) forced Disque to justify every decision he'd made: Who had given him the authority to declare an eight-hour workday, a power that typically rested with Congress? What had made him think that the army's mandate included the creation of a paramilitary unit? Why had he built such elaborate sawmills? The more Disque tried to explain, the sterner the chairman seemed to become.

"Don't make any attempt to philosophize," the chairman scolded. At one point, Disque grew so frustrated that he responded to the chairman, "Don't waive [*sic*] your fingers at me." And then added, "I want the record to clearly indicate the attitude of the chairman."

The endless testimony took its toll on Disque. As a man who had sacrificed his future army career to help serve his country in the forests, he felt it absurd to reevaluate reasonable military decisions in the cold light of peace. The hearings turned Disque's tendencies to assertiveness and self-assuredness into liabilities. Moreover, the constant questioning brought to the surface a latent paranoia—Disque became convinced that the enemies he had made during the war were out for retribution; near the top of his list was Gompers, who had continued to clash with Disque over the creation of the 4L.

Ultimately, the congressional panel found Disque innocent of any malfeasance, but the process had left Disque wholly disillusioned and had smeared his reputation. He retreated to a career in the private sector. In the end, his willingness to tackle the spruce production problem, as he initially feared, had cost him a postwar military career, even if it might have saved the war effort.

The termination of Disque's army career, it should be noted, did not mark the end of the paramilitary labor organization he had created and overseen. Following the armistice, members of the 4L voted overwhelmingly to continue the organization as a peacetime labor body. In Disque's estimation, "After a taste of better living nobody wanted to go back to the old ways." The 4L's continued presence kept the wobblies from regaining their footing, and, in consequence, the IWW would never again play a major role in the Pacific Northwest forests. But the 4L was not an infallible substitute for a peacetime labor union, wobbly or otherwise. The absence of SPD soldiers and of Disque left the organization vulnerable to abuse. Over time, the owners turned it into a promanagement organization and membership dropped accordingly. It finally died in the 1930s during the New Deal. Interestingly, this was roughly the same moment that the airplane industry began shifting from wooden to aluminum construction. Thus, in a fitting twist of fate, the 4L disappeared just as the Sitka spruce trees that had helped lead to its creation ceased being the key to military air power.

S ITKA SPRUCE, of course, was not the only American tree recruited into the war effort. The nation's military operation required an incredible amount of wood, billions of board feet in total. And such immense needs affected commercial forests from coast to coast.

Some of the heaviest use of wood concerned the effort simply to prepare the nation to enter the fight. Almost no facilities existed to house or train troops when America declared war, a result of Wilson's long-standing insistence on formal neutrality. Once war was announced, the army immediately initiated an ambitious program to build temporary wooden shelters, known as cantonments, for the millions of soldiers it anticipated. This approach differed notably from that of earlier wars; as a 1918 article from *American Forestry* noted: "Housing of armies is no longer in tents, but in wooden cities."

Once soldiers arrived at these wooden cities, they discovered that the products from trees would be essential to many aspects of military life. Nearly all supplies arrived in wooden crates and containers; heat was frequently generated using wood fires; standard-issue rifles featured wooden stocks; troops and supplies traveled in wooden railway cars, many of which were hastily constructed in the spring of 1917. The list was seemingly endless, though not surprising. The military was simply transferring many of the conventions of civilian life—where wood remained a ubiquitous, relatively inexpensive option for countless tasks—to wartime needs.

Within the European theater of combat, timber and other forest products were perhaps even more essential than on the home front. The Allied nations had needed to raid their forests to acquire sufficient wood for bridges, rail ties, telegraph poles, hospitals, cantonments, and innumerable other parts of the wartime infrastructure. Additionally, the trench system—a 350-mile-long network of interconnected dugouts that ran along the front from the North Sea to the Swiss border—consumed remarkable quantities of wood: To minimize the standing water that bred disease and wreaked havoc on soldiers' feet, the trench floors were lined with wooden planks, known as "duckboards," which needed to be frequently replaced. Soldiers at the front thus spent significant amounts of time using wood to repair their trenches, not only the floors but also the sides, the parapets, and the wooden platforms where they placed artillery. And should a soldier bravely attempt to cross the barbed-wire-filled no-man's-land, he would pass by countless wooden stakes, millions of which supported the deadly wire matrix all along the front.

For the American army, getting the timber needed to support combat operations in this European theater created a unique challenge. Raw lumber was an especially bulky commodity. Transporting it across the Atlantic was expensive and took up limited shipping space (airplane spruce being a notable exception). Thus, no matter how much wood the United States could produce, there was no simple way to bring sufficient quantities to the front.

Shortly after the nation entered the war, commanders from the United States and the Allies met to find a solution to this dilemma. French representatives noted that their nation, even after three years of fighting, possessed plenty of standing commercial timber. That country's professionally managed forests—the same ones that Gifford Pinchot had so admired as a young man—had withstood the assaults of war. As one French logger quipped, "Our forests have fought several wars before this one." But France's forests were in better shape than their foresters, whose ranks had been decimated during the war. An agreement was soon reached wherein France agreed to provide the U.S. military with trees if the American Expeditionary Force supplied the manpower.

In the spring of 1917, the army put out a call for foresters and loggers to serve as specialized soldiers in the forests of Europe. This request was soon answered by the nation's growing cadre of foresters, whose ranks had swelled dramatically since Pinchot's days as head of the Forest Service. These volunteers, some ten thousand in total, then formed the Tenth Engineers (Forestry), part of the American Expeditionary Force. They headed to France in June 1917.

The need for lumber at the front, however, quickly grew so great that this initial group proved incapable of meeting the American force's demands, which had spiraled to 73 million board feet per month. To remedy this shortage, another unit of equal size headed over in early 1918. This brought the total number of Americans working in the French forests to twenty thousand. Over the course of the war, they produced more than 200 million feet of lumber, half a million cords of fuelwood, and millions more rail ties, barbed-wire stakes, and duckboards. Colonel James Woodruff, the forest unit's commander, proudly told his troops after the armistice: "Your part in winning the war has been as important as that of any other troops in the AEF." And, indeed, this was so, for without sufficient wood supplies, the entire AEF operation would have been compromised.

T HE JOY OF the victory over Germany did not last long before the nation began to reflect on what it had cost. Though America had not endured casualties anywhere near the scale of its European allies, the country had still lost more than 117,000 of its sons and fathers. It was the largest loss of life in a military conflict since the Civil War, and communities across the nation sought ways to pay tribute to the men who had bravely sacrificed their lives for their country.

The traditional approach was to construct monuments of bronze, marble, or stone, symbols meant to endure for centuries as testament to the cost of war. But some now turned to trees, which could stand as living memorials for the fallen.

At first, this idea caused a degree of controversy. An editorial in the *New*

*York Times* from early December 1918 stated, "A memorial of soldiers should have more enduring form." It considered tablets placed on trees "a memorial in too petty and uncertain a style," whereas a planned memorial arch would be "a dignified and enduring monument."

But the movement for memorial trees soon gained a major boost. On Christmas 1918, the American Forestry Association, the nation's most powerful tree advocacy organization, issued a call for a nationwide effort to plant trees in honor of fallen soldiers.

Once the AFA put out its challenge, the response was overwhelming. Periodicals around the country endorsed it through editorials. The *New York Times* described it as "one of the most comprehensive plans of forestration [*sic*] ever undertaken"—no mention was made of the paper's earlier dismissiveness. Civic and church groups banded together to plant memorial trees in groves and along highways, including the recently completed Lincoln Highway, the nation's first transcontinental road. General Pershing, upon returning from Europe, made one of his initial acts the planting of memorial trees in Independence Square, Philadelphia, and in Central Park, New York—much of the famous stand of American elms in the Central Park Mall, which has largely survived into the present, actually began as a memorial to honor soldiers from Manhattan. President Warren G. Harding, who served after Wilson, once declared,

> I find myself altogether responsive to [the AFA's] request for an appeal to the people to plant memorial trees. . . . I can hardly think of a more fitting testimonial of our gratitude and affection than this. It would be not only the testimony of our sentiments, but a means to beautify the country which these heroes have so well served.

To support the memorial tree campaign, the AFA issued large amounts of literature, and most of it contained a short poem called "Trees." The author was Joyce Kilmer, a New Jersey–born poet and editor at the *New York Times*, who had enlisted in 1917 and was killed on the battlefield in France. Before his death, his poem "Trees" had achieved some prominence, but the AFA campaign helped to spread the work's fame much further. Eventually, it would become one of the most famous works of American verse, and millions of schoolchildren would learn its opening stanza, beloved by some, loathed by others: "I think that I shall never see / A poem lovely as a tree."

Memorial plantings, meanwhile, were not the only way that the AFA used trees to help heal the scars of warfare. The organization also looked to provide assistance in Europe. There, years of battle had extinguished not only millions of lives but millions of acres of forests. Where once there had stood healthy stands of trees, there was now tattered wasteland. According to a report that the AFA sponsored, the war had destroyed nearly all of Belgium's forests and more than one and a half million acres in France. This information deeply troubled AFA president Charles Lathrop Pack, a wealthy businessman who would soon found the American Tree Association and author a number of popular books, including *Trees as Good Citizens*.

Pack determined to organize and finance a project to deliver American tree seeds to the war-ravaged regions of Europe. The collection effort, possibly the largest seed gathering in history to that point, involved more than one thousand people and took several years. Pack arranged for the seeds to be delivered on the five-year anniversary of America's entry into the war. In total, 100 million Douglas fir seeds were shipped off to Europe to help rehabilitate the decimated forests. An article in *Outlook* magazine noted, "[T]he trees planted from these seeds will serve not only as a memorial to American soldiers who fell beside their British and French comrades, but will reforest great areas devastated in a cause that was American as truly as it was British or French."

Interestingly, this was not the first time that America had sent trees to France as a sign of friendship. Some of the Douglas firs that Pack had financed would likely have been repopulating American trees that had been sent over 125 years earlier. Recall that in the 1780s the federal government had authorized the famed French botanist André Michaux to send tens of thousands of American trees to his home country, largely as a show of gratitude for that nation's support of America during the Revolutionary War.

## Roosevelt's Tree Army

WORLD WAR I, among its other effects, had strengthened America's global economic position. For the better part of ten years, growth and output increased steadily. This helped the postwar decade earn the designation the "Roaring Twenties." However, much of this new wealth was tied up in speculation schemes and was increasingly concentrated at the very top of the social ladder. By the late 1920s, the rising economic instability and inequality was beginning to threaten the integrity of the entire financial system.

The façade of sound money finally shattered in late October 1929. Over the course of barely a week, the New York Stock Exchange, the nation's largest trading market, lost an unprecedented 30 percent of its value. This fantastic crash marked the start of the worst sustained economic collapse the country had ever experienced. The intricate web of relationships that composed the modern economy quickly unwound beneath a rush of bankruptcies and bad deals.

The Great Depression, as this twelve-year period would soon be known as, wiped out millions of people's life savings overnight. Unemployment skyrocketed. Countless Americans were turned into beggars and vagrants. Millions simply abandoned their homes, turning into a shiftless army of the hopeless. In the cities, many of those who had lost their jobs and homes clustered together in hastily built shantytowns. These destitute communities soon gained the name Hoovervilles, a knock at Republican president Herbert Hoover, who was occupying the Oval Office at the time the crisis began. Nearly every major city featured one or more of these Hoovervilles. There was even one in Central Park, known as "Hoover Valley"—the *New York Times* noted that "the name is officially recognized by Park Department heads." Hoover Valley was located on the site of the present-day Great Lawn, not terribly far from the American elms that had been planted to honor those lost in the war.

As president, Hoover hadn't been able to do much to disconnect his name from the unendurable poverty that wracked the nation. For the most part, he favored the continuation of the same economic policies that had been in place before the crisis. His faith, like that of many Republicans, was that private markets would self-correct if the government got out of their way. But by 1932, three years into the crisis, the economy was reeling and unemployment had reached a dizzying 25 percent. These were not good figures for a president in an election year. And Hoover's chances to retain power grew even dimmer with the emergence of his Democratic challenger, fifty-year-old Franklin Delano Roosevelt—handsome, ambitious, and preternaturally gifted.

From his birth in 1882, Roosevelt had been bred to be a politician and leader. His mother, Sara, a strong, if not controlling, influence in his life, had worked assiduously during her son's formative years in New York State to ensure that he developed these capacities. And, of course, it helped that the young man possessed the proper pedigree. He was not only from a wealthy family, but related to the inimitable bull moose Teddy Roosevelt, both by blood (as fifth cousins) and by marriage (his wife, Eleanor, whom he married in 1905, was Teddy's niece).

With such credentials it was no surprise that Franklin's political career had begun early. At the age of twenty-eight, after several years working as an attorney, he won election to the New York state senate. Soon his talent and ambition pushed him onto the national radar. In 1920, the Democratic Party named him as its vice presidential candidate; his ticket, however, lost to a Republican one led by the photogenic and otherwise feckless Warren G. Harding. Following the loss, Roosevelt's career took a tragic turn; he contracted polio, which cost him the use of his legs. Such a personal catastrophe might have doomed the future of any politician—especially in an era when disabilities were seen as near-insurmountable political liabilities—but Roosevelt was not broken. He worked tirelessly to adapt to a radically altered existence and devised a series of complicated work-arounds to hide the fact that he was crippled. By the time that the Depression arrived in 1929, he had returned to public office as the governor of New York, where he was wildly popular.

This, then, was the opponent who was campaigning against the fast-fading Hoover. But there was another side to Roosevelt, the man who would soon steer the nation through the Great Depression and World War II. Politics was only a portion of his persona. He was also, by all accounts, a tree lover of the highest order, a man who spent his free time, in his own words, "driving around planting lots of trees."

This often overlooked aspect of Roosevelt's nature would profoundly effect his presidency and the nation.

T HE TREES WERE THERE for Roosevelt from the very start. He was born and raised in Hyde Park, New York, at an estate named Springwood, one of those grand landscaped properties that once populated the Hudson River Valley. At Springwood, there were numerous aging specimen trees to admire as well as an adjoining forest of more than four hundred acres. And this served as the young Roosevelt's playground. Eleanor noted that he "knew every tree" on the place. Roosevelt, in reflecting on his youth, described himself as "a small boy [who] took especial delight in climbing an old tree, now unhappily gone, to pick and eat ripe sickle pears."

In his love of sickle pears, a variety first cultivated in America, the young Roosevelt shared something in common with Thomas Jefferson, who once described this fruit as "exceed[ing] anything I have tasted since I left France, & equal[ing] any pear I had seen there." But the parallel stretched further than just pears. Roosevelt's appreciation for trees aligned him with many who had occupied the White House before him, men like Jefferson and Washington, who lived on great estates and developed an interest in trees. And like these men, Roosevelt grew to respect the pastoral life, praising a form of existence that bore much in common with Jefferson's bucolic sensibility of the yeoman farmer supporting democracy.

However, with respect to trees, Roosevelt differed from his predecessors on two levels. First, he showed less interest in horticulture, which by the early twentieth century was no longer the upper-class pursuit it had earlier been.

And second, Roosevelt would develop a keen interest in forestry, a field that had arrived in America at roughly the same time as his birth.

He was only a child when he first discovered the value of professional forestry. In 1891, during a family vacation to Europe, the nine-year-old Roosevelt came upon a municipal forest near Bad Nauheim, Germany, where careful management practices had been in place for two hundred years and ensured a constant supply of timber. As Roosevelt later noted, "[T]he interesting thing to me, as a boy even, was that the people in that town didn't have to pay taxes. They were supported by their own forest." This youthful encounter provided a foundation for Roosevelt's conviction that forestry and tree planting justified themselves not only for conservation reasons but for their long-term economic returns. In believing this, Roosevelt was unknowingly aligning himself with Pinchot, who spent his career advocating for forestry on conservation as well as economic grounds.

Early experiences aside, it was politics, in many respects, that turned Roosevelt toward forestry. His formal interest in the subject, by his own account, began only in 1911, following his election to the New York state senate and a sudden appointment as chair of the Forest, Fish, and Game Committee. As Roosevelt wryly observed, "The fact that this baby senator was made chairman of this particular committee meant that forestry had not progressed far in the State." The chairman's position may not have been a desirable one, but Roosevelt nonetheless felt obliged to educate himself on the areas he now controlled. He turned for advice to none other than Pinchot, the closest confidant of his beloved cousin Teddy.

What happened next would leave an impression on Roosevelt for the rest of his life. At the young senator's request, Pinchot traveled to Albany in order to give a public talk on the value of forestry and the importance of trees. During the talk, the chief forester warned of a potential timber famine and corresponding environmental degradation. To illustrate his point, he projected two slides onto a screen. The first, a Chinese painting from 1510, depicted a lush landscape with abundant water; but in the corner was an ominous sign: a logging chute. Pinchot then flashed the second slide, a photograph of the same landscape in 1900, completely stripped of trees, dry and barren. For Roosevelt, this was a revelatory moment. As he noted, "One need not be an alarmist to foresee that, without intelligent conservation measures, long before half a millennium passes some such contrasting pictures might be possible in our own United States." Roosevelt had come to realize the same principle that George Perkins Marsh had articulated so brilliantly in his 1864 book *Man and Nature*: "Man has too long forgotten that the earth was given to him for usufruct alone, not for consumption, still less for profligate waste."

Inspired by Pinchot's slides and constructive recommendations, Roosevelt determined to address the issue before it was too late. Shortly after hearing the talk, he sponsored one of his earliest pieces of legislation, the Roosevelt-Jones Bill. It sought broadly to expand fire protection and tree-planting facilities across the state. The heart of the legislation was a provision regulating logging on the millions of acres of private lands located within the Adirondack State Park. With this move, Roosevelt joined the continuing campaign to improve protections for the park, a cause that reached back into the nineteenth century and had benefited from the earlier efforts of men like Charles Sprague Sargent and Morris Jesup. But Roosevelt had underestimated the strength of the logging lobby, and his language covering the Adirondack park's privately held lands was removed from the final version of his bill.

Roosevelt's interest in forestry did not stop with advocacy. The same year he ascended to the state senate he had also assumed control over his family's Springwood estate, more than one thousand acres in total. Much of the soil, Roosevelt soon discovered, had been degraded from years of improper management. He saw potential to restore the land by implementing some of the ideas that Pinchot had championed, specifically tree planting. As Roosevelt observed of his family's property, "I can lime it, cross-plough it, manure it and treat it with every art known to science but it has just plain run out—and now I am putting it into trees in the hope that my great-grandchildren will be able to try raising corn again—just one century from now."

Once Roosevelt began planting trees, he was hooked. His youthful enthusiasm for trees converged with his interest in forestry. The first year of his program, 1912, Roosevelt planted an impressive one thousand seedlings—many by his own hand—and this amount would be equaled or exceeded every year thereafter; in fact, for the last fifteen years of his life, he oversaw the planting of at least twenty thousand trees annually. Nelson Brown, dean of the New York State College of Forestry, who was contracted by Roosevelt to help coordinate the expanding forestry activities in Springwood, estimated that his client planted in total more than half a million trees, which covered over 550 acres, nearly half the Springwood estate. There were countless varieties involved, though Roosevelt had his favorites, including Douglas fir and Norway spruce.

Tree planting wasn't just an activity for Roosevelt; it provided something of an identity as well. For many years, when voting in Hyde Park, he listed his profession as "tree-grower" instead of "politician" or "lawyer." And Roosevelt took great pleasure in referring to himself in this fashion, for trees were one of his favorite topics of discussion. As one of his neighbor's sons noted, "FDR used to come over to talk about his tree farm. . . . [H]e and my father would talk about seeds; and thinning, and commiserate on good years and bad. He loved to feel he was using the land to good advantage."

Roosevelt had been a confirmed tree planter for nearly a decade when, in 1921, polio cost him the use of his legs. The days of walking among his acres of planted trees were suddenly gone, but Roosevelt took measures to find other solutions. In particular, he instructed his grounds crew to carve new paths through his forests so that he could drive along them in a specially equipped vehicle. This became one of his favorite activities during the period of convalescence and reflection that followed his illness.

For much of the 1920s, Roosevelt's forestry activities had been confined to his personal properties and various private associations, but that changed in the fall of 1928, following his victory in the New York State governor's race. Back in the public eye, Roosevelt was ready to once more push for tree-based solutions to environmental challenges. This time, the central issue was the state's abandoned or degraded farmlands. Such properties were beginning to pile up. Over the course of several decades, countless farm families had either moved west in search of richer soils or headed into the cities to find work— according to the *Journal of Forestry*, "Between 4,000,000 and 5,000,000 acres [were] now lying idle as a result." Roosevelt sought to use tree planting to renew these overworked soils, just as he had done at Springwood.

The political battle centered on the Hewitt Amendment, a proposed change to the New York Constitution that the state's Reforestation Commission had suggested. It would grant the state authority to purchase lands outside of the Adirondack park—primarily, degraded farms—for the purposes of reforestation and rehabilitation. Roosevelt threw all of his weight as governor behind this amendment, traveling the state to give speeches, pressing his friends to lend their support, rebuffing the protests of the various groups who opposed the measure. His efforts helped to convince the electorate, and in 1931 the Hewitt Amendment became a part of the state constitution.

In the wake of the victory, the *Journal of Forestry* declared, "The present governor, so definitely a believer in forestry as to spend his own money in its practice on his personal estate, enthusiastically supported the measure. . . . As the Nation's largest reforestation project, larger even than that of the federal government, much interest will be shown in its progress. . . . [I]t is now a matter requiring only technical accomplishment." And, of course, Roosevelt was there to ensure the realization of the "technical" side of the measure. Relying on the authority of the Hewitt Amendment as well as Depression-related emergency funding, he instituted a massive program that, among other things, took some ten thousand unemployed men and set them to work reforesting state lands.

Thus, by the time that the 1932 presidential election arrived, Roosevelt possessed more forestry experience than almost any politician in the country. He had been the force behind the most ambitious state reforestation effort in the nation. He had worked through two major political battles over forestry, coming up short with the Roosevelt-Jones Bill of 1912 before triumphing with the Hewitt Amendment. His home at Springwood was a working tree farm, he was a self-proclaimed tree grower by profession, and everyone in Hyde Park knew that trees were among Roosevelt's favorite conversation topics. Now was finally the time for the governor of New York to take the ideas he'd worked out in Hyde Park and Albany to the entire nation.

On July 2, 1932, at the Democratic National Convention in Chicago, Roosevelt became his party's official nominee for president. It was a grand event, one covered by media outlets across the country, and Roosevelt used this moment to inform the public that he saw trees as the way forward, a panacea to relieve unemployment and combat the Depression. He declared: "We know that a very hopeful and immediate means of relief, both for the unemployed and for agriculture will come from a wide plan of the converting of many millions of acres of marginal and unused land into timberland through reforestation." This was the same argument he had used when pushing the Hewitt Amendment, only now he was applying it to the entire nation. And the scale of his proposal increased accordingly. Whereas in New York he had provided reforestation jobs for ten thousand men, he now asserted that "employment can be given to a million men" and that the project would be self-financed through the sale of the resulting timber.

For Americans used to a federal government hesitant to intervene in the economy, this proposal sounded somewhat absurd. A million unemployed men recruited by the government solely to plant trees? How would they be trained and housed? Could tree planting possibly produce enough revenue to cover the cost of the program? Would this be on private land or public land? Who would organize everything? Were there enough trained foresters to oversee the work? These were just a few of the concerns.

Even people who should have been sympathetic to Roosevelt's idea chimed in to voice their discomfort. Charles Lathrop Pack, the man behind the World War I memorial and battlefield trees, wrote Roosevelt on behalf of the American Forestry Association to express his reservations: "Shall we, as foresters and conservation leaders, shut our eyes to the facts?" As Pack saw it, the obstacles to success were too daunting; tree planting simply couldn't accomplish all that Roosevelt imagined.

But Roosevelt remained undeterred. He explained to Pack that his program was, in fact, much broader than his acceptance speech had suggested. "Reforestation" was simply shorthand. He wanted men employed not just in tree planting, but in "all forestry activities which would tend to restore the true forest lands of the United States to normal productiveness." The recruits would work in small camps spread out across the entire nation, wherever local needs existed. The obstacles that had concerned Pack, Roosevelt promised, would be easily overcome.

Over the course of the next few months, the presidential candidate continued to refine his program and to build support, among both the public and the forestry community. The more that people came to appreciate Roosevelt's doggedness and tenacity, the more they came to accept that he might be able to realize his vision. It didn't hurt that he rolled to victory over Hoover with nearly all of the electoral votes (472 to 59), giving him an ironclad mandate.

In January, after Roosevelt had won the election but before his inauguration (then held in March), Gifford Pinchot, who was still one of the most influential conservation voices in the nation, wrote him to say: "[A]s I see it there is no single domestic step that can be taken that will mean so much to the future of the United States as this one, and at the same time none that will meet with such universal approval." Few people's endorsement might have meant more to the president-elect. This was, after all, the very man who had first opened Roosevelt's eyes to the importance of forestry and trees.

Once Roosevelt became president, he wasted little time turning talk into action. On March 9, five days after his swearing-in, with the cheers from the crowds still echoing in his head, he sat down to map out his plan in detail for what he had started to call the Civilian Conservation Corps (CCC). The outline of his proposal by this point went roughly as follows: Approximately 250,000 unemployed young men would be hired by the federal government, using emergency relief funds, to work temporarily in the nation's forests; they would be paid thirty dollars a month, and all but five dollars would be sent automatically to their families; the men would live together in camps, have all their meals provided, and would have access to educational materials (Roosevelt wanted to make sure that his recruits left the CCC feeling mentally and physically rehabilitated, ready to return as productive members of society); the projects would be numerous, but primarily of a simple nature, the sort of work that required energy over experience; the program's administration would be divided between the Forest Service, which would provide expertise, the Department of Labor, which would recruit the workforce, and the army, which would handle transportation and the running of the camps.

On March 21, Roosevelt presented his full vision to Congress. "I propose to create a civilian conservation corps," he declared. This was the start of his domestic agenda, the initial push for social legislation, the first piece in a complicated puzzle of ambitious programs that would soon be known as the New Deal. And time was of the essence. Roosevelt felt that the problems that the Depression presented were too great to allow for further dillydallying: "I estimate that 250,000 men can be given temporary employment by early summer *if you give me authority to proceed within the next two weeks.*"

Roosevelt had issued the challenge. The decision now rested with Congress. It was a seminal moment for his presidency: Would the legislators endorse his agenda or attempt to frustrate it? The *New York Times* suggested that it might be a tough fight: "It must be doubted . . . if his plan will be received with zealous approval in Congress." Some conservatives opposed the plan on principle, as an unwarranted expansion of government and a misuse of relief funds. Left-leaning union groups voiced displeasure as well. The head of the AFL—in a statement that echoed the concerns Gompers had expressed during World War I regarding the 4L—predicted: "The regimentation of labor through enlistment in the Civilian Conservation Corps, under military discipline and military control, will, in my judgment, awaken feelings of grave apprehension in the hearts and minds of labor."

But, in the end, these protests fell flat. Republicans were the minority in both houses, and the labor issue was not enough to dissuade Democrats. On March 31, several days shy of Roosevelt's two-week deadline, Congress passed a law granting him the authority he sought. The following week, on April 5, Roosevelt issued an executive order that formally created the CCC. Eleanor later described this moment as "the one in which my husband took the greatest pleasure" during his first year.

Upon signing the order, Roosevelt put forth another challenge: He wanted the first camp up and running within two weeks.

In an effort to meet this demand, a model camp—little more than a handful of tents in a clearing—was hastily constructed in Virginia's George Washington National Forest. (Though all the original national forests were carved from the western public domain, the government had gained authority in 1911 to purchase eastern lands and convert them into national forests as well.) The army christened this test site "Camp Roosevelt" to honor the man who was the program's driving force. The first recruits, some two hundred young men, arrived on April 17, a few days short of Roosevelt's deadline. They soon found themselves the center of national attention. As explained by an article in *American Forests*, "Hardly a day passed but came photographers, reporters, writers and an endless stream of officials to inspect them, to photograph them, and to write about their work and their lives." Most of the reports were positive. The CCC seemed off to a strong start.

However, progressing from 200 men to 250,000 men was no simple feat. Thousands of camps needed to be constructed, recruitment offices had to be set up around the nation, projects sufficient for a quarter million men needed to be identified and coordinated. The challenges were immense.

Nonetheless, when Roosevelt's deadline arrived, there were, remarkably, more than a quarter million young men enrolled, the largest peacetime government labor force ever assembled. According to the *Atlantic Monthly,* General Douglas MacArthur, who oversaw the effort, boasted that "in the ninety days after the CCC was authorized, the army enrolled 270,000 boys and transported 55,000 of them to camps across the continent, while, in the ninety days after the declaration of war on Germany in 1917, only 181,000 men were mobilized, and only 16,000 were embarked for France."

With so many men suddenly in the forests, it was possible to implement forestry on a scale never before seen. The totals after the first year told much of the story. CCC workers built enough forest protection roads and trails that, according to *American Forests,* if these had been "placed end to end [they] would more than reach around the world." Similarly, the number of firebreaks "if stretched in a continuous line, would twice encircle the boundaries of the United States." Then there were the several hundred million trees planted to rehabilitate overworked lands, a reforestation effort unlike anything the nation or world had known. But this hardly captured the full scope of the CCC's activities. In total, there were more than three hundred distinct tasks. CCC recruits built dams, erected fire towers, collected seeds, improved streams, combated erosion, controlled floods, and constructed recreational campsites. They also fought against tree diseases and pests—their labor was central in the doomed fight against Dutch elm disease. For all their efforts, the men of the CCC soon earned the nickname "Roosevelt's Tree Army."

The original authorization for the CCC had funded only a two-year period, which was set to end in April 1935. But the work of the organization—in improving the forests, in planting trees, in relieving unemployment, in building the character of young and otherwise idle men—seemed far from finished as this deadline began to approach. In October 1934, Roosevelt wrote the CCC's director to say: "This kind of work must go on. I believe that the nation feels that the work of these young men is so thoroughly justified and, in addition, the benefits to the men themselves are so clear that the actual annual cost will be met without much opposition or complaint."

His prediction proved correct. When time came to reauthorize the CCC's funding, Congress not only pushed an extension through with broad bipartisan support, it also increased funding to some $600 million. As a result, hundreds of new CCC camps opened. And by the fall of 1935 the total number of men in the forests had ballooned to over half a million.

The CCC's success soon persuaded Roosevelt to try to expand his vision even further. Several months after the congressional extension, he told a sympathetic audience: "Some of you who are here remember the ribald laughter about planting trees, this 'crazy dream,' this 'political gesture.' Well, . . . I see no reason why I should not tell you that these Camps, in my judgment, are going to be a permanent part of the policy of the United States Government." Roosevelt was proposing to transform a relief organization, one designed to address an acute economic crisis, into a perpetual federal program. If he had his way, it would turn the government into the nation's employer of last resort—a huge expansion of the social welfare state. It would also be a chance for Roosevelt to extend his passion for trees to future generations of young Americans.

The issue reached Congress in the spring of 1937, when the second round of CCC authorizations were set to expire. Roosevelt, at this point, seemed to be at the peak of his powers, having recently won a second term in a landslide election. It thus came as something of a shock when the House, which was majority Democratic, refused to grant him the permanent organization he sought. The *New York Times* called it "the largest Democratic defection in years." The *Chicago Tribune* went even further: "The defeat of the President's proposal was by far the most drastic he has received since he took office."

Some had opposed the plan on the grounds that permanence signaled defeat in the fight against the Depression. Others feared that Roosevelt's proposal, which would have required a reduction in the number of CCC participants for budgeting reasons, might remove camps from their districts, something that no representative wanted to explain to his constituents. Furthermore, the resistance might have been tied to congressional fears about unchecked presidential power on the heels of Roosevelt's controversial plan to pack the Supreme Court with sympathetic justices. As historian John Salmond suggested, "There could hardly be a better way of protesting against what was considered to be a dangerous accretion of power . . . than to refuse to go along . . . on this issue," which House leadership considered "Roosevelt's 'pet.'"

Nevertheless, House opposition to Roosevelt was not meant as a referendum against the CCC itself, which remained incontrovertibly popular. The final legislation, passed in June, extended the program for three more years. It seemed that the CCC might continue on a temporary basis well into the future.

But, in truth, the end was already in sight, even if few realized it. It began in September 1939, when Europe descended once more into total war. America's political leadership, remembering the mistakes of the last war, soon began to advocate increased militarization in anticipation of potential involvement. In

July 1940, the head of the CCC declared: "The Civilian Conservation Corps has a new objective as it marches forward in its eighth year. It is national defense." This, however, was never the program's intended purpose.

Over the next eighteen months, the CCC's numbers began to dwindle as young men left for jobs in war industries and overall unemployment fell to 2 percent. A congressional committee then issued a call for the program's termination in late December 1941, several weeks after the Japanese attack at Pearl Harbor that precipitated America's entrance into the war. Roosevelt fought to save his creation, but it was too late. In the minds of Congress, the CCC was a relief organization, and once war arrived there was no longer any need. The most ambitious government employment program in American history—and one that had put trees at the center of the fight to save the nation's economy—finally met its end in June 1942.

It was a remarkable near-decade-long run. In total, the CCC employed 2.5 million men, who put forth roughly 730,000 man-years of labor. They collectively planted over 3 billion trees, maintained or constructed more than 100,000 miles of trails, developed thousands of new campgrounds, rehabilitated hundreds of millions of acres of state and national forests, and assisted with projects, large and small, that affected the life of nearly every American. It was far and away the most well-regarded New Deal program, one Rex Tugwell, a member of Roosevelt's "Brain Trust," called "too popular for criticism."

There were, nonetheless, some shortcomings: The organization was plagued by charges of militarism; desertion rates were sometimes high; the quality of its conservation work was sometimes questioned; and its record on race relations was spotty—CCC camps were segregated (though, as a point of reference, the army did not formally desegregate until after World War II). But these failings were relatively minor issues in the broader story. Roosevelt had turned his fascination with trees and forestry into a program that fundamentally changed the nation, temporarily relieving unemployment, providing purpose to a generation of young men, implementing forestry on a scale never witnessed before or since, and planting roughly twenty-five trees for every person then living in the country.

The CCC, however, was not actually the most ambitious tree-planting scheme that Roosevelt proposed during his presidency. There was another project, one that sounded almost fantastical. An Iowa congressman would call it "one of the most ridiculous and silly proposals that was ever submitted to the American people." But such criticism wouldn't deter Roosevelt. Trees, he believed, held the key to solving the worst environmental catastrophe of his generation.

## The Shelterbelt

W HEN ROOSEVELT FIRST ASSUMED the presidency in 1933, the nation was in the throes of not only an economic crisis but an ecological one as well. Starting around 1930, a severe drought struck the high plains, the region once known as the "Great American Desert." This might not have been an issue of national importance had the region been uninhabited or kept as grasslands, but such was not the case. During the first thirty years of the twentieth century, the high plains had been populated by several waves of settlers. These pioneers had unknowingly arrived during a period of above-average rainfall, which made the land appear amenable to agriculture. Millions of acres were transformed into farms, the rough sods broken by the plow. But when drought struck, this cropland quickly dried out, and the winds that swept across the area soon stripped off the desiccated topsoil. This created something known colloquially as "black blizzards," dust storms so severe that they could reach the Atlantic Ocean, some two thousand miles away, raining prairie soil all along their path. And the once-fertile farms of the high plains were suddenly left with worthless land, plunging millions into poverty.

One potential solution to this catastrophe, which became known as the "Dust Bowl," first occurred to Roosevelt during his presidential campaign. It was during a day of blistering heat, when his touring train was detained outside Butte, Montana. Roosevelt exited his car and gazed upon a region denuded of trees and other vegetation, the result of noxious fumes from a nearby copper-smelting plant. Though this scene was actually several hundred miles to the west of the Dust Bowl, it nonetheless reminded the future president of the situation unfolding all across the high plains. Roosevelt, who had spent a career using forestry techniques to improve his home at Hyde Park and who had just announced to the country his plans to create the CCC, then had an epiphany: What if the answer to the Dust Bowl also rested with trees?

The concept of using trees to improve the conditions of the Great American Desert was certainly not new. It traced back to the earliest settlements of the mid-nineteenth century. J. Sterling Morton had argued that because "the shade and beauty of trees was everywhere absent . . . our conditions impelled us to plant trees." Then, of course, there was the ill-fated, but powerful, movement claiming that trees would bring the rains, which had resulted in the disastrous Timber Culture Act of 1873. The belief that forests brought the rains, however, had been largely discredited by the end of the nineteenth century, particularly following a period of severe drought across the Great Plains in the 1890s (the last major drought before the Dust Bowl).

Roosevelt, however, wasn't suggesting that tree planting might change the region's climate. Rather, he was considering the possibility that a sufficient quantity of trees might protect the topsoil by creating a shield against the brutal winds that whipped across the region.

This idea was rooted in a principle that farmers had been aware of for eons: By blocking the wind, trees could protect crops and the soil. Examples of trees being used as windbreaks abounded. For instance, California citrus growers routinely planted stands of fast-growing, imported eucalyptus trees to shield their precious orange trees from gusts coming off the Pacific Ocean. As a 1908 pamphlet on eucalyptus explained, "In unprotected orchards, nearly the entire crop is frequently blown from the trees, or so scarred and bruised that the grade and market value are much reduced."

Roosevelt was far from the first to see the potential for windbreaks in the Great American Desert. Many prairie farmers planted trees for this purpose, and Roosevelt's own cousin Teddy had beaten him to the punch by nearly thirty years. At the 1905 American Forestry Congress—the meeting that famously led to the creation of the U.S. Forest Service—the elder Roosevelt had stated, "The use of forests as windbreaks out on the plains, where the tree does not grow unless men help it, is of enormous importance."

What made Roosevelt's 1932 Montana epiphany remarkable, then, was not its originality, but its scale. Roosevelt never hesitated to dream big. The CCC, for example, would become the biggest nonmilitary workforce in U.S. history. Several of his New Deal programs—such as the Tennessee Valley Authority and Central Valley Project—sought to transform tens of millions of acres at once. The Great Plains windbreak would be no different. Roosevelt wanted to build a forest, several miles wide, from the Canadian border straight down into Texas, a giant barrier that would arrest the wind and mitigate the worst consequences of the drought. It would be the ultimate expression of the power of tree planting.

But this wasn't something Roosevelt could undertake immediately upon entering office. There were too many questions to be answered first. Unlike the case of the CCC, where Roosevelt had a clear vision that grew from his experience as governor, the high plains windbreak was far outside his field of knowledge. He may have known plenty about planting trees in the well-watered soils of Hyde Park, but that meant little when dealing with the arid climate of the Great American Desert. Thus, shortly after his inauguration, Roosevelt reached out to the head of the Forest Service for advice.

The chief forester provided a thorough response in August 1933. His memorandum agreed with the president that a windbreak might improve the situation, but argued that a solid forest was impractical and "would take a large area of farmland out of cultivation." A better solution would be to plant hundred-foot-wide strips of trees, spaced apart in intervals, along a belt that ran the length of the United States and occupied roughly one hundred miles.

This new proposal met with the president's approval, and he encouraged its further development. The Forest Service, in response, began to prepare a full report analyzing the many technical, logistical, and political challenges involved. It was a remarkable amount of background research, especially for an administration that tended to implement interesting ideas long before the minutiae were sorted out. But there was reason to proceed cautiously; a project of this magnitude, in a region where tree culture had never thrived, was likely to garner its fair share of hostility.

In the late spring of 1934, the completed Forest Service report reached Roosevelt, and the timing couldn't have been more appropriate. The drought, at this point, seemed to be spiraling out of control. Black blizzards were sweeping across the country. It was raining dust in New York City, Washington, D.C., and even on ships cruising the Atlantic. Those living on the Great Plains were suffering unbearable hardship. To address the worsening situation, Congress announced in June that it was making $525 million available for immediate drought relief efforts.

With the nation abuzz about dust storms, Roosevelt finally announced the proposal that he had been contemplating for nearly two years. On July 11, while on vacation aboard the USS *Houston*, he issued an executive order calling "for the planting of forest protection strips in the Plains Region as a means of ameliorating drought conditions." The proclamation authorized $15 million to be taken from the drought relief funds for this purpose. This would be the first installment of a projected $75 million necessary to construct the world's largest windbreak. The project quickly came to be known as the Shelterbelt.

As Roosevelt anticipated, the July 11 announcement unleashed a storm of controversy. Some of the harshest debates took place within the forestry profession itself. Those who advocated the plan described it as "the most unique and daring forestry undertaking in the history of the country." These proponents believed that forestry had advanced enough since the late nineteenth century to successfully bring trees to the high plains, at least "on the favorable sites." But others worried that the Shelterbelt risked compromising all the work that foresters had done to establish the field as a credible, scientific profession.

The nation's newspaper editors seemed to side mostly with the opposition. One writer artfully summed up their sentiments by quoting the closing line of Kilmer's famed poem: "They pointed out that only God can make a tree . . . that if He had wanted a forest on the wind-scoured prairies of Nebraska and

Kansas, He would have put it there . . . and that for FDR to rush in where The Almighty had feared to tread was not only silly, but possibly blasphemous." And piling on to this mountain of naysaying was a strong majority of Congress. According to historian Wilmon Droze, "To many politicos, the idea of spending $75,000,000 in an area where few voters lived and for a project of uncertain merits was politically unwise, grossly unfair, and hardly in keeping with the promises to balance the budget."

None of this vitriol should have much mattered. The funds, after all, had already been allocated by Congress through the June relief measure. But then Roosevelt's plan hit an unforeseen snag. The nation's comptroller, a Harding appointee who seemed to take joy in holding up monies for some New Deal programs, determined that the president's requested $15 million did not constitute "immediate drought relief" as dictated by the June legislation; the rationale was that tree planting only paid dividends years later.

There was little that Roosevelt could do to circumvent the comptroller. The president may have been the most powerful man in the country, but occasionally the subtle inner workings of the federal bureaucracy proved more powerful still. In the end, Roosevelt was forced to reduce his request to $1 million, simply to fund preliminary work.

It was a trifling amount—especially compared to the $600 million that Congress would soon grant for the CCC—but it was nonetheless a start. The Forest Service used the funds to begin surveying the lands, arrange seedling suppliers, and reach out to farmers whose land they would need to lease for planting. Roosevelt did his part behind the scenes as well to ensure the viability of a program that he had described to Charles Lathrop Pack as "my baby." Ultimately, Shelterbelt work would be able to commence the following growing season, even if the scale was reduced by an amount that must have struck Roosevelt as tragic.

Planting finally began in March 1935. The first tree was put in place at a farm near Mangum, Oklahoma. There was a small ceremony, though it didn't receive much attention. Plantings continued throughout the spring growing season, not only in Oklahoma, but also Texas, Kansas, Nebraska, and the Dakotas. In total, Forest Service and federal relief workers managed to establish 125 miles of Shelterbelt, covering some twenty-five hundred acres.

Tree strips in the Shelterbelt typically included ten rows of vegetation. The outer rows contained small trees or shrubs, most commonly chokecherry, lilac, mulberry, Russian olive, and wild plum. The inner rows featured quick-growing, long-lived, taller trees that had been selected for their tolerance of the unwelcoming climate. Some tree varieties were native, while others had been discovered abroad, often the result of research first conducted by plant explorers from David Fairchild's Office of Foreign Seed and Plant Introduction. The most widely planted species were cottonwood, green ash, and Chinese elm, which each appeared in all six participating states. Other tree types that were popular in specific portions of the Shelterbelt included bur oak, hackberry, honey locust, ponderosa pine, post oak, red cedar, and willow.

The planting of trees was only the first step in a successful Shelterbelt. Once a given tree strip was fully installed, workers needed to construct a fence around the entire area, to protect the seedlings from cattle. They also treated the young growth with poison, which deterred insects and rodents. Finally, they had to return several times to cull any undergrowth that might be sucking moisture from the soil and outcompeting the young trees. When all this was done, a given acre of Shelterbelt was expected to provide protection for about twenty acres of farmland. An article in *American Forests* estimated, somewhat optimistically, "On a fifty-year basis, the cost to the government of an acre protected a year is estimated at four cents."

Once the program had gotten under way, many careworn farmers on the Great Plains embraced it enthusiastically, but in Washington, D.C., it was a different story altogether. Congressmen remained skeptical of the Shelterbelt's merits, convinced that it was a costly boondoggle, a political stunt by Roosevelt to capture the farm vote. In 1936, Congress even allocated $170,000 specifically for the purposes of liquidating the program. But Roosevelt fought back, acquiring several million dollars from the recently created Works Project Administration (WPA), which was another massive relief initiative that contained hundreds of millions of dollars in undesignated funds. The availability of WPA funds allowed Roosevelt to repeatedly counter congressional efforts to defund the Shelterbelt throughout the 1930s.

As the political battle over the Shelterbelt raged in Washington, the Forest Service quietly continued to plant their trees. The secretary of agriculture noted in 1937, "Over 32,000 acres have been planted in two years with emergency funds in spite of limitations by the constant questioning of legal and fiscal authority." By 1938, more than 34.5 million trees had been planted across 107,000 acres. To facilitate the work, a special mechanized tree planter was invented, capable of setting down eight thousand trees during an eight-hour day. The scope of the Shelterbelt program even turned the Forest Service into the largest builder of fences in the world. The endless horizons of the high plains, at least near the ninety-ninth meridian, were beginning to be broken up by the silhouettes of forests in the distance.

But ultimately, the political opposition proved too powerful for the Shelterbelt to survive. By the early 1940s, Roosevelt, the program's creator and staunchest defender, was in poor health and was preoccupied with America's likely entry into World War II. Moreover, two key pieces of federal legislation had been passed during the 1930s that provided alternative approaches to the Shelterbelt. The first, the Soil Conservation Act of 1935, created a new agency, the Soil Conservation Service (SCS), which was authorized to pay farmers for keeping their land uncultivated with the hope that native grasses would return to stabilize the soil. The second, the Norris-Doxey Farm Forestry Act of 1937, allowed the government to devote funds to work cooperatively with farmers looking to improve their woodlots.

In late October 1941, the secretary of agriculture suggested to Roosevelt that the Shelterbelt project ought to be folded into the increasingly popular SCS. Roosevelt, who had been struggling to keep the program alive over congressional hostility for nearly a decade, finally agreed. And in July 1942, after eight years and a total cost of $14 million, the Shelterbelt as an independent program officially came to an end. Many involved, especially foresters who had been impressed by the program's relative success, feared that Roosevelt's willingness to fold the Shelterbelt into the SCS spelled the end of serious tree planting on the high plains. And these concerns were largely borne out in the years that followed. The SCS, populated by agronomists more than foresters, quickly deprioritized the use of tree strips as a soil conservation measure. Plantings dropped from 1,750 miles in 1942 to 65 miles in 1943.

Meanwhile, Roosevelt, the consummate tree planter, soon came to lament the death of the Shelterbelt. At a 1943 White House dinner to honor the king of Saudi Arabia, the topic arose when the president was comparing the Arabian Desert to the Great American Desert. He explained to the audience, "[S]ome years ago we had undertaken a certain project known as Shelter Belt. . . . And I might just as well tell the Congress of the United States now that I am going to revive it, if I live long enough. It's a very excellent thing."

But Roosevelt's days were fast running out. On April 12, 1945, less than a month before America gained victory over the Nazis, the nation's longest-serving president died of a cerebral hemorrhage. An editorial that ran in the *New York Times* the following day summed up the national mood:

> Men will thank God on their knees, a hundred years from now, that Franklin D. Roosevelt was in the White House, in a position to give leadership to the thought of the American people and direction to the activities of their Government, in that dark hour when a powerful and ruthless barbarism threatened to overrun the civilization of the Western World and to destroy the work of centuries of progress.

Though many of Roosevelt's final days were indeed spent buried in affairs of state and the emergencies of war, he was still thinking about his beloved and beleaguered Shelterbelt right up to the ultimate moments. Three days before his death, he had reviewed a new memorandum on the program and sent a letter to its author asking for "a little more material on what tree planting is doing to enable families to improve their yield in crops."

In the end, Roosevelt's grand vision to transform the Great Plains into a forest fell short, but the project nonetheless left its mark on the region. A 1954 evaluation of the Shelterbelt determined that over 220 million trees had been planted on thirty thousand farms. The Forest Service had laid down in total more than 18,600 linear miles of tree strips—and a majority of these, more than 70 percent, survived for decades. During the 1950s and 1960s many of the original Shelterbelt plantings were reinforced or expanded through the private actions of farmers who had come to appreciate the value of tree windbreaks. And today, among the fields and farms of the high plains, some aging stands of cottonwood, green ash, and Chinese elm still attest to the existence of a program initially planned as "the biggest technical job the Forest Service has yet undertaken" but one that became, in the eyes of many, "the most ridiculed project of the New Deal."

## "Careless Matches Aid the Axis"

IN THE HISTORY OF AMERICA, there are few dates more prominent than December 7, 1941. On that morning, the Empire of Japan launched a surprise attack against a U.S. naval installation at Pearl Harbor, Hawaii. It was the deadliest strike on U.S. soil until September 11, 2001. Roosevelt famously labeled it "a date which will live in infamy." The events at Pearl Harbor not only pushed the nation to enter World War II but also shattered a long-held illusion that American territory, far removed from the theaters of combat in Europe and the Pacific, was safe from military attack.

The Japanese confirmed this fear three months after Pearl Harbor with a second strike against the United States. This time the assault was less spectacular, but perhaps more audacious, an attack not on one of the nation's outlying territorial possessions, but the mainland itself. It took place during an evening in late February. Most Americans were huddled around their radio sets, listening to an address that Roosevelt was giving on the war effort. But in Goleta, California (a town adjacent to Santa Barbara), the president's words were suddenly interrupted by the sound of artillery shells exploding. Locals described themselves as being "almost scared to death." The culprit, as newspapers reported the next morning, was a Japanese submarine that had penetrated to within a mile of shore and launched more than a dozen rounds at a local oil refinery. The harm, to everyone's relief, was minimal: a damaged oil well and a small brush fire that started after several orange trees in a nearby grove went up in flames.

But the attack raised concerns that went far beyond the immediate damage. And one of the most serious points of anxiety related to the nation's trees.

Only a few miles inland from the site of this second attack was located the San Padre National Forest. The proximity of this forest to the impact zone highlighted a vulnerability that some in the army, the Forest Service, and other branches of government had been worrying about since before the war began: If Japan could attack the West Coast, then it could potentially set fire to the grand forests that ranged from Washington to Southern California. One month after the submarine attack at Goleta, Roosevelt wrote in a letter: "You are dead right about the danger of forest fires on the Pacific Coast. It is obvious that many of them will be deliberately set on fire if the Japs attack there." In correspondence the following month, the president urged, "[W]e must guard against Japanese incendiary bombs and incendiary fires during the dry season. This is essential for our national future."

It was no exaggeration for Roosevelt to link the safety of the forests with "our national future." World War II had once again turned the nation's trees into a resource of paramount military importance. As in World War I, tree products could be found in nearly all elements of military life: housing, transport, weaponry, containers, fuel. The nation's armed forces would require more than 6 billion board feet for the first year of combat operations alone. As an army major explained to a reporter, "If you could see us use every available piece [of wood] over and over, until nothing is left but slivers, you'd know just how important it is." There would, quite simply, be no way to conduct an effective military campaign without drawing heavily on the country's tree resources and keeping them safe from Japanese attacks.

But the Japanese were not the only threat. In many foresters' estimations, an equal, if not more pressing, concern was the carelessness of the average American. Reports at the time claimed that recklessness with cigarette butts, campfires, and matches caused nine out of ten wildfires, totaling more than a hundred thousand incidents annually. In bad years, this was destroying some 31 million acres, an area larger than the state of Pennsylvania. The danger that individuals posed had also grown more noticeable, to a certain extent, as industrial logging practices and train technology improved in ways that reduced their likelihood of starting fires. The question now had become: How could foresters get the message out to the citizenry and change the way that people thought about their tree resources?

In the spring of 1942, shortly after the Goleta attack, a Southern California forest ranger suggested a potential solution. What if advertising agencies designed a public awareness campaign? It was a novel idea, but one in keeping with the times. The federal government had recently created the War Advertising Council (WAC), an agency tasked with marshaling the resources of private advertising firms in support of the war effort. The same techniques that were used to create demand for products, it was thought, could also drum up support for the war effort.

The suggestion to mount an advertising campaign around fire prevention quickly rose through the bureaucratic channels. Soon representatives of the Forest Service and the National Association of State Foresters were meeting with the WAC. And these conversations led to the creation of a home-front propaganda effort: the Wartime Forest Fire Prevention Campaign.

In late July 1942, the campaign kicked off with a nationally broadcast radio address from the secretary of agriculture. He introduced the campaign's theme, which was summed up in a catchy slogan: "Careless Matches Aid the Axis—Prevent Forest Fires." In the months that followed, this message and others like it blanketed the country. They appeared in 12 million mail inserts, 2 million leaflets, and fifteen thousand billboards. In one campaign poster, a burning match was shown in the hand of a giddy, and grossly caricatured, General Hideki Tojo, the Japanese prime minister. In another image, the heads of Tojo and Hitler floated about a burning forest; beneath them read the words, "Our Carelessness: Their Secret Weapon." Everywhere that people turned they were suddenly being told that their thoughtlessness around forests was tantamount to a direct attack against the country.

Roosevelt, unsurprisingly, threw his weight as chief executive behind the effort. Two weeks after the launching of the campaign, he declared the first week of October to be Fire Protection Week, reviving an idea that had been launched in the 1920s but since fallen out of favor. His official proclamation noted,

> Uncontrolled fire, even in normal times, is a national menace. . . . Today, when every machine is being taxed to its fullest productive capacity, . . . when agents of our enemies are seeking to hinder us by every possible means, it is essential that destructive fire be brought under stricter control in order that victory may be achieved at the earliest date. Nothing less than the united vigilance and effort of all the people will suffice to break the grip of this menace.

Up to this point in the war, the Japanese threat against the forests—which in many respects was the initial impetus for the newfound emphasis on forest fire prevention—had remained theoretical. But soon the situation changed. On the morning of September 9, a forest ranger working a patrol in Oregon's Siskiyou National Forest spotted what appeared to be a Japanese aircraft. A few minutes later he noticed a plume of smoke rising from among the trees. Forest Service agents rushed to the site to combat the flames. While there, they discovered fragments of what seemed to be an incendiary bomb.

It turned out that Japan had indeed recognized the strategic importance of the Pacific Northwest forests. Its military had launched a floatplane from a submarine stationed offshore to fly over the woods and dump a cargo of two eighty-kilogram explosives. The morning after the attack, a headline in the *Los Angeles Times* announced, "Jap Incendiary Sets Forest Fire!"

The surprise air raid—one of two that Japan attempted—only reinforced the idea that all Americans needed to do their part to protect the forests. Shortly after the incident, an editorial in the *Los Angeles Times* cautioned:

> Fires started by carelessness burn just as hotly and destructively as any that might be caused by enemy incendiary bombs. While we are preparing to deal with those the Japs may try to start, we should resolve that preventable fires of domestic origin are not to be tolerated. It may help us in steeling our determination to get into the spirit of "Fire Protection Week."

The campaign against carelessness continued to build as the nation geared up for October's Fire Protection Week.

During this period, a new ally in the fight arrived from, of all places, Disney Studios. In August it had released its fifth animated feature film, the story of Bambi, a fawn who must learn to survive in the forests after his mother is shot by a hunter. It was an immediate hit, filling theaters and garnering three Academy Award nominations. In the film's final act, Bambi's father, the Great Prince, warns his son that the threat to the forest has returned: "It is man. He is here again. . . . We must go deep into the forest. Hurry, follow me!" Suddenly, a forest fire, one presumably started by the action of these hunters, breaks out. Bambi and his friends barely escape from danger, before reuniting on an island in the middle of a river.

While the Disney film hadn't been designed as war propaganda, it still packed a powerful message. And after its release, members of the WAC entered into talks about using Bambi as part of the fire prevention campaign. Walt Disney agreed to loan the image to the federal government for a year, and soon Bambi starred in an official war poster, staring out with big doe eyes, his friends Thumper and Flower by his side. The accompanying message read: "Please, Mister, Don't Be Careless. Prevent Forest Fires. Greater Danger Than Ever!"

The Bambi poster was a hit with the public. And the Advertising Council and Forest Service quickly determined that once the Disney contract ran out, they would need to replace the iconic deer with a new animal advocate, this time something original. During the course of 1944, several ideas were proposed and debated. By summertime, the campaign leadership had settled on a bear, the king of the North American forests. One of those involved suggested in a letter that it was to have a "nose short (Panda type), color black or brown; expression appealing, knowledgeable, quizzical; perhaps wearing a campaign (or Boy Scout) hat that typifies the outdoors and the woods." To realize this vision, the campaign called upon Albert Staehle, an animal illustrator whose work routinely appeared on national magazine covers. Staehle then submitted a drawing of a brown bear wearing blue jeans and a forest ranger hat. The image met with general approval and it was quickly decided to name the character Smokey, supposedly in honor of "Smoky Joe" Martin, the recently deceased assistant chief of the New York Fire Department, whose bravery was legendary. The cause of forest protection suddenly had a new mascot; it was Smokey Bear.

Meanwhile, the Japanese military remained intent on wreaking havoc against the nation's trees. It had recently developed a new technology known as a fire balloon. They were unmanned weapons, filled with highly flammable hydrogen. These balloons were designed to be released in Japan, traveling high in the atmosphere along the newly discovered jet stream, crossing the Pacific Ocean, and finally descending onto America, where the entire hydrogen-filled contraption would explode. In late 1944, at the same moment that Smokey Bear was being born, Japan began launching thousands of these balloons. They threatened to become a plague upon the western forests and potentially cause massive losses of life.

While the danger seemed all too real, technical problems and wet weather prevented nearly all of the balloons from succeeding in starting fires. The Japanese nonetheless proclaimed the operation a success. According to John McPhee, who wrote about this little-remembered episode in *The New Yorker,* "Japanese propaganda broadcasts mentioned great fires and an American populace in panic."

In truth, however, hardly any Americans knew about the campaign. Some had spotted the balloons floating in the western skies, and, in January 1945, *Newsweek* even published a story titled "Balloon Mystery." But that was as far as it got; the nation's Office of Censorship quickly ordered radio stations and media outlets to stay silent on the issue for fear of creating exactly the sort of general panic that Japanese propaganda was suggesting had occurred.

By April 1945, the Japanese military, sensing the program's ineffectiveness and seeing no mention of it in the American media, finally abandoned it. The program had launched a total of ninety-three hundred balloons. Ultimately, the worst damage came the month after the initiative's conclusion, when six people from a Sunday school group were killed by the delayed explosion of a balloon that had landed in an Oregon forest—these were, in fact, the only casualties from enemy combat that occurred in the continental United States during the war.

Following the fire balloon campaign, Japan made no further attempts to harm the nation's forests. The American government, nonetheless, remained on edge. Fear for the safety of the forests was even listed as a reason to sustain the internment of Japanese Americans, one of Roosevelt's most controversial acts as president—a June 1945 decision upholding certain elements of its continuation pointed to "[t]he peculiar vulnerability of Military Area No. 1 to devastating forest fires." Fears of further attacks or sabotage on the forests subsided only in August 1945, when Japan finally surrendered in the wake of America's dropping two catastrophic atomic bombs, one on Hiroshima and one on Nagasaki.

The end of the war, however, did not mean the end of the Cooperative Forest Fire Prevention campaign. Its success in reducing the total number of accidental fires seemed to justify its continuation. Plus, Smokey Bear had quickly won over the American public.

The postwar years saw what had begun as a replacement for Bambi develop into one of the nation's most recognizable images. In 1947, Smokey gained a signature catchphrase, when the Ad Council—the peacetime successor to the War Advertising Council—invented the slogan: "Only YOU can prevent forest fires." Three years later the character was brought to life after a black bear cub that escaped from a forest fire in New Mexico was christened "Smokey" and brought to the National Zoo in Washington, D.C.; it became one of the zoo's most popular attractions. During the 1950s and 1960s, countless celebrities teamed up with the fictional bear in radio advertisements to encourage responsible behavior in the forests.

The character also became an ambassador to the nation's youth. There were Smokey Bear dolls and songs and comic strips. One 1955 headline declared, "'Smokey' Makes Half Million Youngsters Junior Forest Rangers." The bear's popularity with schoolchildren grew so intense that the postal service even created a special ZIP code in 1964 to handle all the fan mail that poured in.

In more recent years, Smokey's celebrity status has diminished somewhat, but he remains an integral part of forest fire prevention in America. Various estimates have suggested that the character's impact in decreasing forest fires has saved the country tens of billions of dollars in forest damage. The campaign has also stood as the nation's longest-running public service announcement.

Of course, Smokey Bear was but one story to emerge from World War II, which was among the most transformative events in human history. The war's end marked a reordering of international power structures, with the United States ascending as the strongest nation in the world. Along with this increase in global influence would come a period of sustained American prosperity, in which living standards rose dramatically for more than twenty years. There would be new opportunities and new conflicts. And the nation's trees, once more, would play an integral role.

# 9

## Postwar Prosperity

Black Walnut

## Wooden Boxes with Picture Windows

WILLIAM LEVITT TOOK a drag from his cigarette, the first of several dozen the forty-year-old would smoke that day. It was October 1, 1947, and he had been anticipating this date for months. Later in the morning, some three hundred veterans and their families would begin to arrive at Nassau County, Long Island, to move into three hundred near-identical houses that Levitt had built for them, seemingly overnight. This day marked the start of what would soon be known as Levittown, the largest planned community in America.

Levitt's eponymous project would symbolize the new American suburbs, which over the next few decades would dominate the national landscape, both literally and figuratively. The suburbs would represent a new kind of domestic norm for the nation, one in which communities were frequently planned by large-scale developers such as Levitt and in which social life became notably insular. Where there once had stood working farms there would be rows upon rows of single-family houses, many of them indistinguishable from one another, each of them containing the hopes and aspirations of a generation of Americans who had just watched their nation triumph in the largest war in history. By and large, the dwellings would be simple in design, readily afford-able, filled with recently developed conveniences, and, to a remarkable degree, dependent on wood, the single most important material in their construction. Though their new residents likely wouldn't take long to contemplate the fact, these homes would owe their existence to America's trees, the unnoticed pillars of suburbia.

The idea of suburbia was not itself a postwar invention. Its history actually predated that of the nation. Historian Kenneth Jackson, author of *Crabgrass Frontier*, observed that written depictions of the suburb—which is to say, a residential area outside but dependent upon an urban center—traced back as far as 593 BCE. Most early American cities featured some variant of suburbs. These communities initially evolved somewhat organically, but in the middle of the nineteenth century, there began to appear fully planned suburban devel-opments. The first of these, located in the eastern foothills of New Jersey's Orange Mountains and constructed in the 1850s, was named Llewellyn Park, in honor of its creator, Llewellyn S. Haskell. He was both a wealthy New York merchant and an adherent of Perfectionism, a religious cult that advocated correct living as a way to attain a perfect earthly existence. His new suburb fea-tured upscale homes and, equally important, extensive landscaping, including a fifty-acre ramble at its center; Haskell, a staunch champion of Central Park, invested more than one hundred thousand dollars to plant trees and other plants. Llewellyn Park aimed to become a picturesque garden community, one that, in the words of an early architectural reviewer, provided "not only a source of health and recreation, but of culture and refinement." It quickly proved to be an attractive alternative for those who could afford the privilege—one of the most famous residents was the inventor Thomas Alva Edison, who lived there for over forty years.

The suburban ideal continued to evolve throughout the nineteenth and early twentieth centuries, and the task of planning and landscaping drew on the talents of many of the nation's preeminent designers, including Frederick Law Olmsted. He once opined, "[N]o great town can long exist without great suburbs."

But the suburbs that appeared in the wake of World War II shared relatively little with the expressive and fashionable enclaves that had inspired Olmsted. Levittown would have almost nothing in common with Llewellyn Park (other than the fact that they each owed their names to their self-aggrandizing developers). As historian Witold Rybczynski once observed, "It's almost as if a sort of amnesia set in and the garden suburb was forgotten."

The primary reason for this shift was that Levittown, like almost all postwar subdivisions, arose not as an alternative to urban life but as a solution to an acute housing crisis. The end of overseas fighting in 1945 had meant the return of some 16 million veterans, many of whom would be starting families and would need places to live. However, since the early 1930s, new-home construction had been somewhat stalled, first due to the economic effects of the Depression and then due to the war, a period when many homebuilders were contracted to meet emergency military housing needs. The lack of immediately available housing forced families to double up and, occasionally, to take more extreme measures. In 1947, two years after the war's end, some 500,000 families were still occupying Quonset huts or other temporary housing. In Chicago, 250 families took up residence in former trolley cars that had been converted into living quarters. In Omaha, one newspaper advertisement declared: "Big Ice Box, 7x17 feet, could be fixed up to live in."

The federal government sought to address the unfolding crisis head-on. As President Harry Truman told Congress in 1945: "A decent standard of housing for all is one of the irreducible obligations of modern civilization. . . . The people of the United States, so far ahead in wealth and productive capacity, deserve to be the best housed people in the world. We must begin to meet that challenge at once." It became a national imperative to ensure that sufficient housing be made available by any means necessary. And faced with the choice of building homes directly—a policy that seemed implausibly socialist—or of providing incentives to private builders, the federal government chose the latter.

Some measures had already been put in place before the crisis hit. Specifically, several acts passed under FDR during the Depression had created a number of housing agencies, which, among other things, provided federally backed mortgage insurance. This system helped to free credit for home loans, but it had not been designed to accommodate the needs of 16 million veterans, many of whom would have limited incomes upon returning from combat. Thus, in 1944, when the government passed the Servicemen's Readjustment Act (better known as the G.I. Bill of Rights), a sweeping set of veteran entitlements, it included the right to purchase a home without a down payment. Two years later, Truman signed the Veterans Emergency Housing Program, which channeled additional resources toward construction. At this point, in the words of Levitt, "Two of the three ingredients of success were there—the demand for housing, and the availability of money. The only thing missing was the product, the house."

Levitt was especially well equipped to provide this final ingredient. Nearly his entire adult life had been spent learning how to build houses. Real estate was the family business. His father, Abraham, had gotten involved in Long Island home construction during the 1920s, first as a supplement to his law profession and later as a full-time vocation. Abraham's business appealed greatly to William, who showed a flair for marketing, a facility with organization, and an unrelenting impulse to get rich. As he later observed, "I wanted to make a lot of money. I wanted a big car and a lot of clothes." William's younger brother, Alfred, found the family business equally attractive, though for different reasons. The more introverted of the two, Alfred had little taste for the industry's unavoidable hustling, but was fascinated with architecture; it was a subject that he'd learned largely through self-study, though he briefly interned with the legendary architect Frank Lloyd Wright. Collectively, the three men formed a brilliant team, soon to be known as Levitt & Sons. Abraham handled the financing, Alfred the design, and William, the world-beater and company president, attended to most everything else.

In the years before the war, Levitt & Sons pursued homebuilding in a relatively traditional fashion, a few projects at a time, each custom-built over the course of several months. Their homes were targeted at upper-middle-class New Yorkers looking for the tranquility of life outside the city. During the 1930s the firm earned some local renown for a small, two-hundred-unit subdivision that they constructed near Manhasset, Long Island. Known as Strathmore, it was full of Tudor-style houses priced between $9,100 and $18,500, and it shared certain elements with earlier high-end suburbs like Llewellyn Park. William, already a master salesman, drummed up interest by having one of the new houses wrapped the whole way round with cellophane, including a gargantuan red cellophane bow that sat above the entryway.

The arrival of war brought new opportunities and challenges to the firm. In 1941, it received a contract from the government to build sixteen hundred military worker homes in Norfolk, Virginia. The contract demanded speed and efficiency on a scale that the Levitts had never before attempted. In response, they began to experiment with mass-production techniques: time-consuming dug-out basements were replaced with poured-cement foundations; walls and roofs were partly preassembled; construction was broken down into simple tasks that could be performed without trained carpenters or unionized labor. Homes became stationary units in a moving assembly line of people; it was Fordism turned on its head. Thanks in large part to these innovations, the Levitts met the government contract ahead of schedule.

The experience transformed the family's outlook on homebuilding, encouraging them to think on a much grander scale. As William explained,

"[I]t proved to us what we had long suspected—that houses could be mass-produced in the field; and it infected us with the fever of mass building. . . . [I]t made us hungry for a full-blown, unhampered try at mass-producing houses." The Levitts began to contemplate a radical new idea in housing: a gigantic planned community, one that transferred the mass-production techniques that their military contract had required to civilian life. "It was a king-sized dream," said William. And it would require the combined efforts of all three family members. Alfred would take charge of designing a home that would be simple to construct and would appeal to popular sentiment. Abraham, who by this point had semiretired and turned his attention to gardening, would handle the landscaping. And William, the wunderkind, would coordinate the rest.

The homes they were about to erect on several thousand acres of potato fields in Nassau County, Long Island, would introduce an aesthetic that still controls much of the American landscape. They would be icons of a new age of prosperity. They would show remarkable innovation. They would feature new technologies and futuristic materials. However, the heart of the Levitt houses would depend solely on trees, just as had been the case in America from the outset.

THOUGH THE FIRST British settlers in New England had emigrated from a country where wood was a scarce commodity, they nonetheless brought with them knowledge of building homes using wood. English carpenters of the era favored a technique known as timber framing: Heavy beams of wood, often eight inches by eight inches, provided structural posts upon which was erected a wooden grid held together with mortise-and-tenon joints. Beyond this basic frame, however, the house contained materials that were often easier to acquire and less expensive than wood: The spaces between the support beams were filled in with bricks, loam, or wattle and daub, and the outer walls were coated with plaster. According to historian James Deetz, when English homes featured wood in the façade, it was primarily as "ostentation," an outward display to "show that [the wealthy] could afford such a luxury." But in America the forests expanded in every direction without end, a repository of timber unlike any the world had ever seen.

Unconstrained by the limitations of English life, the early colonists were free to cut down centuries-old white oaks and hew them into beams of sizes that were practically unknown in England. And the ready availability of good lumber encouraged the colonists to use wood in almost all construction tasks. For example, while builders in England typically constructed roofs from heavy materials such as slate, thatch, and tile, Plymouth colonists used cedar shingles, which were significantly lighter but equally protective. And the same story could be told for nearly all aspects of American homebuilding: Thin wooden strips, known as lath, were stacked horizontally along the structural beams to provide a latticework against which plaster was then applied; thick white pine boards, sometimes more than two feet across, lined the floors; vertical planks, running from the ground to the eaves, were often used to clad the frame; and long, overlapping bands of oak or pine, known as clapboard, covered the external siding. The typical New England home contained so much timber throughout that, but for its size, it might easily have been mistaken for the dwelling of nobility had it existed in the mother country.

While the English-influenced timber-framed home became the most common construction style in early America, it was far from the only one in a pluralistic society. Swedish settlers along the Delaware River introduced the log cabin to America during the seventeenth century. Dutch settlers preferred to build stone houses, examples of which can still be seen throughout New York's Hudson Valley. In the South, homes built of brick predominated in many regions, especially among the well-to-do. Nonetheless, even these non-timber-framed homes depended extensively on lumber, for internal paneling, doors, window frames, ceiling beams, supplemental supports, shutters, staircases, and furniture. Thomas Jefferson, whose Monticello home was built mainly of brick, wrote, "I have thought myself obliged to decline every application which has been made to me for [the sale of] timber of any kind. [W]ithout that resource I could not have built as I have done, nor could I look forward [to life] with any comfort." Wood was, quite simply, the universal American building material.

However, there was always potential to improve upon the methods of wooden construction. Timber framing, in particular, had several pronounced downsides. The technique depended upon extensive joinery, which required time and skilled labor, something that was always expensive in a land of freeholders. Additionally, the amount of heavy timber involved made increasingly less sense as lumber ceased being something locally harvested and became a commodity hauled in from afar.

During the early nineteenth century, carpenters searching for a solution to this dilemma began experimenting with different approaches that took advantage of an emerging technology: cheap, machine-fabricated iron nails. In the 1830s, a Chicago builder discovered that a sound structure could be produced using thinner, two-by-four-inch pine timbers that were precisely spaced, cross-braced, and fastened together with a generous dose of hammering. Skeptical carpenters supposedly joked that a stiff midwestern wind would blow away this curious-looking adaptation like a balloon. Their concerns were quickly disproved, but the dismissive name stuck and the new technique became known as "balloon framing." It quickly gained popularity, and by the turn of the century was the standard building technique throughout America. Whether the façades of individual homes featured clapboard (as in New England), brick (common in the South), or stucco (the most popular choice in the West), they most often contained an underlying structure of two-by-fours, and this continues to the present day.

The balloon frame heralded the end of full-timber framing, but it had little impact on the countless other roles that wood played in home construction. Throughout the nineteenth and early twentieth centuries, many of the techniques that initially worked in New England continued unabated across America. Cedar shingles remained common for roofs and external siding. Lath continued to serve as the base against which plaster was applied. Floors, ceilings, and walls were all frequently paneled with wood. And, unsurprisingly, the furniture that filled these homes almost universally came from the trees that filled the nation's many forests.

By the middle of the twentieth century, however, circumstances began to change. Technological advances and lower manufacturing costs led to a host of new construction materials. Wooden shingles faced competition from facsimiles made of asbestos. The lath-and-plaster method of wall construction began to give way to Sheetrock, a type of paneling that sandwiched gypsum between sheets of heavy paper and that could be directly hammered against wooden studs. Hardwood flooring gained new rivals from asphalt tiling and linoleum. And clapboard competed with aluminum siding. There was an endless array of options: Kimsul insulation, Armstrong's monowall, Kentile asphalt tiles, Congowall, and countless others. These brand-new, brand-named materials began to appear in magazine and newspaper advertisements, which loudly proclaimed their superiority to wooden alternatives. A 1950 ad for Beauty Bonded Formica, a new, resilient, plastic-based compound, provocatively inquired: "Who spanks the children at your house? The hair brush, razor strap, and switch don't get much of a work-out in homes that have formica surfaces. Formica [unlike wood] shrugs off fruit acids, alcohol, boiling water—and even the most elaborate childish messes." Nonetheless, the wooden aesthetic remained so ingrained in American culture that many of these products consciously imitated the lumber they sought to replace—that same 1950 formica ad continued, "Formica's beautiful color patterns and *rich wood grains* never need painting or refinishing."

The midcentury challenges to raw lumber came not only from these new materials but, in equal measure, from the wood-products industry itself. New ways to manipulate wood were constantly arising, fueled through the research and innovation of several groups: the Forest Products Laboratory; private inventors; and large timber companies, like Weyerhaeuser, which continually sought out methods to minimize wooden waste and expand the reach of their market share.

The most important structural wood product—at least in terms of postwar sales—was plywood, which was produced by taking thin sheets of wooden veneer, most frequently from Douglas fir trees, and gluing them against one another such that the direction of the grain alternated in each layer. This manufacturing process made plywood resistant to splitting regardless of where pressure was applied; as a result, it was stronger pound for pound than steel. First invented in 1905, it became practicable for widespread use in the 1930s, following the discovery of waterproof casein-based glues that created a bond as strong as the wood itself. There was seemingly no construction task that plywood couldn't handle. One advertisement proclaimed, "Ask your architect or builder about plywood's advantages for *every* building and remodeling job . . . for sheathing, subflooring, interior paneling, cabinets, built-ins. And remember! Your local retail lumber dealer has fir plywood for all purposes— INTERIOR for all inside applications, waterproof EXTERIOR for outside and marine uses. See him today!"

While plywood was the most widely used manufactured wood product, it was among the least complex. By midcentury, the timber products industry was producing an ever-growing range of composite materials. New production techniques took unsalable bits of lumber—like slabs and edgings—or small-diameter trees and ground them down into particles, flakes, fibers, or pulp, which were then pressed together or mixed with other materials to create new wonder products like particleboard, fiberboard, and hardboard. These, too, competed for the loyalty of consumers and builders through advertising: "Yes, these days home buyers are watching the way a house is built. They want to know if the builder is using these new materials—the kind that make a better house and save money, too—materials like Armstrong's Temlok Sheathing. . . . It's made of strong wood fibers, formed into big boards that are tough and durable. . . . Its light weight, toughness, and large size make it possible to sheath most houses in one day, with almost no waste."

This, then, was the state of home construction at the time the Levitt family determined to embark on their plans for mass fabrication. Homebuilders faced a remarkable array of options. Design styles spanned a broad range, shaped by regional preferences and personal taste. And lumber, while still preeminent for framing, was quickly being replaced by building materials that were largely unheard of a generation before, many of which had been developed by the lumber industry itself.

• • •

WHEN ALFRED LEVITT began to sketch out potential designs for a mass-produced Long Island home in the mid-1940s, he aimed for simplicity, utility, and a certain degree of instinctual Americanness. The home's overall shape would be modeled after the simple New England saltbox, a design older than the nation itself. The building's footprint would be twenty-five by thirty feet, barely larger than the cross-section of a mature giant sequoia. There would be four rooms in total: two bedrooms, a kitchen, and a living room that could double as a dining area—in addition, stairs would lead to an unfinished attic. Alfred's plans also incorporated many of the lessons that his family had learned in Norfolk. Foundations, for instance, would be poured-concrete slabs, which increased production speed and eliminated the need for basements.

For structure, the Levitts stayed loyal to the balloon frame. This wasn't inevitable, however. In an age of new materials, some builders experimented with such alternatives as steel, plastic, and fully prefabricated frames. Sometimes this led to outlandish outcomes, like one builder's proposal for a geodesic dome to be constructed from tetrahedrons of "three-way laminated fiber-glass plastic." But these alternatives did not interest William Levitt, who was far less concerned with conceptual innovation than with economical production. As he explained to a reporter, "A steel frame makes it last as long as the Empire State Building, if that's what you want, but the housewife never sees it—what does she care?"

Although Levitt chose to use traditional balloon framing, he nonetheless introduced several key innovations to the business of constructing homes from wood. Before him, builders had purchased wood from timber companies or relied on contractors to supply them. But Levitt, with an eye to profit margins and the opportunities that economies of scale offered, determined that it would be preferable to control the entire process, from tree to two-by-four. Much like Frederick Weyerhaeuser, who had revolutionized the lumber industry almost a century earlier by purchasing timberlands directly, Levitt bought his own forest in California and constructed a mill to handle the processing. This gave him control over the entire fabrication process, allowing the standardization of each step along the way. As he noted, "Freight cars loaded with lumber went directly into a cutting yard where one man with a power saw cut parts for ten houses in one day. These were bundled into packages, each one containing all the lumber parts for one house, and picked up by fork-lift trucks for reloading and delivery by truck to the house lot."

Beyond the frame, the Levitt home would feature an array of new materials, some wood-based, others not. The initial models used five-sixteenths-inch plywood for external sheathing, upon which was mounted either wood or asbestos shingles. The roofs were covered with asphalt shingles atop asphalt-saturated felt. Interior walls were faced with half-inch gypsum drywall, while the floors were laid with asphalt tiles that sat upon a waterproof emulsion (and beneath this were copper coils that provided radiant heating). Everything was selected to maximize consumer satisfaction, cost-effectiveness, and efficiency. According to Levitt, they "calculated the shape and size and quantity of materials needed for the construction of that house, down to the last two pounds of four-penny finishing nails."

The Levitts paid equal attention to the construction process. It was boiled down to twenty-six major steps, which could be completed with a team of semiskilled, nonunion laborers in several hours start to finish. The short-story writer W. D. Wetherell described the scene in his award-winning 1985 piece *The Man Who Loved Levittown*: "But here's what happens. A truck comes along, stops in front of the house, half a dozen men pile out . . . in fifteen minutes they've put in a bathroom. Pop! Off they go to the next house, just in time, too, because here comes another truck with the kitchen. Pop! In goes the kitchen. They move on one house, here comes the electricians. Pop! Pop! Pop! The house goes up."

The finished product carried an initial price tag of $7,990, a remarkable achievement considering that many builders claimed that it was impossible to erect single-family homes for less than $10,000. And with the generous financing provided through the various federal initiatives, veterans could purchase a Levitt home for zero money down and only $56 per month—the national government's efforts to subsidize postwar housing actually made it more cost-effective to purchase a new Levitt home than to rent many of the apartments in New York City. Once Levitt houses went on the market (first as rental units only but soon exclusively for purchase), veterans—who were the only people that the Levitts initially targeted—lined up to capitalize on the opportunity to finally have a home that they could call their own.

The first residents arrived on October 1, 1947, and the landscape that greeted them was unlike almost anything seen in America up to that time. Row after row of houses, indistinguishable but for their color and the placement of certain windows, stretching out into the distance. Surrounding them was an ocean of grass, trimmed precisely to three inches. And equally striking was the complete absence of mature trees. This, as much as any other factor, symbolized the break between Levittown and the planned garden communities that predated the war. One journalist described the new subdivision as "a horizon broken only by telegraph poles."

This was not to say that planted trees were unimportant in Levittown. Abraham, the patriarch, had insisted that trees form an integral part of the new venture. William described his father as "a modern Johnny Appleseed." If this claim was overstated, it was not necessarily misplaced, for Abraham did demand that each home have an apple tree on its lawn, along with several others. "In developing the landscaping plans," the eldest Levitt explained in 1950, "deciduous trees, as well as evergreens and well-known species of flowering shrubs, had to be included. But, in addition, at least four fruit trees—apple, pear, peach, and cherry—were included in the landscaping for each house. . . . I know that in a few years Levittown, with its 40,000 trees in flower, will be a veritable fairyland."

Abraham's fairyland vision, however, had the consequence of turning planted trees into a mass-produced commodity, just like the homes that they surrounded. Whereas earlier landscape architects, like Andrew Jackson Downing or Olmsted, had thought carefully about the ways that individual trees might complement a particular backdrop, Abraham sought a degree of uniformity that was hitherto unknown in America. As one sociologist argued, the senior Levitt was "the man chiefly responsible [for inventing] the mass produced landscape to go along with its ready-built housing."

Nonetheless, the mass-produced nature of the new environs did little to discourage the new residents, whose numbers grew from an initial three hundred families up to a final, almost incomprehensible, total of seventeen thousand. Levittown was suddenly a small city, but one where everyone had more in common than not. As a *New York Times* reporter explained in 1952, "Nobody keeps up with the Joneses because they almost all have the same income (about $4,000 average). Nobody talks about the war much, because they've all been in it. And most of the men have the same Long Island Rail Road commuting problem—which many have solved by car pools. All this helps cement neighbors into friends." And as friends, these early residents strove to build a community, forming clubs, sharing tools, and scrupulously following the elaborate and sometimes doctrinaire rules of the Levittown Homeowner's Guide: "No fabricated fences . . . will be permitted"; "Mow your lawn and remove weeds at least once a week." The term "Levittowner" became one that these first-generation residents embraced with affection.

The planned community's success transformed William Levitt into a national celebrity and a household name (a term that seemed particularly appropriate). In the summer of 1950, *Time* magazine placed him on its cover and ran an accompanying story that bordered on hagiography. "[T]he leader of the U.S. housing revolution," read the article, "is a cocky, rambunctious hustler with brown hair, cow-sad eyes, a hoarse voice (from smoking three packs of cigarettes a day), and a liking for hyperbole that causes him to describe his height (5 ft. 8 in.) as 'nearly six feet' and his company as the 'General Motors of the housing industry.' His supreme self-confidence—his competitors call it arrogance—is solidly based on the fact that he is the most potent single modernizing influence in a largely antiquated industry."

And Levitt's influence could be seen across the nation. As the *Time* article noted, the Levitt "methods of mass production are being copied by many of the merchant builders in the U.S., who are putting up four of every five houses built today." By 1955, large-scale subdivisions accounted for more than 75 percent of all new residential construction near urban areas. As a result of this, in less than a decade, the nature of American homes changed forever. They were suddenly available for purchase to all but the poorest in society. At the same time, regional variation began to disappear: The communities of small, hastily built houses looked roughly similar, whether one was in Long Island or Los Angeles.

Life in the new suburbia was about more than just owning a home. It was also about being a consumer. A generation raised during the Depression suddenly found themselves living in an age of remarkable prosperity, where many had disposable income. Suburbanites reveled in their newfound ability to purchase modern comforts. The signs of good living in the subdivisions included a car in the garage, a television in the living room, and a full range of appliances in the kitchen.

Levitt, who seemed to possess a preternatural understanding of consumer tastes, made sure that many of these conveniences came preinstalled in his new homes. The living rooms included a built-in Admiral television set. The kitchens contained a refrigerator, stove, and, most important, a fancy Bendix-brand washing machine. About the only feature that didn't smack of modernity was a two-way fireplace, which was technically unnecessary since the floors already contained state-of-the-art radiant heating. But the fireplace provided a touch of nostalgia for America's past, a time when the hearth had been the center of the home. According to Levitt, "It was difficult to say whether the washing machine or the two-way fireplace did more to endear the house to the buyers' hearts."

The new consumer goods displaced many of the traditional roles that wood had played within the home. Gone were the wooden icebox, the wooden washboard, the wood-burning stove. Modernity meant steel, plastic, glass, and synthetics. Nonetheless, the demand for consumer goods also facilitated the introduction of scores of novel tree-based products, just as had been the case with housing materials. By the 1950s, Americans (even if they likely didn't realize it) were surrounded on all sides by products that originated in the nation's forests.

Perhaps the best example of this was the ascendance of disposable paper products. Wood pulp had been used for newspapers since the 1870s, but it took much longer for technology and consumer demand to exploit pulp's full range of possibilities. The pioneer in this field was the Kimberly-Clark Corporation of Wisconsin. Founded in 1872, it began to market disposable paper products in the aftermath of World War I, following its invention of a feminine sanitary napkin known as Kotex. Though this product, according to company chairman John R. Kimberly, was initially "the target of taboos that bordered on the mystical," its eventual acceptance "led to a generation of constant expansion, a growth so compulsive that . . . the company's work force actually expanded during the Depression." Kimberly-Clark's next revolutionary innovation was the Kleenex tissue, introduced during the 1930s. By the postwar period the company had an entire line of products that quickly became indispensable to daily life. As Kimberly noted in 1964, "Consider for the moment the everyday paper products that were, by and large, almost unknown a generation or so ago: paper plates, cups, facial tissues, towels, napkins, place mats, aprons, even throwaway paper diapers." But even this list failed to capture the full range of paper uses in the postwar period. Eggs now came in paper containers, milk was sold in paper cartons, and the countless new appliances arrived inside cardboard boxes. Whereas annual per-capita paper consumption in 1920 had been 145 pounds, by the 1960s it had more than tripled and was the highest in the world.

But disposable paper products were far from the only part of domestic life that tree products had infiltrated by midcentury. In 1942, the Forest Service, seeking to illustrate this point, produced a short film, *The Tree in a Test Tube,* that featured Laurel and Hardy, the famed comic duo. They appeared at the film's outset looking bewildered in reaction to the offscreen narrator's prompt: "Wood, got any?" The narrator continued, "Like most guys you don't realize how many articles made of wood products you carry around." Over the next four minutes, the two baffled comedians proceeded to empty an entire suitcase and trenchcoat's worth of materials, each of which relied on trees. There were plastic-framed glasses, a plastic fountain pen, a plastic cigarette container, a plastic-cased penknife, and a plastic-handled razor; as the narrator noted, "About sixty percent of plastic is wood flour. Powdered wood, my friends." There was a billfold, a hat, and a toilet case, all of which contained imitation leather that had been made with cellulose acetate, another wood derivative. At one point, Hardy cagily extracted a pair of pantyhose from Laurel's wallet, to which the narrator replied, "Oh, sure, your wife's, of course; anyway, they're rayon, another wood product." After all of the comedians' pockets and suitcase compartments had been accounted for, the narrator quipped, "It's a good thing these lads didn't come around here with a trunk; we'd be here for days."

This was one of the great ironies of the postwar period. Though wood was no less important than it had been in earlier times, the average person hardly noticed. This was as true for consumer products as it was for home construction. The suburban world that Levitt helped to create betrayed scant evidence of its utter reliance upon trees—indeed, this dependence was one of the reasons that in Western Europe, where wood was a less available commodity, there arose almost no overnight subdivisions.

By the late 1950s, the wooden wonderland of suburbia was being heralded as a symbol of the triumph of American capitalism. It became an instrumental tool in the ideological battle that the United States was waging against the Soviet Union. As Levitt famously declared, "No man who owns his own house and lot can be a communist. He has too much to do." Government officials even decided to use a typical suburban home as the centerpiece of the 1959 American exhibition in Moscow—Levitt was supposedly asked to provide one of his homes but demurred. The resulting wood-framed model home— which was bisected by a walkway and consequently dubbed "Splitnik," a play on the Soviet satellite Sputnik—served as the site for one of the most famous exchanges of the entire Cold War. While standing near the home's General Electric kitchen, Vice President Richard Nixon and Soviet premier Nikita Khrushchev got into a heated discussion, later dubbed the "Kitchen Debate," over the merits of American capitalism. Khrushchev, who was skeptical that such a home could possibly be available to an average worker, questioned the value of all the modern appliances that lined the walls. Nixon, in response, issued the immortal line: "Would it not be better to compete in the relative merits of washing machines than in the strengths of rockets?"

The suburbs may have offered a projection of strength abroad, but they were increasingly coming under fire on the home front. Critics charged that they stunted social development, left women (few of whom belonged to the workforce) hopelessly isolated, and bred a dangerous degree of conformity. In 1956, John Keats marshaled these claims into a polemic titled *The Crack in the Picture Window*. The title was an allusion to an oversized living room window that the Levitts had begun including in nearly all units they built after 1949. According to Keats, "[I]f there was any cohesive force acting on typical development householders, it would be that of hatred." This sentiment was echoed several years later in sociologist William Whyte's *The Organization Man*, which focused on how the new suburban lifestyle inexorably sapped the spirit of its male inhabitants, who worked long days for large corporations in the city in order to earn enough income to support their suburban families, with which they hardly ever had a chance to spend any time. The subject of suburban alienation subsequently became a trope for a generation of writers, like Raymond Carver and John Updike.

But discontentment was hardly the only problem. Perhaps even more troubling was the issue of race. Though subdivisions originated as a solution to a housing crisis, they quickly evolved into all-white enclaves. Partly this was the result of whites fleeing from cities in reaction to urban decline and the threat of school integration that emerged as a result of the Supreme Court's landmark 1954 ruling in *Brown v. Board of Education,* which declared segregation unconstitutional. But the lily-white nature of suburbs was also facilitated by the builders, who actively excluded African Americans (whether veterans or otherwise) from the communities they had planned. Levitt was no exception. In his words, "We can solve a housing problem, or we can try to solve a racial problem. But we cannot combine the two." There was not a single black resident among the eighty-two thousand people who populated Levittown in its first decade. Civil rights activists repeatedly challenged Levitt's policies, and by the late 1950s the federal courts declared that excluding blacks from planned communities was unconstitutional. Levitt nonetheless remained defiant, violating court pronouncements on the grounds that it was a market necessity.

By the early 1960s, the man who helped introduce suburbia was no longer considered a national hero. His racial politics and an increasing dissatisfaction with the subdivisions that he had built or inspired turned him into something of a pariah. As Wetherell wrote in *The Man Who Loved Levittown,* "What has Levitt ever done? He built these places and never looked back. He made his pile, then didn't want to know nothing." The residents of the third Levittown, in New Jersey, even voted to have the town's name returned to its original Willingboro in 1963. Circumstances quickly grew more difficult for Levitt— in a period of four years, from 1962 to 1966, his father, mother, and brother all passed away. By the end of the decade, Levitt was ready to exit the homebuilding business, and in 1968 sold his company to the International Telephone & Telegraph Corporation (ITT) for $92 million in stock. The transaction netted Levitt $62 million, but much of this evaporated when the share price of ITT later collapsed. He attempted to reenter the mass-housing industry several times during the 1980s, but the original magic was long gone, and those who prepurchased his homes found themselves with nothing but unbuilt promises. He died in early 1994, at the age of eighty-six, his legacy some 140,000 American homes.

Levitt's disappearance from the trade ultimately had little impact on the trend that he'd helped inaugurate. Throughout the second half of the twentieth century, suburbs spread out all across America. As of 1980, some 100 million people, more than 40 percent of the nation, lived in suburbs, a higher proportion than lived in either rural or urban areas. As Kenneth Jackson observed, "By 1985 reasonable people could debate whether the United States was a racist nation, an imperialist nation, or a religious nation, but scarcely anyone could quarrel with its designation as a suburban nation." The suburbs, taken as a whole, represented a dramatic population shift, as great as any in U.S. history. An entire generation moved out of cities and into the surrounding hinterlands.

From the perspective of land use, the rise of suburbia turned millions of acres of farmland, often abandoned or failing, into an endless sea of grass, infinite swaths of green carpeting, broken up only by planted trees and wooden boxes. But the suburban revolution was far from the only significant land-use shift during the postwar period. Major change was also taking place in the nation's private forests, which comprised over 350 million acres, an area more than twice the size of Texas.

## "Timber Is a Crop!"

IN EARLY JUNE 1941—almost exactly six years before the Levitt family stepped onto a worn-out Long Island potato field to break ground on their famous subdivision—another group was gathering, shovels in hand, on the other side of the nation. The property upon which they stood—some 120,000 acres located on the western side of the Cascade Mountains in Washington State—had formerly been covered with Douglas firs, primeval giants whose evergreen tops seemed to scrape against the clouds. But now many of those trees were charred stumps, the casualties of the forest fires that followed on the heels of industrial logging. Lumber companies typically abandoned such holdings once the trees were ruined, but this day marked a new approach. The shovels were for planting new trees, and the land, which belonged to the Weyerhaeuser Timber Company, would soon earn the official designation of "Tree Farm No. 1," first in a movement that would spread across the nation.

The idea that trees could be grown to produce lumber was not a new one by any stretch of the imagination. It was a tenet of European forestry and was something that Pinchot had been advocating throughout his entire career. In his autobiography, he declared, "Trees may be grown as a crop just as corn may be grown as a crop. The farmer gets crop after crop of corn, oats, wheat, cotton, tobacco, and hay from his farm. The forester gets crop after crop of logs, cordwood, shingles, poles, or railroad ties from his forest, and even some return from regulated grazing." In the early decades of the twentieth century, Pinchot's message had already resonated with numerous conservation-minded individuals. Most notable, perhaps, was Franklin Delano Roosevelt.

But the logging industry had largely avoided the practice. Though most lumbermen expressed support for forestry techniques, they chafed at the notion of actually planting trees or undertaking the serious labor required to implement sustainable forestry. It was costly and time-consuming, with the rewards unseen for a generation. And, as they frequently pointed out, the nation's tax system made it more economical to exploit virgin lands and abandon them than to invest in long-term projects.

By the 1930s, however, attitudes among lumbermen toward tree planting and sustainable forestry began to soften. One factor was the continued growth of a forestry consciousness among a generation of loggers. A second was the rise in stumpage prices. A third was growing talk at the state and federal level of alterations to the tax policy that would facilitate the rehabilitation of cutover lands. And, perhaps most important, lumbermen started to worry that the government, which had largely left the industry-owned forests alone out of respect for private property rights, was finally going to insist on regulations if loggers didn't take action. They had reason to fear this. In 1933, the *Copeland Report,* a Senate-sponsored study that provided the most comprehensive review of the country's tree resources to date, concluded "that practically all of the major problems of American forestry center in, or have grown out of, private ownership." It seemed only a matter of time before FDR's administration did something in response.

In the late 1930s the Weyerhaeuser Timber Company, so often at the forefront of the lumber industry, instituted a number of policies designed to demonstrate a reformed attitude. It began by hiring a dedicated public relations executive, and one of his first initiatives was a 1937 advertising campaign built around Pinchot's timeworn slogan "Timber is a crop!" But this was more rhetoric than policy. To show that the firm was serious, Weyerhaeuser executives soon started making plans for a public demonstration of what their sloganeering amounted to. The project, named "Operation Rehab," would take 120,000 acres of burned-over land near Montesano, Washington, and turn it into a showpiece for forestry techniques, including extensive replanting and fire control. During the course of planning, it was suggested that the firm dub their project a "tree farm," a catchy term that seemed likely to resonate with the media and the public. A local newspaper editor then proposed that this inaugural tree farm be named in honor of Charles H. Clemons, a pioneer logger in western Washington. Thus, the Clemons Tree Farm was born. The formal dedication took place on June 12, 1941, before an overflow crowd whose guests included Phil Weyerhaeuser, the grandson of the firm's founder, and Arthur B. Langlie, the governor of Washington.

At the dedication ceremony, Langlie prophesied that "[t]he Clemons Tree Farm . . . may set the pace for millions of acres of such lands throughout the state." This was meant to be an optimistic assessment, but in truth the governor had greatly underestimated the potential scope of tree farms. Five months after the Montesano groundbreaking, the National Lumber Manufacturers' Association resolved that a national tree farm system ought to be instituted. The NLMA's educational arm then put together a loose set of criteria for inclusion in this American Tree Farm System. It would cover "privately owned forest-land dedicated to the growing of forest crops for commercial purposes, protected and managed for continuous production of forest products." This marked the first time that a certification system was put in place to evaluate forest health. Lumbermen whose lands met this definition and who wanted to participate in the program received official signs emblazoned with the words "Tree Farm" in large green letters within a white diamond. These signs promised a degree of free publicity and goodwill from the local communities.

Logging firms rushed to emulate the model that Weyerhaeuser had initiated. Within the first year, the total amount of land designated as tree farms grew from the initial 120,000 acres to more than 5 million. By mid-1942, the idea had expanded beyond the Pacific Northwest and into the South, turning the program into a truly national phenomenon. And it showed no signs of slowing down.

Nonetheless, not everyone embraced tree farms as a sign of progress. Lyle Watts, the chief of the Forest Service, lamented that it amounted to little more than a fanciful public relations stunt designed to ward off government regulation. Speaking before a 1943 meeting of the Society of American Foresters, he said, "I cannot let the misleading publicity of the forest industries pass unchallenged." While he acknowledged that the tree farm movement might represent a positive step forward if "high standards" were maintained, he cautioned, "Unfortunately, mediocre or lower performance has served to qualify some properties for the 'Tree Farm' designation."

Watts's criticisms—more accurate than many of those involved might have publicly acknowledged—were aimed at the major industrial players who had been the earliest adopters of tree farms. But the movement was also rapidly growing beyond the titans of commercial logging. The same year that Watts voiced his concerns, the state of Alabama certified the first nonindustrial property as a tree farm, marking the start of a new era.

Small landholders were a big issue in timber production. As a group, they controlled nearly 300 million acres of commercial forest, almost 60 percent of the total at midcentury (the rest was split between the government, which held nearly 150 million acres, and the forest products industry, which owned the remaining 60 million acres). Bernhard Fernow, the chief of the Division of Forestry before Pinchot, had recognized early on that it was among farmers that the practice of forestry could see the greatest gains. He considered them "the most desirable" candidates, "since they probably form the most stable class of our population, and can devote the most care and attention to the management of their wood lots." But the nation's farmers and small landholders had lagged behind in the implementation of management practices for their woodlands. The tree farm movement, first the province of the large logging firms, eventually developed into a helpful tool for encouraging better management of small timber tracts. It was free to join, it was simple to understand, and it offered additional revenue (as well as tax breaks).

It was also especially well publicized. Throughout the postwar years, the NLMA and its affiliated lobbying arms devoted expansive resources to popularizing the tree farm concept. They retained writers like Stewart Holbrook, the great raconteur of the Pacific Northwest forests, to help sell the idea. They funded radio shows, such as *The Adventures of Peter Pine,* and films, such as *Tomorrow's Trees,* to spread the message of the importance of conservation to a wide audience. And they even recruited celebrity endorsements. In the 1960s, Andy Griffith, perhaps the most recognized television personality of the age, served as an official spokesman for tree farms. In one of his recorded messages, he explained,

> See I'm a tree farmer myself. My tree farm in Dare County, North Carolina, is growing strong. We have 135 acres. . . . So I know what the American tree farm system is all about and I believe in it. . . . There are about 4 million of us private landowners in the United States, and altogether we own nearly sixty percent of this country's commercial land. . . . Without your volunteer effort and help the tree farm program wouldn't be where it is today.

Fueled by such widespread publicity, the tree farm movement grew steadily. By 1959, there were more than 50 million acres nationally controlled by 15,798 participants, the great majority of whom were small landholders. There were tree farms in Maine, where the lumber industry began, in the Lake States, where Weyerhaeuser revolutionized the industry, in the South, where second-generation longleaf pines grew around abandoned lumber towns, and in the Pacific Northwest, where the largest lumber firms resided. Soon tree farms would appear in all fifty states. A 1964 opinion poll determined that 59 percent of Americans had heard of tree farms—remarkably, only 12 percent of them realized that it was an industry-sponsored program.

The American Tree Farm System continued to expand into the early 1990s, when the total amount of certified land topped 90 million acres. In the years that followed, the gross acreage began to shrink, not from lack of interest, but because of the rise of rival certification programs. These included the Sustainable Forest Initiative and the Forest Stewardship Council. Today, hundreds of millions of private forest acres are party to one of these certification programs. And the emphasis on renewable forests has helped allow new growth to continually exceed annual cuttings—a significant achievement in a nation where, in 1918, almost six trees had been harvested for every new one that appeared. The American Tree Farm System, meanwhile, continues into the present and boasts more than ninety thousand members, inheritors of a tradition that began with the Clemons Tree Farm.

The postwar tree farm movement had given a name and purpose to the conservation-minded (and sometimes publicity-minded) owners of the country's private forestland. But quite a different story was unfolding in the nation's public forests during the same period. The issue there wasn't only in producing timber sustainably, but in making room for a new role: recreation. America's emergency reserve of public timberland had slowly evolved into the nation's playground, a site for summer vacations, winter getaways, and weekend hunting trips. And the demand for these activities would increase exponentially in the years following World War II. As a result, private citizens and the government would be forced to reevaluate just what these forests and their trees were actually for.

## A Nation of Vagabonds

A s with suburbia and tree farms, outdoor recreation had a history that greatly predated the form it would assume in America during the twentieth century. The idea of enjoying leisure time among the forests and their trees had been a recurring theme of life in the young nation. It informed the writings of Ralph Waldo Emerson, Henry David Thoreau, and John Muir. It helped inspire the urban parks movement that Frederick Law Olmsted spearheaded. And it brought thousands of well-heeled Americans into the grand hotels of the Catskills. Restless boys retreated to the forests to imitate the exploits of backwoodsmen, while grown men banded together into social clubs devoted to hunting and sport—the ranks of this latter group included President Theodore Roosevelt, founder in 1887 of the Boone and Crockett Club, an open-air fraternity of sorts.

Nonetheless, outdoor recreation was but a minor breeze in the gale of ideas that led to the creation of the national forests in the late nineteenth century. The 1897 Pettigrew Amendment—which outlined the purpose of the newly created national forests and which, Pinchot later determined, was among "the most important Federal forest legislation ever enacted"—did not even acknowledge recreation. It listed only three legitimate uses: "to improve or protect the forest," "[to] secur[e] favorable conditions of water flows," and "to furnish a continuous supply of timber."

This was not to say that no one spared a thought to the recreational potential of these novel creatures of federal authority. Pinchot himself, in the 1907 *Use Book*, the pocket-sized bible of the Forest Service, wrote: "Quite incidentally, also, the National Forests serve a good purpose as great playgrounds for the people." In the sentence that followed, however, he hinted at just why outdoor recreation was little more than an "incidental" concern: "They are used more or less every year by campers, hunters, fishermen, and *thousands of pleasure seekers from the near-by towns.*" This was, to put it mildly, not a very significant figure in a nation of 90 million souls—Central Park alone could boast a number of visitors several factors greater.

The paltry number of forest frolickers likely owed more to logistics than to custom. The government-owned trees could not be reached without expending great effort. Practically none of the new forest reserves—located exclusively in the far West before 1911—were accessible by tourist train, the primary mode of distance travel in the late nineteenth and early twentieth centuries. Thus, public woodlands were functionally off-limits for nearly all Americans. The main exceptions were either the lucky few who lived close by, the devoted naturalists like Muir who gleefully tramped for days on end across any stretch of woodland they could access, or the thoroughly financed adventurers like Teddy Roosevelt who could afford a horse, ample provisions, and a competent guide.

But the inexorable process of development kept motoring along, bringing new opportunities with it. The same era that witnessed the creation of the nation's timber reserves also saw the arrival of the most transformative technology of the twentieth century, the automobile. This new "horseless carriage" promised a degree of mobility and freedom hitherto unknown to the average American.

Of course, delivering on that promise seemed as difficult as chopping down a hickory with a blunt ax. The earliest car models, of which there were thousands, performed unreliably but carried pricetags that only the rich could afford. The automobile thus began as a luxury primarily confined to intracity transport. This situation, however, would soon change, thanks in large part to the efforts of Henry Ford, a mechanic whose name would eventually become synonymous with the idea of mass production.

Ford was born on July 30, 1863, in Dearborn, Michigan, a hamlet five miles away from the city of Detroit. His father was a prosperous farmer, one who pressured his son to adopt the family vocation. But the younger Ford showed little interest in agriculture. At sixteen, he headed to Detroit to apprentice and work with a number of manufacturing concerns, including Westinghouse. It was during this period that he encountered an early model internal combustion engine, a machine that grabbed his imagination as surely as a magnet attracts iron. He nonetheless returned to Dearborn in 1886 when his father offered him forty acres of timberland in exchange for abandoning the machinist trade. Ford thus briefly became a lumberman, though he also used this time to get married and continue his mechanical investigations on the side. As he explained, "[W]hen I was not cutting timber I was working on the gas engines—learning what they were and how they acted." Once all the timber had been cut, Ford packed up his belongings and headed back to Detroit, entering the hurly-burly world of automobiles for good in 1890.

By 1903, he had amassed enough capital and experience to open his own shop, the Ford Motor Company. Six years of experimentation followed, until he and his team—which featured several future titans of the industry, including the Dodge brothers—settled on the idea of focusing all the firm's efforts on the fabrication of a single, standardized design: the Model T. Ford declared, "I will build a motor car for the great multitude." To make good on this promise, he needed not just a solid design—for which the Model T undoubtedly qualified—but also a manufacturing process that could churn out enough cars to meet the seemingly bottomless demand for affordable vehicles. His team began to analyze every facet of production, seeking ways to improve efficiency, accelerate fabrication, and increase scale. Within four years, they had settled on a revolutionary approach that would become the hallmark of modern industry: the assembly line. Complex tasks were broken down into their constituent parts, each of which was assigned to a single worker who remained stationary as his assignment arrived on an automated conveyor belt. The subsequent production numbers told the story: By Ford's calculations, in 1909 his firm had produced 19,000 cars at a price of $950 each, but by 1916 the output had climbed more than forty times, to over 785,000, while the price fell by more than half, to $360. Suddenly, thanks to Ford and his team, the automobile was available to the average American.

Ford believed that his new car was a vehicle as much for pleasure as for productivity. The same speech in which he had announced his plans to build "a motor car for the great multitude" had also included the assurance that it would allow any man to "enjoy with his family the blessing of hours of pleasure in God's great open spaces." Of the two types of Model T, the slightly more expensive one was branded specifically for "touring." As Ford later explained, "The single matter of giving people a chance to move about and see the world is an element which of itself would be sufficient to change the character of the people." And this change in character included the desire to access the forests and trees whose remoteness had thus far kept them segregated from the great majority of Americans.

On this matter, Ford led by example. Over a period of seven years, from 1918 to 1924, he embarked on a series of car camping trips that helped introduce this new form of outdoor recreation to the nation. Ford's celebrity was so immense by this point that anything he did was likely to receive some degree of media coverage, but it was the company he kept that made these outings front-page news. Joining him were three other giants of the era, men whose reputations were of such vast magnitude that it was fitting they could only be contained in the open-air cathedral of the forests. There was Thomas Alva Edison, the wizard of Menlo Park, New Jersey, who, by dint of his 99 percent perspiration, had given the world the incandescent lightbulb, the motion-picture camera, the phonograph, and some thousand other patented devices. There was John Burroughs, the wise man of the Catskills, a naturalist whose writings about nature rivaled those of Muir in popularity and impact. And finally there was Harvey Firestone, the nation's rubber baron, upon whose tires rolled the millions of Model Ts that the Ford Motor Company produced. Collectively, this unlikely grouping would soon be known as "the four vagabonds."

The idea for their car camping trips dated to 1915, when Ford, Firestone, and Edison encountered each other at the World's Fair in San Francisco. The occasion was the celebration of the fair's Edison Day, a testament to the popular reverence that the inventor enjoyed. After the festivities concluded, the threesome determined to travel together by private car to San Diego, where yet another Edison Day was about to be held. According to Firestone, "All of us had such a good time that Mr. Edison proposed that the three of us go camping the next year." An invitation was soon extended as well to Burroughs, who was by then an octogenarian but as lithe as his beard was long. Firestone suggested that he was recruited because Edison "wanted a man along who could tell us about the trees and the birds and the flowers." Ford may have also wanted a chance to proselytize for his product, noting that Burroughs had "developed a grudge against modern progress . . . [and] declared that the automobile was going to kill the appreciation of nature."

Edison selected the Adirondacks as the site for their first trip in the summer of 1916. At the last moment, business obligations forced Ford to withdraw, but the other three traversed more than a thousand miles together, touring by day and sleeping in tents at night. Burroughs wrote, "John Muir would have called it a glorious trip. . . . We cut the heart out of the Adirondacks, and we took a big slice off the Green Mountains." They planned to repeat the adventure the following year, but, as Firestone explained, "[T]he coming of the war found us with our hands too full to take any time off for gadding about."

Circumstances were less chaotic by the summer of 1918, at which point all four men finally set out together. This time their destination was the Great Smoky Mountains of the Southeast (much of which would become a national park in 1934). Though they were seeking to escape among the trees, they nonetheless came equipped with all the conveniences that autocamping afforded. R. J. H. DeLoach, a professor who was one of several guests accompanying the vagabonds, explained,

> The camping equipment was very elaborate. . . . The caravan, so to speak, was always headed by Mr. Edison's 4-cylinder Simplex. Mr. Firestone's Packard came next, followed by two Model-T Fords. Then came two vans, the first of which was called the dining room and kitchen, carrying all the necessary equipment for cooking and serving and an abundance of good food. At the end of the line was the van carrying the tents, cots, bedding, and blankets.

Burroughs, in reflecting on this scene, described his merry band as "a luxuriously equipped expedition going forth to seek discomfort." On their first night they camped in an oak grove about thirty miles southeast of Pittsburgh, and each man began to assume his unique vagabond identity: Edison preferred to read or meditate, Ford would seize an ax and "swing it vigorously till there [was] enough wood for the camp fire." At night, they gathered around the fire, beneath the shadows of the trees, to discuss literature, business, politics, the war, and anything else that came to mind (Ford hadn't yet begun to express the anti-Semitic views that would tarnish his legacy). Such was their rhythm for days on end, as they cruised about some of the most majestic forestland remaining in the East. Firestone considered this 1918 adventure "the best that we ever had."

But it was far from the last. The following year they returned to the Adirondacks for another grand tour. The next summer there was no car camping, but the group did briefly gather at Burroughs's home. While there, a tree-chopping contest broke out between Ford and Burroughs. Firestone noted, "We gave the victory to Mr. Burroughs." This would be the vagabonds' last memory of the great naturalist, for he died soon after. But even without their tree-chopping champion, the car trips continued. In 1921, the remaining three vagabonds set forth into the woods of Maryland with an even grander assemblage and a guest list that included President Warren Harding and his wife. Their final gathering, in 1924, comprised a series of excursions in and around Massachusetts, the most notable of which was a visit to President Calvin Coolidge at his family home in Vermont.

The vagabonds might have continued their forest autocamping adventures beyond 1924, but as Firestone explained, "the publicity which the trips began to gather around them eliminated their object and charm. . . . [I]t became tiresome to be utterly without privacy." Everywhere the group traveled it encountered eager crowds, a phalanx of reporters, and the constant whirring of motion-picture cameras. The attention made it near impossible for the vagabonds to find solitude among the trees, but it also meant that the entire nation was able to glimpse the pleasures of autocamping, something that no doubt pleased Ford.

By the time the vagabonds finally disbanded, millions of Americans had purchased mass-produced automobiles and sought to emulate the escapades of Burroughs, Edison, Firestone, and Ford. The *New York Times* estimated that by the early 1920s nearly 6 million cars a year were being used for autocamping (an impressive figure considering that there were only 10 million cars in the entire nation at that point). In response to this development, there soon appeared an industry of roadside services. Popular touring routes grew crowded with campsites, food vendors, gas stations, billboards, and restaurants. Products targeted at this new booming market also began to appear. In 1923, the Coleman Gas Lamp Company, previously the makers of domestic gas appliances, introduced a camp stove that it marketed as "The Smooth Way to Rough It." Other businesses followed with tents, camp clothes, portable furniture, specially packaged food, and a slew of gadgets and gizmos designed for the outdoors.

The federal government took pains to usher along this new, seemingly unstoppable movement that had appeared on the heels of Ford's innovations. In 1915, Congress passed a law that allowed long-term permits to be issued in the national forests for summer homes, lodges, and other recreation structures. The following year, President Woodrow Wilson signed the Federal Highway Act, the first major legislation devoted to road construction. It included an allocation of $10 million for constructing new roads within the national forests, where the number of visitors had jumped from the "thousands" of Pinchot's day to more than 3 million by 1917 (that same year, visits to the national parks, which had been established with recreation in mind but which had a much smaller total area, were fewer than 250,000).

Shortly after the passage of the Federal Highway Act, the Forest Service commissioned a landscape architect to study the question of forest recreation and autocamping for the first time. This initial review led to further discussions that ultimately prompted the nation's chief forester to caution in 1920: "It is only by the adoption of a sound national recreation policy that the public interests can be safeguarded." The recreation question, by this point, had risen all the way to the highest levels of government. And in 1924, President Calvin Coolidge convened the first National Conference on Outdoor Recreation (NCOR). It was, in certain respects, the era's equivalent of the 1905 American Forest Congress that Teddy Roosevelt had hosted. Secretary of State Elihu Root wrote that the NCOR was a timely response to "one of the most important and necessary readjustments of American life."

The decade that followed this first recreation summit brought more conferences, more federally sponsored studies, and more roads. But the demands that car-owning vacationers placed on the nation's public lands rapidly outpaced the capacity of these measures. Established campsites became crowded and dirty. Roads got jammed with Model T Fords. Acres of trees fell victim to the flames that spread from unattended campfires.

This was the situation facing the nation when Franklin Delano Roosevelt ascended to the presidency in 1933. But the commander in chief soon had the so-called tree army at his disposal, and the CCC placed recreation among its highest priorities. The program's forestry manual noted, "The growth of forest recreation since 1916 has in some sections placed it at the top of the list as a forest value." With hundreds of thousands of young men and hundreds of millions of emergency funds, the CCC quickly revolutionized the recreational potential of the nation's public forests. In total, CCC labor created or improved nearly five thousand public recreation spots. But this represented only half of the work necessary to increase public access to the outdoors: Roads would also be needed so that motorists could reach these CCC-sponsored sites. The tree army met this challenge with equal enthusiasm. The national forests had contained fewer than fifteen thousand miles of roads at the program's outset, but a decade later, that number had increased nearly ten times.

All of this activity turned out to be a mere prelude for the onslaught of recreationists that was about to descend upon the national forests like a horde of leisure-seeking locusts. The era of prosperity that followed the conclusion of World War II meant that suddenly almost every middle-class family both owned a car and had time for vacations (leisure hours had increased 50 percent since 1920). Furthermore, much of the postwar population growth occurred in the West, home to the overwhelming majority of national-forest acreage. In consequence, the number of recreational visitors increased from 10 million in 1945, to 27 million in 1950, to 46 million in 1955, to over 92 million in 1960. It marked a staggering 900 percent augmentation over a fifteen-year period in which the total population only grew by 35 percent.

But recreation was not the only activity that depended on widespread access to the nation's publicly owned trees. Rather, its acceleration corresponded to a new era of intense logging in the national forests. These public trusts had hosted commercial lumbering before World War II, but on a relatively limited scale. The demands of the war and the subsequent housing boom, however, brought new pressures. The 1946 *Report of the Chief of the Forest Service* began by declaring: "Our forests today are not supplying enough timber products. While thousands search desperately for places to live, construction of urgently needed dwellings is hampered by lack of building materials." In the fifteen years following World War II, the total cut of timber in the national forests ballooned from 2.7 billion to 9.4 billion board feet. And sites of timber harvesting—typically done through clear-cutting—rarely provided much recreation potential.

The competing uses of lumbermen and recreationists raised a fundamental question about the nation's publicly controlled trees: Were they stumpage destined to end up as timber and forest products or were they the architecture supporting outdoor leisure? The unenviable task of providing an answer rested with the Forest Service, whose jurisdiction included the overwhelming majority of public woodlands.

The Forest Service already had a policy in place before the surge in postwar use. Known as "multiple use," it dictated that forest acreage serve as many concurrent purposes as possible but that in cases of conflict discretion be employed to select the highest use. This sounded reasonable in theory, but as with so many things, the devil was in the discretion. The Forest Service shared a long relationship with the logging industry, and many foresters still considered timber production to be the preeminent concern. And, of equal importance, the 1897 Pettigrew Amendment, which remained in effect, did not cover recreation. Thus, highest use by statute excluded the needs of autocampers. The upshot was that when the needs of the two factions were at loggerheads, the loggers often seemed to come out ahead of the recreationists.

But the recreation community was evolving into a powerful constituency. It comprised not only millions of individuals interested in conservation, hunting, leisure, and pleasure driving but also corporate interests, such as the American Automobile Association (AAA), which argued: "In evaluating the recreational value of the national forests, the economic importance of travel should not be overlooked." A study that the AAA commissioned found that "motor vacationists spend nearly $10 billion during the course of their journeys." The Forest Service's own literature confirmed these findings and noted that by the mid-1950s outdoor recreation ranked third among American industries, trailing only manufacturing and agriculture. Recognizing the economic and

political strength of the motorist lobby, the lumber and forest products industries tried to appear conciliatory—their joint public relations arm even issued
pamphlets titled "Story Tips for Outdoor Writers," which were peppered with
vignettes showing how loggers worked in chorus with recreationists. Nonetheless, the forces aligned with recreation began to demand reform of the system.

The issue reached Congress in the late 1950s. Legislators soon found themselves torn between the appeals of the recreationist lobby (labeled by its oppo-
nents as advocating a "single use" approach) and of the forest products industry
(labeled by its antagonists as promoting "overuse"). The Forest Service, meanwhile, continued to champion "multiple use" but chafed at any legislation that
might alter its mandate. Congress was soon flooded from all sides with statutory proposals and potential amendments. One congressman, in frustration,
asked, "[H]ow can we possibly put together these various amendments, incorporate them in this bill, and then vote on it[?]" But pressure for a resolution
would not let up.

In mid-1960 Congress passed the Multiple-Use Sustained Yield Act
(MUSYA), the first legislation since the 1897 Pettigrew Amendment to
confront the ultimate purpose of the national forests and their trees. The act
attempted to offer some degree of satisfaction for everyone involved. The Forest Service preserved its discretion in choosing between conflicting uses. The
forest products industry gained some assurance that its access would remain
unfettered—the "sustained yield" requirement was viewed by many as a guarantee that the era of intensive logging would continue. And outdoor enthusi-
asts saw recreation gain a formal statutory endorsement. The first sentence of
the new legislation read: "[I]t is the policy of the Congress that the national
forests are established and shall be administered for outdoor recreation, range,
timber, watershed, wildlife and fish purposes." Recreation was now a top-level
use, equal in stature to timber production. The nation had officially recognized
a new dimension for its publicly owned trees.

Nonetheless, some recreationists and conservationists felt that their side
had lost out in the fight. The year following the act's passage, Michael McCloskey, the future executive director of the Sierra Club, wrote an extended critique
in the *Oregon Law Review*. He argued that the gains for recreationists were
more rhetorical than functional: The act's recognition of recreation had failed
to provide any enforcement beyond the discretion that the Forest Service
already held. McCloskey concluded that if the Act was of major importance
it was only "because of the legal confusion it add[ed] to an already confused
area."

McCloskey's legal analysis was spot-on (as future conflicts would confirm),
but from another perspective the MUSYA could simply be seen as codify-

ing a revolution that had already taken place. By the time the act passed, the Forest Service was in the midst of implementing its most ambitious outdoor recreation program to date, known as "Operation Outdoors," and in 1962 the federal government created the Bureau of Outdoor Recreation. The national forests were now for the people in a way that would have been inconceivable at their founding. It was part of the culture that traced back to Ford and the creation of mass-produced cars. Even if many sites were damaged by clear-cutting, the national forests were still the destination for tens of millions of American families packing up and heading out for vacation. In fact, if one didn't follow the political battles or encounter an active logging site, it would have been easy to assume that the forests were for nothing but recreation. The best example of this might have been the 1960 Winter Olympic Games, which are little remembered but stand out for several reasons: They were the first ones broadcast live; they featured an American ice hockey victory over the Soviet Union (the "forgotten" Miracle on Ice); and they were staged almost entirely on land leased from the Tahoe National Forest in Northern California.

## The End of the Road

WHILE THE NATION'S motor tourists and forest products industries disagreed on many issues, they both tended to be in favor of more road construction. Roads provided the all-important access to the country's trees, whether the product being sought was timber, pulp, or leisure.

But not everyone shared this attitude. To a small minority of recreationists and conservationists, the twentieth-century mania for road building marked mankind's having gone too far in its effort to exert control over nature. The sound of a motor sputtering in the distance meant that the trappings of society always remained within earshot. Solitude was constantly haunted by the specter of the next car horn. A forest (or any other ecosystem) bisected by roads was one that had forever lost a certain degree of its inherent wildness. And once that fell to the imperium of the automobile, it was nearly impossible to resurrect.

This concern would develop into an issue of national prominence during the postwar period. It had become increasingly apparent that if measures weren't taken to protect some public lands from automobile traffic, there would soon be nowhere left to escape from the rumbling of modernity, nowhere left for land to remain undisturbed. And just as a coalition had formed in the late nineteenth century to protect some forests from the rapacious slashing and burning of the lumber industry, so, too, would one now come together to salvage these last stands of wilderness.

The spirit of this group would owe much to John Muir, the great naturalist, writer, national parks champion, and, in his last years, antagonist of Gifford Pinchot. But the movement's true intellectual anchor—a man dubbed "the Jeremiah of wilderness thinking" and "the Commanding General of the Wilderness Battle"—was someone who had actually spent almost his entire career working for Pinchot's Forest Service. His name was Aldo Leopold. He never arose to any position of national prominence, and for most of his lifetime was little known outside forestry circles. But his writings set the foundation for one of the twentieth century's most important environmental movements.

Leopold's life began just as the nation was awakening to the reality that its once illimitable forests and their trees were running out. He was born in Burlington, Iowa, on January 11, 1887, three years before the U.S. Census declared that the frontier was officially exhausted and four years before President Benjamin Harrison proclaimed the first national forest reserve. Like so many Americans, the Leopold family drew their livelihood from the very trees that had suddenly become the subject of so much agitation. Aldo's father, Carl, ran a company that manufactured wooden desks. They were made from the finest cherry, oak, and walnut, and the family business soon gained a national reputation for the quality of its product. The elder Leopold, when not tending to business affairs, spent much of his time immersed in the natural world. He was an avid birder, hunter, and woodsman, pursuits that young Aldo absorbed with the passion of a zealot. Aldo's love of the outdoors and his fear for its long-term survival bred an interest in professional forestry, a field that had just arrived on this side of the Atlantic. By age fifteen, he had determined to become a forester and join the ranks of Pinchot's budding federal agency. Leopold's father urged his son to remain in Iowa and enter the family desk business, but his mother, seeking to provide her son the opportunity he desperately craved, pressured her husband to finance an elite secondary education in the East, with the hope that Aldo might then be able to attend Yale, home to the newly established School of Forestry.

In January 1904, Leopold arrived at the Lawrenceville School in New Jersey. Located between Trenton and Princeton, it was among the nation's oldest boarding schools and featured a campus designed by Frederick Law Olmsted. The school's parklike setting appealed greatly to Leopold, but he spent much of his free time on tramps in the surrounding countryside. A month after arriving he had mastered the terrain for ten miles around, naming the places that captivated his interest: Big Woods, Cat Woods, Fern Woods, Owl Woods, Ash Swamp. The tramps continued unabated throughout the next three semesters. During the fall of 1904, he wrote, "What great satisfaction there is in plowing through the rich brown autumn leaves of the woods on a fine sunny day!" The other students took to calling him "the naturalist."

Leopold nonetheless balanced his love for the surrounding woods with his schoolwork, and, as his mother had hoped, he earned himself a place at Yale for the fall of 1905. He chose to enroll in the university's Sheffield Scientific School, which offered preparatory work in forestry. The long tramps of his Lawrenceville days gradually gave way to the demands of a more rigorous curriculum, but Leopold dutifully made this sacrifice. It was a thrilling moment to be studying forestry. President Roosevelt was expanding the national forests at a breakneck pace, and his loyal deputy Pinchot had just won a campaign to wrest control of the national forests away from the Department of the Interior. Leopold, who entered the Forestry School full-time in the fall of 1906, worked tirelessly to distinguish himself and, in one of his proudest moments, was tapped to join the Society of Robin Hood, the school's elite fraternity. By the time of his graduation in 1909, it was clear that Leopold was going to join the burgeoning ranks of Pinchot's Forest Service, a dream he had been pursuing since before his arrival in the East.

In July 1909, Leopold arrived at Albuquerque, in the New Mexico Territory, to begin his work as an assistant forester. Though much of the Southwest was a desert, the region also hosted a network of woodlands and scrub brush. By the time Leopold appeared on the scene, the Southwest, known to the Forest Service as District 3, contained twenty-one national forests. Leopold soon learned that he had been assigned to the sprawling Apache National Forest, which had been created the previous year from public lands in the Arizona Territory (the forest's name provided a somewhat cruel tribute to the Native American tribe, led by Geronimo, that as late as 1886 had resisted federal efforts to claim their land). The Apache featured a range of forest ecosystems characteristic to the region. Along the canyon stream banks grew a mixture of cottonwoods, sycamores, and willows. Higher up, in the semidesert climate, were oak groves, scrubby hardwoods, and a mixture of juniper and piñon pines. And above this, coating the mountains that burst forth from the landscape, stood endless stands of ponderosa pine. For Leopold, it was a magical setting: rugged and unbroken, its streams flush with trout, its forests full of wild game and trophy-worthy predators. In a word, the land could be best described as wilderness.

Leopold spent most of his next fifteen years working for the Forest Service in District 3. It was a period of vital development for the young naturalist, both personally and professionally. Once he got his bearings in the region (and suffered through the growing pains of a tenderfoot in a strange land), he began to demonstrate the sort of unerring competency that had marked his time at Yale.

By 1913 he was put in charge of the Carson National Forest, one the district's most beautiful landscapes, nestled between the Sangre de Cristo Mountains in the east and the San Juan Mountains in the west. During this same time, he also met Estella Bergere, the elegant daughter of one of New Mexico's most distinguished families. Leopold courted her with the same passion he brought to the study of the natural world, and in 1912 the two married, marking the beginning of a companionship that lasted the rest of his life. By 1919, Estella had given birth to four children, and Leopold had risen to second in command of District 3.

While this was a prosperous decade for the young forester, the same could not necessarily be said of the lands that he was helping to manage. They were beginning to lose the wild character that had so endeared them to Leopold. Loggers and grazers, who had been exploiting the region long before Leopold's arrival, were expanding their activities, largely with the consent and license of the Forest Service. And the predators that stalked the land were beginning to fall victim to the keen-eyed riflework of farmers, herders, and rangers—this "varmint" eradication policy was something that Leopold had wholeheartedly endorsed but would later come to regret and publicly denounce. But most troublesome, at least from Leopold's perspective, was the arrival of motor tourist roads, which progressively sliced the landscape into thinner and thinner strips. When he had begun working in District 3, there had been, in his words, "six immense roadless areas in the Southwestern forests, each larger than half a million acres," but these, too, like the predators, were beginning to disappear. As he explained, "Part of the lost areas were justifiable sacrifices to timber values; part, I think, were the victims of poor brakes on the good roads movement."

Seeking to keep his beloved wild forests from becoming further tamed, Leopold began working to formulate a policy proposal that might offer a way to curb the invasion of motor roads before they had wholly colonized the Southwest. In 1921, he set forth his ideas in a short article that appeared in the *Journal of Forestry* and was titled "The Wilderness and Its Place in Forest Recreational Policy." This article would eventually become one of the most influential pieces ever written on forestry and trees. Its power, in many respects, derived from one sentence, tucked away in the center of the piece, that provided a precise definition of what Leopold aimed to protect: "By 'wilderness' I mean a continuous stretch of country preserved in its natural state, open to lawful hunting and fishing, big enough to absorb a two weeks' pack trip, and kept devoid of roads, artificial trails, cottages, or other works of man."

This language marked a new era for a concept with a very long history. The first English settlers in America had frequently employed the word "wilderness" to describe the entirety of their newfound landscape, and not often in a positive light. William Bradford, the governor of Plymouth Colony, wrote in 1620 that New England contained nothing "but a hidious & desolate wildernes, full of wild beasts & willd men." The term's meaning gradually shed its more nefarious connotations as settlement continued and the threat of Indian attacks diminished. By the mid-nineteenth century, Thoreau was able to write: "[I]n Wildness is the preservation of the World. Every tree sends its fibres forth in search of the Wild." John Muir, whom many saw as a successor to the transcendentalist tradition, took the idea even further, claiming that "[t]he clearest way into the Universe is through a forest wilderness."

When Muir spoke of wilderness, he meant it largely as a counterweight to the idea that trees were provided to man for economic exploitation. Leopold, however, had a much different agenda attached to his definition. As he explained of his view of wilderness, "Very evidently we have here the old conflict between preservation and use, long since an issue with respect to timber, water power, and other purely economic resources, but just now coming to be *an issue with respect to recreation*." As a member of the Forest Service, Leopold accepted that timber mining was a necessary and inevitable use of the nation's trees. But the field of recreation—source of so many discussions in the era of Fordism and autocamping—had opened a new lens through which to understand forests. The question was whether recreational use included something greater than motorized tourism. For Leopold, the answer was obvious. Wilderness, therefore, did not mean "nonuse" (as it might have been understood by Muir) but a particular type of recreational use. Leopold wondered: "[Does] the principle of highest use . . . not itself demand that representative portions of some forests be preserved as wilderness[?]"

Seeing wilderness as a type of forest use was a fairly radical proposition. But Leopold tempered his argument with a host of qualifications. As he wrote in his 1921 article,

> First, such wilderness areas should occupy only a small fraction of the total National Forest area—probably not to exceed one in each State. Second, only areas naturally difficult of ordinary industrial development should be chosen. Third, each area should be representative of some type of country of distinctive recreational value, or afford some distinctive type of outdoor life, opportunity for which might disappear on other forest lands open to industrial development.

This was the plan of a forester and, above all, a pragmatist.

After Leopold published his first wilderness article, he began working to see his policy put into effect. Though most of his southwestern forests had already been traversed by automobile roads, one section of national forest, near the headwaters of the Gila River in New Mexico (which had gained statehood in 1912), remained unbroken. It was, according to Leopold, "an area of nearly half a million acres, topographically isolated by mountain ranges and box canyons," and its remoteness ensured that "no net economic loss would result from the policy of withholding further industrial development, except that timber would remain inaccessible and available only for limited local consumption." Of course, not everyone saw it this way. Leopold encountered staunch resistance from many of his colleagues in the Forest Service who believed that any potential development took priority over wilderness preservation. Leopold's antagonists were, in many respects, simply pursuing the limited mandate of the 1897 Pettigrew Amendment. Leopold nonetheless managed to convince the regional district forester of the soundness of his plan, and on June 3, 1924, the section of the Gila National Forest that Leopold had personally mapped became the first federally designated wilderness area. It was placed under a ten-year wilderness recreation policy that prohibited everything but grazing, water power development, and fire-prevention trails.

At almost the exact same moment that the Gila Wilderness was created, the first National Conference on Outdoor Recreation (NCOR) was convening. Leopold had hoped that it would provide a chance for wilderness policy to gain national attention, but to his dismay the ideas he championed were unmentioned in the concluding resolutions. There had been plenty of talk about car camping, road building, hunting, and sports, but no one yet seemed interested in discussing the need to preserve some sites from the threats these activities posed.

Leopold subsequently determined to redouble his efforts, and in 1925 published a string of forceful articles in defense of wilderness, most notably "The Last Stand of the Wilderness." It warned that "the remaining wild areas in both the Forests and Parks are being pushed back by road construction at a very rapid rate,—so rapid that unless something is done, the large areas of wilderness will mostly disappear within the next decade." In this article, Leopold also demonstrated a new concern with the Lake States, where, he feared, "wilderness canoe trips are about to become a thing of the past, because of the extension of tourist roads and summer resorts into the remnants of wild country." His change in geographical emphasis reflected the altered circumstances of his career. Shortly before the creation of the Gila Wilderness Area, he had been promoted to assistant director of the Forest Products Laboratory in Madison, Wisconsin. Though he would hold the position for only four years, he would stay in Wisconsin for the remainder of his life.

Leopold's new round of advocacy helped to finally push the wilderness idea onto the national stage. When the second NCOR convened in 1926, Leopold was invited to attend. This time the delegates proposed the creation of twenty-one potential wilderness areas. That same year, the U.S. secretary of agriculture personally signed a plan to preserve a portion of Minnesota canoe country as wilderness. And the Forest Service soon initiated a set of policies, known as the L-20 regulations, which provided for the designation and maintenance of "primitive areas" that largely followed the blueprint that Leopold had first proposed.

By the late 1920s, Leopold began devoting less of his time to wilderness preservation and more to wildlife management, one of his other great passions. But new voices began to speak out in defense of wilderness. Perhaps most notable was Robert Marshall, a young New Yorker who shared Leopold's love of the outdoors and contempt for the excesses of automobile tourism. In 1930, when Marshall was twenty-nine, he published an article in *Scientific Monthly* titled "The Problem of the Wilderness." It rehashed many of the points that Leopold had first set forth (even quoting from him directly), but took the appeal a step further than the original wilderness thinker had ever attempted: "To carry out this program it is exigent that all friends of the wilderness ideal should unite. . . . There is just one hope of repulsing the tyrannical ambition of civilization to conquer every niche on the whole earth. That hope is the organization of spirited people who will fight for the freedom of the wilderness." Five years after issuing this call to arms, Marshall—who had inherited a sizable fortune following the death of his father—used his wealth to found the Wilderness Society. The new organization brought together many of the leading thinkers on the subject of America's disappearing wilderness. The founding members included Benton MacKaye, the main force behind the Appalachian Trail, Robert Sterling Yard, the executive secretary of the National Parks Association, and Leopold, who was brought in to serve as an advisor.

The formation of the Wilderness Society coincided with Leopold's embarking on a new round of advocacy. He felt that his voice was needed to counteract a danger posed by Roosevelt's Tree Army: In its crusade to improve the public forests, the CCC was threatening to destroy all the wilderness that remained there. The problem was not merely limited to public forests but affected all the public lands that fell under the jurisdiction of the New Deal's many acronym-bearing agencies. As Leopold later observed, "A roadless marsh is seemingly as worthless to the alphabetical conservationist as an undrained one was to the empire-builders. Solitude, the one natural resource still undowered of alphabets, is so far recognized as valuable only by ornithologists and cranes."

Leopold's writings during the Depression continued to hammer away at the need to distinguish wilderness recreation from motorized tourism, but he also began to highlight a new rationale: that wilderness served as a "land laboratory." As he explained:

> All wilderness areas, no matter how small or imperfect, have a large value to land-science. The important thing is to realize that recreation is not their only or even their principal utility. . . . The science of land health needs, first of all, a base-datum of normality, a picture of how healthy land maintains itself as an organism.

In arguing this, Leopold was drawing on the emerging field of ecology, particularly the work of Frederic Clements, an American plant ecologist who argued that any given ecosystem must be understood as a living organism in which every component, from the soil to the animals to the trees, formed an interconnected superstructure. It was Leopold's contention that foresters could not develop plans for the management of healthy and productive forests without understanding how they functioned in their most primitive state.

The expanded intellectual arguments for wilderness facilitated its growth as a matter of policy. Wilderness was no longer just a question of recreation, but also one of land use and science, where even a few thousand acres might justify special protection. Thanks in part to this shift, the nation's budding roadless network saw great gains throughout the Depression years. The Forest Service promulgated new rules, known as the U Regulations, that allowed for increased amounts of "primitive areas." The National Park Service embraced the wilderness concept as well (sometimes using it as a tool to wrest acreage away from national forests). And the Bureau of Indian Affairs created more than 1.5 million acres of wilderness, largely at the urging of Marshall, who worked there in the early thirties. (Marshall's impact would likely have been even greater had he not died of heart failure in 1939, at age thirty-eight.)

While the amount of designated wilderness was growing steadily, it nonetheless lacked the protections that members of the Wilderness Society desired. The regulations put in place by the Forest Service, National Park Service, and other federal agencies did not have the force of law and failed to explicitly prohibit development. This became increasingly problematic in the postwar era when the demands on the forests for lumber and recreation exploded. In the mid-1940s, Leopold wrote, "Lumber shortages during the war gave the impetus of military necessity to many road extensions, legitimate and otherwise. At the present moment, ski-tows and ski-hotels are being promoted in many mountain areas, often without regard to their prior designation as wilderness."

This was among Leopold's last pronouncements on wilderness. Shortly after writing it, he suffered a heart attack while fighting a grass fire that had broken out near his property in Wisconsin. By the time his neighbors discovered him, the great champion of wilderness was already dead. He was sixty-one years old.

Leopold's death was mourned by all in the wilderness community, but it received little national attention. The *New York Times* buried the brief obituary on page 27 and described Leopold simply as "the author of several books and magazine articles on forest and game management." Remarkably, the word "wilderness" appeared nowhere. Even after almost twenty-five years of advocacy, Leopold's crusade hadn't warranted a single mention. This glaring omission reflected the cold reality that wilderness preservation remained a concept unfamiliar to the average American.

But that was about to change. The Wilderness Society, at this point under the leadership of the indefatigable Howard Zahniser, planned to turn the cause into front-page news. Building public awareness would be the initial step in a long-term campaign, one whose ultimate goal was the passage of comprehensive federal wilderness legislation.

The organization set its focus on a controversy brewing in Dinosaur National Monument, a 320-square-mile region that stretched across the Colorado-Utah border. The area had been incorporated into the National Park System by President Franklin Delano Roosevelt, but in the late 1940s the Bureau of Reclamation began making plans for a billion-dollar dam project that would flood a portion of the region known as Echo Park. To those in the conservation movement, the situation was uncomfortably familiar. A nearly identical dispute had arisen almost forty years earlier, when John Muir and Gifford Pinchot had squared off over the potential construction of a dam in the Hetch Hetchy Valley of the Yosemite National Forest. That conflict had raged in the headlines for months before Congress finally sided with Pinchot and authorized the project. Echo Park offered a chance for redemption.

Zahniser and the Wilderness Society mobilized all their resources, firing off polemics and lobbying congressmen. The issue quickly assumed national importance and morphed into a referendum on wilderness. At one of the early federal hearings, held in 1950, a conservationist stated bluntly: "[L]et's open this to its ultimate and inevitable extent, and let's settle . . . once and for all time . . . whether we may have . . . wilderness areas . . . in these United States." The fight raged for more than five years, with the future of the wilderness movement hanging in the balance. At first, it seemed the dam would inevitably gain approval; there were simply too many corporate interests and too many western congressmen supporting it. But Zahniser ensured that the pressure from the wilderness lobby never subsided. An endless stream of articles, speeches, and mailers gradually turned public sentiment against the project. In 1955, one western congressman lamented that the dam's proponents possessed "neither the money nor the organization to cope with the resources and mailing lists" of the opposition. The campaign concluded in mid-1956, when Congress passed legislation banning any dam building in Echo Park.

It was a moment of great celebration for the Wilderness Society. Historian Roderick Nash observed, "At this juncture the Echo Park victory gave promise that statutory wilderness preservation might be more than a dream." Zahniser soon began lobbying his allies in Congress to endorse this next step, a federal Wilderness Act. The proposed legislation, which Zahniser had first drafted several years earlier, would call for the creation of a National Wilderness Preservation System to cover more than 60 million acres in 160 regions of the national forests, national parks and monuments, Indian reservations, and national wildlife refuges and ranges.

The issue reached the Senate floor in early 1957, but quickly became subsumed by the larger struggle over national forest recreation. The proposed Multiple-Use Sustained Yield Act was intended to set forth broadly the permitted uses of the national forests, and many felt that this ipso facto covered wilderness. The Forest Service, in particular, endorsed this attitude, largely to preserve its discretion over wilderness zones—some argued that the agency's support for MUSYA arose largely from the legislation's potential to derail a Wilderness Act. As negotiations wore on, Zahniser's bold plan was whittled down to a single insipid sentence tagged to the end of MUSYA's first paragraph: "The establishment and maintenance of areas of wilderness are consistent with the purposes and provisions of this Act." The leader of the wilderness movement had temporarily been outflanked.

But the fight was far from over. The Wilderness Bill continued to receive strong public support and gained a new ally in early 1961, when John F. Kennedy ascended to the presidency. Kennedy wanted wilderness preservation to be part of his ambitious domestic program. He found widespread support in the Senate but encountered intense resistance in the more conservative House. The stalemate dragged out through two legislative sessions and seemed unlikely to break, but then an assassin's bullet pierced the young president's skull, and a mourning nation began to demand that Congress push through the domestic agenda of the fallen leader. Leaders in the House and Senate worked throughout the first half of 1964 to resolve their differences. The final step was a backroom negotiating session in late summer, when New Mexico senator Clinton Anderson, who had been championing the bill for years, made a number of crucial concessions as the price of gaining permanent federal recognition of the wilderness ideal.

On September 3, 1964, at a ceremony in the White House Rose Garden, President Lyndon Johnson signed the Wilderness Act into law. Notably absent from the gathering was Howard Zahniser, the legislation's most tireless advocate. He had died unexpectedly in April, four months shy of seeing his life's work realized. As one House leader observed, "[L]ike the patriarch of old [he] was denied the opportunity to experience his moment of victory." Of course, it was far from a total victory. Congressional negotiations had led to the inclusion of a twenty-year exemption for mineral prospecting and extraction. And Zahniser's original wilderness network was reduced from 60 million acres to just 9.1 million acres, spread out over fifty-four sites in the national forests.

Still, those 9.1 million forest acres represented a remarkable achievement, a shift in the way that Americans conceptualized their relationship to nature, forests, and trees. President Johnson, in his first report on the new National Wilderness Preservation System, proclaimed,

> Only in our country have such positive measures been taken to preserve the wilderness adequately for its scenic and spiritual wealth. In the new conservation of this century, our concern is with the total relation between man and the world around him. Its object is not only man's material welfare but the dignity of man himself. . . . Generations of Americans to come will enjoy a finer and more meaningful life because of these actions taken in these times.

In the decades that followed, the National Wilderness Preservation System expanded dramatically. The original 9.1 million acres doubled and then doubled again as conservation advocates around the nation fought to have new lands protected from any form of development. Eventually, some in the environmental movement began to fear the statutory protection for wilderness had inadvertently facilitated an extremist reverence for unadulterated nature that failed to appreciate the curious paradox that modern wilderness was, by definition, land being actively managed by the government. As William Cronon wrote in 1995, "[T]he trouble with wilderness is that it quietly expresses and reproduces the very values its devotees seek to reject." Nonetheless, the wilderness program, largely unchanged since its inception in 1964, remains hugely popular, and today includes nearly 110 million acres in 757 sites.

•　•　•

THE POSTWAR YEARS had produced fundamental shifts in the American landscape. Farms and fields yielded to suburbs; private forests began to function as tree plantations; public forests became sites of leisure; and great swaths of land were transformed into official wilderness. The sum total of these changes affected hundreds of millions of acres across the nation.

This period had also seen a remarkable change in the way that people thought about trees. On the one hand, wood had become much less conspicuous in daily life. This was especially true in suburbia, where new homes masked the debt they owed to trees and tree products. On the other hand, the nation's forests had grown much more accessible to the average American thanks to the automobile and the policies it inspired. Forests had become the subject of renewed political debate and broad publicity campaigns. Trees were beginning to seem part of a world segregated from domestic life but increasingly worthy of veneration.

These shifts in attitudes and in land use had arisen in large part due to the prosperity that followed World War II. But they were merely the preface to a major social movement, one inspired by trees and yet much more comprehensive in scope. Conservation was about to evolve into environmentalism.

# 10

## The Environmental Era

Sugar Maple

### Nelson's New Day

THE UNITED STATES had enjoyed more than two decades of sustained economic growth following World War II. American corporations not only led the world in manufacturing, they produced more than 40 percent of the world's finished products. The middle class swelled. Average living standards exceeded those of anywhere else on earth. It became commonplace to own a home, a car, a television, and countless other luxuries. But all of this producing and consuming had come with a hidden cost.

The first major wakeup call came with the publication of Rachel Carson's *Silent Spring* in 1962. Her book presented a devastating, frightening account of the toxins that had spread across the landscape in the postwar years. Dangerous chemicals, she warned, could be found everywhere. They were in the by-products of unregulated manufacturing, in the runoff from industrial agriculture, and in the pesticides that were used to control problems like Dutch elm disease.

As the 1960s wore on, the effects of this toxic stew began to surface across the nation. America's lakes and rivers were turning into industrial sinks. Lake Erie, once a thriving fishery, was essentially dead by the mid-1960s. The Cuyahoga River in Ohio was covered in a near-constant oily slick that occasionally burst into flames. Industrial smokestacks built near sprawling urban environments were filling the surrounding atmosphere with nonstop streams of pollutants. Air quality in many cities was becoming perilous, and cases of asthma appeared on the rise.

Despite mounting evidence of a crisis, these issues garnered relatively little public attention. They rarely appeared on television or in newspapers—not surprising, since no major media outlets had journalists devoted to such themes. They gained somewhat more traction on college campuses, which had evolved into hotbeds of civic activism. But even there, most of the political energy went toward fighting for civil rights, opposing the Vietnam War, and trying to build a counterculture.

Without public pressure, politicians saw little need to act. President Richard Nixon paid lip service—his January 1969 inaugural speech mentioned "protecting our environment and enhancing the quality of life"—but his administration hesitated to fully embrace a potential regulatory scheme that seemed complicated, costly, and likely to alienate some within the business community. Many in Congress followed the president's lead. And in their inaction, air quality continued to deteriorate, lakes and rivers continued to go fetid, toxic chemicals continued to coat the landscape, municipal drinking water continued to turn sour, and fragile ecosystems continued to degrade.

It might have continued this way further into the future but for Gaylord Nelson, the junior senator from Wisconsin. Through his efforts, a new holiday would soon appear and a new movement would coalesce.

Nelson was born on June 4, 1916, in Clear Lake, Wisconsin, a small village in the northern part of the state. His hometown fell within the region that had once contained endless stands of pristine white pines, the same mythic spires that had entranced Frederick Weyerhaeuser. But by the time of Nelson's birth, the primeval trees were long gone, victims of the industrial lumbering boom led by Weyerhaeuser's syndicate. As Nelson wrote, "We wiped [the forest] out in an eyewink of history and left behind fifty years of heartbreak and economic ruin." Nelson grew up as a witness to the problems that followed when industry showed little regard for natural resources, such as trees. It was an experience that would shape his worldview and set the path for his future career.

After serving in World War II, Nelson decided to enter state politics. He was a staunch Progressive, formed in the mold of "Fighting Bob" La Follette, the legendary Wisconsin senator. The Progressives at the time were still part of the Republican Party, but this alliance crumbled when Robert La Follette, Jr., who had inherited his father's Senate seat, lost a heated 1946 primary contest to Joseph McCarthy, a little-known conservative who would soon mature into one of the most controversial demagogues in the nation. McCarthy's victory pushed the Progressives into the arms of the state Democratic Party, and Nelson, who won a state senate seat in 1948, became one of the party's young lions.

In 1958, Nelson successfully ran for governor. The conservationist impulse that had been formed among the cut-over pine forests of northern Wisconsin now began to assert itself. During his inaugural address, he declared, "We need more parks and playgrounds, more wetlands, more stream improvement, better use of our lakes and streams, and more careful husbanding of our wilderness areas." At first, Nelson struggled to turn his rhetoric into action, but during his second term as governor he managed to push through a massive conservation initiative that would cement his reputation as "the conservation governor." Known as the Outdoor Recreation Act Program (ORAP), Nelson's plan used a penny tax on cigarettes to fund a $50 million war chest for the acquisition of state land. U.S. Secretary of the Interior Stewart Udall described ORAP in 1961 as "a landmark in conservation history . . . the boldest conservation step ever taken on a state level in the history of the United States."

In early 1962, Nelson announced that he would not seek a third term as governor. Though he remained popular, he felt that he "had achieved practically everything that [he] could achieve." He set his sights on the U.S. Senate, where the longer terms would relieve some of the campaigning pressures and where he could bring his conservation cause to the federal level. The senatorial race that followed was a close one, but Nelson triumphed with almost 53 percent of the vote. By this point, it was beyond evident that conservation would be his main focus moving forward. He told a reporter shortly after winning the election, "I think the most crucial domestic issue facing America . . . is the conservation of our natural resources."

During his first trip to Washington as a senator-elect, Nelson requested a special meeting with Attorney General Robert F. Kennedy, the president's brother and chief advisor. The subject at issue was the possibility of the president's embarking on a national conservation speaking tour, something that no sitting president had ever done. In Nelson's view, federal conservation efforts could not advance until the issue's profile was raised nationally, and the chief executive's bully pulpit seemed like the best place to start. President Kennedy, who saw himself as a champion of natural-resource protection, responded positively when he learned of Nelson's suggestion. And in May 1963, it was announced that the president would embark on a five-day conservation tour later in the fall.

Nelson was brimming with anticipation when the trip finally began in mid-September. The first destination was Milford, Pennsylvania, where the president dedicated the family home of Gifford Pinchot as a national monument and paid homage to the greatest conservationist of an earlier era. The trip then headed west, including a special stop in Wisconsin during which Kennedy publicly thanked Nelson for suggesting the speaking tour. The speeches quickly piled up as Kennedy visited ten more states throughout the greater West. But to Nelson's dismay, the effect that he had been hoping for didn't seem to be materializing. His initial optimism began to transform into resignation. The president's speeches, he wrote, "didn't have much sweep or drama to them." Even worse, the media that covered the president seemed more concerned with his thoughts on foreign policy than with the stated purpose of the trip. By the time the itinerary was completed, Nelson concluded that it had been "poorly conceived" from the start and that its ultimate impact was negligible. However, it would become, in his words, "the germ of the idea" that ultimately defined his personal legacy and reordered the national political agenda.

Six years passed before this germ of an idea finally blossomed. In August 1969, Nelson was carrying out a smaller conservation speaking tour of his own when he stopped in Santa Barbara, California. The city was in the midst of a catastrophe: Six months earlier an offshore oil platform blowout had released up to a hundred thousand barrels of crude oil into the Santa Barbara Channel and nearby beaches. It was the worst oil spill in U.S. history (and would remain so until the *Exxon Valdez* disaster of 1989, itself eclipsed by the *Deepwater Horizon* explosion of 2010). The scenes of environmental degradation around Santa Barbara shook Nelson to his core. He wanted to do something, but didn't know what. Then, on the way to another tour stop, Nelson read an article about the effectiveness of recent college campus teach-ins in raising awareness about the war in Vietnam. As Nelson explained, "[T]he idea occurred to me that we could get political attention by having a nationwide environmental day patterned after the[se] Vietnam teach-in[s]."

It took Nelson a month to develop this initial burst of inspiration into a practical plan, and he finally went public with the rudiments of his proposal in mid-September. During a speech in Seattle before the Washington Environmental Council, he declared, "I am convinced that the same concern the youth of this nation took in changing this nation's priorities on the war in Vietnam and on civil rights can be shown for the problems of the environment." He suggested that a single day be set aside in the spring for a national teach-in devoted to what he called "The Crisis of the Environment."

Nelson's use of the term "environment" hinted at how his thinking had changed over the course of a decade. In the late 1950s and early 1960s, he had spoken primarily of natural-resource protection, especially for the purposes of recreation and wilderness. But over time his outlook—like that of many conservationists—began to broaden. Toxins and dangerous chemicals had entered the discourse following the publication of *Silent Spring*. Air and water pollution had grown in importance as their effects began to resonate across the landscape. A concern for aesthetics had emerged in the middle of the decade, when Lady Bird Johnson, wife of President Lyndon Johnson, spearheaded a campaign to "Keep America Beautiful." Excessive consumption was being recast from a symbol of prosperity to an indicator of irresponsible resource use. Runaway population growth—the subject of Paul Ehrlich's 1968 bestseller *The Population Bomb*—was seen as a looming threat to the stability of society and the supply of raw materials. The word "environment" encompassed all of these new perspectives as well as the older ones.

To Nelson's surprise, his environmental teach-in announcement in Seattle was covered by the nation's two main wire services—the Associated Press and the United Press. Their interest prompted further exposure in the nation's daily newspapers and on some television news broadcasts. According to Nelson, by the time he returned to his office in Washington, D.C., "the response by letter and phone was overwhelming. Inquiries were flooding in from all across the country."

His senatorial office was ill-equipped to handle the onslaught of attention. Nelson appealed to some of his supporters for seed money and used their contributions to set up an independent nonprofit, The Environmental Teach-In, Inc. He then recruited Paul McCloskey, a Republican congressman from California, to serve as co-chair—Nelson's hope was that this move might counteract any accusations of partisanship. The next step was to find someone to handle the day-to-day planning and organization. The job went to Dennis Hayes, a twenty-five-year-old student at Harvard Law School. Hayes had initially inquired about helping to coordinate the Boston-area teach-in, but his enthusiasm and dedication made a strong impression on Nelson and McCloskey. They asked him to consider running the entire show. Hayes soon accepted, dropped out of Harvard for a semester, and began assembling a staff, most of whom were equally young, passionate, and inexperienced.

Nelson now needed to select an actual date. It was, after all, somewhat difficult to mobilize around the notion that a teach-in would take place "probably in April," a phrase Nelson's office had initially used in promoting the event. Nelson's primary concern was that the teach-in occur at a time that would allow all schoolchildren and college students to participate. The date, therefore, could not fall around the Easter/Passover holidays. Nor could it hit near a weekend, at least not if the college participants were going to be clearheaded. Nelson's team eventually settled on Wednesday, April 22.

But that date was already spoken for, at least on the calendars of many conservationists and schoolteachers. It was the anniversary of the birth of J. Sterling Morton, the father of Arbor Day. In Morton's home state of Nebraska, Arbor Day had been observed on April 22 since 1885, the year it became an official state holiday. Several other states also used this date, and even those that didn't tended to recognize the holiday toward the end of April—the majority placed it on the fourth Friday of the month, which in 1970 would fall on April 24. Thus, Nelson's teach-in would either conflict directly with Arbor Day or preempt it by two days and siphon off much of the energy.

This potential double-booking, however, generated little outcry. It may have been that the teach-in was conceived as a one-time event, so no one thought much about the overlap. Or, perhaps, it was that tree planting was viewed as a component of the teach-in, just as conservation had become one aspect of the broader concern for the environment.

Nelson, who knew firsthand the importance of trees and the consequences that stemmed from their abuse, made little mention of the Arbor Day conundrum. His only concern was mobilizing as many students as possible.

And, to his delight, college students were already beginning to mobilize on their own. The *New York Times* discussed this phenomenon in a front-page story in late November 1969. It was headlined: "Environment May Eclipse Vietnam as College Issue." According to the article, "From Maine to Hawaii, students are seizing on the environmental ills from water pollution to the global population problem, campaigning against them, and pitching in to do something about them." The two accompanying photos showed a group of University of Minnesota students conducting a mock funeral for a gasoline engine and a crowd of women wearing surgical masks and protesting smog in Los Angeles. The article ultimately treated all of this activity as a preview of what was soon to follow, explaining, "Already students are looking forward to the first 'D-Day' of the movement, next April 22."

The *Times'* use of the phrase "D-Day" revealed an early confusion over just what the teach-in ought to be called. Nelson referred to it, rather dispassionately, as the "Environmental Teach-In." The official title simply didn't concern him. He claimed that "[w]hatever name was attached to it didn't matter one way or the other." But not everyone shared this attitude. Organizers and the media toyed with a variety of different options as the date approached. The official title never actually changed, but in the popular consciousness the teach-in was beginning to be known as "Earth Day."

Regardless of what the day was called, one thing seemed clear: The purpose was to foment political change. Nelson had stressed this point from the outset, and he began developing a legislative agenda to support the anticipated demonstrations. In late January, he presented his plan on the floor of Congress in a speech titled "An Environmental Agenda for the 1970s." One of his senatorial colleagues described it as "a Magna Carta on the environmental rights to which our fellow citizens feel themselves entitled." The speech contained the outlines of more than a dozen pieces of legislation, ranging from bans on specific chemicals, such as DDT, to sweeping reforms, such as a proposed constitutional amendment that would guarantee every citizen "the inalienable right to a decent environment." Nelson, who had spent much of the 1960s watching the environmental legislation he sponsored get passed over, realized that this new agenda would be hopeless unless the April 22 demonstrations were truly transformative.

As the date approached, it started to appear that Nelson just might get the support he desperately sought. More than two thousand universities, two thousand community civic groups, and ten thousand elementary and secondary schools had committed to participate. Mayor John Lindsay of New York City agreed to close a two-mile stretch of Fifth Avenue so that demonstrators would have ample space to march. Every major news broadcast blocked off space in its schedule for special coverage. And politicians, sensing the importance of the event, rushed to get involved—so many congressmen planned to give speeches that the legislative session for April 22 was actually canceled.

Much of the credit for this surge in enthusiasm belonged to Hayes and his staff, but in many ways the fervor was a truly grassroots phenomenon. Earth Day seemed to tap into the zeitgeist of the times. As Nelson liked to say, "The real story is that we didn't have to organize Earth Day. It organized itself."

When dawn broke on April 22, students on college campuses across the nation began gathering to welcome the day with readings and vigils. They went on to join local cleanups, partake in protests, plant trees, and attend speeches and rallies. The precise nature of Earth Day depended on where one looked. The issues could be local or general; the participants young or old; the tone hopeful or fearful, often both.

The largest demonstration took place in Manhattan. Several hundred thousand New Yorkers packed the stretch of Fifth Avenue that Mayor Lindsay had declared traffic-free. Many were just out to enjoy an atmosphere free of car honks and exhaust fumes, but countless tens of thousands also headed down to Union Square, where a full slate of Earth Day events transformed the scene into an "ecological carnival," according to a *New York Times* reporter. There were folks singers, rock bands, chanters, and politicians eager to shake hands.

The square's lawn hosted a nonstop Frisbee game, while on nearby Seventeenth Street a block-long polyethylene bubble offered the chance to breathe pure, filtered air—however, the *Times* observed that the enclosure "carried unmistakable whiffs of marijuana." The revelry and demonstrating continued straight through to midnight, when the floodlights were shut off and the streets were once again opened to traffic.

The day, taken as a whole, was not without its failures and controversies. In some cities, such as Washington, D.C., turnout was a good deal lower than expected. And in almost all cases, the day's events lacked involvement from African Americans. One of the teach-in organizers told CBS News that a prominent black leader told him, "You're part of a Nixon trick. You are basically doing what Nixon wants you to do, take energy away from the black issue, take energy away from the war issue." Nixon, for his part, declined to participate in Earth Day. Dan Rather of CBS described the administration's attitude as "one of benign neglect" and suggested that Nixon viewed Earth Day as a partisan stunt by Democrats. This critique was taken even further by those on the Far Right, such as the John Birch Society, which painted the teach-ins as a secret communist plot—it was an unfortunate coincidence that April 22 happened to be the birthday of Vladimir Lenin. Criticism came as well from the Left, with the influential college group Students for a Democratic Society condemning the day as an establishment con.

Nonetheless, when the dust had finally settled, and the cars returned to the streets, and the sun rose on April 23, Nelson was able to claim success. The media estimated that 20 million people had participated, a full 10 percent of the U.S. population. Hayes's organization called it "the largest, cleanest, most peaceful demonstration in America's history." And even those who failed to join in could not avoid hearing about the events. As the *New York Times* observed, "There were so many TV specials, summaries and schedule changes during the course of Earth Day that no single set of eyes could hope to keep abreast of all that was offered on the home screen, let alone the radio."

The momentum from Earth Day helped to finally push Nelson's cause onto the nation's political agenda. The ideas that he had first proposed in his "Environmental Agenda for the 1970s" speech now began to gain widespread support. Several months after Earth Day, the Environmental Protection Agency was created, and the ensuing years saw the passage of landmark environmental laws such as the Clean Air Act (1970), the Clean Water Act (1972), the Endangered Species Act (1973), the Safe Drinking Water Act (1974), the Toxic Substances Act (1976), and the Comprehensive Environmental Response, Compensation and Liability Act (1980, also known as Superfund). The 1970s had turned into the "environmental decade," and Nelson remained at the center of an environmental movement that had come of age around the day that he created.

However, by 1980 the national mood was shifting. Nelson's environmental leadership became a liability in a time of rising conservatism. He lost his Senate seat in the same election that lifted Ronald Reagan to the White House.

By this point, Nelson was sixty-four years old. Retirement was an obvious option, but Nelson was not yet ready to abandon the issues that he had been championing for more than thirty years. He accepted an offer to serve as counselor for the Wilderness Society, where he could carry on the legacy of Leopold, Marshall, and Zahniser. In 1995, he received the Presidential Medal of Freedom, the nation's highest civilian honor. At the presentation ceremony, President Bill Clinton said, "As the father of Earth Day he is the grandfather of all that grew out of that event." Nelson died ten years later, on July 3, 2005. The *New York Times* obituary described him as "the architect of America's modern environmental movement."

Earth Day, meanwhile, had taken on a life of its own. Though Nelson had intended it as a onetime affair, many of the organizers and participants wanted to see it institutionalized. April 22 soon became an unofficial day of environmental awareness in America, and the idea gradually spread to other nations. For the twentieth anniversary in 1990, activities were held in more than 140 countries. Global involvement was estimated at 200 million people. The annual celebrations continue to serve as a showcase for leading environmental concerns.

Earth Day's institutionalization, however, also abraded the status of Arbor Day. Trees were no longer a stand-alone concern, but part of a broader outlook. If further evidence of this shift was needed, perhaps it could be found in the decision of the Yale School of Forestry—the nation's oldest—to change its name in 1972 to the Yale School of Forestry and Environmental Studies.

Nonetheless, the rise of environmentalism did not mean that Americans had stopped paying attention to their woody resources. Rather, in the years ahead, the fate of the nation's trees would continue to demand public attention, and one of the greatest forest battles in the history of the nation was looming on the horizon.

## The Forest or the Trees?

O N APRIL 2, 1993, the scene in downtown Portland, Oregon, was chaos and cacophony. Logging trucks snaked along the streets and honked their horns. Helicopters buzzed overhead. Tens of thousands of demonstrators—split into two rival factions—gathered in the rain to march and chant and hold up placards: "For a Forester, Every Day Is Earth Day"; "Clinton, Gore, Cut No More"; "We Support Our Timber Industry."

The real action, however, was unfolding away from the public square. In a conference room nearby, where C-SPAN cameras were broadcasting live and reporters from national media outlets jockeyed for space, sat Bill Clinton, the newly elected president; Al Gore, his environmentally oriented vice president; and a full third of their cabinet. They had come to listen. And they had come to seek a solution for a crisis over the region's great forests, the very same tree-filled landscape that had once captivated Frederick Weyerhaeuser, had once provided the Sitka spruce that altered the course of World War I, had once produced the Douglas fir timber that sustained the postwar housing boom, and that now was locked up by court order. It was a day that had the potential to affect tens of thousands of jobs, tens of millions of forest acres, and, quite likely, the future of logging itself.

Yet this controversy—grand enough to summon a president and his cabinet from three thousand miles away, powerful enough to bring an entire industry to its knees—had begun, innocently enough, over the future of an owl that few had ever seen.

The animal in question, which by the time of Clinton's appearance had become among the most studied creatures in history, was commonly known as the northern spotted owl. The word "spotted" referenced the flecks of white that dotted its chocolate plumage and helped distinguish it from other owl species. The word "northern" conveyed its range. It was the northernmost of three spotted owl subspecies, its territory extending from the lower reaches of British Columbia, through Washington and Oregon (where its numbers were highest), and into parts of Northern California. Within this region, it typically made its home in the snags and hollows of trees whose provenance often pre-dated that of the nation.

Europeans had first identified the northern spotted owl in the mid-nineteenth century, but the subspecies, which hunted at night and lived in the deep woods, garnered almost no attention until the late 1960s. It was then that a young wildlife biologist, Eric Forsman, first encountered the owl's distinctive hoot, "a kind of barking sound," as he described it. Intrigued, Forsman began to seek out the reclusive creature and, along with several other researchers, started to map its habitat. As they gathered data, they realized that the owls nested almost exclusively in the undisturbed, unlogged forests that were known as "old growth."

This type of monarchical forest had once covered nearly the entire region. But centuries of lumbering had exhausted almost all of the old growth that was not held in public trust, mainly as national forest. Even this remaining portion—about 10 million acres spread across a 24-million-acre area—was rapidly falling to the lumberman's ax, a consequence of the postwar decision to expand industrial access to the national forests. Unless something changed, the northern spotted owl's demise seemed inevitable.

There had been a time when such a concern would have been met with blank stares, if not outright mockery and charges of lunacy. Daniel Boone, the embodiment of the frontier spirit, had not protected forest animals; he had killed them (and did it barehanded, according to the legends). In the race to settle the continent, Americans had lustfully, even gleefully, decimated the buffalo, eradicated the passenger pigeon, and slaughtered numerous other species. Sportsmen like Teddy Roosevelt had demonstrated some concern for the perpetuation of animals, but only those that counted as game. Predators and anything too small to serve as a mounted trophy remained dependent on their wits.

It was only during the era of Aldo Leopold that a more encompassing view of wildlife began to emerge. Leopold's own conversion had taken place early in his career, when he was stationed in the Southwest and hunting wolves as part of the Forest Service's varmint eradication policies. In a famous passage, he wrote,

> We reached the old wolf in time to watch a fierce green fire dying in her eyes. I realized then, and have known ever since, that there was something new to me in those eyes—something known only to her and to the mountain. I was young then, and full of trigger-itch; I thought that because fewer wolves meant more deer, that no wolves would mean hunters' paradise. But after seeing the green fire die, I sensed that neither the wolf nor the mountain agreed with such a view.

Leopold's new perspective gained increasing traction among conservationists with the growing acceptance of ecology, which gave equal weight to all the organisms in a given environment. The forests were no longer just about the trees, but about the entire spectrum of life, from bacteria to fungi to insects to predators, like the wolf and the spotted owl. The health of a forest could be measured not in board feet but in biodiversity.

The need to protect this biodiversity subsequently became one of the tenets of the post–Earth Day environmental movement. The decade-long legislative reformation that Senator Nelson helped spearhead included the passage of the Endangered Species Act in 1973. The new law created a system through which endangered or threatened plants and animals could have their numbers protected and, ideally, increased.

Nixon applauded the ESA as a measure that would give the federal government the "needed authority to protect an irreplaceable part of our national heritage—threatened wildlife." But the act was much more than that. Whether or not Nixon realized it, he had just authorized one of the most powerful tools in the history of conservation. And as the spotted owl saga would soon demonstrate, it was impossible to protect the endangered wildlife without preserving the entire ecosystem that sustained it.

The ESA, however, was not the only step that Congress took to protect biodiversity. In 1976, it passed the National Forest Management Act, a sweeping set of reforms that, among other things, heightened the Forest Service's obligations to protect threatened species. Whereas the 1960 MUSYA had simply listed wildlife protection as one of the five main uses for the national forests, this new act authorized an independent scientific council to promulgate specific regulations for the management of wildlife. The resulting regulations, adopted in 1982, required the Forest Service to manage habitats "to maintain *viable* populations of existing native and desired non-native vertebrate species in the planning area." Thus, even if a species wasn't specifically listed under the ESA, it might still necessitate special protection if its home range was located within a national forest.

Such was the case with the northern spotted owl. By the early 1980s, it had been subject to a decade's worth of research, and almost all the studies confirmed the subspecies' near-absolute dependence on the old growth that was largely contained in national forests. In 1983—one year after the "viability" regulation was enacted—the Forest Service recognized the northern spotted owl as a key "indicator species" to forest health, and the agency subsequently proposed a special management plan for the national forests in Oregon.

However, it was a limited, conservative plan designed to minimize any impact on logging activities. Many in the Forest Service had remained committed to maximizing timber production above all other uses. This attitude was, broadly speaking, loyal to the vision of Pinchot and in the early twentieth century would have seemed downright progressive.

But times had changed. The rise of ecological thinking meant that many— biologists and environmentalists in particular—felt that a perspective that privileged logging was shortsighted, backward, and ultimately a danger to the long-term health of forests. By the mid-1980s, national environmental groups began to direct their legal resources toward challenging the government's management of the northern spotted owl. (Their ultimate goal was widely acknowledged to be the protection of the old-growth forest itself; however, as a matter of legal strategy, it seemed efficacious to champion a threatened species and indirectly preserve the forests as a type of vulnerable habitat.) Advocacy groups filed lawsuits against the Forest Service as well as the Bureau of Land Management (BLM), which also controlled some old-growth acreage and which was similarly obliged to factor biodiversity into its land-use planning.

The northern spotted owl, the size of a football, had been transformed into a political football. And it was being tossed around in the battle over old growth and in the ideological clash between the production-minded groups who saw the trees for the forest and the ecologically minded groups who saw the forest for the trees.

Despite all of this attention, the owl was not yet even listed under the ESA. The Fish and Wildlife Service, which executed the act, had initially reviewed the issue in 1981. At the time, the scientific case was still being built and it was decided that listing was unwarranted. The science quickly grew more conclusive, but the politics was another matter. The FWS was understood to be beholden to President Reagan, a man who considered environmentalism a threat almost on a par with communism. During his first term, Reagan had appointed James Watt to lead the Department of the Interior, which oversaw the FWS. Watt's antiregulatory policies were so extreme—and his personal politics so offensive—that he was forced to step down in 1983 amid a wave of popular outrage. As for Reagan's attitude toward trees, it could be summed up in two statements that are well known in certain environmental circles. The first was made during his campaign for governor of California, "A tree is a tree. How many more do you have to look at?" The second is a paraphrase of comments he made during the 1980 presidential campaign: "Trees cause more pollution than automobiles." In late 1987, the FWS officially denied the northern spotted owl listing for a second time.

It was a temporary setback for the environmentalists, but they still had an ever-growing scientific literature and they still had the courts. An appeal of the FWS decision was filed in federal court, and in 1988, a judge ruled that the agency's decision had been unconstitutionally "arbitrary and capricious or contrary to law." Shortly after this, a different judge held that the BLM's plan for the spotted owl was inadequate. Suddenly, the possibility that the spotted owl might upend the logging industry seemed very real.

Many loggers were already worried about their future job security. Increased automation was rendering some jobs superfluous, and competition from Canada and the southern pine plantations was threatening profit margins. If the old-growth forests were to be locked up, it could mean the disappearance of tens of thousands of jobs overnight. The livelihood of entire communities was at stake. Panic began to grip many in the Pacific Northwest. Bumper stickers appeared that read "I love spotted owls . . . fried." The logging industry, worried about its access to the green gold of the old growth, stoked the fires and rallied locals in defense of the status quo. To many of the people who depended on the forests—few of whom considered themselves opposed to environmentalism—the issue seemed less about traditional logging versus ecological stewardship than about owls versus jobs.

The situation was spiraling toward crisis until Mark Hatfield and Brock Adams—the U.S. senators from Oregon and Washington, respectively—stepped in to allay the tension that threatened to tear their states apart. They fashioned a plan that would temporarily grant approval for the BLM and Forest Service spotted owl plans, but would also create an interagency scientific committee (ISC) to study the issue further and report back in a year. Their plan gained approval from Congress and was enacted in 1989. For the moment, a crisis had been averted.

But it was to be a brief moment indeed. The newly created ISC was staffed with experts on spotted owl research, including Eric Forsman, the researcher who first drew attention to the spotted owl, and Jack Ward Thomas, an ecologically minded biologist in the Forest Service. Their report, which appeared in mid-1990 and contained more than four hundred pages, only reinforced what environmentalists had been arguing for years: "We have concluded that the owl is imperiled over significant portions of its range because of continuing losses of habitat from logging and natural disturbances. Current management strategies are inadequate to ensure its viability." Several weeks later, the FWS released its long-awaited, court-ordered decision. It declared that the spotted owl was "threatened throughout its range by the loss and adverse modification of the suitable habitat as the result of timber harvesting and exacerbated by catastrophic events such as fire, volcanic eruption, and wind storms." Then, the following spring, a federal district judge in Washington, William Dwyer, ruled that the Forest Service's 1988 management plan failed to meet the "viability" requirements as concerned the spotted owl. He issued an injunction, effective immediately, to shut down all logging operations in the national forests of Oregon and Washington. More than 20 million acres were suddenly locked up.

The panic now returned with renewed intensity. Mills shut down. Loggers got pushed into unemployment lines. Communities watched helplessly as their income streams dried up. Debates raged in the local papers, in the local bars, and on the streets. The crisis was consuming the Pacific Northwest, and it soon spilled over into national politics as America geared up for a presidential election.

The incumbent, President George H. W. Bush, viewed environmentalism somewhat more charitably than had his predecessor, Ronald Reagan. But Bush's support for natural-resource protection ended rather abruptly once it threatened to impede economic growth. Of the spotted owl, he memorably said during the 1992 campaign, "And yes, we want to see that little furry, feathery guy protected and all that. But I don't want to see 40,000 loggers thrown out of work." This was the classic "owls versus jobs" dichotomy that the lumber industry promoted (though its statistics put potential job losses well above one hundred thousand), and Bush's stance largely ignored the underlying issues, namely the survival of old growth and the clash of worldviews between strict productivity and ecologically informed logging.

Bush's Democratic challenger was Arkansas governor Bill Clinton, a baby boomer who had come of age in the post–Earth Day era. Clinton seemed to embrace many of the tenets of environmentalism and even named Senator Al Gore, one of the most outspoken environmentalists in Congress, as his running mate. Clinton's view of the Pacific Northwest crisis did not conform to the popular "owls versus jobs" framing, but attempted instead to capture the larger themes. As he explained, "We could remove all the restrictions on logging tomorrow and even put more people to work. . . . But then in a few years we'd have no trees at all to log. So the issue is, how can we have a stable logging environment and keep a significant number of people working and still preserve the old-growth forest, and by the way, the spotted owl." Clinton offered few concrete proposals, but promised, if elected, to convene a forest conference so that he and his top staff could "listen, hammer out alternatives, and then take a position that . . . will try to be fair to the people whose livelihoods depend on this and fair to the environment that we are all obligated to maintain."

Clinton ended up winning the 1992 election and stayed true to his word. Barely two months after he was sworn in as the nation's forty-second president, he and his top staff traveled across the nation to Portland, Oregon, for the promised forest conference. The event offered an opportunity for both the lumber industry and the environmental movement to project their strength and to spread their sound-bite-ready messages to a national media that had descended upon the city. Many lumber mills gave their workers the day off and bused them to Portland to protest. The owl supporters, for their part, drew large crowds with the promise of a massive rock concert to feature Neil Young, Kenny Loggins, and Carole King. President Clinton, the great empathizer, the man who had popularized the phrase "I feel your pain," spent the day in a conference room with his top advisors, listening to the stories of nearly fifty local representatives from all sides of the controversy.

The conference itself, as Clinton had predicted, produced no immediate solutions, but it led the president to authorize a new scientific commission and to set a breakneck, sixty-day deadline for comprehensive recommendations covering all the federal lands involved. This new commission was led by Jack

Ward Thomas, the Forest Service biologist who had been chairman of the ISC. He oversaw the hurried production of a massive one-thousand-page report that was released on July 1, only one month past Clinton's ambitious deadline. The report laid out ten potential management scenarios, and Clinton selected option nine. The details of this option were complex, reflecting more than two decades of scientific research and policy analysis. But in the broadest terms, it placed 77 percent of the 24 million acres of federal lands that fell within the owl's range in protective reserves; it reduced timber harvesting in the unreserved lands to 25 percent of the 1980s levels; and it expanded monitoring activities to a host of potentially vulnerable species besides the northern spotted owl. As Thomas later noted, "[T]he northern spotted owl was addressed as but one of many species and ecosystem components to be dealt with in forest ecosystem management."

On April 13, 1994, the heads of both the Forest Service and the BLM signed a Record of Decision implementing a revised version of option nine, which became known as the Northwest Forest Plan (NFP). The Record of Decision explained: "This represents the first time that two of the largest federal land management agencies . . . have developed and adopted a common management approach to the lands they administer throughout an entire ecological region." The ecological approach, with its concern for the totality of the forest and its trees, had now been implemented at the highest levels of government.

The passage of the NFP, however, did not instantly end the long-standing controversy. Both sides filed lawsuits to contest its validity. But much of the combative energy disappeared in late 1994, when Judge Dwyer—whose 1991 injunction had triggered an earlier panic—ruled that the NFP, at last, satisfied the "viability" requirement.

The effects of the NFP quickly began to reshape the economy of the Pacific Northwest. Timber production from federal lands dropped 90 percent. Men whose families had been harvesting the land for generations found themselves unemployed. Some towns were utterly devastated. But overall job loss numbers were smaller than most had feared, and the spotted owl soon ceased being a national priority.

The underlying issues, however, were far from resolved. In the 2007 book *War in the Woods,* historian Samuel Hays argued that the Pacific Northwest controversy represented merely one chapter in a larger, national struggle between "commodity forestry" and "ecological forestry." Perhaps the largest theme of his book was that "forest issues were being adopted into political party agendas." Clinton had helped to put the Democrats in the ecological camp, not only through his brokering the NFP but also through his eventual appointment of Jack Ward Thomas as head of the Forest Service. Clinton's successor, George W. Bush, subsequently worked to roll back many of the protective measures that had been previously instituted, including parts of the NFP. The fights will likely continue into the future.

As for the "furry, feathery guy" that started it all, the outlook is less than inspiring. The protections instituted under the NFP slowed its decline, but total numbers have been dropping by about 3 percent a year. The largest threat, however, is no longer the destruction of old growth but the encroachment of a rival bird, the barred owl, a hardier species that seems to be steadily outcompeting its threatened cousin. Eric Forsman told the *New York Times* in July 2011, "I've certainly become much less confident as the years have gone by. . . . If you'd asked me in 1975, 'Can we fix this problem?' I'd have said, 'Oh yeah, this problem will go away.'" In the end, it may prove that the spotted owl helped to save a forest, but that the forest could not return the favor. If the spotted owl disappears, it will still live on as testament to America's ability to save its last great stands of continental old growth from the pressures of economic development.

And its ultimate importance extended even beyond the nation's borders. As *Time* magazine noted in 1990, on the eve of the ESA listing, "From Brazil to Japan, the decision will be carefully observed. The stakes are that high. . . . It will . . . enhance or diminish U.S. credibility overseas, as America tries to influence other nations to husband their natural resources and protect their endangered species." The nation, for centuries focused only on the fate of its own forests, had finally awoken to the importance and vulnerability of trees outside its sovereign territory.

## Save the Rain Forest!

DEEP WITHIN THE tropical rain forests of Brazil's Amazonian watershed, Francisco "Chico" Mendes made his living extracting natural latex from massive rubber trees that thrived in the hot, humid conditions. It was simple, traditional labor that caused little damage to the trees or to the surrounding ecosystem. But by the 1980s it was also an imperiled lifestyle. Land speculators wanted to burn down Mendes's forest and transform it into pasturage for cattle.

As the leader of the regional rubber-tappers union, Mendes had been spearheading a fight to protect his trees. He eventually began working together with several environmentalists from the United States and other developed nations. They promised exposure, influence, and money; and by the mid-1980s, Mendes was spending much of his time traveling around the developed world to bear witness to the unfolding crisis of tropical forest destruction. But this was the sort of advocacy that made enemies of dangerous men, and Mendes knew as much.

On December 5, 1988, having recently returned to Brazil from an international tour, Mendes wrote, "I do not wish flowers at my burying, because I know they will go and root them up in the forest. . . . I go [home] to a meeting with death. I am not a fatalist, only a realist. I have already denounced who wishes to kill me and no measures whatsoever have been or will be taken." Barely three weeks later, his prediction came to pass. Hit men hired by land speculators shot him dead in his own back doorway.

Mendes's murder garnered relatively little coverage in the national press of his home country. There, it was the death of a minor labor leader, something that occurred with uncomfortable frequency. In America, however, it was major news. The *New York Times* placed the story on page one, and other media outlets followed its lead. Within weeks, several Hollywood studios began courting Mendes's widow for the film rights to her husband's life story. Bidders included Robert Redford, Steven Spielberg, Ted Turner, and Warner Bros.

It was a curious reaction to the death of a man that few Americans had ever heard of, but one that made more sense given the era's broader context. The nation's populace was in the midst of an awakening about the fate of the tropical rain forests, and Mendes had suddenly given the cause a human face. As a *New York Times* reporter noted in April 1989, "Mr. Mendes has emerged as a martyr for this nation's growing environmental movement. . . . In death, the union leader has become a worldwide symbol of the effort to slow the destruction of Brazil's massive rain forest."

The movement that Mendes symbolized seemed to have arisen almost overnight. Indeed, the tropical rain forests had barely warranted a thimble's worth of press coverage before the late 1980s. But this belied a more complicated evolution in the way Americans thought about the global environment and, in consequence, the trees and forests beyond the nation's boundaries.

A useful date to mark the beginning of this process—if only symbolically— was Christmas Eve 1968, almost precisely twenty years before Mendes's murder. It was then that Bill Anders, a young astronaut aboard *Apollo 8*, captured the first image of earth from space. People were finally able to see the planet in its true form. There were no political boundaries, no sharp lines, no features grafted on by cartographers. It was just a blue and white orb, floating ethereally against a sea of infinite darkness. The day after the photo was taken, Archibald MacLeish, the Pulitzer Prize–winning poet and essayist, wrote, "To see the earth as it truly is, small and blue and beautiful in that eternal silence where it floats, is to see ourselves as riders on the earth together, brothers on that bright loveliness in the eternal cold—brothers who know now they are truly brothers."

This ideal of global brotherhood soon became a background theme for Senator Nelson's April 22 environmental teach-in. (Its adopted name of "Earth Day" certainly reflected this sensibility.) Though many of the teach-in's leading issues were local or national in character, a significant number were overtly international: pollution of the oceans, threats from nuclear fallout, the environmental consequences of the Vietnam War. The rhetoric of globalism suffused many of the speeches that poured forth on that April 22. Some even made direct reference to the newfound awareness that the *Apollo 8* photograph had produced. As future Illinois senator Adlai Stevenson III said during his Earth Day talk, "We have reached for the moon and beyond, and looking back through space we have been confronted by the insignificance of the planet which sustains us."

Two years after Earth Day, this emerging global environmental outlook was made the subject of a major U.N.-sponsored conference that took place over eleven days in Stockholm, Sweden. Known as the Conference on the Human Environment, it brought together delegates from more than one hundred nations. America sent a delegation, though its role in organizing was minimal. It was but one strong voice in a European-centered chorus—nations across Europe had recently experienced similar environmental awakenings. The strongest backer of the conference, in fact, was its host nation, Sweden.

The conference marked what many environmentalists and historians identified as the beginning of an organized international environmental movement. Though the delegates did not attempt to negotiate any binding agreements, they did agree on a statement of principles, a sort of foundational text for a new type of global environmental politics. It included twenty-six points, largely written as affirmations of cooperation and broad promises to confront the threats from industrialized production.

The declaration's loose and somewhat vague wording reflected a fundamental limitation. There was no global authority on environmental issues. They could only be addressed with the help and support of sovereign governments. The political lines that had seemed to disappear when earth was viewed from space became quite conspicuous and indelible when rhetoric morphed into policy.

This was especially true for forests, which were not directly mentioned anywhere in the conference's declaration. As the American experience had amply demonstrated, trees were some of the greatest natural resources that any nation possessed. Billions, and in some cases trillions, of dollars were waiting to be sawed and pulped and processed. And this did not count the value of the underlying soil for agriculture or of the mineral and petroleum deposits buried underground. Developing nations, which contained nearly all of the world's tropical resources, had not yet chopped through their virgin growth to nearly the same extent as the United States. Any U.N. declaration opposing rain forest destruction thus contained undertones of rich nations telling poor ones how to manage their resources. To call for protection of rain forests, therefore, was to impose something of a double standard.

But many in the international environmental community saw the issue differently. The world's temperate forests—such as those in much of Europe and America—were relatively young, having appeared only after the retreat of Ice Age glaciers. Tropical rain forests, on the other hand, had evolutionary histories that stretched back unbroken for millions of years. This longer time-line had allowed for the development of highly site-specific, interdependent biotic communities. No one was certain exactly how much ecological diversity existed within the tropical rain forests, but by the 1970s biologists were beginning to estimate that it likely amounted to more than one-half of all species on earth. Rain forest destruction, therefore, meant not only the loss of trees, but potentially of millions of life forms, only the tiniest fraction of which had been discovered, let alone studied. Three months after the Stockholm conference, the American journal *Science* published an article highlighting this point. It concluded: "[T]he sole fact that thousands of species will disappear before any aspect of their biology has been investigated is frightening. This would mean the loss of millions and millions of years of evolution. . . . We urgently suggest that, internationally, massive action be taken to preserve this gigantic pool of germ plasm by the establishment of biological gene pool reserves from the different tropical rain forest environments of the world."

If the situation already seemed urgent in 1972, it would grow only more desperate in the subsequent years. Annual tropical rain forest destruction climbed steadily through the 1970s. At the close of the decade, the United Nations attempted to quantify the damage and issued a report citing an annual rate of thirty thousand square miles either logged or burned over, an area close in size to South Carolina.

The largest culprits were tropical timber harvesters. They cut through an estimated seventeen thousand square miles of global rain forests each year, mostly to provide tropical hardwoods to markets in the developed world. America was a particularly significant purchaser. Even before the nation's independence, colonists had been importing commercial amounts of hardwoods from nations across Latin America and Africa. (The slave trade was even referred to, morbidly, as the trade "in ebony wood.") Such species as ebony, mahogany, rosewood, and teak were among the most desired veneers for luxury furniture. Another popular hardwood species in America, though for a much different purpose, was ipê. Known also as the trumpet tree for its brilliant display of horn-shaped flowers, it was chopped down for its durable, rot-resistant wood. American cities in the postwar years began importing ipê for use in benches, boardwalks, and piers. When the world-famous Coney Island Boardwalk was rehabilitated during the 1960s, Brooklyn used ipê.

After the timber trade, the most destructive industry to the rain forests was cattle ranching. The U.N. 1979 report estimated that it burned through nearly six thousand square miles per year in the effort to create new pasturage. If that wasn't ecologically troubling enough, the pasturage that ranchers created remained fertile for only two to five years before the soil began to exhaust and erode. This reckless land use nonetheless remained profitable because of a surging global demand for beef, especially in America. The nation's postwar population displayed a somewhat insatiable appetite for red meat, especially with the arrival of fast food restaurants. Much of the cattle raised on former rain forest land was destined to be ground up and sandwiched between a hamburger bun somewhere in America.

In the years following the U.N. report, both cattle ranching and tropical timber harvesting continued their march of destruction at a steady pace. The overall rate of tropical forest loss, however, spiraled even higher. Much of the responsibility for this increase rested with settlers and small farmers. Faced with unequal property systems that concentrated fertile land among a small elite, they infiltrated the rain forests, slashing and burning in an effort to create new space for agriculture. And the poor soils meant that settlers needed to carve out new fields every few years. Adding to this pressure was a new wave of massive infrastructure projects, such as highways, hydropower dams, and mining facilities. Local governments were often too indebted to fund these projects independently, but they frequently found financing from multilateral development banks (MDBs). The MDBs were controlled by Western countries and were more interested in positive economic returns than in negative ecological consequences. Once again, the fingerprints of the developed world were all over the charred stumps of the rain forests.

By the mid-1980s, due to these new development stresses, rain forest loss was estimated to be topping fifty thousand square miles a year. Adrian Cowell, a British journalist and documentarian who worked closely with Chico Mendes, labeled this period "The Decade of Destruction."

The deepening of the rain forest crisis corresponded with—and, in part, facilitated—a growth of international environmentalism. The United Nations had first created an environmental program in the wake of the Stockholm Conference. The White House began to display an interest in the international environmental movement several years later—in 1977, President Jimmy

Carter ordered a report on the global environment and its potential impact on American life by the year 2000. Soon, new nonprofit organizations began to form to deal specifically with international environmental challenges. Two of the largest were America-based: the World Resources Institute (WRI) (founded 1982) and Conservation International (founded in 1987).

By the early 1980s, this new submovement within environmentalism was beginning to work toward formulating a practicable plan to address rain forest destruction. One possibility was an international treaty, but the political momentum was absent among the developing countries that controlled the trees. A more feasible option was for the movement simply to put its money where its mouth was and offer to pay for the outcomes it desired. While the nonprofits were well capitalized, they could not command billions of dollars, the amount necessary given the scale of destruction. The international environmentalists thus looked to build bridges with other funding sources. These included the U.S. government and the United Nations (both of which oversaw international aid organizations with vast budgets) as well as the deep-pocketed MDBs (which were already embroiled in rain forest politics).

Gradually, a loose coalition formed, and in July 1985, a group of international organizations—including the World Bank, the WRI, the U.N. Development Program, and the U.S. Agency for International Development—declared that they had devised a Tropical Forestry Action Plan (TFAP) to combat deforestation. The plan called for a staggering $8 billion to be donated over five years for preservation, reforestation, and rehabilitation projects in fifty-six nations. As a representative for the U.N. Development Program explained, "Hitherto we've just piddled around with this problem. . . . Now we are telling the world this is a global problem and this is what it will cost to fix, and we're asking for billions."

Despite early optimism, the plan sputtered. Interagency squabbling hampered effective administration. Potential donors hesitated to commit such large amounts, and the money that was raised produced less impact than hoped for. Some developing nations simply refused to participate, wary that the financial support would cost them political sovereignty. Still, TFAP set out a preliminary path for the potential use of funds from the developed world to address environmental challenges abroad.

Directed aid, however, was not the only way to make money talk. Some in the American rain forest movement targeted the U.S. corporations whose behavior encouraged tropical deforestation. In mid-1987, the Rain Forest Action Network (RAN)—a two-year-old San Francisco–based nonprofit—called for a boycott of the fast food chain Burger King, which annually was importing seven hundred thousand steers raised on land cleared from Central

American rain forests. The boycott quickly gained widespread coverage from national media that were beginning to embrace the rain forest issue. An article in *Newsweek* quipped, "Lunch isn't what it used to be. . . . Partly because it takes 55 square feet to produce enough grazing area for a single all-beef patty (let's not even *discuss* Double Whoppers), at least 260 rain-forest acres disappear each day." Within a few weeks of the boycott's being announced, Burger King caved to the public pressure and promised that it would no longer purchase south-of-the-border beef. It was a major victory, and set a precedent for other companies that profited from rain forest destruction.

At this point, it was beginning to seem like the multipronged approaches of the environmental movement had a real chance to change the fate of the rain forests. The *New York Times* published an article in October 1987 titled "Concern for Rain Forest Has Begun to Blossom." It described the save-the-rain-forest campaign as making "slow but certain progress." The head of the RAN told the *Times* reporter, "What's happening now is very exciting. . . . [T]here's more to be done in the United States to save the rain forest than in countries like Brazil because a lot of American tax dollars and American companies are financing destructive rain forest projects."

As media reports increased, the issue began to grab the attention of the great tastemakers in American culture: entertainers. Among the first to embrace the issue was the long-touring band the Grateful Dead. In mid-1988, it announced that it would perform a benefit concert for the rain forests at New York City's Madison Square Garden. Frontman Jerry Garcia told the *New York Times*, "We've never called on our fans to align themselves with one cause or another, and we've always avoided making any political statements. . . . But this is an issue that is life-threatening and we hope that we can empower our own audience to act." Dozens of major musical acts followed the Grateful Dead's lead, including the Rolling Stones, who donated five hundred thousand dollars from their 1989 Steel Wheels tour to rain forest protection.

By early 1989, the rain forests were being described as "the hottest political cause since world hunger." That spring, a sort of celebrity debutante ball for the save-the-rain-forest campaign took place in New York City. It was called "Don't Bungle the Jungle," and its twenty-one hundred attendees included a roster of America's glitterati: designer Calvin Klein, musician Billy Joel, actress Tatum O'Neal, model Iman, and artist Kenny Scharf, who served as cohost. The guests were treated to an evening of live music, with performances by the B-52s, the Del Fuegos, the Grateful Dead's Bob Weir, and even Madonna, who was not only the biggest musical act in America at the time but also the benefit's other cohost. Clad in a blond wig and see-through blouse, she told the star-studded crowd, "When the trees go down, the whole system collapses. . . .

The tropical forests produce oxygen for the world. You know, air, we need it to breathe. . . . Every second an area of rain forest the size of a football field disappears. . . . At this rate in 50 years the entire rain forest may be gone—forever." The gravity of this statement was somewhat undermined later in the evening when Madonna began dancing provocatively with comedian Sandra Bernhard. In the flurry of tabloid speculation that followed, Bernhard griped to *People* magazine, "The rain forest is dying. What do you care more about, the rain forest or our sexuality?" *People*'s response: "The rain forest. Really."

Americans were now being bombarded from all sides with calls to save the rain forests. The *New York Times* alone ran more than fifty stories on the rain forests during 1989. Documentaries and special reports filled the airwaves. Stores began stocking clothing adorned with images of endangered species. Supermarkets carried cereal boxes and snack packs that displayed cartoon scenes of tropical forest life. Colleges held rain forest vigils. There was even a rain forest exhibit on the National Mall in Washington, D.C., for the twentieth anniversary of Earth Day.

In the midst of this activity, *USA Today* produced a short, tongue-in-cheek article titled "Evolution of the '80s Man." The final evolutionary phase, from 1988 onward, was described as the "Gentler Man." According to the article, his "mission was to nurture, prolong life and save the planet. . . . [H]e contributed time and money to save the rain forests." This may have been a caricature, but it captured a remarkable development in the way average Americans thought about trees. They no longer needed to be physically located in the United States to justify concern. The growth of ecology, the rise of the international environmental movement, the martyrdom of Mendes, and a sudden celebrity and commercial push had worked together to help stamp rain forest protection onto Americans' ethical map (though most might have struggled to locate a tropical forest region on an actual map).

And Americans were not the only ones whose attitudes were changing. Brazil, which controlled more rain forest than any other nation, was also undergoing a transformation. Its government had long chafed at the work of the international environmental movement, viewing it as a threat to political sovereignty. As late as 1989, the Brazilian president was still questioning the movement's entire premise: "We cannot accept the developed world's manipulation of the ecology issue to restrict Latin America's autonomy and progress. . . . It is the developed countries which should be giving explanations for the destruction of the environment." Barely a year later, however, a newly elected president announced that his administration was going to reverse course, support the goals of international environmentalism, and accept aid to save the rain forests. This turnabout partly reflected economic necessity—

Brazil, like many developing nations, was trapped in a worsening cycle of debt and could not easily turn down aid. But there was more going on, a deeper shift in priorities that owed much to the work of local environmental groups. Brazil even agreed to host an upcoming Earth Summit that would mark the twentieth anniversary of Stockholm.

Following Brazil's about-face, the international environmental movement continued to expand its actions, both in the Amazon and throughout the tropical world. Much of the progress relied on links with local and indigenous communities whose leaders were carrying on the legacy of Mendes and other, lesser-known, rain forest defenders. The combined impact of these activities helped to break the pattern of accelerating forest loss that had marked the "Decade of Destruction." But the pace still remained alarmingly high, and pressures to develop the rain forests would only increase, especially as populations swelled and global markets demanded ever more resources.

America's save-the-rain-forest campaign never officially ended, but it only managed to sustain its peak level of popular interest for several years in the early 1990s. The special news reports gradually slowed down. The celebrities— most of them anyway—moved on to new feel-good trends. The save-the-rain-forest T-shirts disappeared from the racks. The much-anticipated Chico Mendes movie was scrapped.

In some respects, America's concern for the rain forests did not so much disappear as become subsumed. A new international environmental threat— one that affected not only the rain forests but every tree on earth—was beginning to seem even more worrisome. To put it simply, the world was starting to heat up.

## Carbon Copies

THE EARLY MONTHS of 1988 were record setting, at least as far as temperature was concerned. Mercury was everywhere on the rise. Meteorologists began pronouncing it the hottest year since official record-keeping began in the mid-nineteenth century. Then the summer arrived, and the situation only worsened. Heat waves rumbled across the nation. Droughts reached a scale unknown in some places since the Dust Bowl. On July 4, *Time* magazine ran a cover story simply called "The Big Dry." The punishing conditions were front-page news and top-of-the-hour television.

In the midst of this, an unusual number of fires began to appear in the Yellowstone region. This was one of the sacred cathedrals of America's arboretum. Part of it—the portion containing the grand geyser named Old Faithful— served as the nation's first national park. It had been authorized by President

Ulysses S. Grant in 1872. Nineteen years later, President Benjamin Harrison had designated over one million adjacent acres as the nation's first federal timber reserve (later to become America's first national forest). All of these tree-filled acres were at risk if the fires spread.

Federal officials tried to contain the outbreaks from the very start, but the summer's unrelenting heat stoked the blazes like a cosmic bellows. Individual fires swelled and then linked together, forming massive walls of flame that rolled across the tree canopy. At the height of the crisis, more than nine thousand firefighters were dispatched in an effort to contain nature's fury. But all was in vain. The wildfire would not relent until the midautumn arrival of cooler, wet weather. By that point, more than one-third of the park—nearly one million acres—had been consumed. How many moose perished was anyone's guess.

It was the worst forest fire in the history of the National Park Service, and Americans wanted answers for what had happened to their cherished trees and the ecosystem they supported. Some questioned the agency's tactical decisions. Others suggested that the fire was an unavoidable—indeed, necessary—response to an overabundance of mature timber. But the clearest culprit—at least to a nation suffering beneath triple-digit temperatures—was the heat wave itself. The all-important question, then, became: Just why was it so brutally hot?

A potential answer had appeared on the front page of the *New York Times* on June 24, just as the Yellowstone fires were beginning. The headline read: "Global Warming Has Begun, Expert Tells Senate." According to the article:

> [T]he higher temperatures can now be attributed to a long-expected global warming trend linked to pollution. . . . Until now, scientists have been cautious about attributing rising global temperatures of recent years to the predicted global warming caused by pollutants in the atmosphere, known as the "greenhouse effect." But today [a top government scientist] told a Congressional committee that it was 99 percent certain that the warming trend was not a natural variation but was caused by a buildup of carbon dioxide and other artificial gases in the atmosphere. . . . The current drought [is] a foretaste of what the country [will] be facing in the years ahead.

Other media outlets soon picked up on the story. Within weeks, "The Greenhouse Effect" was featured on the cover of *Newsweek.*

As the summer wore on, and the droughts deepened, and the Yellowstone fires raged, the cries of global warming grew louder. Americans were inundated with terrifying accounts of the impending day of reckoning that their own behavior had supposedly brought about. According to Spencer Weart, author of *The Discovery of Global Warming,* "Up to this point . . . global warming had been generally below the threshold of public attention," but the issue suddenly broke through. A poll conducted in the aftermath of the brutal 1988 summer found that 79 percent of Americans had become aware of the greenhouse effect.

THE ORIGINS OF the climate change discourse reached back to the early nineteenth century and a French scientist named Joseph Fourier. He had wanted to understand what factors produced the earth's stable, temperate climate. Based on his calculations of incoming solar heat energy and of outgoing infrared radiation, the earth should have been extremely cold. In the late 1820s, he postulated, correctly, that the warmer observed temperatures were somehow due to insulation that the earth's atmosphere provided. Fourier compared the situation to a box covered with a pane of glass, where sunlight entered and much of the heat could not escape. (This powerful but inapt image would later give rise to the term "greenhouse effect.")

In the late 1850s, John Tyndall, an English scientist, picked up where Fourier had left off. The atmosphere, he speculated, might be able to trap heat if gas molecules absorbed infrared radiation. Most scientists at the time believed that all gases were transparent in this regard, but Tyndall discovered that coal gas—mostly methane—broke this supposed rule. According to Weart, Tyndall "found that for heat rays, this gas was as opaque as a plank of wood." Tyndall's subsequent experiments proved that other atmospheric gases, including carbon dioxide, were similarly absorptive. (In a continuation on Fourier's glass box analogy, these gases would later be dubbed "greenhouse gases.") Tyndall explained, "As a dam built across a river causes a local deepening of the stream, so our atmosphere, thrown as a barrier across the terrestrial [infrared] rays, produces a local heightening of the temperature at the Earth's surface."

Tyndall had identified the mechanism behind Fourier's insulation speculation, but his research stopped there. It was another forty years before a Swedish scientist named Sven Arrhenius offered a precise relationship between greenhouse gases and global temperature. Arrhenius determined—in a rough but remarkably accurate calculation (at least based on present estimates)—that a doubling of atmospheric carbon dioxide would raise the Earth's average temperature by five to six degrees Celsius.

The role of mankind in all of this meant little to the early climate theorists. Their worldview treated nature, in its broadest dimensions, as a force well beyond man's reach. And, from an atmospheric sense, this had largely been true during the nineteenth century. Theories of climate change were thus viewed as somewhat abstruse philosophizing, perhaps useful for understanding geological shifts like Ice Ages, but hardly relevant to anything in the near term.

This consensus view, however, began to fracture in 1938. That year, a British engineer named Guy Stewart Callendar stood before the Royal Meteorological Society in London and declared that the world was indeed warming and that man was to blame. His claim threatened the very foundation of man's relationship to nature. It was practically heresy. But Callendar remained adamant. His calculations showed a discernible warming trend, and the simplest explanation for him was the millions of tons of greenhouse gases that poured forth from the world's refineries, power plants, automobiles, and factories. The entire industrial system had been built around extracting energy from carbon-rich coal and petroleum (the so-called fossil fuels). But their combustion released huge volumes of carbon dioxide.

Many initially dismissed Callendar's contentions as either incorrect or wildly speculative. The skeptics questioned whether it was even possible to measure global average temperature or carbon concentrations. These were—and still are—valid concerns. But researchers across diverse fields found innovative ways to track temperature and carbon over time. Glaciologists would study air bubbles trapped in ancient ice cores. Paleobotanists would analyze sediment from peat bogs. Meteorologists would set up carbon sensors in the most remote corners of the globe. Dendrochronologists would measure the width of tree rings from millennia-old specimens. The early evidence was far from conclusive, but suggested that Callendar might have been correct.

By the early 1960s, climate researchers were recommending that fossil fuels be treated as a type of pollutant. Their case was not yet sufficient to sustain a Rachel Carson–style polemic, but the federal government did acknowledge the concern in a 1965 report on environmental pollution. One of the report's sections bore the title "Carbon Dioxide From Fossil Fuels—The Invisible Pollutant." It noted, "Through his worldwide industrial civilization, Man is unwittingly conducting a vast geophysical experiment. Within a few generations he is burning the fossil fuels that slowly accumulated in the earth over the past 500 million years." In the period between the federal report and the scorching summer of 1988, the climatic threats from fossil fuels appeared occasionally in the nation's public discourse, particularly during the energy crises of 1973 and 1979.

Fossil fuel combustion, however, was not the sole source of greenhouse gases. Carbon was the basic building block of all organic material, including trees. When forests grew, they sucked carbon dioxide from the atmosphere through photosynthesis and converted much of it into wood. Conversely, when trees decayed or caught fire, they released much of this stored carbon as $CO_2$. Nature maintained a general degree of balance between these two processes. But this homeostasis was threatened by man-made deforestation, which transformed forests from giant reservoirs of solid-state carbon into greenhouse gas factories.

For many years, the link between deforestation and global warming received little attention. It was not even mentioned in the 1965 report on environmental pollution. At the time, forest coverage in the developed world had largely stabilized, and almost no one was paying attention to the world's tropical forests. But then came the international environmental movement and the "Decade of Destruction." By the mid-1980s, some climate scientists were speculating that deforestation contributed a staggering 20 percent of total greenhouse gas emissions.

This rough estimation was reinforced in 1987, when scientists used satellites to monitor Amazonian destruction for the first time. What they found was shocking. Their satellites detected more than 170,000 fires between June and October, the so-called burning season. Smoke clouds spiraled twelve thousand feet into the air. One of the lead researchers observed, "There is enough to compare it to the outburst of a very large volcano." The following year—during the torturous summer of 1988—the *New York Times* ran a front-page story with the headline: "Vast Amazon Fires, Man-Made, Linked to Global Warming." As the article explained, "In the case of carbon dioxide . . . the forest destruction is doubly harmful. . . . The dwindling forest cover becomes not only less efficient in absorbing and removing this 'greenhouse gas,' but the fires also add new, huge volumes of it." Saving the rain forests and their trees was no longer just a matter of biodiversity protection, but one of global climate stability.

The path forward, at this point, was unclear. Combatting global warming would require an unprecedented international effort. The cost of neutralizing tropical deforestation alone—assuming the political obstacles could be overcome—was placed in the hundreds of billions of dollars. And this would only address a fraction of the total greenhouse gas emissions. The majority came from fossil fuels, which powered the global industrial economy. Developed nations could not spend their way past the problem even if they had wanted to.

Still, some in the environmental movement believed that there was reason to be Pollyannaish.

The year before the 1988 heat wave, the international community had come together and negotiated a comprehensive treaty to address a different global environmental crisis: the depletion of the stratospheric ozone layer (which provided a natural shield against ultraviolet radiation). That treaty, known as the Montreal Protocol, had set standards controlling the manufacture of chlorofluorocarbons (CFCs), a chemical compound that was popular in aerosol sprays but that lingered in the upper atmosphere and destroyed ozone. The passage of the Montreal Protocol had been the greatest international environmental success to date (far outpacing the save-the-rain-forest campaign). It suggested that nations could work together to address some types of global challenges.

But the science of ozone depletion was simpler than that of climate change. If the Montreal Protocol model were to be followed, a necessary first step would be the establishment of a scientific consensus that governments could rely upon. Policymakers required some uniform baseline data before they could commence informed negotiations. In December 1988, the United Nations announced the creation of a new agency to address this deficiency. Known as the Intergovernmental Panel on Climate Change (IPCC), it promised to bring together experts from around the world to sift through and interpret the flood of scientific literature. And every few years, the IPCC's findings would be published in a report—the closest approximation of an international consensus.

The IPCC issued its First Assessment Report in September 1990. It was a doorstopper, but all the analysis and statistics could be boiled down to a few phlegmatic phrases: "Our judgment is that global-mean surface air temperature has increased by between $0.3^\circ$ and $0.6^\circ$C over the last hundred years. . . . [T]he size of this warming is broadly consistent with predictions of climate models, but it is also of the same magnitude as natural climate variability." This was a rather tepid way to describe what many scientists considered a warming crisis. It even failed to attribute any definite responsibility to the actions of mankind. As Weart explained, "Under pressure from the industrial interests, as well as from the mandate to make only statements that virtually every knowledgeable scientist could endorse, the IPCC's consensus statements were highly qualified and cautious. This was not mainstream science so much as conservative, lowest-common-denominator science." Nevertheless, the report did represent an international consensus, one that could serve as a starting point for negotiations at the upcoming 1992 Earth Summit in Rio de Janeiro, Brazil.

It was inevitable that the United States would play a key role in any potential negotiations. In addition to being the world's largest economic and military power, America was also unrivaled at producing greenhouse gases—about one-quarter of total global emissions were estimated to come from America; and since the U.S. population only composed 4 percent of the planet's population, Americans were on average the earth's worst polluters. Consequently, any plan to combat global warming seemed to require their participation.

The administration of President George H. W. Bush was divided over how to approach the Earth Summit. Some advisors considered climate change a threat to national security and pressed for strong leadership. Others scoffed at the entire hullaballoo, labeling it nothing more than environmentalist hand-wringing and junk science. Bush, for his part, supported additional climate change research, but tended to chafe at any measures that threatened short-term economic growth, something any serious international effort to halt global warming would likely require.

Bush's refusal to promise support for a climate change treaty at Rio prompted a wave of criticism in the media and in Congress, where Senator Al Gore led the attack. The outrage prompted the Bush administration to publicly reverse course. But then, when the Earth Summit arrived in June 1992, the U.S. delegation opposed the calls of many nations—mostly from Western Europe and certain low-lying island states—for aggressive reforms. America did, however, agree to a nonbinding climate convention, akin to the 1972 Stockholm Declaration on the Human Environment. This represented a degree of progress.

Bush flew down to Rio toward the end of the summit and declared, "We've signed a climate convention. . . . Let me be clear on one fundamental point. The United States fully intends to be the world's preeminent leader in protecting the global environment. We have been that for many years. We will remain so."

After Rio, conditions grew more favorable for the eventual U.S. approval of a binding treaty. The Democrats—who tended to both acknowledge the threat of climate change and to support the expansion of international law—won the 1992 presidential election. Al Gore, the new vice president, had authored a book, *Earth in the Balance,* in which he wrote: "I favor an international treaty limiting the amounts of $CO_2$ individual nations are entitled to produce each year." His influence on President Bill Clinton's administration strengthened U.S. commitment to the negotiation process that had started around the Earth Summit and was leading toward a new conference at Kyoto, Japan, in December 1997. Furthermore, two years into Clinton's first term, the IPCC published its second report. Its key language—quoted widely in the media—read: "The balance of evidence suggests that there is a discernible human influence on global climate." The scientific consensus had begun to harden.

Nevertheless, negotiations surrounding the potential treaty were hard fought. As with the rain forest debate, nations on each side of the development curve argued over principles of justice. Poorer countries wanted the wealthier ones—the source of most of the world's greenhouse gases—to bear the brunt of the burden. Conversely, some wealthy nations argued that the warming crisis demanded that all countries, especially fast-growing ones like India and China, needed to trim emissions. In either case, the impact would be especially high in the United States, the world's great greenhouse gas emitter.

Continued U.S. resistance nearly shuttered the treaty, but at the last minute, Gore flew to Kyoto to help hammer out a resolution. The upshot was a binding agreement, but one as watered down as a dose of homeopathic medicine. Known as the Kyoto Protocol, it split the world into two groups, Annex I and Annex II—in the roughest sense these annexes represented, respectively, the developed and developing world. Annex II countries faced few obligations; Annex I countries pledged to reduce $CO_2$ emissions an average of 5.2 percent below 1990 baseline levels (which were based on data in the IPCC report). Several key provisions for how this would be measured, meanwhile, were tabled for a future conference.

The Kyoto Protocol was not only limited, it was not even enforceable at first. Many nations, including the United States, required supplemental legislative approval before their international commitments could be ratified. The protocol's terms stated that it would only become law upon ratification by fifty-five countries that represented, collectively, more than 55 percent of total Annex I emissions as of 1990. The United States alone accounted for over 36 percent of this total. Its cooperation therefore was essential.

In late 2000, a follow-up conference was held in the Hague to sort out the issues that Kyoto had left unresolved. The thorniest question concerned the tree resources of large Annex I nations such as Canada, Russia, and the United States. As the *New York Times* reported, "After 11 days of draining and unwieldy bargaining by 170 countries . . . all the issues had been narrowed to just this one: How much credit should big forested countries get for all that photosynthesis?" In the end, to quote the *Times* piece, "the negotiators got lost in the trees." They reached an impasse over a difference of only 20 million tons of forest-related carbon credits, a paltry percentage of the 6 billion tons of $CO_2$ that the world was producing annually.

In the midst of this, America faced a new presidential election. The contest to replace Clinton was the closest in recent history and served in part as a referendum on climate change, such was the importance each aspirant gave to global warming. The Democratic candidate, Vice President Gore, vowed to continue his advocacy and make the issue a centerpiece of his presidential agenda. The Republican, George W. Bush, a Texas governor with close ties to the petroleum industry, sought to discredit the entire movement.

Bush's controversial, Supreme Court–aided victory laid to rest any hopes that the United States would join Kyoto or otherwise address climate change in the near term. The new president staffed his administration with veterans of the energy sector—his vice president, Dick Cheney, was the former CEO and chairman of Halliburton, one of the world's largest oil field service suppliers.

Early in Bush's second term, the Kyoto Protocol reached the Annex I 55 percent threshold. This meant that it had been ratified by almost all of the nations in the developed world, except the United States. America, in holding out, joined an elite club of corrupt and broken states. (But it was a fast-collapsing fraternity that would be down to a single, stubborn member by 2010.) The elder Bush's 1992 promise about America being a global leader had come true, only it was now a leadership of opposition against a monolithic environmental consensus.

The younger Bush administration's hard-line stance engendered strong opposition from environmentalists and scientists at home. In 2004, for example, forty-eight American Nobel laureates signed a petition endorsing Democratic challenger John Kerry and rebuking Bush's dismissive treatment of global warming. It read: "By ignoring scientific consensus on critical issues such as global climate change, [President Bush and his administration] are threatening the Earth's future." Perhaps the most influential single voice on this environmental counterfront was Bush's vanquished presidential rival. Gore had initially retreated from public life following his election defeat, but he eventually began traveling the country giving lectures on the impending climate catastrophe that he felt was awaiting America. In 2006, his lectures were turned into a documentary film, *An Inconvenient Truth,* which became a runaway success. It grossed more than $23 million and won the Oscar for best documentary. An accompanying book sat comfortably on the bestseller list for months.

Gore's call of alarm was strengthened when the IPCC released its Fourth Assessment Report in 2007. The science had grown increasingly sophisticated as high-speed computers allowed for more complex climate modeling, and the new data only reaffirmed the arguments floating around since the time of Callendar. The report concluded, "Most of the observed increase in global average temperatures since the mid-twentieth century is *very likely* due to the observed increase in anthropogenic [i.e., man-made] greenhouse gas concentrations." The international scientific community had now endorsed a position that treated man-made global warming as a near certainty. Nothing short of Darwin's theory of evolution seemed to demonstrate a greater degree of scientific consensus.

In late 2007, it was announced that the year's Nobel Peace Prize was going to be awarded jointly to Al Gore and the IPCC. Many saw the decision as a political gesture, a staunch rebuff of those, like President Bush, who refused to act in the face of mounting evidence. The speech that the chairman of the Norwegian Nobel Committee gave at the award ceremony in Oslo, Norway, did little to dispute this. In praising Gore, the chairman said:

> Political defeats can also bring good results! Again and again, Gore has hammered in his message, not least to Americans. The USA is, along with China, the great polluter. But that also entails a responsibility for becoming the leader in emission reduction. . . . We all have a responsibility, small countries and large, all mankind, but the heaviest responsibility rests on the rich nations, which to a large extent created global warming.

Nonetheless, President Bush, the self-appointed Decider, was not known as a man who changed his mind, even in the face of rising criticism or new information. His position remained fixed.

The election of Barack Obama seemed to offer a new direction. However, by the time the new president assumed office, the nation was in the grip of an all-consuming economic crisis. Political energy went toward health care reform and saving the country's struggling financial system. To complicate matters further, Bush's denial of global warming became Republican Party orthodoxy. The average American and many media outlets seemed convinced that a scientific controversy existed, regardless of the overwhelming consensus expressed through the IPCC.

As the United States waits, signs of climate change continue to appear. The record temperatures of 1988 were topped five times in the first decade of the new millennium. Extreme weather—which computer models predict as a consequence of climate change—appears to be increasing as well: Hurricane Katrina; record flooding along the Mississippi; killer blizzards in the Midwest and Northeast; severe droughts across Texas and parts of the Southeast; heavy rains in Southern California. Scientists acknowledge that no individual event conclusively proves climate change, but trends are becoming noticeable. And nowhere is this more evident than among America's trees, the pillars of the landscape.

The great 1988 blaze at Yellowstone, for instance, appears to have been the start of a new era of rising wildfires. A 2011 study of the Yellowstone region found that the rates of burning have increased over the past twenty years at a pace unknown in the last ten millennia. And the situation in Yellowstone is being repeated all across the nation. The total forest acreage consumed annually by wildfire is reaching levels not seen in a hundred years, since the peak of unregulated industrial logging. At a 2011 Senate hearing on wildfires, the head of the Forest Service testified, "Our scientists believe this is due to a change in climate."

Recent years have also seen a proliferation of tree diseases and pests. The list is a long one indeed. In New York City, for example, a quarantine is in effect to contain an infestation of Japanese long-horned beetles, which destroy maple trees. Cities across the Midwest are losing their ash trees to a pest known as the emerald ash borer. In California and parts of the West, millions of oak trees are falling victim to an illness that's been named "Sudden Oak Death." Some of these problems likely stem from the same international forces that produced chestnut blight and Dutch elm disease; however, many seem to be worsened by—if not entirely the result of—changing climate conditions, such as warmer winters and wetter summers.

Even more alarming, small shifts in climate seem to be leading to a higher overall rate of tree deaths. This was the conclusion of a 2009 article in *Nature*. It found that tree mortality rates in the western United States and Canada had doubled, and it suggested rising temperatures were a likely cause. As the climate continues to alter, trees will struggle to stay rooted. Some speculate that global warming will soon eliminate the famous Joshua trees from the national park in California that bears their name.

The federal and state agencies that oversee the nation's forests and trees have been forced to formulate new management strategies. In 2010, the Forest Service published the *National Roadmap for Responding to Climate Change*. The report noted, "Most of the urgent . . . management challenges of the past 20 years, such as wildfires, changing water regimes, and expanding forest insect infestations, have been driven, in part, by a changing climate. Future impacts are projected to be even more severe." Climate change is threatening to undermine a century's worth of progress in forestry. In July 2011, the Fish and Wildlife Service for the first time identified climate change as the main factor causing the endangerment of a tree species, the whitebark pine. (The agency determined that official listing was "precluded by higher priority actions.")

Trees, however, may not be mere victims. Many see them as potential saviors as well. A 2011 study published in *Nature* claimed that forests are even more effective at absorbing carbon dioxide than previously thought. Each year, the researchers found, trees lock away roughly 2.4 billion tons of solid carbon in their wood fiber. If the study's numbers are accurate, then the world's forests are absorbing an amount equivalent to one-third of total man-made $CO_2$ production.

The utility of trees has made them a centerpiece of countless climate change initiatives. One of the most popular tactics is old-fashioned tree planting, plain and simple. The elder President Bush—always a fan of low cost environmental programs—recognized this early on. As the *New York Times* reported in January 1990:

> With insufficient credit, President Bush has just broken with former President Reagan's doctrine of killer trees. Mr. Reagan seemed to condemn trees, calling them a source of pollution. On the opposite principle that they absorb pollution, Mr. Bush has announced a plan to plant a billion new trees a year for 10 years. . . . The 10 billion new trees should in time absorb 13 million tons of carbon dioxide a year, or 5 percent of the U.S. annual emissions of the gas, according to the President's budget report.

Similarly ambitious programs were subsequently enacted by nonprofit groups, local governments, and the Forest Service.

A related approach involves the creation of markets that set a price on tree planting based on the expected amount of carbon dioxide that will be absorbed. This technique works best when carbon emissions are taxed, as is the case for many Annex I members of the Kyoto Protocol. While America does not yet place any penalty on carbon pollution, in 2007 the Forest Service and the American Forest Foundation announced the creation of a voluntary market where environmentally minded individuals or corporations could pay six dollars in exchange for tree plantings estimated to absorb one metric ton of $CO_2$ from the atmosphere. A few tree farms and forests are now being managed primarily as so-called carbon sinks.

Creating these new carbon sinks, of course, matters little if the established ones—like the tropical rain forests—keep disappearing at accelerating rates. The international environmental movement continues to advocate the policy of compensating poorer nations for forest stewardship. The issue was a central concern of the 2009 U.N. Climate Change Conference in Copenhagen, Denmark. What resulted was the approval of a framework for an ambitious program—something of an improved and expanded version of TFAP—known as Reducing Emissions Through Deforestation and Forest Degradation (REDD). Many environmentalists see REDD as a key to climate change mitigation moving forward. But like so many aspects of international environmentalism, REDD's success may depend on whether the United States ultimately lends its full support.

Finally, scientists are directing research toward projects looking to exploit the carbon-dioxide-consuming qualities of trees. Breakthroughs in genetics may allow the widespread introduction of genetically modified, fast-growing "supertrees" (with all the ecological risks that entails). Programs are also under way to design a synthetic tree, a tall structure containing carbon dioxide catchers that could work a thousand times faster than its natural counterpart. Americans in the future may travel in forests of newly invented trees (real or artificial). Perhaps they will imagine it has always been that way, just as many in the present mistakenly think that America's tree canopy has been fairly stable throughout the nation's history.

T HE BROAD TREND of the past century has been toward better stewardship of America's tree resources. History provides abundant evidence to support this claim. Professional forestry expanded from a small group of dedicated Progressives to the boardrooms of Fortune 500 companies. Technological advances allowed logging companies to reduce waste and process all parts of the tree. The nation's wilderness gained protection through the tireless efforts of conservationists. The management of forests developed to encompass an ecological view that valued not only trees, but the entire ecosystem they supported. America now creates more new forest each year than it degrades through overuse.

The journey has been neither straightforward nor certain. Along the way have been many obstacles, and some outright failures. Threats of a "timber famine" lingered into the mid-twentieth century. Diseases decimated two of the nation's most beloved species. Logging and pollution severely reduced the numbers of many others. Fears over job security nearly allowed the country's last stands of old-growth forest to be wiped out. The tropical rain forests continue to fall. Climate change is but the latest—and perhaps most consequential—challenge to the nation's forests.

# Epilogue

Franklinia

OUR TREES ARE living history. Each has a story to share, though it is well guarded, locked away in eternal silence. Uncovering these hidden tales requires a degree of tenacity. One must develop a feel for the many factors that determine why any given tree arrived at a particular spot and why it subsequently survived. Rarely in our nation does a tree's life involve no intervention, direct or indirect, from mankind. Perhaps the tree in question was planted intentionally. Perhaps it sprouted from some chopped-down predecessor. Perhaps it is but one specimen in a forest that populated a neglected field or appeared from the ashes of a fire. In writing *American Canopy*, I have attempted to make the nation's treescape more legible, to show how these trees shaped our society and how we shaped them in turn.

Geographers estimate that the original forest cover of the continental United States measured close to one billion acres. That figure declined gradually over the course of three hundred years, reaching a historic low around

600 million acres in the early twentieth century. The total amount of forest then began to stabilize and slowly recover. Today, the nation's continental forest measures roughly 750 million acres. From one perspective, then, our trees tell a tale of redemption, of unchecked consumption and dependence being tempered by prudence and effective management.

But a more careful review forces us to look beyond this somewhat triumphalist description of a forest that fell and then rose. America contains not one great forest but many, and their evolutions differ. Woodlands in the East, for instance, have made great gains as abandoned farms and fields gradually returned to forests; those in the West have shrunk under pressure from industrial logging. Moreover, forest quantity is not the same as forest quality. The contemporary forest often differs greatly from its forebear. The giant monarchs are nearly all gone. The unregulated diversity of nature has often been circumscribed—indeed, some managed forests contain a single commercial species for miles on end. And even in unmanaged forests, the trees have changed: Many of our once prominent native species have fallen to diseases, aggressive logging, or introduced competitors—changes that cannot be undone.

The national statistics also overlook our impact on trees outside of the country. But our forest footprint is ultimately international—importation rates for many forest products have been rising steadily for years. In the age of global warming, Americans can no longer afford to speak of "our trees" and "their trees."

Changes take place not only within these sylvan worlds but also within our understandings about them. The language we use to describe forests has shifted immensely. Colonial notions of savagery and fear eventually transformed into environmental refrains of rejuvenation and salvation. We started as a people who saw tree clearing as the key to our survival and expansion. We became a people who found a moral imperative in reintroducing trees across the landscape, whether it be a cutover forest or a paved-over metropolis. We developed an American society through the beneficence of these trees, their wood the foundation of our industrial economy and our domestic life. As we matured, our daily intimacy with trees and their products gradually diminished. We transformed trees into a commodity, grown and harvested afar, then sawed and pulped and processed until the final product seemed stripped of anything natural. Today, objects that appear wooden are often facsimiles, their grains and textures stamped on during fabrication.

Our progress might suggest that we have tamed our trees and unlocked their secrets. We have studied them to the cellular level and beyond. But our mastery remains superficial. History has shown that trees and forests refuse to submit to our dominion. Though we have learned much, we are still tormented by fires and diseases. Our remarkable advances in forest management face constant revision as we learn more of ecology. There are limits to how far we can exert our will over nature. This is a lesson worth keeping in mind as we explore new frontiers in tree genetics and trust in our technological prowess to combat a climate crisis.

The trees and forests are not passive actors, despite what appearances may suggest. They channel our collective behaviors and influence the way we think. American attitudes toward resource consumption were formed against a backdrop of seemingly unlimited access to wood. The country's industrial expansion differed from that of Europe in large part because of trees, which allowed (perhaps even encouraged) a style of development that favored speed and immediacy over permanence. It may well be that the reason Americans today consume more than any other nation traces back to the once limitless bounty of their forests.

But this aspect of American identity hardly suggests the full extent to which trees have shaped and continue to shape national culture. The woods have been the source for many of the country's traditional folk heroes, from Johnny Appleseed to Daniel Boone to Paul Bunyan. An American style of literature first emerged when writers such as James Fenimore Cooper began reflecting on the great tree-filled wilderness that stretched across the continent's interior. We are all inheritors of the municipal parks movement of the mid-nineteenth century, the national parks program that John Muir inspired, the forestry crusade of Gifford Pinchot and Theodore Roosevelt, the alphabetical conservationism practiced under Franklin Roosevelt, the wild regions saved by men like Aldo Leopold, and the regulatory framework of the post–Earth Day generation. With all of this as the basis for our modern culture, it is understandable why most Americans feel an affinity for trees.

Trees also manage to provide a counterbalance to the excesses and alienation of modern life. Henry David Thoreau realized as much when, in 1845, he fled Concord, Massachusetts, for two years of contemplation in nearby Walden Woods. But the life that Thoreau temporarily escaped would seem downright pastoral by current standards. What would he make of the present day, surrounded by technology, further removed from the tactile sensations of the real world?

As we rush headlong into the twenty-first century, the physicality of trees seems more vital than ever. The modern workplace and home are becoming increasingly antiseptic. Americans now spend their days staring into computer screens that receive information as if by magic. Daily life seems alarmingly virtual. Trees provide the antidote. The smell of pine needles, the crunch of autumn leaves, the roughness of bark are all reminders that we are a part of nature. Tree hugging, in its most literal sense, offers a reconnection with the physical world, the world of our forefathers. The forests and their trees are a sanctuary for the spirit. To enter them is to seek renewal.

Rarely do these trees receive the public attention that they deserve. Gone are the fears of a "timber famine" that might destroy the economy. Our success in preserving our forests from total destruction has made it easy to overlook them altogether. Trees appear frozen in time, and the invisibility of gradual change can make problems difficult to spot. The nation tends to rediscover its tree resources only in periods of catastrophe. The rest of the time many of us motor along with indifference, leaving the issue to the government, corporations, and the permanent environmental movement. But this is a risky approach. America's forests and trees are more necessary now than ever.

# Acknowledgments

I HAVE BEEN CARRYING the project that would become *American Canopy* with me for more than half a decade. During that time, many people have provided support, counsel, and encouragement. I can only imagine that even the most resolute among them began to weary of the constant talk of trees. (And not just trees, but tree history at that!) I hope that the final result will justify their patience.

My research would have been unimaginably more difficult without the support of two of the world's great libraries. The early months of reading and investigating were spent beneath the painted clouds of the New York Public Library's Main Reading Room. Later, I was granted access to the Library's Allen Room, a phenomenal writing space where the walls are lined with the published works of former Room members. Particular thanks go to Jay Barksdale, a superb research librarian and a composer of some of the most erudite emails I have ever witnessed. I have also had access to the library resources of Yale University for the past two years as part of my graduate work. The breadth of the collections and the speed of the service continually exceeded what seems possible, let alone reasonable. Many Yale librarians have provided me with assistance, but a special debt of gratitude is owed to John Nann, who opened my eyes to the full potential of some of the electronic collections and who kindly answered far too many emails with the subject line "Another Quick Question."

Yale also provided me with a wonderful intellectual community. Members of the History Department have been especially generous with their time and enthusiasm. I'd like to thank, in particular, Joanne Freeman, Naomi Lamoreaux, Gil Joseph, Glenda Gilmore, Paul Sabin, and Patrick Cohrs. Additionally, some of the ideas in the later chapters were debated and refined during semiregular, informal Thursday-evening gatherings with a small cast that reliably included Shafqat Hussein, Isaiah Wilner, Jose Ramirez, and Todd Holmes.

A special word of appreciation is owed to two people who graciously read and commented on the entire manuscript: John Demos and David Oshinsky. Each is a friend, a mentor, and a role model. Their thoughts proved invaluable in completing the book.

Long before the manuscript was completed, it was a sketch of an idea that I brought to my agents at William Morris Endeavor, Eric Simonoff and Eric Lupfer. They both embraced the project from the outset and have provided endless guidance along the way. My only grievance is that three Erics trying to work together can sometimes produce rather confusing emails. My editor at Scribner, Colin Harrison, brought wisdom, experience, and a great sensitivity to the challenges of writing American history. Over meals around Midtown, he guided me through innumerable problems and reminded me about the importance of failing upward. Others at Scribner also contributed their considerable talents throughout the editing and production process. These included Rex Bonomelli, Kelsey Smith, Kate Lloyd, and Katie Rizzo.

My friends provided constant, and appreciated, reminders that there is more to life than trees and writing. I owe particular debts of gratitude to Brent Barton, Chesa Boudin, Cole Ferguson, Alec Flyer, Nate Harper, Meredith Mackey, and Eric Stern. Most of all, I want to thank my girlfriend, Emilie Walgenbach, who has been by my side since I began work on this book. When she is around, it is impossible for my spirits to not be high or my stomach not to be full.

Finally, my family has been a wellspring of love and support. My grandparents—Bea and Al, and Roz and Milt, all of whom are still active and healthy—sent me countless good wishes and gladly shared their own memories of trees in America. My sister, Lainie, can make me laugh in a way that's all her own. And she remains a model for me, as she has since the days of matching Halloween costumes and Margaret Chase Smith impressions. Her husband, Adam, joined our family while I was in the midst of writing *American Canopy* and has felt from the start like a brother. My parents, Beth and Ira, remain willing to go to any lengths to help me. They've worked tirelessly to provide me with every opportunity. My father, a historian in his own right, was the first person with whom I discussed the book, and he was instrumental in shaping it through every step of the process. His eyes have passed over the pages so many times that I fear there are some passages he now knows better than I do.

Without all of this support, *American Canopy* could not have been written. That being said, the omissions and errors—both the inevitable and the avoidable—are mine and mine alone.

# Notes

## Introduction: The Death of Prometheus

2    *"offers a richer":* John Muir. *The Mountains of California.* New York: The Century Co., 1894, 154.

2    *The* National Geographic *article:* Edmund Schulman. "Bristlecone Pine, Oldest Known Living Thing." *National Geographic* 113, no. 3 (1958): 361.

3    *"a dead crown":* Donald R. Currey. "An Ancient Bristlecone Pine Stand in Eastern Nevada." *Ecology* 46 (1965): 565.

3    *"present along a single":* Ibid.

3    *"was like many":* Carl T. Hall. "Staying Alive: High in California's White Mountains grows the oldest living creature ever found." *San Francisco Chronicle,* August 23, 1998, SC-1.

3    *"Cut 'er down":* Michael P. Cohen. *A Garden of Bristlecones: Tales Change in the Great Basin.* Reno: University of Nevada Press, 1998, 72.

5    *"the wooddes [were]":* E. G. R. Taylor, ed. "Document 46: Discourse of Western Planting by Richard Hakluyt, 1584." In *The Original Writings & Correspondence of the Two Richard Hakluyts* (vol. II). Nendeln, Liechtenstein: Kraus Reprint Limited, 1967, 225.

6    *"Well may ours":* James Hall. *Notes on the Western States; containing descriptive sketches of their soil, climate, resources and scenery.* Philadelphia: Harrison Hall, No. 72 S. Fourth Street, 1838, 101.

## 1: From Discovery to Revolution

12    *"I marvaile not":* Richard Hakluyt. *Divers voyages touching the discoverie of America and the Ilands . . .* London: Thomas Woodcocke, dwelling in paules Church-yard, at the signe of the blacke beare, 1582, The Epistle.

12    *"for the manifolde":* Taylor, 211.

13    *"the Contrie":* Ibid., 222.

13    *"all the commodities":* Ibid., 211.

13    *"So that were there":* Ibid., 281.

13    *"the present wante":* Ibid.

14    *"Never so much [oak]":* William Harrison. *The Description of England: The Classic Contemporary Account of Tudor Social Life.* Dover Publications, 1994, 279.

15    *"agreed that the New World":* Howard Mumford Jones. "The Colonial Impulse: An Analysis of the 'Promotion' Literature of Colonization." *Proceedings of the American Philosophical Society* 90, no. 2 (1946): 143.

15    *"And England posessing":* Taylor, 315.

15    *"mightie greate wooddes":* Ibid., 224.

16    *"no man can let":* Antoin E. Murphy, ed. "A Tract Against the High Rate of Usurie (1641) by Sir Thomas Culpepper." In *Monetary Theory: 1601–1758.* London: Routledge, 1997, 4–5.

17  *He determined, among other things:* Henry S. Burrage. *Gorges and the Grant of the Province of Maine 1622: A Tercentenary Memorial.* Augusta: for the State of Maine, 1923, 47–48.

18  *"I heare not":* A. G. Bradley, ed. "John Chamberlain. Letter to Dudley Carleton, 7 July, 1608." In *Travels and Works of Captain John Smith (part I),* Edward Arber, ed. New York: Burt Franklin, n.d., xcii.

18  *"[N]either the scattered Forrest":* Peter Mancall, ed. "Anonymous. A True Declaration of the Estate of the Colonie in Virginia (Issued by the Virginia Company) 1610." In *Envisioning America: English Plans for the Colonization of North America, 1580–1640.* Boston, New York: Bedford Books, 1995, 129, 132.

19  *"The ardent Love":* Foster Watson. *Richard Hakluyt.* London: Sheldon Press, 1924, 29.

19  *"necessitie calling them":* William Bradford. *Bradford's History "Of Plimoth Plantation."* Boston: Wright & Potter Printing Co., State Printers, 1898, 97.

19  *"soone lost both":* Ibid., 98.

20  *"gave a sodaine jerk up":* Henry Martyn Dexter. *Mourt's Relation or Journal of the Plantation at Plymouth.* Boston: John Kimball Wiggin, 1865, 25.

20  *"whole countrie":* Bradford, 95.

20  *"so incompassed with woods":* Dexter, 63.

20  *"always cost a great":* Ibid., 51.

20  *"halfe a quarter":* Ibid., 65.

21  *"Here is good living":* Francis Higginson. *New-Englands Plantation with the Sea Journal and Other Writings.* Salem, MA: Essex Book and Print Club, 1908, 102.

21  *"Trees both in hills":* William Wood. *New England's Prospect.* London: Tho. Cotes, for John Bellamie, at the three Golden Lyons in Corne-hill, neere the Royall Exchange, 1634, 18.

21  *"2 hoggsheads":* Bradford, 130.

21  *"That for the preventing":* William Brigham, ed. *The Compact with the Charter and Laws of the Colony of New Plymouth.* Boston: Dutton and Wentwork, 1836, 28.

22  *"[they would] dig":* Cornelis Van Tienhoven. *Information Relative to Taking up Land in New Netherland, in the Form of Colonies or Private Boweries, 1650.* In E. B. O'Callaghan. *The Documentary History of the State of New-York,* vol. IV. Albany: Charles Van Benthuysen, 1851, 31.

22  *"so much paines":* Wood, 19.

22  *"as bigge as":* Ibid.

25  *"the great necessity":* George Louis Beer. *The Old Colonial System, 1660–1754, Part I: The Establishment of the System, 1660–1688 (vol. I).* New York: Macmillan, 1912, 81, fn. 1.

26  *The initial shipment had occurred:* William Strachey. *The Historie of Travaile in Virginia Brittania.* London: Hakluyt Society, 1849, 130.

26  *"There is also the very good":* Samuel Pepys. *The Diary of Samuel Pepys.* London, New York: Macmillan, 1905, 445.

27  *A 1736 article: The American Weekly Mercury,* March 1–March 8, 1736, 3.

27  *"When the male flowers":* Donald Culross Peattie. *A Natural History of North American Trees.* Boston: Houghton Mifflin Company, 2007, 28.

27  *"an Assortment of":* The *New-Hampshire Gazette, and Historical Chronicle,* April 14, 1775, 3.

28  *the white pines were:* John Wentworth to the Earl of Hillsborough, December 4, 1771, taken from Governor Wentworth's letter-books in the archives at Concord, New Hampshire. In "The King's Woods." *Proceedings of the Massachusetts Historical Society* 54 (1920–1921): 53.

28  *"48 out of 50":* Ibid.

29  *"[H]ere everyone's hand":* Maurice Cary Blake. "A Mast-Fleet Letter of 1709." *Proceedings of the Massachusetts Historical Society* 78 (1966): 136.

29  *"Nothing can Doe":* Ibid.

30  *"never had right":* Robert Greenhalgh Albion. *Forests and Sea Power: The Timber Problem of the Royal Navy, 1652–1862.* Hamden, CT: Archon Books, 1965, 254.

31  *"in the Execution":* "Benning Wentworth to Roger Wolcott, June 25, 1753." *Collections*

*of the Connecticut Historical Society,* vol. XV. Hartford: Connecticut Historical Society, 1916, 310.

31 *"was a man of sound":* Timothy Dwight. *Travels; in New-England and New-York,* vol. IV. New Haven: Timothy Dwight, 1822, 162.

31 *"singled out one man":* John Wentworth to the Earl of Hillsborough, October 22, 1770. In Paul Wilderson. *Governor John Wentworth & the American Revolution: The English Connection.* Hanover, NH: University Press of New England, 1994, 163.

31 *This approach to enforcement:* "The King's Woods," 56.

32 *"especially when all":* The *New-Hampshire Gazette, and Historical Chronicle,* August 21, 1767, 1.

32 *"to make use of":* Journals *of Each Provincial Congress of Massachusetts in 1774 and 1775.* Boston, 1838, 139, n. 4. In William R. Carlton. "New England Masts and the King's Navy." *New England Quarterly* 12, no. 1 (1939): 11.

33 *"the lack of masts":* Albion, 282.

33 *"peeping out":* Malcolm Freiberg. "An Unknown Stamp Act Letter." *Proceedings of the Massachusetts Historical Society,* Third Series, 78 (1966): 140.

34 *"How Glorious is":* Ibid., 141.

34 *"[t]hree Guineas was":* Ibid., 140.

34 *"with great solemnity":* Ibid., 141.

34 *"the Affair at Liberty Tree":* Connecticut Courant, February 17, 1766, 2.

34 *Local carpenters pruned:* Boston Evening Post, February 17, 1766, 2.

35 *"What better thing":* Quoted in Eric Sloane. *A Reverence for Wood.* New York: Funk, 1965, 75.

35 *"a good deal above":* Francis Bernard. *Letters to the Ministry from Governor Bernard, General Gage, and Commodore Hood.* Salem, MA: Samuel Hall, near the Town-House, 1769, 18.

35 *"an Idol for the Mob":* Douglass Adair and John A. Schutz, eds. *Peter Oliver's Origin & Progress of the American Rebellion: A Tory View (1781).* Palo Alto, CA: Stanford University Press, 1961, 54.

36 *"tore [the effigies]":* Boston Evening Post, November 4, 1765, 3.

36 *"I do hereby":* Boston News-Letter and New-England Chronicle, December 19, 1765, supp. 2.

36 *"regaled themselves on":* Boston Post Boy, May 19, 1766, 2.

36 *"as a standing monument":* Boston News-Letter and New-England Chronicle, May 22, 1766, supp. 2.

37 *The grantor stated that:* Newport Mercury, April 14–April 21, 1766, 3.

37 *A letter posted in:* Boston Evening Post, April 6, 1767, 2.

37 *"the everlasting Remembrance":* Boston Post Boy, August 18, 1767, 3.

38 *The traders posted:* Broadside. "Tradesmen's Protest Against the Proceedings of the Merchants." Boston: E. Russell, next the Cornfield, Union Street, November 3, 1773, collection of the Massachusetts Historical Society.

38 *"impossible for [them]":* Essex Gazette, November 2–November 9, 1773, 59.

39 *"After a long Spell":* Connecticut Courant, September 4, 1775, 2.

39 *"The tree of liberty":* Thomas Jefferson. "Letter to Colonel Smith, November 13, 1787." In H. A. Washington, ed., *The Writings of Thomas Jefferson: Being His Autobiography, Correspondence, Reports, Messages, Addresses, and Other Writings, Official and Private,* vol. II. New York: John C. Riker, 1853, 319.

## 2: The Fruits of Union

41 *"zealously testified":* Benjamin Smith Barton. *Philadelphia Medical and Physical Journal,* part I, vol. I. Philadelphia: T. & G. Palmer, 116, High-Street, 1804, 121–22.

41 *"[h]e seemed to have been":* Ibid., 117.

41 *"most of his medicines":* Ibid.

41 *In September 1728, Bartram:* Technically, several other gardens predated his. In 1694, German Pietists, for example, inaugurated a garden on the lower Wissahickon Creek

in order to grow and study medicinal plants. Bartram's garden, nonetheless, was the most well-known, historically important, and comprehensive, and the first created by a native-born American.

42 *"I was on top of the tree":* William Darlington. *Memorials of John Bartram and Humphry Marshall with Notices of Their Botanical Contemporaries.* Philadelphia: Lindsay & Blakiston, 1849, 227.

42 *"encouraged [him] to persist":* Barton, 118.

42 *"to the curious in Europe":* Ibid.

43 *"Thee need not collect":* Peter Collinson to John Bartram, March 12, 1735. Darlington, 73.

43 *"exert[ing] thyself out":* Collinson to Bartram, December 14, 1737. Darlington, 105.

43 *"There is nothing more":* Batty Langley. *New Principles of Gardening.* London: A. Bettesworth and J. Batley in Pater-Noster Row; J. Pemberton in Fleetstreet; T. Bowles in *St. Paul's Church-Yard;* J. Clarke, under the Royal Exchange; and J. Bowles at Mercer's Hall in Cheapside, 1728, x.

43 *"planted out about ten thousand":* Collinson to Bartram, September 1, 1741. Darlington, 145.

43 *"[They] are suspected both":* Collinson to Bartram, March 30, 1751. Darlington, 367.

43 *"transport[ing] the rogue":* Collinson to Bartram, August 21, 1766. Darlington, 282.

44 *"within less than half a century":* Mark Catesby. Preface to *Hortus Britanno Americanus; or, a Curious Collection of Trees and Shrubs, the Produce of the British Colonies in North America.* London: W. Richardson and S. Clark for John Ryall, 1763, iii.

44 *"As to the Society":* Collinson to Bartram, July 10, 1739. Darlington, 132.

44 *"And as the Wildernesses":* "A Copy of the Subscription Paper, for the Encouragement of Mr. John Bartram, promised in our last." *Pennsylvania Gazette,* March 17, 1742, 3.

45 *"Americans have not zeal":* Bartram to Collinson, December 18, 1742. Darlington, 162.

45 *"all new-discovered plants":* "A Proposal for Promoting Useful Knowledge Among the British Plantations in America," May 14, 1743. Reprinted in Jared Sparks. *The Works of Benjamin Franklin,* vol. VI. Philadelphia: Childs & Peterson, 602 Arch St., 1840, 14–17.

45 *"nearly the whole load":* Carl van Doren. "The Beginnings of the American Philosophical Society." *Proceedings of the American Philosophical Society* 87 (1943): 287.

45 *"The communication between":* Benjamin Franklin to Bartram, May 27, 1777. Darlington, 406.

46 *"more of the North American":* Bartram to Collinson, September 30, 1763. Darlington, 254.

46 *"the greatest natural botanist":* Samuel Miller. *A Brief Retrospect of the Eighteenth Century,* vol. III. London: J. Johnson, St. Paul's Churchyard, 1805, 232. Linnaeus's quotation appears in nearly all Bartram biographies, though the original source appears to be lost.

46 *"Boxes of seeds":* Humphry Marshall. *Arbustrum Americanum: The American Grove, or, An Alphabetical Catalogue of Forest Trees and Shrubs.* Philadelphia: Joseph Crukshank, in Market-Street, Between Second and Third-Streets, 1785, back page.

47 *"study the productions":* Henry Savage, Jr., and Elizabeth Savage. *André and François André Michaux.* Charlottesville: University Press of Virginia, 1986, 34.

47 *Additionally, of the eighteen:* Ibid., 275–76.

47 *One shipment from March 1786:* Ibid., 63.

47 *"on a par with all":* Ibid., 35.

48 *"The greatest service":* Thomas Jefferson. "Appendix to Memoir: Note G." In Thomas Jefferson Randolph, ed. *Memoirs, Correspondence, and Private Papers of Thomas Jefferson.* London: Henry Colburn and Richard Bentley, New Burlington Street, 1829, 144.

48 *"Before this scheme":* Bartram to Collinson, September 30, 1763. Darlington, 254–55.

48 *"Jefferson and several other":* Caspar Wistar to Moses Marshall, June 20, 1792. Darlington, 570.

48    *"I proposed to several":* Charles Sprague Sargent. *Journal of André Michaux, 1787–1796.* *Proceedings of the American Philosophy Society* 26, no. 129 (1888), 89–90. Author's translation.

48    *"Bound by all manner":* André Michaux. "Exposition of the Basis upon which I have resolved to undertake the journey to the West of the Mississippi." In Savage and Savage, 131.

49    *one of Jefferson's greatest:* Jefferson to Benjamin Barton, February 27, 1803. In H. A. Washington, ed., *The Writings of Thomas Jefferson,* vol. IV. New York: H. W. Derby, 1861, 470.

50    *"I can't tell a lie, Pa":* M. L. Weems. *The Life of George Washington; with Curious Anecdotes Equally Honourable to Himself and Exemplary to His Young Countrymen.* Philadelphia: Joseph Allen, 1833, 13–14.

50    *"[W]e went through":* Jared Sparks. *The Writings of George Washington,* vol. II. Boston: Russell, Odiorne, and Metcalf, and Hilliard, Gray, and Co., 1833, 416.

51    *"If he does that":* Garry Wills. *Cincinnatus: George Washington and the Enlightenment.* New York: Doubleday, 1984, 13.

51    *"I am become a private citizen":* Washington to Marie-Joseph Paul Yves Roch Gilbert du Motier, Marquis de Lafayette, February 1, 1784. George Washington Papers at the Library of Congress, 1741–1799: Series 2, Letterbooks.

51    *"Plantations . . . are now":* Washington to William Grayson, January 22, 1785. George Washington Papers at the Library of Congress, 1741–1799: Series 2, Letterbooks.

51    *His journal read: The Diaries of George Washington,* vol. 4. January 12 and 28, 1785. Donald Jackson and Dorothy Twohig, eds. *The Papers of George Washington.* Charlottesville: University Press of Virginia, 1978, 75, 81.

52    *"[e]mployed all day":* Ibid., 88. February 11, 1785.

52    *"the greatest part of the day":* Ibid., 97. March 3, 1785.

52    *"[T]hese Trees [are]":* Washington to Lund Washington, August 19, 1776. In *The Magazine of History* 2 (June–December 1905), 148–49.

52    *"tho' stored with".* *The Diaries of George Washington,* vol. 5. June 10, 1787. Donald Jackson and Dorothy Twohig, eds. *The Papers of George Washington.* Charlottesville: University Press of Virginia, 1979, 166–67.

52    *"did not answer":* *The Diaries of George Washington,* vol. 5. October 10, 1789. Ibid., 458.

53    *"I am once more seated":* Washington to James Anderson, April 7, 1797. George Washington Papers at the Library of Congress, 1741–1799: Series 2, Letterbooks.

53    *"[T]hose trees which":* Washington to the Chevalier de Chastellux, June 2, 1784. In Jared Sparks, ed. *The Writings of George Washington,* vol. IX, part III. Boston: Ferdinand Andrews, 1839, 48.

56    *"We were sadly disappointed":* Collinson to Bartram, February 1759. Darlington, 217.

56    *"They have no apple":* Jefferson to Madison, October 28, 1785. In George Bancroft. *History of the Formation of the Constitution of the United States of America,* vol. I, 3rd edition. New York: D. Appleton and Company, 1883, 465.

57    *"Learn, reader, to prize":* "In Honor of American Beer and Cyder." *Pennsylvania Mercury,* July 15, 1788, 3.

57    *"Cider is to be":* Henri L. Bourdin et al., eds. *Sketches of Eighteenth Century America: More "Letters from an American Farmer" by St. John de Crèvecoeur.* New York: Benjamin Blom, 1972, 49.

57    *"a new apple orchard":* Ibid., 102.

58    *"[W]ithin three years":* Peter Hatch. *The Fruits and Fruit Trees of Monticello.* Charlottesville: University Press of Virginia, 1998, 17.

59    *"he would go off":* "The History of the Life of Johnny Appleseed [From (Hovey's) Horticultural Magazine]." *Boston Evening Transcript,* April 18, 1846, 4.

59    *"Refusing all offers":* "Johnny Appleseed: A Pioneer Hero." *Harper's New Monthly Magazine* 43, no. 258 (November 1871): 833.

60    *"After talking about his nurseries":* *Ohio Liberal,* August 13, 20, 1873. In Robert Price. *Johnny Appleseed: Man and Myth.* Bloomington: Indiana University Press, 1954, 113.

60  *"intended for the purpose":* Report of the Society for Printing, Publishing and Circulating the Writings of Emanuel Swedenborg. Manchester, England, January 14, 1817. In Price, 120.

61  *"The gradual change":* L. H. Bailey. *The Apple-Tree.* New York: Macmillan, 1922, 62.

62  *"Serene, not sullen":* Lord Byron. *Eulogy on Colonel Boon, and Choice of Life.* In *Life and Adventures of Colonel Daniel Boon.* Brooklyn, NY: C. Wilder, 1823, 42.

62  *"The spit was":* Increase Mather. *An Essay for the Recording of Illustrious Providences.* Boston and London: George Calvert at the Sign of the Half-moon in Pauls Church-yard, 1684, 126.

62  *"[S]ettling ye back":* Calendar of Virginia State Papers I, 1742, 235. In Frederick Jackson Turner. *The Frontier in American History.* New York: Henry Holt, 1950, 50, n. 31. See also Floy Perkinson Gates. "The Historical Dictionary of American English in the Making." *American Speech* 6, no. 1 (October 1930): 38.

63  *Crèvecoeur, for example:* J. Hector St. John. *Letters from an American Farmer.* Dublin: John Exshaw, in Grafton Street, near Suffolk Street, 1782, 46.

63  *"[They] cut his head off":* John Filson. *The Discovery, Settlement and Present State of Kentucke.* Wilmington: James Adams, 1784, 48.

63  *"Many dark and sleepless":* Ibid.

64  *"he might have accumulated":* "Miscellaneous Articles: Colonel Boone." *Niles' Weekly Register,* from March to September 1816—vol. x. Baltimore: Franklin Press, 1816, 261.

65  *"[My] object was":* J. K. Paulding. *The Backwoodsman.* Philadelphia: M. Thomas, 1818, To The Reader.

65  *"hardly admissable":* William I. Paulding. *Literary Life of James K. Paulding.* New York: Charles Scribner, 1867, 94.

65  *"embraced a crude effort":* J. F. Cooper. Introduction to *The Spy.* London: Henry Colburn and Richard Bentley, 1831, ix.

65  *"a state of society":* Ibid., x.

66  *"early specimens will be":* J. K. Paulding. "National Literature," 1820. In Launcelot Langstaff. *Salmagundi,* vol. II. New York: Harper & Brothers, 1835, 271.

66  *"There was a peculiarity":* J. F. Cooper. *The Pioneers, or The Sources of the Susquehanna.* Boston: Houghton, Osgood and Company, 1880 (reprint), 9–10.

67  *"I'll turn my back":* Ibid., 229.

68  *"was the universal material":* Lewis Mumford. *Technics and Civilization.* New York: Harcourt, Brace & Co., 1934, 119.

68  *"society pervasively":* Brooke Hindle, ed. *America's Wooden Age: Aspects of its Early Technology.* Tarrytown, NY: Sleepy Hollow Restorations, 1975, 3.

68  *"One year with another":* Bourdin, 144.

69  *"will of course grow scarcer":* Benjamin Franklin. "An Account of the New-Invented Pennsylvania Fireplaces." In Jared Sparks, ed. *The Works of Benjamin Franklin,* vol. VI. Boston: Charles Tappan, 1844, 36.

69  *According to one historian:* John Richards. "Woodworking Machinery." *Journal of the Franklin Institute* (June 1870).

70  *"It would be difficult":* Alexis de Toqueville. *Democracy in America,* vol. I. Translated by Henry Reeve. Cambridge: Sever and Francis, 1863, 376.

## 3: The Unrivaled Nature of America

72  *In it, the narrator:* Mark Twain. *The Celebrated Jumping Frog of Calaveras County, and Other Sketches.* New York: C. H. Webb, 1867, 7, 15.

72  *"All thoughts of hunting":* "The Mammoth Trees of California." *Hutchings' California Magazine* 3, no. 9 (March 1859): 386.

72  *"[N]ow, boys, do you":* Ibid.

73  *"from 16 to 18 fathoms":* W. F. Wagner, ed. *Leonard's Narrative: Adventures of Zenas Leonard, Fur Trader and Trapper, 1831–1836.* Cleveland: Burrows Brothers Company, 1904, 180.

73  *"This tree employed"*: "The Mammoth Trees of California," 390–91.

74  *"dreadfully shocked"*: "The Big Tree at the World's Fair." *Daily Placer Times and Transcript* (San Francisco, California), June 27, 1853, 2.

74  *"[I]n taking its proportions"*: Ibid.

74  *"Nobody who has"*: "Wonder of the World at Big Tree Pavilion." Broadside, New York: Powers & Macgowan, 1871.

74  *"The average attendance"*: J. Otis Williams. *Mammoth Trees of California.* Boston: Alfred Mudge & Son, 1871, 48.

74  *"[I]t really seemed that"*: "The Mighty Cedars of California." *Daily Picayune*, August 3, 1856, 2.

75  *"The stump has been"*: "Our California Correspondence." *New York Herald*, November 23, 1857, 2.

75  *"[H]owever incredible it"*: "The Mammoth Trees of California," 390.

75  *Horace Greeley, the editor:* Horace Greeley. *An Overland Journey, from New York to San Francisco, in the Summer of 1859.* New York: C. M. Saxton, Barker & Co., 1860, 312, 315.

75  *"vast beyond any thing"*: William Cullen Bryant. *Picturesque America or, The Land We Live In.* New York: D. Appleton and Company, 1894 (revised edition; 1872), 304.

75  *"it is only a country"*: "The Mammoth Trees of California." *Hedderwick's Miscellany*, no. 2 (October 11, 1862), 29.

76  *"[I]t must have been"*: C. F. Winslow. "The Mammoth Trees of California." *Ohio State Journal*, November 1, 1854, 1.

76  *"[M]any a towering mountain"*: E. Louise Peffer. "Memorial to Congress on an Agricultural College for California, 1853." *Agricultural History* 40, no. 1 (January 1966): 56.

77  *Hutchings considered any cuttings:* "The Mammoth Trees of California," 391.

77  *"[I]t is the duty"*: *New York Herald*, December 17, 1854. In Berthold Seemann. "On the Mammoth-tree of Upper California." *Annals and Magazine of Natural History* (Third Series), no. 15 (March 1859): 172.

77  *"for public use, resort"*: *An Act authorizing a Grant to the State of California of the "Yosemite Valley," and of the Land embracing the "Mariposa Big Tree Grove,"* June 30, 1864.

77  *"At the present time the only [sequoia] grove"*: Gifford Pinchot. *A Short Account of the Big Trees of California.* Washington, D.C.: Government Printing Office, 1900.

78  *"Probably there is no part"*: A Lady (Susan Fenimore Cooper). *Rural Hours.* New York: George P. Putnam, 1850, 144, 190.

78  *And while she:* Ibid., 188, 206.

79  *"He is as ugly as sin"*: Julian Hawthorne. *Nathaniel Hawthorne and His Wife, A Biography*, vol. I. Boston and New York: Houghton Mifflin, 1884, 291.

79  *"essences unchanged by"*: Ralph Waldo Emerson. *Nature.* Boston: James Munroe and Company, 1836, 7.

79  *"In the presence of"*: Ibid., 11–13.

80  *"man of genius"*: Ralph Waldo Emerson. "The American Scholar: An Oration Delivered Before the Phi Beta Kappa Society, at Cambridge, August 31, 1837." *The Works of Ralph Waldo Emerson, Volume I: Miscellanies.* London: Macmillan, 1884, 90.

80  *While he rationalized:* Bradford Torrey, ed. *The Writings of Henry David Thoreau: Journal, 1850–September 15, 1851*, vol. II. Boston: Houghton Mifflin, 1906, 23, 25.

81  *"I went to the woods"*: Henry D. Thoreau. *Walden; or, Life in the Woods.* Boston: Ticknor and Fields, 1854, 98.

81  *"a perfect forest mirror"*: Ibid., 204.

81  *"in the midst of a young forest"*: Ibid., 124.

81  *"Instead of calling on"*: Ibid., 217–18.

82  *"something savage"*: Henry David Thoreau. *The Maine Woods.* Boston: Ticknor and Fields, 1864, 70.

82  *"The mass of men"*: Thoreau, *Walden*, 10.

82  *"the woodchoppers have"*: Ibid., 208.

83  *"Our village life would"*: Ibid., 339.

83 *"How many a man":* Ibid., 117.

83 *"[Thoreau] loved Nature":* Ralph Waldo Emerson. "Biographical Sketch of Thoreau." In Henry David Thoreau. *The Succession of Forest Trees and Wild Apples.* Boston and New York: Houghton Mifflin, 1887, 29.

84 *"I suppose that I have not":* Thoreau to Myron B. Benton, March 21, 1862. In F. B. Sanborn. *The Writings of Henry David Thoreau, Vol. VI: Familiar Letters.* Boston: Houghton Mifflin, 1906, 400.

86 *"Among all the materials":* Andrew Jackson Downing. *A Treatise on the Theory and Practice of Landscape Gardening, Adapted to North America.* New York: Wiley and Putnam, 1841, 44.

86 *William Cullen Bryant, for example:* "A New Park." *New York Evening Post,* July 3, 1844.

86 *"far more so, in many":* Andrew Jackson Downing. "A Talk About Public Parks and Gardens." In *Rural Essays.* New York: Leavitt & Allen, 1860, 139.

86 *"health, good spirits":* Ibid., 142.

87 *Public parks, according to Downing:* Ibid., 144–45.

87 *"Five hundred acres is":* "The New-York Park." In *Rural Essays,* 149–50.

87 *"Never was a more desolate":* "A Ramble in Central Park." *Harper's New Monthly Magazine,* vol. LIX, no. CCCLIII (October 1879): 691.

89 *"what else can I do":* Frederick Law Olmsted to John Hull Olmsted, September 11, 1857. In Charles E. Beveridge and David Schuyler, eds. *The Papers of Frederick Law Olmsted, Volume III: The Creation of Central Park, 1857–1861.* Baltimore: Johns Hopkins University Press, 1983, 79.

89 *"a democratic development":* Olmsted to Parke Godwin, August 1, 1958. In *The Papers of Frederick Law Olmsted, Volume III,* 3.

89 *"a mob of lazy":* Olmsted to the Board of Commissioners of the Central Park, January 22, 1861. In *The Papers of Frederick Law Olmsted, Volume III,* 314.

89 *"I should have had nothing":* Olmsted to Mariana Griswold Van Rensselaer, May 22, 1893. In *The Papers of Frederick Law Olmsted, Volume III,* 67.

90 *Their submission was:* Frederick Law Olmsted and Calvert Vaux. *Description of a Plan for the Improvement of the Central Park: "Greensward."* New York: Aldine Press, 1858 (reprinted 1868).

90 *"For the purpose":* Ibid., 14–15.

90 *"The north-east section":* Ibid., 33–34.

91 *"chiefly directed to":* Olmsted. "Park." In George Ripley and Charles A. Dana, eds. *The New American Cyclopedia: A Popular Dictionary of General Knowledge, Volume XII: Mozambique–Parr.* New York: D. Appleton and Company, 1861, 773.

91 *"It would have been difficult":* Olmsted. "Public Parks and the Enlargement of Towns." *Public Parks.* Brookline, MA: n.p., 1902, 57.

91 *"to select immediately":* Olmsted to the Board of Commissioners of the Central Park, October 16, 1857. In *The Papers of Frederick Law Olmsted, Volume III,* 108.

91 *"No tree or shrub":* Olmsted. "Instructions to All Engaged in Moving or Planting Trees or Shrubs," June 27, 1860. In *The Papers of Frederick Law Olmsted, Vol. III,* 255.

91 *"specimens of every tree":* Third Annual Report of the Board of Commissioners of the Central Park. New York: William C. Bryant & Co., 1860, 42. See also Philip J. Pauly. *Fruits and Plains: The Horticultural Transformation of America.* Cambridge, MA: Harvard University Press, 2007, 174.

91 *"or nearly ten millions":* Olmsted. "Statistical Report of the Landscape Architect." *Third General Report of the Board of Commissioners of the Department of Public Parks for the Twenty Months, from May 1, 1872, to December 31, 1873.* New York: William C. Bryant & Co., 1875, 350.

92 *"[T]he Central Park in New York":* "Cities and Parks." *Atlantic Monthly* VII, no. XLII (April 1861): 421.

92 *"the finest work of art":* "Editor's Easy Chair." *Harper's New Monthly Magazine,* August 1863, 419.

92 *"No one . . . can doubt":* "Public Parks and the Enlargement of Towns," 71.

92    *"slovenliness [as] a":* Ira Rutkow. *Bleeding Blue and Gray: Civil War Surgery and the Evolution of American Medicine.* New York: Random House, 2005, 35.

93    *"In the first two years":* George Perkins Marsh. *Man and Nature; or, Physical Geography as Modified by Human Action.* New York: Charles Scribner, 1864, 296.

93    *"the fountainhead of":* Lewis Mumford. *The Brown Decades: A Study of the Arts in America, 1865–1895.* New York: Harcourt, Brace & Co., 1931, 78.

93    *"it was the general opinion":* Charles Lanman. "George Perkins Marsh." *Literary World* xiii, no. 21 (October 21, 1882): 353.

94    *"I have had occasion both":* Marsh to Asa Gray, May 9, 1849. Quoted in George Perkins Marsh (David Lowenthal, ed.). *Man and Nature.* Cambridge, MA: Harvard University Press, 1965, xviii.

94    *"For instance my father":* Marsh to Spencer Fullerton Baird, May 21, 1860. In Caroline Crane Marsh, compiler. *The Life and Letters of George Perkins Marsh,* vol. 1. New York: Charles Scribner's Sons, 1888, 422–23.

94    *"It was well for me":* David Lowenthal. *George Perkins Marsh: Prophet of Conservation.* Seattle: University of Washington Press, 2000, 37.

95    *"The arts of the savage":* Marsh. "Address Delivered Before the Agricultural Society of Rutland County (September 30, 1847)." In Stephen C. Trombulak, ed. *So Great a Vision: The Conservation Writings of George Perkins Marsh.* Hanover, NH: Middlebury College Press, 2001, 5.

95    *"[T]rees are no longer":* Ibid., 16–17.

95    *Marsh went so far:* Ibid., 16.

96    *"that whereas [many]":* Marsh to Spencer Fullerton Baird, May 21, 1860. In Marsh, *Life and Letters,* 422.

96    *"to show the evils":* Marsh to William Henry Seward, July 7, 1863. In Lowenthal, *George Perkins Marsh,* 267.

96    *"Man alone":* Marsh, *Man and Nature,* 36, 39–40.

96    *"Man has too long":* Ibid., 35.

97    *"With the disappearance".* Ibid., 214, 216.

97    *"[W]e have not yet bared":* Ibid., 228.

## 4: Forests of Commerce

99    *"a part of the great":* Quoted in "The Age of Steam and Its Marvels—Movement of the Iron Horse 'Across the Continent.'" *Brotherhood of Locomotive Engineers' Monthly Journal* 3 (1869): 294.

100   *"We have the honor":* Ibid., 193.

100   *The multiple speakers:* Quoted in "The Celebration of the Completion of the Pacific Railroad, in Salt Lake City, May 11, 1869." *Latter-Day Saints' Millennial Star,* June 19, 1869, 397.

101   *"the rails are of pine":* Philip Thomas et al. "Rail Road." *Niles' Weekly Register,* June 23, 1827.

101   *"A twenty-foot bar":* "Wooden Railways." *Scientific American,* April 15, 1871.

102   *"To any engineer":* David Stevenson. *A Sketch of the Civil Engineering of North America.* London: John Weale, 1859 (second edition), 146.

103   *"a whirlwind of bright sparks":* Charles Dickens. *American Notes for General Circulation,* vol. 1. London: Chapman and Hall, 186, Strand, 1842, 165.

103   *"They used dry pitch-pine":* Judge J. L. Gillis to William H. Brown, June 24, 1870. Quoted in William H. Brown, *The History of the First Locomotives in America.* New York: D. Appleton and Company, 1871, 190–91.

104   *"The moment of passing":* "Observations on some points relating to the Construction of Rail-roads." *Journal of the Franklin Institute* 12 (1833): 155.

104   *"among the very best":* "Destruction of Our Forests." *New York Times,* October 21, 1874.

104   *"It is estimated that":* "Railroad Consumption of Timber." *Annapolis Gazette,* July 15, 1873.

105   *"That devilish Iron Horse":* Thoreau, *Walden,* 208.

105    *"Even where railroads":* Andrew S. Fuller. *The Forest Tree Culturist: A Treatise on the Cultivation of American Forest Trees.* New York: Geo. E & F. W. Woodward, No. 37 Park Row, 1866, 12.

106    *"saw how often brewers":* Frederick Weyerhaeuser. "Some Recollections of Grandfather's Early Days." In Louise L. Weyerhaeuser. *Frederick Weyerhaeuser: Pioneer Lumberman.* Minneapolis: McGill Lithograph Company, 1940, 23.

106    *"the work didn't suit":* Ibid., 25.

106    *"expecting to learn":* Ibid., 26.

106    *"The secret of this":* Ibid., 27.

109    *"Upon the rivers which":* Congressional Globe, 32nd Congress, 1st Session, 1851–52, App. 25: 851. Quoted in Jenks Cameron. *The Development of Governmental Forest Control in the United States.* Baltimore: Johns Hopkins University Press, 1928, 135.

109    *"the stalwart sons":* Congressional Globe, 32nd Congress, 1st Session, App., 389. Quoted in Cameron, 138, n. 25.

110    *The local paper described it:* Rock Island Daily Union, August 12, 1869. Quoted in Ralph W. Hidy, Frank Ernest Hill, and Allan Nevins. *Timber and Men: The Weyerhaeuser Story.* New York: Macmillan, 1963, 30.

111    *"The Chippewa valley might":* Frederick E. Weyerhaeuser. *A Record of the Life and Business Activities of Frederick Weyerhaeuser, 1834–1914.* Unpublished manuscript, 127, 169. Quoted in *Timber and Men,* 43.

111    *"For a mill man":* Matthew G. Norton. *The Mississippi River Logging Company: An Historical Sketch,* n.p. 1912, 13.

111    *"Many members of the Mississippi":* Quoted in *Timber and Men,* 42.

112    *"This was enough to":* Norton, 15–16.

113    *"He could see from":* Ibid., 42.

114    *"saw the importance":* Ibid., 56.

114    *"to cover and govern":* Quoted in *Timber and Men,* 74.

114    *"[H]is associates place him":* "A Pine Land King: Earning a Dollar a Day Thirty Years Ago, Now Controlling $100,000,000." *Times Picayune,* quoting the *Milwaukee Sentinel,* November 9, 1887.

114    *"can hardly be comprehended":* Norton, 82.

114    *"[Weyerhaeuser] has at last":* "A Great Lumber 'Combine.'" *New York Times,* May 28, 1888.

115    *The first historian of lumbering:* George W. Hotchkiss. *History of the Lumber and Forest Industry of the Northwest.* Chicago: George W. Hotchkiss, 1898, 641.

115    *"Trees, trees everywhere":* Peter Pernin. "The Great Peshtigo Fire: An Eyewitness Account." *Wisconsin Magazine of History* 54 (1971): 247.

116    *"To my mind":* Isaac Stephenson. *Recollections of a Long Life, 1829–1915.* Chicago: privately printed, 1915, 163.

116    *"the forests and brush":* Ibid., 175.

117    *"It is as though you":* Green Bay Advocate, October 5, 1871. Quoted in "Great Peshtigo Fire," 250.

117    *"Unless we have rain":* Marinette and Peshtigo Eagle, October 7, 1871. Quoted in Stewart Holbrook. *Burning an Empire: The Story of American Forest Fires.* New York: Macmillan, 1943, 65.

117    *"There seemed to be a vague":* "Great Peshtigo Fire," 252.

117    *"This sound resembled":* Ibid., 254.

118    *"[the banks] were covered":* Ibid., 257.

118    *"we struggled all night":* Stephenson, 176.

119    *"a scene with whose":* "Great Peshtigo Fire," 260.

119    *"there was nothing left":* Stephenson, 180.

119    *"In the glory of this":* New York Tribune, October 20, 1871. Quoted in Alfred L. Sewell. *The Great Calamity!* Chicago: Alfred L. Sewell, 1871, 94.

119    *"[W]here the forest had":* Stephenson, 176.

120    *"the fire [was] directly":* Ibid., 186.

120    *"I was pleased to find"*: C. C. Washburn. "Governor's Message." *Journal of the Proceedings of the Twenty-Sixth Annual Session of the Wisconsin State Senate.* Madison: Atwood & Culver, 1873, appendix, 24.

121    *"The BellCart will go"*: *Boston Post-Boy,* March 9, 1767, 2.

122    *"Who shall write"*: "Discoveries in Making Paper." *New York Tribune,* April 16, 1866.

122    *"Paper is too high"*: "Paper Mills." *New England Farmer,* February 1867.

122    *"Industry and science had"*: "Discoveries in Making Paper."

123    *"if [the owners] succeed"*: Ibid.

123    *"Poplar wood," wrote*: "Paper from Wood." *Ohio Farmer,* September 19, 1868.

123    *"Poplar wood wanted"*: *Philadelphia Inquirer,* May 11, 1866.

123    *"In our own country"*: "The Exhaustion of Our Timber Supply." *Bankers' Magazine and Statistical Register,* January 1877.

124    *"With the rapidly increasing"*: "Ten Thousand Tons Daily." *Maine Farmer,* August 2, 1894.

125    *"The invention of wood pulp"*: "Manufacture of Paper Pulp from Wood." *Scientific American* 45 (1881): 296.

125    *"Some philosopher has said"*: "Ten Thousand Tons Daily."

125    *"At first, wood pulp was used"*: "Our Wood Pulp Industry." *Scientific American* 65 (1891): 121.

126    *"[T]he original forests cannot"*: Gifford Pinchot. *The Adirondack Spruce.* New York: Critic Co., 1898, 1, 31.

128    *"There is scarcely"*: U.S. Department of Agriculture. *Report of the Commissioner of Agriculture for the Year 1883.* Washington, D.C.: Government Printing Office, 1883, 452–53.

## 5: A Changing Consciousness

130    *"I remember that we"*: J. Sterling Morton. "Address." In *Council Journal of the Legislative Assembly of the Territory of Nebraska, Sixth Session.* Nebraska City: Thomas Morton of the Nebraska City News, 1860, 169.

131    *"as a vigorous and colorful"*: James C. Olson. *J. Sterling Morton.* Lincoln: University of Nebraska Press, 1942, vii.

131    *"must die, and a few years"*: Morton, "Address," 176.

131    *"defrauded [Nebraskans]"*: Ibid., 172.

131    *"his farm . . . is one"*: A. C. Edmunds. *Pen Sketches of Nebraskans.* Lincoln, NE: R. & J. Wilbur, 1871, 251.

131    *"to prepare and publish"*: *Transactions.* Nebraska State Horticultural Society, 1871, 17. In Olson, 162.

132    *"There is comfort in"*: Ibid., 163.

132    *"Resolved, That, Wednesday"*: *Fourth Annual Report of the President and Secretary of the Nebraska State Board of Agriculture.* Lincoln, NE: Journal Company, State Printers, 1873, 222.

133    *"The newspapers of the State"*: Robert Furnas. *Arbor Day.* Lincoln, NE: State Journal Company, 1888, 8.

133    *"There is a true triumph"*: *Omaha Daily Herald,* April 17, 1872. In Olson, 165.

133    *"the whole people of the state"*: Furnas, 9.

133    *"shall hereafter, in a popular sense"*: See N. H. Egleston. *Arbor Day: Its History and Observance.* Washington, D.C.: Government Printing Office, 1896, 16.

133    *"No observance ever sprang"*: Ibid.

133    *"Arbor Day' . . . is not like"*: Ibid., 22.

135    *"I do not believe that"*: *Report of the Commissioner of the General Land Office for the Year 1867.* Washington, D.C.: Government Printing Office, 1867, 135.

135    *"to improve the climatic conditions"*: Egleston, 77.

136    *"to encourage the growth"*: *Congressional Globe and Appendix, Second Session, Forty-Second Congress, Part II.* Washington, D.C.: F. & J. Rives & Geo. A Bailey, 1872, 1129.

136    *"The object of this"*: Ibid., 4464.

136    *"I have never seen": Annual Report of the Commissioner of the General Land Office for the Year 1885.* Washington, D.C.: Government Printing Office, 1885, 51.

136    *"[B]y the timber-culture act":* J. Sterling Morton. "Arbor Day." *Outing* 7 (1885): 319.

138    *"to encourage manly":* William H. H. Murray. *Adventures in the Wilderness; or, Camp-Life in the Adirondacks.* Boston: Fields, Osgood & Co., 1869, 8.

138    *"[The Adirondack] region is now": New York Times,* February 13, 1872.

139    *"Within an easy day's ride": New York Times,* August 9, 1864.

139    *"The interests of commerce":* Verplanck Colvin. "Ascent of Mount Seward and Its Barometrical Measurement." New York State Senate Documents, 1871, No. 68. Republished in *The Twenty-Fourth Annual Report of the New York State Museum of Natural History.* Albany: Argus Company, 1872, 180.

139    *"to inquire into the expediency":* An Act to Appoint Commissioners of Parks for the State of New York, May 23, 1872. In *Laws of the State of New York,* vol. II. Albany: V. W. M. Brown, 1872, 2006.

140    *It determined that protecting: Documents of the Senate of the State of New York, Ninety-Sixth Session—1873,* vol. 4. Albany: Argus Company, 1873, 3.

140    *"Without a steady":* Ibid., 10.

140    *"The matter is reduced": New York Tribune,* November 27, 1883. In Frank Graham, Jr. *The Adirondack Park: A Political History.* New York: Knopf, 1978, 97.

141    *"There is nothing":* New York (State) Forestry Commission. *Report of the Forestry Commission Appointed by the Comptroller Pursuant to Chapter 551, laws of 1884.* Albany: Legislative printers, 1885, 17.

141    *"it is an open boast":* Ibid.

142    *"The lands now or":* An Act to establish a forest commission, and to define its powers and duties and for the preservation of forests, May 15, 1885. In *Laws of the State of New York, passed at the One Hundred and Eighth Session of the Legislature.* Albany: Banks & Brothers, 1885, 482.

142    *"We are not responsible":* "The Mountains Denuded." *New York Times,* September 22, 1889.

143    The New York Times *warned:* "That Adirondack Park." *New York Times,* January 22, 1890.

144    *"a future timber supply":* An Act to establish the Adirondack park and to authorize the purchase and sale of lands within the counties including the forest preserve, May 20, 1892.

144    *"all revenues from":* Roswell P. Flower. "Memorandum filed with Assembly bill, chap. 707, to establish the Adirondack Park." In Charles Z. Lincoln, ed. *State of New York Messages from the Governors,* vol. IX. Albany: J. B. Lyon Company, 1909, 146.

144    *"It would seem that":* "Lumbering on State Lands." *Garden and Forest,* April 18, 1894, 151.

144    *"I am convinced":* Alfred L. Donaldson. *A History of the Adirondacks.* New York: Century Co., 1921, 188.

144    *"You have brought":* Ibid., 190.

144    *"The lands of the State":* New York State Constitution of 1894, Article VII, Section 7.

145    *"in a month's worship":* Ralph L. Rusk, ed. *The Letters of Ralph Waldo Emerson,* vol. 6. New York: Columbia University Press, 1939, 154.

146    *"a great many dried":* James Bradley Thayer. *A Western Journey with Mr. Emerson.* Boston: Little, Brown and Company, 1884, 90.

146    *"talked of the trees":* Ibid., 101.

146    *"You are yourself a sequoia":* John Muir. "The Forests of the Yosemite Park." *Atlantic Monthly* 85 (1900): 506.

146    *"[Muir] is more wonderful":* John Swett. "John Muir." *Century Magazine* 46 (1893): 120.

146    *"fond of everything":* John Muir. "My Boyhood." *Atlantic Monthly* 110 (1912): 577.

147    *"Fire was not allowed":* Quoted in Ray Stannard Baker. "John Muir." *Outlook* 74 (1903): 367.

147    *"I felt neither pain":* Ibid., 371.

147    *"This affliction has":* Quoted in Linnie Marsh Wolfe. *Son of the Wilderness: The Life of John Muir.* New York: Alfred A. Knopf, 1945, 105.

147 *"joyful and free"*: John Muir. *A Thousand-Mile Walk to the Gulf.* Boston: Houghton Mifflin, 1916, 1.

148 *"We are now in the mountains"*: John Muir. *My First Summer in the Sierra.* Boston: Houghton Mifflin, 1911, 20–21.

148 *"Few men whom I"*: Charles Sprague Sargent. "John Muir." *Sierra Club Bulletin* 10 (1916): 37.

148 *"No other coniferous forest"*: John Muir. "The Wild Parks and Forest Reservations of the West." *Atlantic Monthly* 81 (1898): 27.

149 *During his first eighteen months:* John Muir. "The Bee-Pastures of California." *Century Magazine* 24 (1882): 226.

149 *"The groves were God's"*: Parke Godwin, ed. *The Poetical Works of William Cullen Bryant,* vol. 1. New York: D. Appleton and Company, 1883, 130.

149 *"Thousands of tired"*: Muir, "Wild Parks and Forest Reservations of the West," 15.

150 *"[l]ike Thoreau"*: Ibid., 16.

150 *"I can't make my way"*: Robert Underwood Johnson. *Remembered Yesterdays.* Boston: Little, Brown and Company, 1923, 279–80.

150 *"Obviously the thing"*: Ibid., 287.

151 *"These king trees"*: John Muir. "The Treasures of the Yosemite." *Century Magazine* 40 (1890): 487.

151 *"[T]he bill cannot too quickly"*: John Muir. "Features of the Proposed Yosemite National Park." *Century Magazine* 40 (1890): 667.

152 *"[T]he Yosemite bill is"*: Johnson to Muir, October 3, 1890. University of the Pacific Library Holt-Atherton Special Collections. Available at www.oac.cdlib.org.

152 *"To John Muir more"*: "John Muir." *New York Times,* December 25, 1914.

153 *"How would you like"*: Gifford Pinchot. *Breaking New Ground.* New York: Harcourt, Brace, 1947, 1.

153 *"As a boy it was"*: Ibid., 2.

153 *"an amazing question"*: Ibid., 1.

154 *"something far outside"*: Ibid.

154 *"Forestry has excited"*: *Report of the Commissioner of Agriculture for the Year 1875.* Washington, D.C.: Government Printing Office, 1876, 211.

154 *"thought only of forest"*: Pinchot, *Breaking New Ground,* 1.

154 *"What I learned outside"*: Ibid., 4.

155 *"[M]y future profession welled"*: Ibid., 6.

155 *"[The French forests] were divided"*: Ibid., 13.

156 *"he had accomplished"*: Ibid., 9.

156 *"the finest private residence"*: Karl Baedeker. *The United States with an Excursion into Mexico.* Revised third edition. Leipzig: Karl Baedeker, 1904, 432.

156 *"the beginning of practical"*: Pinchot, *Breaking New Ground,* 50.

157 *"slipped through Congress"*: Ibid., 85.

157 *"That the President"*: 26 Stat. 1095, Section 24.

158 *"a commission composed"*: "Topics of the Time: The Need of a National Forest Commission." *Century Magazine* 49 (1895): 635.

159 *"Heavy rain during"*: Linnie Marsh Wolfe, ed. *John of the Mountains: The Unpublished Diaries of John Muir.* Madison: University of Wisconsin Press, 1979, 357.

159 *"[T]he birth of the Father"*: *Report of the National Academy of Sciences for the Year 1897.* Washington, D.C.: Government Printing Office, 1898, 18.

159 *"I will veto"*: Johnson, *Remembered Yesterdays,* 300.

160 *"Except for the Act of 1891"*: Pinchot, *Breaking New Ground,* 116.

160 *"[E]verybody I consulted"*: Ibid., 135–36.

161 *"I had the honor"*: Ibid., 145.

162 *"Public opinion throughout"*: *Papers Relating to the Foreign Relations of the United States, with the Annual Message of the President Transmitted to Congress December 3, 1901.* Washington, D.C.: Government Printing Office, 1902, xxvi.

163 *"It is doubtful whether"*: Theodore Roosevelt. *An Autobiography.* New York: Macmillan Company, 1913, 436.

163   *"The Bureau has":* N. W. McLeod. "The Lumberman's Interest in Forestry." *Proceedings of the American Forest Congress.* Washington, D.C.: H. M. Suter Publishing Company, 1905, 99.

163   *"Mr. Weyerhaeuser wishes me":* F. E. Weyerhaeuser. "Interest of Lumbermen in Conservative Forestry." Ibid., 141.

163   *"Irrigation and forestry are":* James Hill. "Letter from Mr. James J. Hill." Ibid., 290.

164   *"For us in the Forest Service":* Pinchot, *Breaking New Ground,* 258–59.

164   *"always be decided":* Ibid., 261–62.

164   *"Forest reserves are open":* Gifford Pinchot. *The Use of the National Forest Reserves.* Washington, D.C.: Government Printing Office, 1905, 6.

164   *"In a word, the Federal Government":* George L. Knapp. "The Other Side of Conservation." *North American Review* 191 (1910): 465–81.

164   *"The poor sawmills!":* "Another National Blunder." *Forestry & Irrigation* IX (1903): 261.

164   *"than during all previous":* Roosevelt, *An Autobiography,* 441.

165   *"nothing more than":* Ibid., 422.

165   *"In its broad sense":* Gifford Pinchot. "How Conservation Began in the United States." *Agricultural History* 11 (1937): 265.

165   *"Pinchot is a socialist":* Archibald Butt to Mrs. Lewis F. Butt, April 12, 1910. Quoted in Archibald Willingham Butt. *Taft and Roosevelt: The Intimate Letters of Archie Butt, Military Aide, Vol. 1.* Garden City, NY: Doubleday, Doran & Company, Inc., 1930, 328.

166   *"Dam Hetch Hetchy!":* John Muir. "The Hetch-Hetchy Valley." *Sierra Club Bulletin* 6 (1908): 220.

167   *"Gifford Pinchot is the man":* Roosevelt, *An Autobiography,* 429.

## 6: New Frontiers

168   *"As the orange industry":* James Ingraham. Address before the Women's Club of Miami, November 12, 1920. Quoted in *History of Florida: Past and Present,* vol. 1. Chicago: Lewis Publishing Company, 1923, 64.

169   *"No, sir":* Quoted in Edwin Lefevre. "Flagler and Florida." *Everybody's Magazine* XII (1910): 183.

169   *"merely stations in the great forest":* William Cullen Bryant. "A Letter from William Cullen Bryant: Some Observations and Reflections on East Florida." *Friends' Intelligencer* XXX (1873): 121.

169   *"On the more fertile":* Ibid.

170   *"You can use $50,000":* History of Florida, 66.

170   *"to prove [Tuttle's] point":* Quoted in David Leon Chandler. *Henry Flagler: The Astonishing Life and Times of the Visionary Robber Baron who Founded Florida.* New York: Macmillan, 1986, 168.

170   *"How soon can you arrange":* History of Florida, 65.

171   *"There were hundreds":* Ibid.

172   *"The oranges . . . were":* "Report of the Committees of Award at the Fifth Annual Fair and Cattle-Show of the California State Agricultural Society." In *Transactions of the California State Agricultural Society During the Year 1858.* Sacramento: John O'Meara, State-Printer for California, 1859, 121.

172   *"We wish to form":* J. W. North. "A Colony for California." Knoxville, TN, March 17, 1870. Reprinted in Tom Patterson. *A Colony for California: Riverside's First Hundred Years.* Riverside, CA: Press-Enterprise Company, 1971, 19.

172   *"Its course is eleven miles":* The County of San Bernardino, California, and its Principal City. San Bernardino, CA: Board of Trade, 1888, 52–54.

173   *"[She] was anxious":* P. H. Dorsett et al. *The Navel Orange of Bahia; with Notes on Some Little-Known Brazilian Fruits.* United States Department of Agriculture, Bulletin No. 445, February 10, 1917, 5.

173 *"We . . . sampled":* Quoted in A. H. Naftzger. "Orange-Growing in California." In T. G. Daniells, ed. *California: Its Products, Resources, Industries and Atrractions.* Sacramento, CA: W. W. Shannon, 1904, 73.

173 *"The Washington Navel stands":* O. P. Chubb. "California Citrus Fruits, Markets, Etc." In *Second Biennial Report of the California State Board of Forestry for the Years 1887–88.* Sacramento: J. D. Young, 1888, 219.

174 *"The premiums won":* Edward J. Wickson. *The California Fruits and How to Grow Them.* San Francisco: Dewey & Co., 1889, 439.

174 *"Los Angeles and the southern":* Sunset XXVI (1911): 3.

174 *"With all the trees":* Wickson, 439.

175 *"The cultivation of the orange":* L. M. Holt. "The Future of Citrus Culture in California." In *Official Report of the Ninth Fruit Growers' Convention of the State of California.* Sacramento, CA: J. D. Young, 1888, 74.

175 *"was largely believed":* Kevin Starr. *Inventing the Dream: California Through the Progressive Era.* New York: Oxford University Press, 1985, 143.

176 *"If specialized farming":* Carey McWilliams. *Factories in the Field: The Story of Migratory Farm Labor in California.* Boston: Little, Brown and Company, 1939, 65.

176 *"California citrus culture":* J. Eliot Coit. *Citrus Fruits.* New York: Macmillan, 1915, 10.

177 *"the demand for choice":* Holt, 220.

178 *"Sunkist has been advertised":* Don Francisco. "Putting California Citrus on the Map." *Advertising Age,* October 1917, 37.

178 *The title read:* "Drink an Orange!" *Simmons' Spice Mill XXXIX* (1916): 74.

178 *"Try it for ten days": Good Housekeeping,* January 1917, inside cover.

179 *"People in the United States":* John McPhee. *Oranges.* New York: Farrar, Straus and Giroux, 1967, 7–8.

179 *"extinction of the forests":* Charles S. Sargent. *Report on the Forests of North America (Exclusive of Mexico).* Washington, D.C.: Government Printing Office, 1884, 489.

180 *"The country between":* Ibid.

180 *Sargent's* Report *estimated:* F. P. Baker. "Report on the Condition of Forests, Timber-Culture, Etc., in the Southern and Western States." In Nathaniel H. Egleston, ed. *Report on Forestry,* vol. IV. Washington, D.C.. Government Printing Office, 1884, 108.

180 *"The stately trunks":* F. V. Emerson. "The Southern Long-Leaf Pine Belt." *Geographical Review* VII (1919): 81.

180 *"It is to the extreme South":* Baker, 106.

180 *"Southern pine is rapidly":* M. B. Hillyard. *The New South.* Baltimore: Manufacturers' Record Co., 1887, 40.

181 *"English and Northern capitalists":* Baker. "Report by States Respecting Their Forest Condition." In Egleston, *Report on Forestry,* 194.

182 *"one of my best":* Grover Cleveland to unknown, June 17, 1904. Reprinted in C. W. Goodyear. *Bogalusa Story.* Buffalo, NY: privately printed, 1950, 52.

183 *"We're going to build":* Ibid., 43.

184 *"A belt of this size":* Ibid., 74.

184 *"This is at present":* John Liston. "The Great Southern Lumber Company." *General Electric Review* XI (1908): 254.

185 *"For miserable shacks":* William D. Haywood. "Timber Workers and Timber Wolves." *International Socialist Review* XIII (1912): 106.

185 *"The fight will be":* Ibid., 110.

186 *"[t]he success of the entire labor":* Quoted in Stephen H. Norwood. "Bogalusa Burning: The War Against Biracial Unionism in the Deep South, 1919." *Journal of Southern History* 63 (1997): 612.

186 *"a reign of terror":* Frank Morrison. "Report on Situation at Bogalusa, Louisiana, by President of Louisiana State Federation of Labor." In Herbert J. Seligmann. *The Negro Faces America.* New York: Harper & Brothers Publishers, 1920, 313.

186 *"was to turn the Black men":* Quoted in Art Shields. *On the Battle Lines, 1919–1939.* New York: International Publishers, 1986, 182.

187    *"you can practically":* Advertisement. *Lumber* LXX (1922): 45.

187    *"real forest management":* Elwood R. Maunder. "Go South, Young Man: An Interview with J. E. McCaffrey." *Forest History* 8 (1965): 10.

188    *"[O]ne acre of":* Stewart H. Holbrook. *Holy Old Mackinaw: A Natural History of the American Lumberjack.* New York: Macmillan, 1956, 161.

188    *"No other American tree":* Charles Sprague Sargent. *The Silva of North America, Volume XII.* Boston: Houghton Mifflin, 1898, 91–92.

189    *"A stand of ponderosa":* Stewart H. Holbrook. *Far Corner: A Personal View of the Pacific Northwest.* New York: Macmillan, 1952, 243.

190    *"[T]he prairies . . . must":* Sargent, *Report,* 489.

190    *"The shrewd deal":* Charles P. Norcross. "Weyerhaeuser—Richer than John D. Rockefeller." *Cosmopolitan* XLII (1907): 258.

190    *In 1908:* S. A. D. Puter. *Looters of the Public Domain.* Portland, OR: Portland Printing House, 1908.

191    *"Say, you've heard":* William B. Laughead and W. H. Hutchinson. "The Birth of Paul Bunyan." *Forest History* 16 (1972): 46.

191    *"when he was but":* Frank Shay. *Here's Audacity! American Legendary Heroes.* New York: Macaulay Company, 1930, 163.

191    *"Picture a bent":* Rexford Tugwell. "The Casual of the Woods." *Survey,* July 3, 1920, 472.

192    *"As a community":* Ibid., 473.

192    *"block upon block":* Holbrook, *Far Corner,* 247.

193    *"I am a Pinchot man":* Quoted in Robert E. Ficken. "Gifford Pinchot Men: Pacific Northwest Lumbermen and the Conservation Movement, 1902–1910." *Western Historical Quarterly* 13 (1982): 166.

193    *"overshadow that":* "Weyerhaeuser—Richer Than John D. Rockefeller," 252.

194    *"The entire Northwest":* Quoted in Virgil Wirt. "Weyerhaeuser, Lumber Monarch." *Colman's Rural World* 67 (1914): 14.

194    *"This great domain":* Charles Edward Russell. "The Mysterious Octopus: Story of the Strange and Powerful Organization that Controls the American Lumber Trade." *The World To-Day* XXI (1912): 1747.

194    *"I've heard professional":* Holbrook, *Far Corner,* 233, 240.

195    *"The forest . . . is":* Ibid., 233.

195    *"[N]ature would have":* Emanuel L. Philipp. "Legislative Measures for Forest Conservation." In *The Forest Products Laboratory: A Decennial Record, 1910–1920.* Madison, WI: Democrat Printing Company, 1921, 91.

196    *"To make the most":* William B. Greeley. "Forests and National Prosperity." In *Decennial Record,* 125–26.

196    *"The properties upon":* B. E. Fernow. *Annual Report of the Division of Forestry for 1886.* Washington, D.C.: Government Printing Office, 1887, 37–38.

196    *"not germane to":* Quoted in Fernow. "Forestry Investigations and Work of the Department of Agriculture." In *Report upon the Forestry Investigations of the Department of Agriculture, 1897–1898.* Washington, D.C.: Government Printing Office, 1899, 16.

197    *"in bringing in to use":* Hearings Before the Committee on Agriculture, 59th Congress, 2nd Session. Washington, D.C.: Government Printing Office, 1907, 172.

197    *"the consolidation of these":* An Oral History Interview with McGarvey Cline, 1961, 4. Available at: http://www.foresthistory.org/ASPNET/People/Scientists/Cline.aspx.

197    *"[T]hat a laboratory":* Hearings, 173.

197    *"It can not take you":* Ibid., 176.

197    *"will save many":* Ibid., 181.

198    *"Cline conceived":* Quoted in *Decennial Record,* 21–22.

198    *"I have had few decisions":* Quoted in "Wisconsin Gets Forest Laboratory." *Conservation* XV (1909): 239.

199    *"a combined annual":* Carlisle P. Winslow. "The Forest Products Laboratory." In *Decennial Record,* 116.

## 7: Under Attack

201  *"that the entire shipment"*: J. G. Sanders to L. O. Howard, January 19, 1910. Reprinted in Roland M. Jefferson and Alan E. Fusonie. *The Japanese Flowering Cherry Trees of Washington, D.C.: A Living Symbol of Friendship*. Washington, D.C.: Agricultural Research Service, 1977, 50.

202  *"a perpetual reminder"*: Eliza Ruhamah Scidmore. "The Cherry-Blossoms of Japan: Their Season a Period of Festivity and Poetry." *Century Magazine* 79 (1910): 643.

202  *"The miracles of Japanese"*: Eliza Ruhamah Scidmore. *Jinrikisha Days in Japan*. New York: Harper & Brothers, 1891, 77.

202  *"It is not only the national flower"*: Scidmore. "Cherry-Blossoms of Japan," 643–44.

203  *"[S]ince they had"*: Ibid., 653.

203  *"a prairie boy"*: David Fairchild. *The World Was My Garden*. New York: Charles Scribner's Sons, 1938, 15.

203  *"a turning point"*: Ibid., 12.

203  *"was to 'direct my destiny'"*: Ibid., 31.

203  *"[Lathrop] began to lay"*: Ibid., 84.

203  *"philosophy of free"*: Ibid., 168.

204  *"The greatest service which"*: Thomas Jefferson. *Note G of the Appendix to His Memoir*. In Thomas Jefferson Randolph, ed. *The Writings of Thomas Jefferson, vol. 1*. Charlottesville, VA: F. Carr, and Co., 1829, 144.

204  *"I have rarely been"*: Fairchild, 254.

204  *"one of our chief"*: Ibid., 410.

205  *"to do something towards"*: Ibid., 411.

205  *"aroused the enthusiasm"*: Ibid., 412.

205  *"I [had] determined"*: Mrs. William Howard Taft. *Recollections of Full Years*. New York: Dodd, Mead & Company, 1914, 361.

206  *"I have taken the matter"*: Helen Taft to Eliza Scidmore, April 9, 1909. In Carl Sferrazza Anthony. *Nellie Taft: The Unconventional First Lady of the Ragtime Era*. New York: HarperCollins, 2005, 245.

207  *"determined to raise"*: Philip J. Pauly. "The Beauty and Menace of the Japanese Cherry Trees: Conflicting Visions of American Ecological Independence." *Isis* 87 (1996): 67.

208  *"the fact that very old"*: Charles Marlatt to Secretary of Agriculture James Wilson, January 19, 1910. Reprinted in *Japanese Flowering Cherry Trees*, 53–54.

208  *"We have been importing"*: "Wounding the Japanese Sensibilities." *New York Times*, January 31, 1910.

208  *"the greater number"*: Fairchild, 413.

208  *"[T]he only way to solve"*: Richmond Hobson. "The National Defense." Reprinted in Edwin DuBois Shurter, ed. *American Oratory of To-Day*. Austin, TX: South-West Publishing Company, 1910, 233.

209  *"As this paper goes"*: Scidmore. "Cherry-Blossoms of Japan," 643.

209  *"To be honest about it"*: Ozaki Yukio, Fujiko Hara, trans. *The Struggle for Constitutional Government in Japan: The Autobiography of Ozaki Yukio*. Princeton, NJ: Princeton University Press, 2001, 232.

209  *"[W]e are more than satisfied"*: Ozaki Yukio to Spencer Cosb, February 2, 1912. Reprinted in Fairchild, 413.

210  *"This second sending"*: Charles Marlatt. "Statement of Mr. C. L. Marlatt, Chairman of the Federal Horticultural Board, United States Department of Agriculture." *House Report No. 980 and Hearings before the Committee of Agriculture*. Washington, D.C.: Government Printing Office, 1919.

211  *"when the blossoming"*: Roosevelt, *An Autobiography*, 354.

211  *"They are plump"*: H. G. O. Blake, ed. *Autumn: From the Journal of Henry David Thoreau*. Boston: Houghton Mifflin, 1894, 404.

211  *"[T]he chestnut mast is"*: Frederick Law Olmsted. *A Journey in the Back Country*. New York: Mason Brothers, 1860, 224.

212 *"a greater variety"*: P. L. Buttrick. "Commercial Uses of the Chestnut." *American Forestry* 21 (1915): 961.

213 *"[C]hestnuts were like"*: Richard C. Davids. *The Man Who Moved a Mountain*. Philadelphia: Fortress Press, 1970, 17.

213 *"At last when the tree"*: Buttrick, 961–62.

214 *"[T]his fungus may be"*: W. A. Murrill. "A Serious Chestnut Disease." *Journal of the New York Botanical Garden* 7 (1906): 148.

214 *"liable to fall into"*: Ibid., 152.

215 *"Thousands of trees"*: "Chestnut Trees Face Destruction." *New York Times*, May 21, 1908.

215 *"[I]t is essentially"*: Haven Metcalf and J. Franklin Collins. *The Control of the Chestnut Bark Disease*. Washington, D.C.: Government Printing Office, 1911, 11.

215 *"efficient and practical means"*: Ibid., 14.

215 *"The mere fact that"*: *The Pennsylvania Chestnut Blight Conference*. Harrisburg, PA: C. E. Aughinbaugh, Printer to the State of Pennsylvania, 1912, 108–9.

216 *A participant from New York*: Ibid., 20.

216 *"I do not believe in"*: Ibid., 201.

216 *"Meyer was not"*: Fairchild, 405.

217 *"[I]t seems necessary"*: Winthrop Sargent to Governor John Tener, December 9, 1913. In *Final Report of the Pennsylvania Chestnut Tree Blight Commission*. Harrisburg, PA: Wm. Stanley Ray, State Printer, 1914, 12.

217 *"What happens as"*: "Pennsylvania Chestnut Trees to Be Sold to Save Timber Left by Blight: Gifford Pinchot, Forester, Explains the Action." *American Nut Journal* 12 (1920): 91.

217 *"a botanical Maginot line"*: Susan Freinkel. *American Chestnut: The Life, Death, and Rebirth of a Perfect Tree*. Berkeley: University of California Press, 2007, 73.

217 *"Last summer when"*: Fairchild, 406.

218 *"They cannot be used"*: C. A. Sheffield. "The Elms Go Down." *Atlantic* 182 (October 1948): 22.

218 *"[It] suggests a fountain"*: "An Avenue of Elms." *Garden and Forest*, April 19, 1893, 172.

218 *"the most magnificent vegetable"*: François André Michaux. *The North American Sylva*, vol. 3. Philadelphia: Thomas Dobson.—Solomon Conrad, 1819, 86.

219 *"the oldest and noblest"*: "The American Elm." *Garden and Forest*, June 11, 1890, 281.

219 *"New Haven, known"*: Charles Dickens. *American Notes for General Circulation*, vol. 1. London: Chapman and Hall, 186, Strand, 1842, 183.

220 *"a new longing"*: Thomas Campanella. *Republic of Shade: New England and the American Elm*. New Haven, CT: Yale University Press, 2003, 69.

220 *"one of the most generally"*: Andrew Jackson Downing. *A Treatise on the Theory and Practice of Landscape Gardening, Adapted to North America*. New York: Wiley and Putnam, 1841, 106.

220 *"The Elms of New England!"*: Henry Ward Beecher. *Norwood; or, Village Life in New England*. New York: Charles Scribner & Company, 1867, 4–5.

220 *"free-soilers in their"*: Bradford Torrey, ed. *The Writings of Henry David Thoreau: Journal, Vol. VIII*. Boston: Houghton Mifflin, 1906, 140.

221 *"It can live in"*: Berton Roueche. "A Great Green Cloud." *New Yorker*, July 15, 1961, 36.

221 *"$650,000,000 would be"*: American Forestry Association. *The American Elm: Its Glorious Past, Its Present Dilemma, Its Hope for Protection*. Washington, D.C.: American Forestry Association, 1937, 5.

223 *"There was a general"*: George Hepting. "The Threatened Elms: A Perspective on Tree Disease Control." *Journal of Forest History* 21 (1977): 92.

223 *"A half a million dollars"*: "The American Elm—Now or Never." *American Forests* 40 (1934): 521.

224 *"The first phase"*: "Fight on Elm Disease Continues." *American Forests* 41 (1935): 290.

224 *"the formal beginning"*: Richard Campana. *Arboriculture: History and Development in North America*. East Lansing: Michigan State University, 1999, 148.

224    *"Federal and state officials":* American Forestry Association, *American Elm,* 21.
225    *"We have been told":* "Wallace Asked to Clarify Charge Elms Are Doomed." *American Forests* 42 (1936): 132.
225    *"After eighteen years":* American Forestry Association, *American Elm,* 10.
225    *"Dutch elm disease and":* Campanella, 155.
225    *"It is true that":* "The Case of the Elms." *American Forests* 47 (1941): 31.
226    *"the spray would be":* "To Fight Elm Beetle: Englewood Starts Battle Today to Save 3,500 Trees." *New York Times,* May 5, 1947, 25.
226    *"To the public":* Rachel Carson. "A Report At Large: Silent Spring II." *New Yorker,* June 23, 1962, 40.
227    *"learning to live":* Hepting, 96.

## 8: Trees as Good Soldiers and Citizens

229    *In his own words: Hearings Before Subcommittee No. 1 (Aviation) of the Select Committee on Expenditures in the War Department, House of Representatives,* vol. 2. Washington, D.C.: Government Printing Office, 1919, 1364.
229    *"Equipped with a splendid":* South Haven (Mich.) *News,* December 6, 1912. Quoted in Harold M. Hyman. *Soldiers and Spruce: Origins of the Loyal Legion of Loggers and Lumbermen.* Los Angeles: University of California Press, 1963, 29.
230    *"stronger ounce for ounce":* Edward J. Fenton. "Plywood Takes to the Skies." *American Forests* 48 (July 1942): 296.
230    *"the very best":* Wilbur Wright. "Experiments and Observations in Soaring Flight." *Journal of the Western Society of Engineers* VIII (1903): 415.
230    *"We have found it":* Quoted in P. J. Dickerscheid. "When Wright Bros. Flew, Only W.Va. Spruce Would Do." Associated Press, October 14, 2009.
231    *"a very beautiful":* John Muir. "The Great Forests of Washington." *Pacific Monthly* VIII (1902): 149–50.
231    *"the Northwest had":* Hyman, 44.
231    *"Your spruce will":* Quoted in E. A. Sterling. "Flying on Wings of Spruce." *American Forestry* XXIV (1918): 133.
232    *"Being mostly men":* Brice P. Disque. "How We Found a Cure for Strikes." *System: The Magazine of Business* XXXVI (1919): 379.
232    *"spread through the region":* Robert L. Tyler. "The United States Government as Union Organizer: The Loyal Legion of Loggers and Lumbermen." *Mississippi Valley Historical Review* 47 (1960): 436.
232    *"conciliatory spirit":* Hyman, 72.
233    *"[U]nless present conditions":* "Report of President's Mediation Commission to the President of the United States." *Sixth Annual Report of the Secretary of Labor.* Washington, D.C.: Government Printing Office, 1918, 20.
233    *"wakes up and thoroughly":* Hearings, vol. 3, 3932.
233    *"presented the thing":* Hearings, vol. 2, 1371.
233    *"made it a matter":* Ibid., 1364.
234    *"The I.W.W. . . . is":* Carleton H. Parker. "The I.W.W." *Atlantic Monthly* CXX (1917): 662.
234    *"a radical departure":* History of the Spruce Production Division, United States Army and United States Spruce Production Corporation (n.p., n.d.), Introduction IV. For a discussion of this work's authorship see Hyman, 3, fn. 3.
234    *"improve the living":* "How We Found a Cure for Strikes," 383.
235    *"[Disque] has full":* Quoted in Hyman, 123.
235    *It was also possible:* See Robert E. Ficken. "The Wobbly Horrors: Pacific Northwest Lumbermen and the Industrial Workers of the World, 1917–1918." *Labor History* 24 (1983): 325–41.
235    *"Its sole hold":* Ralph Winstead. "Enter a Logger: An I.W.W. Reply to the Four L.'s." *Survey,* July 3, 1920, 477.

236    *"I can't understand any":* Hearings, vol. 2, 1403.

236    *"the industry would probably":* Ibid., 1404.

237    *"[T]he Director of Aircraft Production":* History of the Spruce Production Division, Introduction V.

237    *"the most ambitious":* "The Race for Airplane Spruce and Ship Timbers." *American Forestry* XXIV (1918): 323.

238    *"Before America entered":* Quoted in "The Truth at Last." *Weekly by George Harvey* 2 (February 22, 1919): 15.

238    *"[Disque's] operation, in my opinion":* Hearings, vol. 3, 3214.

238    *"that without [Disque's] efforts":* Ibid., vol. 2, 1428.

239    *"Don't make any":* Ibid., 1406.

239    *"Don't waive [sic]":* Ibid., 1405.

239    *"After a taste of better":* "How We Found a Cure for Strikes," 382.

240    *"Housing of armies":* "Spruce for Airplanes—The Eyes of the Allied Armies." *American Forestry* XXIV (1918): 324.

241    *"Our forests have":* William Greeley. *Forests and Men.* New York: Arno Press, 1972, 92.

241    *"Your part in winning":* J. A. Woodruff. "An Appreciation." *American Forestry* XXV (1919): 1092.

241    *An editorial in:* "Tree Tablets in Central Park." *New York Times,* December 3, 1918, 14.

242    *"one of the most comprehensive":* "Urge Memorial Trees—Forestry Association Enlarges Scope of the Planting Program." *New York Times,* December 26, 1918, 14.

242    *"I find myself altogether":* Quoted in Charles Lathrop Pack. *Trees as Good Citizens.* Philadelphia: J. B. Lippincott Company, 1922, 116.

242    *"I think that I shall":* Joyce Kilmer. *Trees and Other Poems.* New York: George H. Doran Company, 1914, 19.

243    *"[T]he trees planted from":* "Seeds of International Friendship." *Outlook* 130 (1922): 680.

244    *"the name is officially":* "25 in Park Shanties Politely Arrested." *New York Times,* September 22, 1932, 3.

245    *"driving around planting":* Press Conference, Hyde Park, October 26, 1937, 4:30 p.m. Quoted in Edgar B. Nixon, ed. *Franklin D. Roosevelt & Conservation 1911–1945,* vol. II. Washington, D.C.: Government Printing Office, 1957, 141.

245    *"knew every tree":* Eleanor Roosevelt. *Franklin D. Roosevelt and Hyde Park: Personal Recollections of Eleanor Roosevelt.* Washington, D.C.: Government Printing Office, 1949, 8.

245    *"a small boy [who]":* "Address at the Laying of the Cornerstone of the Franklin D. Roosevelt Library, Hyde Park, New York. November 19, 1939." In Samuel Irving Rosenman, ed. *The Public Papers and Addresses of Franklin D. Roosevelt,* vol. 8. New York: Macmillan, 1941, 580.

245    *"exceed[ing] anything I have tasted":* Jefferson to Timothy Matlack, October 19, 1807. Quoted in Edwin Betts, annotator. *Thomas Jefferson's Garden Book, 1766–1824: With Relevant Extracts from His Other Writings.* Philadelphia: American Philosophical Society, 1944, 352.

246    *"[T]he interesting thing":* Roosevelt. Speech at Clarksburg, West Virginia, October 29, 1944. Reprinted in Nixon, vol. II, 603.

246    *"The fact that this baby":* Roosevelt. "Governor Franklin D. Roosevelt's Address to the New York State Forestry Association, 17th Annual Meeting, Albany, N.Y., Feb. 27, 1929." Reprinted in Nixon, vol. I, 69. The forest at Nauheim made such a strong impression on Roosevelt that he also chose it as a site for his honeymoon. See *Franklin D. Roosevelt and Hyde Park,* 8.

246    *"One need not be":* Roosevelt. "A Debt We Owe." June 1930. Reprinted in Nixon, vol. I, 72.

246    *"Man has too long":* George P. Marsh. *Man and Nature.* New York: Charles Scribner, 1864, 35.

247    *"I can lime it":* Roosevelt to Hendrik Willem van Loon, February 2, 1937. Reprinted in Nixon, vol. II, 11.

247  *he listed his profession:* "The Election." *Time* XLIV (November 13, 1944): 19. "There, at the polls, where he gave his occupation to Inspector Mildred M. Todd as 'tree-grower,' he enthusiastically accepted a piece of candy from Miss Todd, [and] entered the booth munching."

247  *"FDR used to come over":* Quoted in John F. Sears. "Grassroots Democracy: FDR and the Land." In Henry L. Henderson and David B. Woolner, eds. *FDR and the Environment.* New York: Palgrave Macmillan, 2005, 12.

248  *"Between 4,000,000":* "New York Increases Its Lead in State Forestry." *Journal of Forestry* XXX (1932): 2.

248  *"The present governor, so":* Ibid., 1–2.

249  *"employment can be given":* Roosevelt. Acceptance Speech, Democratic National Convention, Chicago, July 2, 1932. Reprinted in Nixon, vol. I, 112.

249  *"Shall we, as foresters":* "Reforestation as a Means of Emergency Employment: Is It Really Practical or Altogether Wise." Enclosure in a letter from Charles L. Pack to James O. Hazard, July 11, 1932. Reprinted in Nixon, vol. I, 116.

250  *"all forestry activities which":* James O. Hazard to Charles L. Pack, July 19, 1932. Reprinted in Nixon, vol. I, 117.

250  *"[A]s I see it there":* Pinchot to Roosevelt, January 20, 1933. Reprinted in Nixon, vol. I, 131–32.

251  *"I estimate that":* Roosevelt message to Congress, March 21, 1933. Reprinted in Nixon, vol. I, 143–44.

251  *"It must be doubted":* "Making Employment." *New York Times,* March 22, 1933, 16.

251  *"The regimentation of labor":* Quoted in "Quick Job Action Sought." *New York Times,* March 22, 1933, 1.

251  *"the one in which my husband":* Eleanor Roosevelt. *This I Remember.* New York: Harper & Brothers, 1949, 135.

251  *"Hardly a day passed":* Erle Kauffman. "'Roosevelt'—Forest Camp No. 1." *American Forests* 39 (1933): 252.

252  *"in the ninety days":* Jonathan Mitchell. "Roosevelt's Tree Army: II." *New Republic,* June 12, 1935, 129.

252  *"if stretched in":* "C.C.C. Work Accomplishments for the First Year." *American Forests* 40 (1934): 322.

252  *"This kind of work":* Roosevelt to Robert Fechner, October 6, 1934. Reprinted in Nixon, vol. I, 329.

253  *"Some of you who":* Roosevelt. Speech at Lake Placid, New York, September 14, 1935. Reprinted in Nixon, vol. I, 431.

253  *"the largest Democratic":* "House Votes Down a Permanent CCC." *New York Times,* May 12, 1937, 6.

253  *"The defeat of the President's":* "House Extends but Won't Vote Permanent CCC." *Chicago Tribune,* May 12, 1937, 1.

253  *"There could hardly be":* John A. Salmond. *The Civilian Conservation Corps, 1933–1942: A New Deal Case Study.* Durham, NC: Duke University Press, 1967, 157.

254  *"The Civilian Conservation Corps has":* James J. McEntee. "The CCC and National Defense." *American Forests* 46 (1940): 309.

254  *It was far and away:* Rexford G. Tugwell. *The Democratic Roosevelt: A Biography of Franklin D. Roosevelt.* New York: Doubleday, 1957, 331.

254  *"one of the most ridiculous":* Quoted in Nixon, vol. I, 494.

255  *"the shade and beauty":* J. Sterling Morton. "Arbor Day." *Outing* 7 (1885): 319.

256  *"In unprotected orchards":* State Board of Forestry. *A Handbook for Eucalyptus Planters.* Sacramento, CA: W. W. Shannon, 1908, 34.

256  *"The use of forests":* Theodore Roosevelt. "The Forest in the Life of a Nation." *Proceedings of the American Forest Congress.* Washington, D.C.: H. M. Suter Publishing Company, 1905, 8.

256  *"would take a large":* "Forest Planting Possibilities in the Prairie Region." Enclosure from Robert Y. Stuart to Henry A. Wallace, August 15, 1933. Reprinted in Nixon, vol. I, 203.

257  *"for the planting of forest":* Executive Order 6793, July 11, 1934. Reprinted in Nixon, vol. I, 319.

257  *"the most unique":* "A Tree Belt for the Prairie States." *American Forests* 40 (1934): 343.

257  *"on the favorable sites":* Ovid Butler. "The Prairie Shelter Belt." *American Forests* 40 (1934): 398.

257  *"They pointed out that":* Arthur H. Carhart. "Shelterbelts: A 'Failure' that Didn't Happen." *Harper's* CCXXI (October 1960): 75.

258  *"To many politicos":* Wilmon H. Droze. "The New Deal's Shelterbelt Project 1934–1942." In Harold M. Hollingsworth and William F. Holmes, eds. *Essays on the New Deal.* Austin: University of Texas Press, 1969, 25.

258  *Roosevelt did his part:* Quoted in Wilmon Droze. *Trees, Prairies, and People: A History of Tree Planting in the Plains States.* Denton: Texas Woman's University, 1977, 51.

259  *"On a fifty-year basis":* "Wallace Praises Prairie Tree Planting." *American Forests* 45 (1939): 377.

259  *"Over 32,000 acres":* Henry A. Wallace, Secretary of Agriculture, to Roosevelt, March 13, 1937. Reprinted in Nixon, vol. II, 30.

260  *"[S]ome years ago":* Roosevelt. Toast to King Abdul Aziz Ibn Saud of Saudi Arabia, September 30, 1943. Reprinted in Nixon, vol. II, 581.

260  *"Men will thank God":* "Franklin D. Roosevelt." *New York Times,* April 13, 1945, 16.

261  *"a little more material":* Roosevelt to Morris L. Cooke, April 9, 1945. Reprinted in Nixon, vol. II, 644.

261  *"the biggest technical job":* This is a quotation from Raphael Zon, the Forest Service researcher generally seen as the central player in the technical and research aspects of the Shelterbelt. See Norman J. Schmalz. "Forest Researcher Raphael Zon." *Journal of Forest History* 24 (1980): 35.

261  *"the most ridiculed project":* Carhart, 75.

261  *Locals described themselves:* "U-Boat Wastes 25 Shells Just as President Makes Speech." *Washington Post,* February 24, 1942, 1.

262  *"You are dead right":* Roosevelt to Senator Elbert D. Thomas, March 16, 1942. Reprinted in Nixon, vol. II, 547.

262  *"[W]e must guard against":* Roosevelt to Harold D. Smith, Bureau of the Budget, June 17, 1942. Reprinted in Nixon, vol. II, 557.

262  *"If you could see us":* James Stevens. "The Forests' Role in Victory." *American Forests* 49 (1943): 208.

263  *"Careless Matches Aid":* "Wartime Forest Fire Prevention Campaign Launched." *American Forests* 48 (1942): 353.

263  *"Our Carelessness":* See *"Remember—Only You . . ." Forty Years of Preventing Forest Fires.* Forest Service Pamphlet, 1984.

263  *"Uncontrolled fire, even":* "A Proclamation," August 5, 1942. Reprinted in *American Forests* 48 (1942): 435.

264  *"Jap Incendiary Sets":* Los Angeles Times, September 15, 1942, 1.

264  *"Fires started by carelessness":* "Help to Prevent Fires That Aid Japs!" *Los Angeles Times,* October 4, 1942.

264  *"It is man":* Walt Disney's *Bambi,* 1942.

265  *"Please, Mister":* See *"Remember—Only You . . ."*

265  *"nose short":* Ibid.

265  *"Japanese propaganda broadcasts":* John McPhee. "Balloons of War." *New Yorker,* January 29, 1996, 59.

266  *"[t]he peculiar vulnerability":* "Alien Exclusion Ruling Upheld in Court Decision." *Los Angeles Times,* June 2, 1945.

266  *In 1947, Smokey:* See *"Remember—Only You . . ."*

266  *"'Smokey' Makes Half":* Daily Boston Globe, October 16, 1955.

## 9: Postwar Prosperity

269    *"not only a source"*: "Landscape-Gardening: Llewellyn Park." *Crayon* IV (August 1857): 248.

269    *"[N]o great town can"*: Frederick Law Olmsted. "To the Riverside Improvement Company," September 1, 1868. In S. B. Sutton, ed. *Civilizing American Cities: A Selection of Frederick Law Olmsted's Writings on City Landscapes.* Cambridge, MA: MIT Press, 1971, 295.

270    *"It's almost as if"*: Witold Rybczynski. "How to Build a Suburb." *Wilson Quarterly* 19 (1995): 125.

270    *"Big Ice Box"*: Quoted in "The Great Housing Shortage." *Life* 19 (December 17, 1945): 27.

270    *"A decent standard of housing"*: Harry S. Truman. Special Message to Congress Presenting a 21-Point Program for the Reconversion Period, September 6, 1945. See John T. Woolley and Gerhard Peters, eds. *The American Presidency Project* (online). www.presidency.ucsb.edu. Santa Barbara, CA.

270    *"Two of the three"*: William J. Levitt. "A House Is Not Enough: The Story of America's First Community Builder." In Sidney Furst and Milton Sherman, eds. *Business Decisions That Changed Our Lives.* New York: Random House, 1964, 64.

271    *"I wanted to make"*: "Up from the Potato Fields." *Time* 56 (July 3, 1950): 70.

272    *"[I]t proved to us"*: "A House Is Not Enough," 63.

272    *"It was a king-sized"*: Ibid., 64.

272    *According to historian James Deetz:* James Deetz. *In Small Things Forgotten: The Archaeology of Early American Life.* Garden City, NY: Anchor Books, 1977, 103–4.

273    *"I have thought to myself"*: Quoted in Edwin Betts, annotator. *Thomas Jefferson's Garden Book, 1766–1824: With Relevant Extracts from His Other Writings.* Philadelphia: American Philosophical Society, 1944, 339.

274    *A 1950 ad:* Advertisement. *American Home,* May 1950, back cover (emphasis mine).

275    *"Ask your architect"*: Advertisement. *American Home,* April 1950, 153.

275    *"Yes, these days"*: Advertisement. *American Home,* March 1950, 76.

276    *"three-way laminated"*: Phyllis Kelly and Richard Hamilton, eds. *Housing Mass Produced: 1952 Housing Conference.* Cambridge, MA: Albert Farwell Bemis Foundation, 1952, 20.

276    *"A steel frame makes"*: Quoted in Eric Larrabee. "The Six Thousand Houses That Levitt Built." *Harper's* (September 1948): 87.

276    *"Freight cars loaded"*: "A House Is Not Enough," 67.

277    *Interior walls were faced:* See "A Complete House for $6,990." *Architectural Forum* 86 (1947): 70–72.

277    *"calculated the shape"*: Ibid., 64.

277    *"But here's what happened"*: W. D. Wetherell. *The Man Who Loved Levittown.* Pittsburgh: University of Pittsburgh Press, 1985, 5.

277    *"a horizon broken "*: "Six Thousand Houses That Levitt Built," 81.

277    *"a modern Johnny Appleseed"*: "A House Is Not Enough," 68.

278    *"In developing the landscaping"*: Abraham Levitt. "Fruit Is Fine for Little Gardens." *American Home* (January 1950): 72.

278    *"the man chiefly responsible"*: Quoted in David Kushner. *Levittown: Two Families, One Tycoon, and the Fight for Civil Rights in America's Legendary Suburb.* New York: Walker & Company, 2009, 153.

278    *"Nobody keeps up"*: Ralph G. Martin. "Life in the New Suburbia." *New York Times,* January 15, 1950, 40.

278    *"No fabricated fences"*: Levitt & Sons. Your "Homeowner's Guide." N.p., n.d., 18–19.

278    *"[T]he leader of the U.S."*: Quoted in "Up from the Potato Fields," 67

279    *"methods of mass"*: Ibid., 68.

279    *"It was difficult to say"*: "A House Is Not Enough," 69.

280     *"the target of taboos":* John R. Kimberly. "Better to Use, Cheap Enough to Throw Away: The Disposable Paper Product." In *Business Decisions That Changed Our Lives,* 153,155.

280     *"Consider for the moment":* Ibid., 154.

280     *They appeared at the film's:* Available at http://www.youtube.com/watch?v=yquh UMgmRgY (last accessed December 2, 2011).

281     *"No man who owns":* "Six Thousand Houses That Levitt Built," 84.

281     *"Would it not be better":* Quoted in Rick Perlstein, ed. *Richard Nixon: Speeches, Writings, Documents.* Princeton, NJ: Princeton University Press, 2008, 95.

281     *"[I]f there was any":* John Keats. *The Crack in the Picture Window.* Boston: Houghton Mifflin, 1957, xvii.

282     *"We can solve":* Quoted in Craig Thompson. "Growing Pains of a Brand-New City." *Saturday Evening Post* 227 (August 7, 1954): 72.

282     *"What has Levitt":* Wetherell, 19.

283     *"By 1985 reasonable":* Jackson and Twohig, 284.

283     *"Trees may be grown":* Pinchot, *Breaking New Ground,* 31.

284     *"that practically all":* Forest Service. *A National Plan for American Forestry.* Washington, D.C.: Government Printing Office, 1933, v.

284     *"[t]he Clemons Tree Farm":* Quoted in Richard Lewis. "Tree Farms." In Richard C. Davis, ed. *Encyclopedia of American Forest and Conservation History, Vol. II.* New York: Macmillan, 1983, 654.

285     *"privately owned forest-land":* American Forest Products Industries. *Tree Farms: Planning a Program.* Washington, 1947, 2. Quoted in Paul F. Sharp. "The Tree Farm Movement: Its Origins and Development." *Agricultural History* 23 (1949): 41.

285     *"I cannot let":* "Public Regulation of Forest Lands Debated." *American Lumberman* (October 16, 1943): 34.

285     *"Unfortunately, mediocre":* Forest Service. *Report of the Chief of the Forest Service.* Washington, D.C.: Government Printing Office, 1943, 13.

286     *"the most desirable":* Bernhard Fernow. *Annual Report for the Division of Forestry for 1886.* Washington, D.C.: Government Printing Office, 1887, 166.

286     *"See I'm a tree farmer":* Four Andy Griffith PSAs, Box 53, American Tree Farm System Records, Library and Archives, Forest History Society, Durham, NC.

288     *"the most important Federal":* Pinchot, *Breaking New Ground,* 116.

288     *It listed only three:* 16 U.S.C. §475 (1897).

288     *Pinchot himself:* Gifford Pinchot. *The Use of the National Forests.* Washington, D.C.: Government Printing Office, 1907, 24 (emphasis mine).

289     *"[W]hen I was not cutting":* Henry Ford with Samuel Crowther. *My Life and Work.* New York: Doubleday, Page & Company, 1922, 29.

289     *"I will build":* Ibid., 73.

289     *The subsequent production:* Ibid., 145.

289     *"enjoy with his family":* Ibid., 73.

289     *"The single matter of":* Henry Ford with Samuel Crowther. *Moving Forward.* New York: Doubleday, Page & Company, 1930, 113.

290     *"All of us had":* Harvey S. Firestone with Samuel Crowther. *Men and Rubber: The Story of Business.* New York: Doubleday, Page & Company, 1926, 194.

290     *"wanted a man along":* Ibid., 196.

290     *"developed a grudge":* Ford, *My Life and Work,* 237.

290     *"John Muir would have":* Quoted in Firestone, 199.

291     *"[T]he coming of the war":* Ibid., 201.

291     *"The camping equipment was":* R. J. H. DeLoach. "In Camp with Four Great Americans." *Georgia Review* XIII (1959): 44.

291     *"a luxuriously equipped":* John Burroughs. *Under the Maples.* Boston: Houghton Mifflin, 1921, 109.

291     *"swing it vigorously":* Firestone, 209.

291     *"the best that we ever had":* Ibid., 201.

291     *"We gave the victory":* Ibid., 227.

292   *"the publicity which"*: Ibid., 188.
293   *"It is only by"*: Henry S. Graves. "A Crisis in National Recreation." *American Forestry* XXVI (1920): 391.
293   *"one of the most important and necessary"*: *National Conference on Recreation*. Washington, D.C.: Government Printing Office, 1925, 13.
293   *"The growth of forest recreation"*: *CCC Forestry*. Washington, D.C.: Government Printing Office, 1937, 279.
294   *"Our forests today are not"*: USDA Forest Service. *Report of the Chief of the Forest Service, 1946*. Washington, D.C.: Government Printing Office, 1946, 1.
294   *"motor vacationists spend"*: Howard Baker, testimony on H.R. 1972, Hearings before the Committee on Agriculture, "Disposition of Moneys from the National Forests," 83rd Congress, 1st Session (March 11, 12, 1953), 129. Quoted in Paul W. Hirt. *A Conspiracy of Optimism: Management of the National Forests Since World War Two*. Lincoln: University of Nebraska Press, 1994, 153.
295   *"[H]ow can we possibly"*: 106 Cong. Rec. 11722 (1960).
295   *"[I]t is the policy"*: 74 Stat. 215 (1960).
295   *"because of the legal"*: Michael McCloskey. "Note and Comment: Natural Resources— National Forests—the Multiple-Use Sustained Yield Act of 1960." *Oregon Law Review* 41 (1961): 50.
297   *"the Jeremiah of wilderness thinking"*: Harvey Broome. "Origins of the Wilderness Society." *Living Wilderness* 5 (July 1940): 13.
297   *"the Commanding General"*: Robert Marshall to Aldo Leopold, February 21, 1930. Quoted in Paul S. Sutter. *Driven Wild: How the Fight Against Automobiles Launched the Modern Wilderness Movement*. Seattle: University of Washington Press, 2002, 5.
297   *"What great satisfaction"*: Aldo Leopold. "A Tramp in November." In Susan L. Flader and J. Baird Callicott, eds. *The River of the Mother of God and Other Essays by Aldo Leopold*. Madison, WI: University of Wisconsin Press, 1991, 35.
299   *"Part of the lost areas"*: Aldo Leopold. "Origin and Ideals of Wilderness Areas." *Living Wilderness* V (July 1940): 7.
299   *"By 'wilderness' I mean"*: Aldo Leopold. "The Wilderness and Its Place in Forest Recreational Policy." In Flader and Callicott, 79.
300   *"but a hidious"*: Bradford, 95.
300   *"[I]n Wildness is"*: Henry David Thoreau. "Walking." In *The Writings of Henry David Thoreau, Vol. IX: Excursions*. Boston: Houghton Mifflin, 1893, 275.
300   *"[t]he clearest way into the Universe"*: Linnie Marsh Wolfe, ed. *John of the Mountains: The Unpublished Journals of John Muir*. Madison: University of Wisconsin Press, 1979, 313.
300   *"Very evidently we have"*: "Wilderness and Its Place in Forest Recreational Policy," 79 (emphasis mine).
300   *"[Does] the principle"*: Ibid., 78.
300   *"First, such wilderness"*: Ibid., 79.
301   *It was, according to Leopold*: Ibid., 81.
301   *"the remaining wild areas"*: Aldo Leopold. "The Last Stand of the Wilderness." *American Forests and Forest Life* 31 (1925): 602.
301   *"wilderness canoe trips"*: Ibid., 603.
302   *"To carry out this program"*: Robert Marshall. "The Problem of the Wilderness." *Scientific Monthly* 30 (February 1930): 148.
302   *"A roadless marsh is"*: Aldo Leopold. *A Sand County Almanac*. New York: Oxford University Press, 1949, 101.
303   *"All wilderness areas"*: Aldo Leopold. "Wilderness as a Land Laboratory." *Living Wilderness* VI (July 1941): 3.
303   *"Lumber shortages during"*: Leopold. *Sand County Almanac*, 190–91.
304   *"the author of several books"*: "Dr. Aldo Leopold, A Conservationist." *New York Times*, April 22, 1948, 27.

304    *"[L]et's open this":* William Voigt, Jr. "Proceedings before the United States Department of the Interior: Hearings on Dinosaur National Monument, Echo Park and Split Mountain Dams" (April 3, 1950), 415, Department of the Interior Library, Washington, D.C. Quoted in Roderick Nash. *Wilderness and the American Mind.* New Haven: Yale University Press, 1974 (revised), 210.

305    *"neither the money":* Congressional Record, 84th Congress, 1st Session, 101 (June 28, 1955), 9386. Quoted in Nash, 218.

305    *"At this juncture":* Ibid., 221.

305    *"The establishment and maintenance":* 74 Stat. 215 (1960).

306    *"[L]ike the patriarch":* Congressional Record, August 20, 1964, 20630. Quoted in Richard A. Baker. "The Conservation Congress of Anderson and Aspinall, 1963–64." *Journal of Forest History* 29 (1985): 119.

306    *"Only in our country":* Lyndon Johnson. Special Message to the Congress Transmitting Report on the National Wilderness Preservation System. February 8, 1965. See *The American Presidency Project.*

306    *"[T]he trouble with wilderness":* William Cronon. "The Trouble with Wilderness; or, Getting Back to the Wrong Nature." In Cronon, ed. *Uncommon Ground: Toward Reinventing Nature.* New York: W. W. Norton & Company, 1995, 80.

## 10: The Environmental Era

309    *"protecting our environment":* Richard Nixon. "Inaugural Address," January 20, 1969. Online by Gerhard Peters and John T. Woolley. *The American Presidency Project.*

309    *"We wiped [the forest] out":* Gaylord Nelson and the editors of *Country Beautiful. America's Last Chance.* Waukesha, WI: Country Beautiful Corporation, 1970, 8.

310    *"We need more parks":* Nelson. "Inaugural Address," January 5, 1959. Wisconsin Historical Society, Nelson Collection, mss 1020, Box 231, Folder 59 (hereafter Nelson Collection).

310    *"a landmark in conservation":* "Recreation Race Is Seen for US Space." *Milwaukee Journal,* September 23, 1961. See also Thomas R. Huffman. *Protectors of the Land and Water: Environmentalism in Wisconsin, 1961–1968.* Chapel Hill: University of North Carolina Press, 1994, 42.

310    *"had achieved practically":* Quoted in Bill Christofferson. *The Man from Clear Lake: Earth Day Founder Senator Gaylord Nelson.* Madison: University of Wisconsin Press, 2004, 158.

310    *"I think the most crucial":* Godfrey Sperling, Jr. "The State of Government." *Christian Science Monitor,* January 3, 1963, 13.

311    *"the germ of the idea":* Nelson. "Statement at Madison Beyond War Ceremony," December 8, 1990. Nelson Collection, Box 230, Folder 11.

311    *"[T]he idea occurred":* Nelson to Dr. Frank Stanton, President, Columbia Broadcasting System, April 7, 1971. Nelson Collection, Box 2, Folder 15.

311    *"I am convinced":* Quoted in Charles Russell. "College Teach-Ins on Environmental Crisis Proposed." *Seattle Post-Intelligencer,* September 21, 1969. See also Christofferson, 303.

312    *"the response by letter":* Nelson to Hans Janitschek, August 9, 1993. Nelson Collection, Box 231, Folder 43.

312    *"probably in April":* "Environmental Teach-In Planned." *Gaylord Nelson Newsletter,* November 1969. Nelson Collection.

313    *"Already students are":* Gladwin Hill. "Environment May Eclipse Vietnam as College Issue." *New York Times,* November 30, 1969, 1.

313    *"[w]hatever name was":* Nelson to Janitschek, 3.

314    *"a Magna Carta":* "Senate Joint Resolution 169—Introduction of a Joint Resolution Relating to an Environmental Agenda for the 1970's." *Congressional Record* 116 (January 19, 1970): S86.

314    *"the inalienable right":* Ibid., S81–S85.

314    *"The real story is":* Nelson to Janitschek, 3.

315 *"carried unmistakable whiffs":* Joseph Lelyveld. "Millions Join Earth Day Observances Across the Nation: Mood Is Joyful as City Gives Its Support." *New York Times,* April 23, 1970, 1, 7.

315 *"You're part of a Nixon":* Transcript of CBS News Special. "Earth Day: A Question of Survival," 21–22. Nelson Collection, Box 157, Folder 11.

315 *Dan Rather of CBS:* Ibid., 29.

315 *"the largest, cleanest":* Environmental Action, ed. *Earth Day—The Beginning.* New York: Arno Press & The New York Times, 1970, no page number.

315 *"There were so many":* Jack Gould. "TV: The Campaign for an Unspoiled Environment." *New York Times,* April 23, 1970, 56.

316 *"the architect of America's":* Keith Schneider. "Gaylord A. Nelson, Founder of Earth Day, Is Dead at 89." *New York Times,* July 4, 2005, B6.

316 *Tens of thousands:* See Timothy Egan. "Clinton Under Crossfire at Logging Conference." *New York Times,* April 3, 1993, 6. See also Frank J. Murray. "Clinton Tries to Keep a Lot in the Air." *Washington Times,* April 3, 1993, A3.

317 *"a kind of barking sound":* Quoted in William Dietrich. *The Final Forest: The Battle for the Last Great Trees of the Pacific Northwest.* New York: Simon & Schuster, 1992, 47.

318 *"We reached the old wolf":* Leopold, *Sand County Almanac,* 130.

319 *"needed authority to protect":* Richard Nixon. "Statement on Signing the Endangered Species Act of 1973," December 28, 1973. *The American Presidency Project.*

319 *"to maintain* viable*":* 36 C.F.R. §219.9 at 47 F.R. 43037, September 30, 1982 (emphasis mine).

320 *"A tree is a tree":* Ronald Reagan, Speech before the Western Wood Products Association, March 12, 1966. See *Sacramento Bee,* March 12, 1966. See also Lou Cannon. *Governor Reagan: His Rise to Power.* New York: Public Affairs, 2003, 177.

320 *"Trees cause more":* See Martin Schram. "Nation's Longest Campaign Comes to an End." *Washington Post,* November 4, 1980, A6. Schram wrote, "So, too, there was the incongruous specter of the former governor of California criticizing overregulation of automobile emissions standards—buttressing his claim with the contention that trees cause more pollution than automobiles." Schram's paraphrase was based on controversy from earlier in the campaign. At the August Democratic National Convention, Senator Edward Kennedy had criticized Reagan, stating, "The same Republicans who are talking about preserving the environment have nominated a man who last year made the preposterous statement, and I quote: 'Eighty percent of air pollution comes from plants and trees.' And that nominee is no friend of the environment." See Edward Kennedy. "The Work Goes On, the Cause Endures, the Hope Still Lives." *Washington Post,* August 13, 1980, A13. In response, Reagan observed, "I know Teddy Kennedy had fun at the Democratic convention when he said that I had said that trees and vegetation cause 80% of the air pollution in this country. . . . Well, now he was a little wrong about what I said. First of all, I didn't say 80%, I said 92%—pardon me, 93%. And I didn't say air pollution. I said oxides of nitrogen. And I am right." See Jack Nelson. "Pollution Curbed, Reagan Says; Attacks Air Cleanup." *Los Angeles Times,* October 9, 1980, B1, 20. The *Los Angeles Times* article went on to note, "Experts at the EPA said that Reagan apparently had mixed up chemical terms. 'Nitrogen dioxide comes only from man-made sources,' one said. 'Plants and trees produce most of the nitrous oxide in the atmosphere, and that is harmless to mankind.'" Ibid., 20.

320 *"arbitrary and capricious":* See Department of the Interior. *Endangered and Threatened Wildlife and Plants; Determination of Threatened Status for the Northern Spotted Owl.* June 26, 1990, 26118.

320 *"I love spotted owls":* Ted Gup. "Owl vs. Man." *Time* 135 (June 25, 1990), 60.

321 *"We have concluded that":* Interagency Scientific Committee. *A Conservation Strategy for the Northern Spotted Owl.* Portland, OR, 1990, 1.

321 *"threatened throughout its":* *Determination of Threatened Status for the Northern Spotted Owl,* 1990, 26114.

322 *"And yes, we want":* "Excerpted Remarks with Community Leaders in Portsmouth, New Hampshire," January 15, 1992. *The American Presidency Project.*

322 *"We could remove all":* William J. Clinton. "Remarks at the Children's Town Meeting," February 20, 1993. *The American Presidency Project.*

322 *"listen, hammer out":* Clinton. "The President's News Conference," March 23, 1993. *The American Presidency Project.*

323 *"[T]he northern spotted owl was":* Bruce G. Marcot and Jack Ward Thomas. *Of Spotted Owls, Old Growth, and New Policies: A History Since the Interagency Scientific Committee Report.* Portland, OR: U.S. Department of Agriculture, 1997, 11–12.

323 *"This represents the first time":* Forest Service and Bureau of Land Management. *Record of Decision for Amendments to Forest Service and Bureau of Land Management Planning Documents within the Range of the Northern Spotted Owl.* April 13, 1994.

323 *"forest issues were being":* Samuel Hays. *War in the Woods: The Rise of Ecological Forestry in America.* Pittsburgh: University of Pittsburgh Press, 2007, xv.

324 *"I've certainly become":* Quoted in William Yardley. "20 Years Later, A Plan to Save Spotted Owls." *New York Times,* July 1, 2011, 12.

324 *"From Brazil to Japan":* "Owl vs. Man," 158.

325 *"I do not wish flowers":* Zuenir Ventura. "O Acre de Chico Mendes." *Jornal do Brasil,* July 5, 1989. Quoted in Kenneth Mazwell. "The Mystery of Chico Mendes." *New York Review of Books,* March 28, 1991.

325 *"Mr. Mendes has emerged":* James Brooke. "A Death in the Amazon, From Symbol to Script." *New York Times,* April 12, 1989, A4.

325 *"To see the earth":* Archibald MacLeish. "A Reflection: Riders on Earth Together, Brothers in Eternal Cold." *New York Times,* December 25, 1968, 1.

326 *"We have reached":* Adlai Stevenson III. "Too Little, Too Late." In Stevenson, *Earth Day—The Beginning,* 51.

327 *"[T]he sole fact that thousands":* A. Gomez-Pompa, C. Vasquez-Yanes, and S. Guevara. "The Tropical Rain Forest: A Nonrenewable Resource." *Science* 177 (1972): 765.

327 *The slave trade was:* See James C. Scott. *Domination and the Arts of Resistance: Hidden Transcripts.* New Haven, CT: Yale University Press, 1990, 53.

329 *"Hitherto we've just":* Erik Eckholm. "U.N. and Aid Groups Seek to Save Dwindling Third World Forests." *New York Times,* July 29, 1985, A11.

330 *"Lunch isn't what":* "Hamburgers Are Killing Trees." *Newsweek,* cx, September 14, 1987, 74.

330 *"What's happening now":* Jane E. Brody. "Concern for Rain Forest Has Begun to Blossom." *New York Times,* October 13, 1987.

330 *"We've never called":* "Grateful Dead Plans Benefit for Rain Forests." *New York Times,* September 16, 1988.

330 *"the hottest political cause":* Peter P. Swine. "Tropical Chic: Saving the Rain Forests from Their Saviors." *New Republic,* January 30, 1989, 18.

330 *"When the trees go down":* Woody Hochswender. "The Jungle Is Given a Certain Cachet." *New York Times,* May 26, 1989, B3.

331 *"The rain forest is dying":* "Gal Pals Sandra Bernhard and Madonna Monkey Around to Save the Jungle." *People* 31, June 12, 1989, 55.

331 *"mission was to nurture":* Tom Gliatto et al. "Evolution of the '80s Man." *USA Today,* November 27, 1989, 4D.

331 *"We cannot accept":* Quoted in Andrew Hurrell. "Brazil and the International Politics of Amazonian Deforestation." In Hurrell and Benedict Kingsbury. *The International Politics of the Environment: Actors, Interests, and Institutions.* Oxford, UK: Clarendon Press, 1992, 405, 406.

333 *"[T]he higher temperatures can":* Philip Shabecoff. "Global Warming Has Begun, Expert Tells Senate." *New York Times,* June 24, 1988, A1.

334 *"Up to this point":* Spencer Weart. *The Discovery of Global Warming.* Cambridge, MA: Harvard University Press, 2003, 154.

334 *"found that for heat rays":* Ibid., 3.

334    *"As a dam built"*: John Tyndall. "Futher Researches on the Absorption and Radiation of Heat by Gaseous Matter" (1862). In Tyndall, *Contributions to Molecular Physics in the Domain of Radiant Heat.* New York: Appleton, 1873, 117. See also Weart, 4.

335    *"Through his worldwide"*: Environmental Pollution Panel, President's Science Advisory Committee. *Restoring the Quality of Our Environment.* The White House: 1965, 126.

336    *"There is enough to compare"*: Marlise Simons. "Vast Amazon Fires, Man-Made, Linked to Global Warming." *New York Times,* August 12, 1988, A1.

336    *"In the case of carbon dioxide"*: Ibid.

337    *"Our judgment is that"*: J. T. Houghton et al., eds. *Climate Change: The IPCC Scientific Assessment.* New York: Cambridge University Press, 1990, xii.

337    *"Under pressure from the industrial"*: Weart, 162.

338    *"We've signed a climate convention"*: George Bush. "The President's News Conference in Rio de Janeiro," June 13, 1992. *The American Presidency Project.*

338    *"I favor an international treaty"*: Al Gore. *Earth in the Balance: Ecology and the Human Spirit.* Boston: Houghton Mifflin, 1992, 345.

338    *"The balance of evidence"*: J. T. Houghton et al., eds. *Climate Change 1995: The Science of Climate Change.* New York: Cambridge University Press, 1996, 5.

339    *"After 11 days"*: Andrew C. Revkin. "The Tree Trap." *New York Times,* November 26, 2000.

340    *"By ignoring scientific consensus"*: Scientists and Engineers for Change. "48 Nobel Laureates Endorse John Kerry: An Open Letter to the American People," June 21, 2004. See also Al Gore. *An Inconvenient Truth: The Planetary Emergency of Global Warming and What We Can Do About It.* Emmaus, PA: Rodale Press, 2006, 269.

340    *"Most of the observed"*: IPCC, 2007. *Climate Change 2007, Synthesis Report.* Contribution of Working Groups I, II, and III to the Fourth Assessment Report of the Intergovernmental Panel on Climate Change (Core Writing Team, R. K. Pachauri and A. Reisinger, eds.). IPCC, Geneva, Switzerland, 5.

341    *"Political defeats can also"*: Available at http://www.nobelprize.org/nobel_prizes/peace/laureates/2007/presentation-speech.html.

342    *"Our scientists believe this"*: Tiffany Stecker. "Climate Change Link to Fires Ignites Senate Committee." *New York Times,* June 15, 2011.

342    *"Most of the urgent"*: USDA Forest Service. *National Roadmap for Responding to Climate Change,* July 2010, 1.

342    *"precluded by higher"*: U.S. Department of the Interior. *Endangered and Threatened Wildlife and Plants; 12-Month Finding on a Petition to List Pinus albicaulis as Endangered or Threatened with Critical Habitat,* 2011, 1.

343    *"With insufficient credit"*: "Topics of the Times; Trees of Life." *New York Times,* January 30, 1990.

# Bibliography

## Periodicals

American Forests
American Home
American Lumberman
*The Atlantic Monthly*
Boston Evening Post
Boston News-Letter and New-England Chronicle
*The Century Magazine*
*The Chicago Tribune*
*The Christian Science Monitor*
Environmental History
Forest History
Garden and Forest: A Journal of Horticulture,
    Landscape Art and Forestry
Harper's
*The Horticulturist*
Hutchings California Magazine

Journal of Forest History
Journal of Forestry
Life
Living Wilderness
Los Angeles Times
National Geographic
Newsweek
*The New Yorker*
New-York Evening Post
*The New York Times*
New York Tribune
Scientific American
Southern Lumberman
Time
*The Washington Post*

## Published Sources

Albion, Robert. *Forests and Sea Power: The Timber Problem of the Royal Navy, 1652–1862.* Hamden, CT: Archon Books, 1965.

American Forestry Association. *The American Elm: Its Glorious Past, Its Present Dilemma, Its Hope for Protection.* Washington: American Forestry Association, 1937.

———. *Proceedings of the American Forest Conference.* Washington, D.C.: H. M. Suter Company, 1905.

American Tree Association. *Forestry Almanac.* Washington, D.C.: American Tree Association, 1924, 1926, 1929, 1933.

Barker, Rocky. *Scorched Earth: How the Fires of Yellowstone Changed America.* Washington, D.C.: Island Press, 2005.

Bender, Thomas. *Towards an Urban Vision.* Baltimore: Johns Hopkins University Press, 1982.

Beveridge, Charles E., and David Schuyler, eds. *The Papers of Frederick Law Olmsted, Volume III: The Creation of Central Park, 1857–1861.* Baltimore: Johns Hopkins University Press, 1983.

Blanchard, Newton, et al. *Proceedings of a Conference of Governors.* Washington, D.C.: Government Printing Office, 1908.

Booth, Brian. *Wildmen, Wobblies & Whistle Punks: Stewart Holbrook's Lowbrow Northwest.* Corvallis: Oregon State University Press, 1992.

Bradford, William. *Bradford's History "Of Plimoth Plantation."* Boston: Wright & Potter Printing Co., State Printers, 1898.

Brown, Nelson Courtlandt. *Forest Products: The Harvesting, Processing, and Marketing of Materials other than Lumber.* New York: John Wiley and Sons, 1950.

Bryant, William Cullen. *Picturesque America.* New York: D. Appleton and Company, 1872.

Burroughs, John. *Under the Maples.* Boston: Houghton Mifflin, 1921.

Cameron, J. *The Development of Governmental Forest Control in the United States.* Baltimore: Johns Hopkins Press, 1928.

Campana, Richard. *Arboriculture: History and Development in North America.* East Lansing: Michigan State University Press, 1999.

Campanella, Thomas. *Republic of Shade: New England and the American Elm.* New Haven, CT: Yale University Press, 2003.

Carhart, Arthur. *Timber in Your Life.* Philadelphia: Lippincott, 1954.

Carlsen, Spike. *A Splintered History of Wood: Belt-Sander Races, Blind Woodworkers, and Baseball Bats.* New York: HarperCollins, 2008.

Carr, Ethan. *Wilderness by Design: Landscape Architecture and the National Park Service.* Lincoln: University of Nebraska Press, 1999.

Carrier, Lyman. *The Beginnings of Agriculture in America.* New York: McGraw-Hill, 1923.

Carroll, Charles. *The Timber Economy of Puritan New England.* Providence, RI: Brown University Press, 1973.

Carson, Rachel. *Silent Spring.* Greenwich, CT: Fawcett Publications, Inc., 1962.

Carter, Susan B., et al. *Historical Statistics of the United States.* New York: Cambridge University Press, 2006.

Chandler, David Leon. *Henry Flagler: The Astonishing Life and Times of the Visionary Robber Baron who Founded Florida.* New York: Macmillan, 1986.

Chernow, Ron. *Washington: A Life.* New York: Penguin Press, 2010.

Christofferson, Bill. *The Man From Clear Lake: Earth Day Founder Senator Gaylord Nelson.* Madison: University of Wisconsin Press, 2004.

Clark, Clifford Edward. *The American Family Home, 1800–1960.* Chapel Hill: University of North Carolina Press, 1986.

Clepper, Henry. *Professional Forestry in the United States.* Baltimore: Published for Resources for the Future by the Johns Hopkins Press, 1971.

Coates, Peter. *American Perceptions of Immigrant and Invasive Species: Strangers on the Land.* Berkeley: University of California Press, 2006.

Coman, Edwin, and Helen Gibbs. *Time, Tide, and Timber: A Century of Pope & Talbot.* Stanford, CA: Stanford University Press, 1949.

Compton, Wilson. *The Organization of the Lumber Industry.* Princeton, NJ: Princeton University Press, 1916.

Cooper, James Fenimore. *The Pioneers or The Sources of the Susquehanna, 1823.* Reprint, Boston: Houghton, Osgood and Company, 1880.

Cooper, Susan Fenimore. *Rural Hours.* New York: George P. Putnam, 1850.

Council on Environmental Quality and the Department of State. *The Global 2000 Report to the President: Entering the Twenty-First Century.* Washington, D.C.: Government Printing Office, 1980 (three volumes).

Cowell, Adrian. *The Decade of Destruction: The Crusade to Save the Amazon Rain Forest.* New York: Henry Holt, 1990.

Cox, Thomas, et al. *This Well-Wooded Land: Americans and Their Forests from Colonial Times to the Present.* Lincoln: University of Nebraska Press, 1985.

Cronon, William. *Changes in the Land.* New York: Hill and Wang, 1983.

———. *Nature's Metropolis: Chicago and the Great West.* New York: W. W. Norton, 1991.

———, ed. *Uncommon Ground: Toward Reinventing Nature.* New York: W. W. Norton, 1995.

Crosby, Alfred W. *The Columbian Exchange: Biological and Cultural Consequences of 1492.* Westport, CT: Greenwood Publishing Company, 1972.

———. *Ecological Imperialism: The Biological Expansion of Europe, 900–1900.* Cambridge, UK: Cambridge University Press, 1986.

Cunningham, Isabel S. *Frank N. Meyer: Plant Hunter in Asia.* Ames: Iowa State University Press, 1984.

Dana, Samuel T. *Forest and Range Policy: Its Development in the United States*. New York: McGraw-Hill, 1980.

Darlington, William. *Memorials of John Bartram and Humphry Marshall*. Philadelphia: Lindsay and Blakiston, 1849.

Davis, Richard C. *Encyclopedia of American Forest and Conservation History*. New York: Macmillan, 1983 (two volumes).

Deetz, James. *In Small Things Forgotten: The Archaeology of Early American Life*. Garden City, NY: Anchor Press/Doubleday, 1977.

Defebaugh, James. *History of the Lumber Industry in America*. Chicago: American Lumberman, 1906–7 (two volumes).

De Forest, Elizabeth K. *The Gardens and Grounds at Mount Vernon: How George Washington Planned and Planted Them*. Mount Vernon, VA: Mount Vernon Ladies' Association of the Union, 1982.

Demos, John. *Little Commonwealth: Family Life in Plymouth Colony*. New York: Oxford University Press, 1970.

Dickens, Charles. *American Notes for General Circulation*. London: Chapman and Hall, 186, Strand, 1842.

Dietrich, William. *The Final Forest: The Battle for the Last Great Trees of the Pacific Northwest*. New York: Simon & Schuster, 1992.

Division of Forestry. *A Short Account of the Big Trees of California*. Washington, D.C.: Government Printing Office, 1900.

Donahue, Brian. *The Great Meadow: Farmers and the Land in Colonial Concord*. New Haven, CT: Yale University Press, 2004.

Donaldson, Alfred. *A History of the Adirondacks*. New York: Century Co., 1921.

Downing, Andrew Jackson. *Rural Essays*. New York: Leavitt & Allen, 1860.

———. *Treatise on the Theory and Practice of Landscape Gardening, Adapted to North America*. New York and London: Wiley and Putnam; Boston: C.C. Little & Co., 1841.

Droze, Wilmon Henry. *Trees, Prairies, and People: A History of Tree Planting in the Plains States*. Denton, TX: Texas Woman's University, 1977.

Dunlap, Riley E., and Angela G. Mertig, eds. *American Environmentalism: The U.S. Environmental Movement, 1970–1990*. Philadelphia: Taylor & Francis, 1992.

Dwyer, Augusta. *Into the Amazon: Chico Mendes and the Struggle for the Rain Forest*. Toronto: Key Porter Books, 1990.

Egan, Timothy. *The Big Burn*. Boston: Houghton Mifflin Harcourt, 2009.

Egleston, Nathaniel H., ed. *Arbor Day: Its History and Observance*. USDA Report no. 56. Washington, D.C.: Government Printing Office, 1896.

———. *Report upon Forestry*. Washington, D.C.: Government Printing Office, 1882.

Emerson, George. *A Report on the Trees and Shrubs Growing Naturally in the Forests of Massachusetts*. Boston: Dutton and Wentworth, State Printers, 1846.

Environmental Action, ed. *Earth Day—The Beginning*. New York: Arno Press & The New York Times, 1970.

Environmental Pollution Panel, President's Science Advisory Committee. *Restoring the Quality of Our Environment*. The White House: 1965.

Fairchild, David. *The World Was My Garden: Travels of a Plant Explorer*. New York: Charles Scribner's Sons, 1939.

Faragher, John Mack. *Daniel Boone: The Life and Legend of an American Pioneer*. New York: Henry Holt, 1992.

Fernow, Bernhard. *Annual Report of the Division of Forestry for 1886*. Washington, D.C.: Government Printing Office, 1887.

———. *A Brief History of Forestry in Europe and the United States and Other Countries*. Toronto: University of Toronto Press, 1907.

Ficken, Robert E. *The Forested Land: A History of Lumbering in Western Washington*. Seattle: University of Washington Press, 1987.

Firestone, Harvey, with Samuel Crowther. *Men and Rubber: The Story of Business*. Garden City, NY: Doubleday, Page & Company, 1926.

Flader, Susan L., and J. Baird Callicott, eds. *The River of the Mother of God and Other Essays by Aldo Leopold*. Madison: University of Wisconsin Press, 1991.

Fleming, J. R. *Historical Perspectives on Climate Change*. New York: Oxford University Press, 1998.

Flint, Timothy. *Biographical Memoir of Daniel Boone: The First Settler of Kentucky*. Cincinnati: N. and G. Guilford and Co., 1833.

Ford, Henry, with Samuel Crowther. *My Life and Work*. New York: Doubleday, Page & Company, 1922.

Forest Products Laboratory. *Wood in American Life*. Madison, WI: Forest Products Laboratory, 1976.

Freinkel, Susan. *American Chestnut: The Life, Death, and Rebirth of a Perfect Tree*. Berkeley: University of California Press, 2007.

Fries, R. F. *Empire in Pine: The Story of Lumbering in Wisconsin, 1830–1900*. Madison: State Historical Society of Wisconsin, 1951.

Furnas, Robert. *Arbor Day*. Lincoln, NE: State Journal Company, 1888.

Furst, Sidney, and Milton Sherman, eds. *Business Decisions That Changed Our Lives*. New York: Random House, 1964.

Gannett, Henry, ed. *Report of the National Conservation Commission*. Washington, D.C.: Government Printing Office, 1909 (three volumes).

Gess, Denise, and William Lutz. *Firestorm at Peshtigo: A Town, Its People, and the Deadliest Fire in American History*. New York: Henry Holt, 2002.

Gollner, Adam Leith. *The Fruit Hunters: A Story of Nature, Adventure, Commerce, and Obsession*. New York: Scribner, 2008.

Goodyear, C. W. *Bogalusa Story*. Buffalo, NY: privately printed, 1950.

Gore, Al. *Earth in the Balance: Ecology and the Human Spirit*. Boston: Houghton Mifflin, 1992.

———. *An Inconvenient Truth: The Planetary Emergency of Global Warming and What We Can Do About It*. Emmaus, PA: Rodale Press, 2006.

Graham, F., Jr. *The Adirondack Park: A Political History*. New York: Alfred A. Knopf, 1978.

Greeley, William B. *Forests and Men*. Garden City, NY: Doubleday, 1951.

———, ed. *Timber Depletion, Lumber Prices, Lumber Exports, and Concentration of Timber Ownership*. Report on Senate Resolution 311 ("The Capper Report"). Washington, D.C.: Government Printing Office, 1920.

Green, Harvey. *Wood: Craft, Culture, History*. New York: Viking, 2006.

Hakluyt, Richard. *Divers voyages touching the discoverie of America, and the Ilands adiacent unto the same, made first of all by our Englishmen, and afterward by the Frenchmen and Britons: And certaine notes of advertisements for observations, necessarie for such as shall hereafter make the like attempt, with two mappes annexed hereunto for the plainer understanding of the whole matter*. London: Thomas Woodcocke, dwelling in Paules Church-yard, at the signe of the blacke beare, 1582.

———. *The Principall Nauigations, Voiages and Discoueries of the English Nation: Made by Sea or Ouer Land, to the Most Remote and Farthest Distant Quarters of the Earth at Any Time within the Compasse of these 1500 Yeeres*. London: By George Bishop and Ralph Newberie, deputies to Christopher Barker, printer to the Queenes most excellent Maiestie, 1589 and 1598–1600.

Harris, David. *The Last Stand: The War Between Wall Street and Main Street over California's Ancient Redwoods*. New York: Times Books, 1995.

Harvey, Mark. *A Symbol of Wilderness: Echo Park and the American Conservation Movement*. Albuquerque: University of New Mexico Press, 1994.

Hatch, Peter. *The Fruit and Fruit Trees of Monticello: Thomas Jefferson and the Origins of American Horticulture*. Charlottesville: University of Virginia Press, 2007.

Haynes, Richard. *An Analysis of the Timber Situation in the United States, 1952 to 2050*. Portland, OR: Pacific Northwest Research Station, USDA, 2003.

Hays, Samuel. *The American People and The National Forests: The First Century of the U.S. Forest Service*. Pittsburgh: University of Pittsburgh Press, 2009.

———. *Beauty, Health, and Permanence: Environmental Politics in the United States, 1955–1985.* New York: Cambridge University Press, 1987.

———. *Conservation and the Gospel of Efficiency: The Progressive Conservation Movement, 1890–1920.* Cambridge, MA: Harvard University Press, 1959.

———. *Explorations in Environmental History: Essays.* Pittsburgh: University of Pittsburgh Press, 1998.

———. *War in the Woods: The Rise of Ecological Forestry in America.* Pittsburgh: University of Pittsburgh Press, 2007.

Hecht, Susanna, and Alexander Coburn. *The Fate of the Forest: Developers, Destroyers, and Defenders of the Amazon.* London and New York: Verso, 1989.

Hendrick, U. P. *A History of Agriculture in the State of New York.* Albany: New York State Historical Society, 1933.

———. *A History of Horticulture in America to 1860.* New York: Oxford University Press, 1950.

Hidy, Ralph W., Frank Ernest Hill, and Allan Nevins. *Timber and Men: The Weyerhaeuser Story.* New York: Macmillan, 1963.

Hindle, Brooke. *America's Wooden Age: Aspects of Its Early Technology.* Tarrytown, NY: Sleepy Hollow Press, 1975.

———. *Material Culture of the Wooden Age.* Tarrytown, NY: Sleepy Hollow Press, 1975.

Hirt, Paul. *A Conspiracy of Optimism: Management of the National Forests Since World War Two.* Lincoln: University of Nebraska Press, 1994.

Holbrook, Stewart. *Burning an Empire: The Story of American Forest Fires.* New York: Macmillan, 1943.

———. *Far Corner: A Personal View of the Pacific Northwest.* New York: Macmillan, 1952.

———. *Holy Old Mackinaw: A Natural History of the American Lumberjack.* New York: Macmillan, 1956.

———, ed. *Promised Land: A Collection of Northwest Writing.* New York: McGraw-Hill, 1945.

Hotchkiss, George W. *History of the Lumber and Forest Industry of the Northwest.* Chicago: G. W. Hotchkiss & Co., 1898.

Hough, Franklin. *Report Upon Forestry.* Washington, D.C.: Government Printing Office, 1878, 1880.

Hulme, Mike. *Why We Disagree About Climate Change: Understanding Controversy, Inaction, and Opportunity.* New York: Cambridge University Press, 2009.

Humphreys, David. *Forest Politics: The Evolution of International Cooperation.* London: Earthscan Publications, 1996.

Hurrell, Andrew, and Benedict Kingsbury. *The International Politics of the Environment: Actors, Interests, and Institutions.* Oxford, UK: Clarendon Press, 1992.

Hurst, J. Willard. *Law and Economic Growth: A Legal History of the Lumber Industry in Wisconsin, 1836–1915.* Cambridge, MA: Harvard University Press, 1964.

Huth, Hans. *Nature and the American: Three Centuries of Changing Attitudes.* Berkeley: University of California Press, 1957.

Hyman, Harold. *Soldiers and Spruce: Origins of the Loyal Legion of Loggers and Lumbermen.* Los Angeles: University of California Press, 1963.

IPCC, 2007: Climate Change 2007: Synthesis Report. Contribution of Working Groups I, II, and III to the Fourth Assessment Report of the Intergovernmental Panel on Climate Change (Core Writing Team, R. K. Pachauri and A. Reisinger, eds.). IPCC, Geneva, Switzerland.

Jackson, Donald, and Dorothy Twohig, eds. *The Papers of George Washington.* Charlottesville: University Press of Virginia, 1978.

Jackson, Kenneth. *Crabgrass Frontier: The Suburbanization of the United States.* New York: Oxford University Press, 1985.

Jacoby, Karl. *Crimes Against Nature: Squatters, Poachers, Thieves and the Hidden History of American Conservation.* Berkeley: University of California Press, 2001.

Jefferson, Roland M., and Alan E. Fusonie. *The Japanese Flowering Cherry Trees of Washington, D.C.: A Living Symbol of Friendship* (National Arboretum Contribution, 4). Washington, D.C.: Agricultural Research Service, USDA, 1977.

Jensen, Vernon H. *Lumber and Labor.* New York: Farrar & Rinehart, Inc., 1945.

Johnson, Robert Underwood. *Remembered Yesterdays.* Boston: Little, Brown and Company, 1923.

Keats, John. *The Crack in the Picture Window.* Boston: Houghton Mifflin, 1957.

Kelly, Barbara M. *Expanding the American Dream: Building and Rebuilding Levittown.* Albany: State University of New York Press, 1993.

Kilmer, Joyce. *Trees and Other Poems.* New York: George H. Doran Company, 1914.

Kinney, J. P. *The Development of Forest Law in America.* New York: John Wiley & Sons, Inc., 1917.

Kushner, David. *Levittown: Two Families, One Tycoon, and the Fight for Civil Rights in America's Legendary Suburb.* New York: Walker & Company, 2009.

Lapham, I. A., J. G. Knapp, and H. Crocker. *Report on the Disastrous Effects of the Destruction of Forest Trees Now Going on so Rapidly in the State of Wisconsin.* Madison, WI: Atwood & Rublke, State Printers, Journal Office, 1867.

Laszlo, Pierre. *Citrus: A History.* Chicago: University of Chicago Press, 2007.

Leopold, Aldo. *A Sand County Almanac.* New York: Oxford University Press, 1949.

Lewis, James G. *The Forest Service and the Greatest Good: A Centennial History.* Durham, NC: Forest History Society, 2005.

Lillard, Richard. *The Great Forest.* New York: Alfred A. Knopf, 1947.

Little, Charles. *The Dying of the Trees: The Pandemic in America's Forests.* New York: Viking, 1995.

Loewenthal, David. *George Perkins Marsh, Prophet of Conservation.* Seattle: University of Washington Press, 2000.

MacCleery, Douglas. *American Forests: A History of Resiliency and Recovery.* Washington, D.C.: U.S. Department of Agriculture, 1992.

Magee, Judith. *Art and Science of William Bartram.* University Park: Pennsylvania State University Press, 2007.

Maher, Neil M. *Nature's New Deal: The Civilian Conservation Corps and the Roots of the American Environmental Movement.* New York: Oxford University Press, 2008.

Major, Judith K. *To Live in the New World: A. J. Downing and American Landscape Gardening.* Cambridge, MA: MIT Press, 1997.

Malone, Joseph. *Pine Trees and Politics: The Naval Stores and Forest Policy in Colonial New England, 1691–1775.* Seattle: University of Washington Press, 1964.

Manning, Robert, Jr. *The History of the Massachusetts Horticultural Society.* Boston: Society, 1880.

Marcot, Bruce G., and Jack Ward Thomas. *Of Spotted Owls, Old Growth, and New Policies: A History Since the Interagency Scientific Committee Report.* Portland, OR: U.S. Department of Agriculture, 1997.

Marsh, Caroline Crane. *Life and Letters of George Perkins Marsh.* New York: Charles Scribner's Sons, 1888 (two volumes).

Marsh, George Perkins. *Man and Nature; or, Physical Geography as Modified by Human Action.* New York: Charles Scribner, 1864.

Marshall, Humphry. *Arbustrum Americanum: The American Grove.* Philadelphia: Printed by Joseph Crukshank, in Market-Street, between Second and Third-Streets, 1785.

Marx, Leo. *The Machine in the Garden: Technology and the Pastoral Ideal in America.* New York: Oxford University Press, 1964.

Maxwell, Robert S., and Robert D. Baker. *Sawdust Empire: The Texas Lumber Industry, 1830–1940.* College Station: Texas A&M University Press, 1983.

McCloskey, Michael. *Sierra Club Executive Director: The Evolving Club and the Environmental Movement, 1961–1981,* an oral history conducted in 1981 by Susan R. Schrepfer, Sierra Club History Series, Regional Oral History Office, Bancroft Library, University of California, Berkeley, 1983.

McCormick, John. *Reclaiming Paradise: The Global Environmental Movement.* Bloomington: Indiana University Press, 1989.

McManis, Douglas. *European Impressions of the New England Coast, 1497–1620.* Chicago: University of Chicago, 1972.

McMartin, Barbara. *The Great Forest of the Adirondacks.* Utica, NY: North Country Books, 1994.

McPhee, John. *Oranges.* New York: Farrar, Straus and Giroux, 1967.

McWilliams, Carey. *Factories in the Field: The Story of Migratory Farm Labor in California.* Boston: Little, Brown and Company, 1939.

Meine, Curtis. *Aldo Leopold: His Life and Work.* Madison: University of Wisconsin Press, 1988.

Merrill, Perry H. *Roosevelt's Forest Army: A History of the Civilian Conservation Corps, 1933–1942.* Montpelier, VT: Perry H. Merrill, 1981.

Miller, Char. *Gifford Pinchot and the Making of Modern Environmentalism.* Washington: Island Press, 2001.

M'Mahon, Bernard. *The American Gardener's Calendar.* Philadelphia: Printed by B. Graves, no. 40, North Fourth-Street, for the author, 1806.

Mohr, Charles. *History of the U.S. Forest Products Laboratory.* Washington, D.C.: U.S. Department of Agriculture, 1971.

Money, Nicholas P. *The Triumph of the Fungi: A Rotten History.* New York: Oxford University Press, 2006.

Morrison, Ellen Earnhardt. *Guardian of the Forest: A History of the Smokey Bear Program.* Alexandria, VA: Morielle Press, 1976.

Muir, John. *Nature Writings.* New York: Penguin Books, 1997.

Mumford, Lewis. *Technics and Civilization.* New York: Harcourt Brace & Co., 1934.

Murphy, Kathryn. *New Housing and Its Materials, 1940–1956.* Washington, D.C.: Government Printing Office, 1958.

Nakashima, George. *The Soul of a Tree: A Master Woodworker's Reflections.* Tokyo: Kodansha International, 1988.

Nash, Roderick. *American Environmentalism: Readings in Conservation History.* New York: McGraw-Hill, 1990.

———. *Wilderness and the American Mind.* New Haven, CT: Yale University Press, 1967.

National Assessment Synthesis Team, eds. *Climate Change Impacts on the United States: The Potential Consequences of Climate Variability and Change.* New York: Cambridge University Press, 2000.

Nelson, Charles. *A History of the U.S. Forest Products Laboratory.* Madison, WI: Forest Products Laboratory, 1971.

Nelson, Gaylord, with Susan Campbell and Paul Wozniak. *Beyond Earth Day: Fulfilling the Promise.* Madison: University of Wisconsin Press, 2002.

Nixon, Edgar B., ed. *Franklin D. Roosevelt and Conservation, 1911–1945.* Hyde Park, NY: Franklin D. Roosevelt Library, 1957 (two volumes).

Norton, Matthew. *The Mississippi River Logging Company: An Historical Sketch.* N.p., 1912.

Ohanian, Nancy. *The American Pulp and Paper Industry, 1900–1940: Mill Survival, Firm Structure, and Industry Relocation.* Westport, CT: Greenwood Press, 1993.

Olson, James. *J. Sterling Morton.* Lincoln: University of Nebraska Press, 1942.

Olson, Sherry H. *The Depletion Myth: A History of Railroad Use of Timber.* Cambridge, MA: Harvard University Press, 1971.

Orsi, Richard. *Sunset Limited: The Southern Pacific and the Development of the American West.* Berkeley: University of California Press, 2005.

Outland, Robert. *Tapping the Pines: The Naval Stores Industry of the American South.* Baton Rouge: Louisiana State University Press, 2004.

Pack, Charles Lathrop. *Trees as Good Citizens.* Philadelphia: J. B. Lippincott Company, 1922.

Paulding, James. *The Backwoodsman.* Philadelphia: M. Thomas, 1818.

Pauly, Philip. *Fruits and Plains: The Horticultural Transformation of America.* Cambridge, MA: Harvard University Press, 2007.

Peattie, Donald Culross. *A Natural History of North American Trees.* Boston: Houghton Mifflin, 2007.

Pennsylvania Chestnut Tree Blight Commission. *The Publications of the Pennsylvania Chestnut Tree Blight Commission, 1911–1913.* Harrison, PA: Wm. Stanley Ray, State Printer, 1915.

Perlin, John. *A Forest Journey: The Role of Wood in the Development of Civilization.* New York: W. W. Norton, 1989.

Pinchot, Gifford. *Breaking New Ground.* New York: Harcourt, Brace and Company, 1947.

———. *The Fight for Conservation.* New York: Doubleday, Page and Company, 1910.

———. *The Use of the National Forest Reserves.* Washington, D.C.: Government Printing Office, 1905.

Pollan, Michael. *Botany of Desire: A Plant's Eye View of the World.* New York: Random House, 2001.

Powell, Fred. *The Bureau of Plant Industry: Its History, Activities and Organization.* Baltimore: Johns Hopkins Press, 1927.

Price, Robert. *Johnny Appleseed, Man and Myth.* Bloomington: Indiana University Press, 1954.

Puter, S. A. D. *Looters of the Public Domain.* Portland, OR: Portland Printing House, 1908.

Pyne, Stephen. *Fire in America: A Cultural History of Wildland and Rural Fire.* Princeton, NJ: Princeton University Press, 1982.

Record, Samuel. *Identification of the Economic Woods of the United States.* New York: J. Wiley & Son, 1912.

Rector, William G. *Log Transportation in the Lake States Lumber Industry, 1840–1918: The Movement of Logs and Its Relationship to Land Settlement, Waterway Development, Railroad Construction, Lumber Production, and Prices.* American Waterways Series no. 4. Glendale, CA: Arthur H. Clark, 1953.

Revkin, Andrew. *The Burning Season: The Murder of Chico Mendes and the Fight for the Amazon Rain Forest.* Boston: Houghton Mifflin, 1990.

Rodgers, Andrew Denny. *Bernhard Eduard Fernow: A Story of North American Forestry.* Princeton, NJ: Princeton University Press, 1951.

Roosevelt, Theodore. *Theodore Roosevelt: An Autobiography.* New York: Macmillan, 1913.

Rozenzweig, Roy. *The Park and the People: A History of Central Park.* Ithaca, NY: Cornell University Press, 1992.

Rybczynski, Witold. *A Clearing in the Distance: Frederick Law Olmsted and America in the Nineteenth Century.* New York: Scribner, 1999.

Sachs, Aaron. *The Humboldt Current: Nineteenth-Century Exploration and the Roots of American Environmentalism.* New York: Viking, 2006.

Sackman, Douglas. *Orange Empire: California and the Fruits of Eden.* Berkeley: University of California Press, 2005.

Sale, Kirkpatrick. *The Green Revolution: The American Environmental Movement, 1962–1992.* New York: Hill & Wang, 1993.

Salmond, John A. *The Civilian Conservation Corps, 1933–1942: A New Deal Case Study.* Durham, NC: Duke University Press, 1967.

Sargent, Charles Sprague. *Report on the Forests of North America.* Washington, D.C.: Government Printing Office, 1884.

Savage, Henry, and Elizabeth Savage. *André and François André Michaux.* Charlottesville: University Press of Virginia, 1986.

Schenck, Carl Alwin. *The Biltmore Story: Recollections of the Beginning of Forestry in the United States.* St. Paul: Minnesota History Society, 1955.

Schiebinger, Londa. *Plants and Empire: Colonial Bioprospecting in the Atlantic World.* Cambridge, MA: Harvard University Press, 2004.

Shabecoff, Philip. *A Fierce Green Fire: The American Environmental Movement.* New York: Hill & Wang, 1993.

Shurtleff, Harold R. *The Log Cabin Myth: A Study of the Early Dwellings of the English Colonists in North America.* Cambridge, MA: Harvard University Press, 1939.

Sitton, Thad, and James H. Conrad. *Nameless Towns: Texas Sawmill Communities, 1880–1942.* Austin: University of Texas Press, 1998.

Sloane, Eric. *A Reverence for Wood.* New York: Funk, 1965.

Smith, Henry Nash. *Virgin Land: The American West as Symbol and Myth.* Cambridge, MA: Harvard University Press, 1950.

Spongberg, Stephen. *A Reunion of Trees: The Discovery of Exotic Plants and Their Introduction into North American and European Landscapes.* Cambridge, MA: Harvard University Press, 1990.

Starr, Kevin. *Inventing the Dream: California Through the Progressive Era.* New York: Oxford University Press, 1985.

Steen, Harold, ed. *The Conservation Diaries of Gifford Pinchot.* Durham, NC: Forest History Society, 2001.

———, ed., *History of Sustained-Yield Forestry: A Symposium.* Santa Cruz, CA: Forest History Society, 1984.

———. *The United States Forest Service: A History.* Seattle: University of Washington Press, 1976.

Steinberg, Ted. *Down to Earth: Nature's Role in American History.* New York: Oxford University Press, 2002.

Steiner, Jesse. *Americans at Play: Recent Trends in Recreation and Leisure Time Activities.* New York: McGraw-Hill, 1933.

Stephenson, Isaac. *Recollections of a Long Life, 1829–1915.* Chicago: privately printed, 1915.

St. John de Crèvecoeur, J. Hector. *Letters from an American Farmer.* Dublin: Printed by John Exshaw, 1782.

Stoll, Steven, ed. *U.S. Environmentalism Since 1945: A Brief History with Documents.* New York: Palgrave Macmillan, 2007.

Stone, Christopher D. *Should Trees Have Standing? Toward Legal Rights for Natural Objects.* Los Altos, CA: W. Kaufmann, 1974.

Strauss, Steven H., and H. D. Bradshaw. *The Bioengineered Forest: Challenges for Science and Society.* Washington, D.C.: Resources for the Future, 2004.

Sutter, Paul. *Driven Wild: How the Fight Against Automobiles Launched the Modern Wilderness Movement.* Seattle: University of Washington Press, 2002.

Swain, Donald C. *Federal Conservation Policy, 1921–1933.* Berkeley: University of California Press, 1963.

Taylor, E. G. R., ed. *The Original Writings & Correspondence of the Two Richard Hakluyts.* Nendeln, Liechtenstein: Kraus Reprint Limited, 1967 (two volumes).

Thoreau, Henry David. *The Maine Woods.* Boston: Ticknor and Fields, 1864.

———. *The Succession of Forest Trees and Wild Apples.* Boston and New York: Houghton Mifflin, 1887.

———. *Walden; or, Life in the Woods.* Boston: Ticknor and Fields, 1854.

Trombulak, Stephen C., ed. *So Great a Vision: The Conservation Writings of George Perkins Marsh.* Hanover, NH: University Press of New England, 2001.

Tucker, Richard. *Insatiable Appetite: The United States and the Ecological Degradation of the Tropical World.* Berkeley: University of California Press, 2000.

Twining, Charles E. *George S. Long: Timber Statesman.* Seattle: University of Washington Press, 1994.

———. *Phil Weyerhaeuser: Lumberman.* Seattle: University of Washington Press, 1985.

Udall, Stewart. *The Quiet Crisis.* New York: Holt, Rinehart and Winston, 1963.

U.S. Bureau of the Census. *Historical Statistics of the United States, Colonial Times to 1970.* Washington, D.C.: Government Printing Office, 1975.

U.S. Forest Service. *A National Plan for American Forestry ("The Copeland Report").* Washington, D.C.: Government Printing Office, 1933.

———. *National Roadmap for Responding to Climate Change.* 2010.

———. *"Remember—Only You . . ." 1944 to 1984, Forty Years of Preventing Forest Fires, Smokey's 40th Birthday.* Washington, D.C.: Government Printing Office, 1984.

————. *Timber Depletion, Lumber Prices, Lumber Exports, and Concentration of Timber Ownership.* Washington, D.C.: Government Printing Office, 1920.

Weart, Spencer. *The Discovery of Global Warming.* Cambridge, MA: Harvard University Press, 2003.

Weber, Gustavus A. *The Plant Quarantine and Control Administration: Its History, Activities and Organization.* New York: Brookings Institute, 1930.

Weeks, Horace Lyman. *A History of Paper Manufacturing in the United States, 1690–1916.* New York: Burt Franklin, 1916.

Weyerhaeuser, Louise. *Frederick Weyerhaeuser: Pioneer Lumberman.* Minneapolis: McGill Lithograph Company, 1940.

White House Committee on Environment and Natural Resources, National Science and Technology Council. *Scientific Assessment of the Effects of Global Change on the United States.* Washington, D.C.: Government Printing Office, 2008.

Whitney, Gordon. *From Coastal Wilderness to Fruited Plain: A History of Environmental Change in Temperate North America, 1500 to the Present.* New York: Cambridge University Press, 1994.

Whyte, William. *The Organization Man.* New York: Simon & Schuster, 1956.

Wickson, Edward J. *The California Fruits and How to Grow Them.* San Francisco: Dewey & Co., 1889.

Wiebe, Robert. *The Search for Order, 1877–1920.* New York: Hill & Wang, 1967.

Williams, Michael. *Americans and Their Forests: A Historical Geography.* New York: Cambridge University Press, 1989.

Wills, Gary. *Cincinnatus: George Washington and the Enlightenment.* Garden City, NY: Doubleday, 1984.

Wolfe, Linnie Marsh. *John of the Mountains: The Unpublished Journals of John Muir.* Boston: Houghton Mifflin, 1938.

————. *Son of the Wilderness: The Life of John Muir.* New York: Alfred A. Knopf, 1945.

Wood, William. *New England's Prospect.* London: Tho. Cotes, for John Bellamie, at the three Golden Lyons in Corne-hill, neere the Royall Exchange, 1634.

Woolner, David, and Henry Henderson. *FDR and the Environment.* New York: Palgrave Macmillan, 2005.

Worster, Donald. *Dust Bowl: The Southern Plain in the 1930s.* New York: Oxford University Press, 1979.

————. *Nature's Economy: The Roots of Ecology.* San Francisco: Sierra Club Books, 1977.

————. *Passion for Nature: The Life of John Muir.* New York: Oxford University Press, 2008.

Wulf, Andrea. *The Brother Gardeners: Botany, Empire, and the Birth of an Obsession.* London: William Heinemann, 2008.

————. *The Founding Gardeners: How the Revolutionary Generation Created an American Eden.* London: William Heinemann, 2011.

Yaffee, Steven. *The Wisdom of the Spotted Owl: Policy Lessons for a New Century.* Washington, D.C.: Island Press, 1994.

Young, Alfred F. *Liberty Tree: Ordinary People and the American Revolution.* New York: New York University Press, 2006.

# Index

# About the Author

Eric Rutkow, a graduate of Yale University and Harvard Law School, has worked as a lawyer on environmental issues. He splits his time between New York City and New Haven, Connecticut, where he is pursuing a doctorate in American history at Yale. *American Canopy* is his first book.